The Writing Teacher's Sourcebook

The Writing Teacher's Sourcebook

Gary Tate

TEXAS CHRISTIAN UNIVERSITY

Edward P.J. Corbett

OHIO STATE UNIVERSITY

New York   Oxford
OXFORD UNIVERSITY PRESS
1981

Copyright © 1981 by Oxford University Press, Inc.

Library of Congress Cataloging in Publication Data
Main entry under title:

The Writing teacher's sourcebook.

  Bibliography: p
  1. English language—Rhetoric—Study
and teaching—Addresses, essays, lectures.
I. Tate, Gary. II. Corbett, Edward P. J.
PE1404.W74   808'.042'071173   80–21473
ISBN 0-19-502878-3

Printed in the United States of America

Printing (last digit): 9 8 7 6 5 4 3 2

To
Charlie and Priscilla

Preface

Since we published *Teaching Freshman Composition* in 1967 and *Teaching High School Composition* in 1970, a great number of formal courses in the teaching of composition have been added to the curriculum in the colleges and universities, and a remarkable amount of good material on the teaching of composition has been published in journals and in books. Both of these developments constitute evidence of the improved status and the growing sophistication of the teacher of writing. It is difficult now to find many academics who seriously contend that any unusually competent native speaker of the language is qualified to teach composition. The growing demand in the schools for courses in writing has been accompanied by a realization of the need for professional training in the teaching of writing. This increasing sense of professionalism has not only elevated the status of composition teachers but has stimulated composition teachers to do the kind of thinking and research that can improve the state of the art. Some of the best of the recent literature on the teaching of composition has been produced by young teachers only three or four years out of graduate school.

Whereas ten years ago we had to search long and hard for enough good articles to fill an anthology, our problem in preparing this collection was the difficulty we encountered in making selections from the plethora of excellent articles available to us. We eased the difficulty of making choices by adopting some rather arbitrary guidelines. (1) Since we wanted to cover a wide range of the concerns of composition teachers, we decided to limit the number of articles on any one aspect of composition. So if one of your favorite articles on, say, invention or assignments is not in this collection, its absence may be a result of our decision to limit the number of articles on any one subject. (2) We decided to include only one article by any author. That arbitrary decision excluded many fine articles. (3) After much deliberation, we decided to exclude excerpts from books and monographs. That decision ruled out the reprinting of chapters or smaller sections from such notable books as Mina Shaughnessy's _Errors and Expectations,_ James Moffett's _Teaching the Universe of Discourse,_ William F. Irmscher's _Teaching Expository Writing,_ and Janet Emig's _The Composing Processes of Twelfth Graders._ (4) Although a half-dozen or so of the articles in our collection are included in one or another of the currently available anthologies,[1] we occasionally made a choice among competing essays solely on the grounds that a particularly excellent essay was not available in any of the other anthologies. By that decision, we have facilitated access to a number of articles that would otherwise be available to readers only in the pages of the sometimes hard-to-get journals.

It should not come as any surprise that the majority of the articles in this collection were taken from such NCTE publications as _College English, College Composition and Communication, English Journal,_ and _Research in the Teaching of English._ The number of articles on composition has increased noticeably in all of the NCTE publications in the last ten years. _College Composition and Communication,_ the NCTE quarterly journal devoted primarily to composition, has provided almost half of the articles in this collection. But at least a fourth of the articles came from non-NCTE journals. We are sure, however, that we have overlooked some of the estimable articles on composition that appeared in some of the regional journals published in this country.

Once we had made our selection of articles, we had to decide on the arrangement of the selections. An obvious principle of organization was to group the articles according to select categories. We discovered, however, that some of the articles did not fit decisively into any of the categories we experimented with, and some of the articles straddled the boundaries of two or three of the categories. We had to settle finally on three categories of the broadest sort: General, Theory, and Practice. Within each of those broad categories we found clusters of essays that deal with a similar or a related topic, and we have indicated those clusters

1. See, for instance, _Contemporary Rhetoric: A Conceptual Background with Readings,_ ed. W. Ross Winterowd (New York: Harcourt Brace Jovanovich, 1975); _Rhetoric and Composition: A Sourcebook for Teachers,_ ed. Richard L. Graves (Rochelle Park, N.J.: Hayden Book Co., 1976); _Children and Writing in Elementary School: Theories and Techniques,_ ed. Richard L. Larson (New York: Oxford University Press, 1975); _Composition and Its Teaching,_ ed. Richard C. Gebhardt (Columbus, Ohio: Ohio Council of Teachers of English Language Arts, 1979); _Ideas for English 101: Teaching Writing in College,_ eds. Richard Ohmann and W. B. Coley (Urbana, Ill.: National Council of Teachers of English, 1975).

by spatial groupings in the Table of Contents. But we ultimately despaired of being able to provide apt headings for these subdivisions. Those who use the book will be more interested in what the essays have to say than in how the essays might be properly classified.

In our two previous anthologies, we provided an extensive listing of additional readings at the back of the book. It was our experience, however, that those bibliographies were so overwhelming, for both the prospective and the veteran teacher of composition, that few, if any, of the additional readings ever got read. We decided that in this collection, we would list, at the end of each of the clusters, only a few related readings. Furthermore, we decided that in the Additional Readings, we would not list any of the books and articles cited in the footnotes in the previous cluster of articles. Serious students and teachers of composition will eventually focus their interest, and when they do, they will not be satisfied with our meager bibliographies. They will turn to the more extensive bibliographies provided in *Teaching Composition: 10 Bibliographical Essays,* ed. Gary Tate (Fort Worth: Texas Christian University Press, 1976) and to the series of annotated bibliographies that Richard L. Larson published in the May issue of *College Composition and Communication* from 1975 to 1979.

We are sad that we had to leave a number of first-rate articles on the cutting-room floor. Fortunately, many of these excluded articles will remain readily accessible in bound periodicals in college libraries. But we are glad that we have been able to bring together between the covers of one book some of the most intellectually exciting and pedagogically useful articles that have been published on composition in this country in the last twenty years. We hope that this collection will prompt other teachers to share the fruits of their experience, their thinking, and their research. But above all, we hope that this collection will encourage all of us to become more knowledgeable and more effective teachers of writing.

Fort Worth
Columbus
August 1980

G.T.
E.P.J.C.

Contents

Contents

General

WILLIAM RILEY PARKER

Where Do English Departments Come From?

My topic-question—Where do English departments come from?—is not intended to be funny, but my answer may strike you as at least ironic. I shall try to answer with something clearer and more illuminating than "Out of the everywhere into the here." I shall try, in fact, to be very definite, and I want you to know at the outset my purpose. If this were a sermon instead of a history-lesson, I would take my text from Cicero, who said, you will remember, "Not to know what happened before one was born is always to be a child." He said this, of course, in Latin, which is the language in which English studies began and, to some extent, long continued, and which is still a language that all serious students of English literature had better know, despite the fact that we are now allowing it to disappear from our public schools. But that is a sermon for another occasion. Cicero's dictum points up my purpose on this one. Even if history does not truly repeat itself, knowledge of it may, at least sometimes, give current problems a familiar, less formidable look. Moreover, neglect of experience, personal *or recorded,* condemns us to repeating its follies. To live intellectually only in one's own time is as provincial and misleading as to live intellectually only in one's own culture. These truisms, if you will accept as well as forgive them, apply to the history of the teaching of English as much as they apply to the history of other matters. And they apply to the recent as well as the distant past. It can be most useful to know with certainty how raw and how new some of our problems really are. So let us begin with recognition of a simple fact: the teaching of English, as a constituent of college or university education, is only about 100 years old, and *departments* of English are younger

From *College English,* 28 (February, 1967), 339–351. Reprinted by permission of the National Council of Teachers of English.

still. Let me underline this by defining "English." A recent dictionary will tell you, not to your great surprise, that it can mean "English language, literature, or composition when a subject of study." It may surprise you, however, to know that you will *not* find this definition or anything like it in the 1925 Webster's unabridged dictionary or in the thirteen-volume *Oxford English Dictionary*. Its absence from these is significant. Its absence from the new Random House dictionary is shocking.

Since I am myself an English teacher, I cannot resist answering my question about the origins of English teaching, first with a flourish of rhetoric, and finally with what I hope will be a full and clear explication. If I may begin by twisting a tired Shakespearean adage, it is a wise child that knows his own parents. "English" as a recognized academic subject was not self-begotten, nor did it spring fully armed from the forehead of ancient rhetoric. It is a normal and legitimate child. It is not a foundling. Present-day professors and graduate students of English should be more aware, therefore, of its once proud parents, both of whom are still very much alive—though living apart. The child, grown to vigorous manhood, is today somewhat ashamed of both, and sees as little of them as possible. Proud of its own accomplishments, confident in its present prestige, it would like to forget its origins. A little more than fifty years ago, after neglecting its mother for some time, it became alienated from her, and became more than ever its father's son. Then, exactly ten years later, it broke with its father. Since increased maturity and a sense of maturity sometimes carry the promise of reconciliation in such domestic tragedies, there is still the possibility, of course, that the child will some day not only feel proud of its parents but even be willing to learn something from them.

As I have said, English was born about 100 years ago. Its mother, the eldest daughter of Rhetoric, was Oratory—or what we now prefer to call public speaking or, simply, speech. Its father was Philology or what we now call linguistics. Their marriage, as I have suggested, was shortlived, and English is therefore the child of a broken home. This unhappy fact accounts, perhaps, for its early feeling of independence and its later bitterness toward both parents. I date the break with the mother, however, not from the disgraceful affair she had with Elocution, but rather from the founding of the Speech Association of America in 1914, which brought, as was hoped, the creation of many departments of speech. I date the break with the father, not from his happy marriage to Anthropology, but from the founding of the Linguistic Society of America in 1924, and the developing hostility of literary scholars to non-prescriptive grammar, new terminology, and the rigors of language study. Splinter groups form when their founders feel their interests neglected, and English teachers, absorbed in what they considered more important business, were indeed neglecting speech by 1914 and losing all vital concern with linguistics by 1924.

I might go on to speak of the unfortunate divorce of linguistics and speech, who, in my unromantic opinion, were obviously "meant for each other." Optimists like me can hope for an eventual family reunion, but pessimists will, of course, point out that this is impossible because, with the passage of time, the parents have actually forgotten each other and the child has almost forgotten the parents. Because there is an element of truth in this charge, I choose to begin by telling (or reminding) you of the family history; reconciliation requires *remembrance* along with wisdom and good will.

But now I must drop this domestic metaphor, and turn to the prosaic details of the history of English studies and of the teaching and eventual departmentalization of English language and literature.

To prevent some potential confusion, let us recall that English *studies*—or serious scholarship or criticism devoted to English language or literature—are much older than any *teaching* of English. English studies date from Tudor times, and are a fruit of the English Renaissance and Reformation. Let me hammer this point home with some illustrations; if in every instance I have not yet found the very first example of a now familiar phenomenon of our field, I very much hope that you will correct me. Serious linguistic scholarship on English begins in the 1560's with the work of Laurence Nowell, John Josselin, William Lambarde, and Archbishop Matthew Parker on Anglo-Saxon. Serious biographical and bibliographical scholarship on English literature begins even earlier, in the 1540's, with the impressive Latin catalogues of John Leland and Bishop John Bale. Important lexicographical scholarship also dates from the sixteenth century, though the first really English dictionary was Robert Cawdrey's, as late as 1604. Unless you choose to begin with Caxton or, perhaps, Polydore Vergil, serious editing of important English authors is inaugurated by Thomas Speght's Chaucer in 1598, which, in a prefatory life, also gives us, to the best of my knowledge, the first separate biography of an English literary figure written because he was a literary figure. Francis Thynne's prompt review of Speght's edition is probably our first example of scholarly reviewing; as you may recall, it greatly influenced Speght's second, revised edition of 1602. The first publication of variant readings of a single work was in 1640, by John Spelman. T. S. Eliot was not the first poet to annotate his own work (in *The Waste Land*, 1922); Thomas Watson did this for his *Hekatompathia* in 1582. Perhaps the first annotation of separate works begins with the notes by "E.K." on Spenser's *Shepheardes Calender* of 1579 and John Selden's notes on Drayton's *Poly-*

Olbion of 1613. The first whole volume to be devoted to annotation of a single literary work was Patrick Hume's 321 closely printed pages on *Paradise Lost* in 1695. Recognizable criticism of English literature dates from the sixteenth century, and the collection of critical opinion on authors begins with Sir Thomas Pope Blount in 1690 and 1694. Source study of English drama begins with Langbaine in 1691. Perhaps the first truly scholarly biography, with ample footnotes and indication of sources, was Thomas Birch's life of Milton in 1738.

One could easily go on; it is fun to collect "firsts"; but perhaps I have said enough to remind you that there was a considerable and venerable tradition of serious scholarship and criticism on English language and literature long before there was any continuous teaching of these subjects. I have to put it this way, carefully, because Archbishop Ussher and the Spelmans, father and son, tried hard to have it otherwise: a chair of Anglo-Saxon was actually established at Cambridge in the 1640's, but the English civil war and the deaths of both the Spelmans and the first and only holder of the chair, Abraham Wheloc, aborted this experiment, and Cambridge did not have another professor of Anglo-Saxon until 1878, and did not have a professor of English literature until 1911. It is interesting to speculate on what the history of our profession might have been like had the academic study of English actually begun in 1640, two years after Harvard College opened. But Harvard was not to have a professor of English until 1876, when, ironically, it granted its first Ph.D in English to a man who never entered the teaching profession. Oxford had a professorship of poetry as early as 1708, but this was to mean classical poetry only, until long after the teaching of English literature had otherwise established itself as an academic subject. Even Matthew Arnold, who in 1857 broke all traditions by lecturing in English instead of in Latin, never thought of himself as a professor of English. Oxford did not have a university chair of English literature until 1904. When the Modern Language Association of America was founded in 1883—only eighty-three years ago—twenty leading institutions were represented at the organizational meeting in New York, and at all twenty of these institutions there were only thirty-nine faculty members in English.

I stress these dates in order to remind you that the teaching of English is a Johnny-come-lately—a fact that has some relevance to any answer given the question "Why can't Johnny read?" Our research and criticism are old; our jobs are new. Our profession as scholars demonstrates richly the lessons learned from four centuries of experience; our profession as teachers is still wrestling strenuously and confusedly with initial problems that mass education has suddenly and greatly aggravated. As scholars we have matured; as teachers we—the same people—are still children in our ignorance or innocence, still fumbling and faddish and lacking well-defined goals. These, I realize, are strong statements, and I mean to explain and support them before I finish. Meanwhile, however, let me say that I *think* I am talking to you about one of the central problems of our profession—and one which, in my experience, is almost never discussed.

When, where, and by whom the formal teaching of English began at any level of education is not, I believe, known, and probably will never be known. From very early times it inevitably formed some part of the "petties" (or primary, elementary education as conducted in the parish, or under private tutors, or however). Exactly when it extended upward into secondary education, in private day or boarding schools, is only approximately known; "grammar schools" were originally designed to teach *Latin* grammar; but in the second half of the eighteenth century a slowly increasing number of such schools in English were professing what was called an "English education," in contrast to the usual classical education preparatory to a university, as their aim. This term is now potentially misleading; it embraced considerably more than English language, literature, or composition, but it normally included composition or "rhetoric" in the mother tongue. On this side of the Atlantic, when Benjamin Franklin published in 1750 his *Idea of an English School,* he had in mind a very radical idea indeed—a utilitarian education for citizenship conducted entirely in the English language. Naturally, it was never tried, but a compromise was attempted. An academy in Philadelphia opened in 1751 with a so-called "English School," and when the academy became a college in 1755 (later to be called the University of Pennsylvania), the second head of its English School, Ebenezer Kinnersley, was given the title Professor of the English Tongue and Oratory. Significantly, he was both a Baptist clergyman and a scientist; his experiments in electricity were second in importance only to those of his friend Franklin. Even more significantly, the title given to Kinnersley, who was probably our first college professor of English in any sense, contained the word "Oratory." Oratory, you may remember, I have called the mother of "English." We shall see in a moment how this happened, but meanwhile let us notice that when Kinnersley resigned in 1773, his successor at Pennsylvania, the lawyer James Wilson, actually gave some lectures on English literature.

In order to understand this momentous development we must turn, not to England, but to Scotland. During the four decades from, roughly, 1742 to 1783, George Campbell, Henry Home (Lord Kames), the philosopher-historian David Hume, the political economist Adam Smith, and other influential Scotsmen agreed on the importance of the arts of public speaking and reading, not only for prospective clergymen, but also for educated citizens in general. As a young man, Adam Smith lectured on rhetoric and literature at Kirkcaldy in 1748–51. Another member of this "Scottish school of rhetoric," the popular Edinburgh preacher Hugh Blair, began to read lectures on composition in the University late in 1759, and the following year the town council made him professor of rhetoric. The experiment was given both significance and permanence in April 1762 with the founding of a regius professorship of rhetoric and belles-lettres, to which Blair was appointed. Rhetoric was, of course, one of the oldest subjects in university education, but something now happened to it. Blair held this post until 1783, and, unlike the Oxford Professor of Poetry, who had a similar opportunity, he chose to lecture in English on English literature. Moreover, when he resigned in 1783 he published his lectures and thus gave other institutions a popular textbook, which Yale adopted in 1785, Harvard in 1788, and Dartmouth in 1822. Blair's was not the only textbook available, however, and the titles of some other influential ones may help me to make the point I am now concerned with. There were, for example, John Ward's two-volume *System of Oratory* (1759) and Thomas Sheridan's *Lectures on Elocution* (1763); and William Enfield's *The Speaker* (1774) quickly became, and long remained, the authoritative anthology of "recitations" from Shakespeare, Sterne, Pope, and more recent writers.

In an age that produced Charles Fox and Edmund Burke in England and Patrick Henry and James Otis in America, the atmosphere was right for a mushrooming of popular interest in oratory and "elocution." What had caused this, I suspect, was the dramatic development of parliaments in the eighteenth century, and the emergence of great orators who were not clergymen. In the second half of the eighteenth century the idea caught on quickly in America, inside, and even more outside, classrooms. The coming century was to witness the fame of Henry Ward Beecher, John Calhoun, Henry Clay, Stephen Douglas, Robert Ingersoll, Wendell Phillips, Daniel Webster, and others—to say nothing of a short, simple address delivered at a place called Gettysburg. Early teachers of "English" were also, usually, teachers of speech. As in ancient Greece and Rome, the art of "rhetoric" once again embraced non-clerical oratory.

In 1806 the Boylston professorship of rhetoric and oratory was founded at Harvard, and the first appointee was John Quincy Adams, who later became President of the United States, thus setting a provocative prededent for all future teachers of English! Adams' lectures, published in 1810, were the first attempt by an American to reunite rhetorical theory with classical doctrines. The Boylston professor from 1819 to 1851 was Edward Tyrrel Channing, teacher of Dana, Emerson, Holmes, and Thoreau. The first half of the nineteenth century in the new republic was a time of many public lectures, of lyceums and other popular societies for literary and liberal education, of literary and debating societies on college campuses, and, in general, of much amateurish and informal attention to both rhetoric and belles-lettres. Although Emerson's famous "American scholar" address was delivered in 1837, it is important to remember that this was *not* a time that produced in America any literary or linguistic scholarship of real substance, and the professor of English language and literature did not immediately emerge. In the United States before 1860 only a very few colleges ventured to mention English literature as a subject in their catalogues or announcements. Dartmouth dared to do so in 1822. In 1827 Amherst offered "Lectures in English and American Literature" as part of a bravely projected modern course of study to parallel the traditional one for the ancient languages and literatures, but the offering was soon withdrawn. Another American pioneer was Middlebury, whose 1848–49 catalogue announced "Critiques on the British and American Classics" as a course in the third term of the junior year, and this offering survived for some decades. On the other hand, Oberlin College considered Shakespeare unsuitable for mixed classes until 1864. The regius professorship at Edinburgh and the Boylston professorship at Harvard were harbingers of things to come, but were not, essentially, first steps in the development of an academic discipline that could demand, and get, equal recognition with the classical languages. For such a revolutionary change in established patterns of education some other factors were necessary— among them, a new, scientific linguistics, a new and rigorous methodology adaptable to literary studies, and a new concept of liberal education. These three factors were all to emerge during the last three quarters of the nineteenth century, but their impacts and results were to be different in the United States from what they were in England.

There were only seven universities in the entire British Isles from 1591 to 1828, a period in which more than *seventy* colleges or universities were founded in America, to survive down to our own day. In 1828, however, what is now University College, London, opened as the University of London, and during the remainder of the nineteenth century the number of British universities *doubled*. This "red-brick" explosion of higher education in England, which tardily reflects a similar phenomenon in the United States, is complex in its origins, but one of the factors was popular reaction against exclusiveness and traditionalism in the curriculum, especially the domination of the classical languages. It is not, therefore, mere coincidence that the sudden proliferation of universities in England produced formal instruction in the modern languages, including English, and even in English literature. Nor is it coincidence that both Oxford and Cambridge were the last universities in the entire English-speaking world to establish professorships in English language and literature. Even after they had reduced to meaningless formalities the medieval exercises in the Schools, the narrow system of written final examinations which succeeded, in 1780 and 1800, prevented the growth of any new kind of learning. The entrenched classical curriculum was not only reconfirmed in the venerable universities which had been looked up to as models by Harvard, Yale, and other institutions; effective means had been found to discourage any possible competition. Moreover, until as late as 1871 graduates of Cambridge and Oxford still had to subscribe to the Thirty-nine Articles, proving their adherence to the Church of England. This fact accounts for the growth during the eighteenth century of the many nonconformist academies, which served as theological seminaries for non-Anglicans, and often, not incidentally, were receptive to ideas of an "English" education. Although it soon added an Anglican college, King's, the new University of London began as a *non-sectarian* institution, and it is not surprising, therefore, that when it opened its doors on Gower Street in 1828, it had a professor of English language and literature. His name was Thomas Dale; he was a popular preacher in London and an old-fashioned high church evangelical; in his first year as professor he wrote and published *An Introductory Lecture to a Course upon the Principles and Practice of English Composition.* Dale was the author of seventy some other works, including some minor poetry, a translation of Sophocles, and an edition of the poems of William Cowper. We need not be ashamed of England's first English professor. We shall meet many other clergymen as English professors in the decades to follow, in both Great Britain and the United States. The fact is significant; until another new university, the Johns Hopkins, insisted that English professors needed a special kind of preparation, the literacy and oratorical skills and genteel acquaintance with literature that clergymen presumably had were considered preparation enough. What eventually made that preparation seem inadequate was the development of a new scientific linguistics and a new historical criticism.

For my personal edification I have tried to trace the growth of the teaching of English in many dozens of institutions in Great Britain, the United States, Canada, and elsewhere, and I wish there were time to give you some of the more interesting details, and to name some of the more interesting people. One other phenomenon, however, I must not fail to mention, for it is important to what I shall later want to say about the departmentalization of our subject. Unlike Thomas Dale of London, many early professors of English were simultaneously professors of modern *history.* This was the case at Cornell, Toronto, Manchester, Queen's University (Belfast), Queen's College (Cork), the University colleges at Cardiff and Liverpool, and elsewhere. On the other hand, one year after Springhill College, Birmingham, opened in 1838, it appointed the *Edin-*

burgh reviewer Henry Rogers as its professor of English literature and language, mathematics, and mental philosophy. By the time of the commencement of the American Civil War, the embryonic or new universities of England had made English a familiar if not yet wholly acceptable part of the curriculum, and the ancient Scottish and Irish universities then followed suit in their own way. Aberdeen, founded in 1494, in 1860 led the way with the appointment of Alexander Bain as professor of logic and English. This was not an unnatural combination; logic as an academic subject used to be associated with rhetoric, and argumentative composition was even thought of as a branch of logic. In any case, logic and English were not separated at Aberdeen until 1894. At St. Andrews the early professorship embraced logic, metaphysics, and English literature. Dublin University, which had been founded in 1591, in 1855 finally attached to the normal duties of its professor of oratory the obligation to give instruction in English literature, but when this man gave up the post in 1866 to become professor of Greek, Dublin appointed Edward Dowden as its first professor of English, a post he held until his death in 1913.

These titular details, with their suggestions of compromise and uncertainty about the sufficient substance of English as an academic subject, make a revealing background for the stubborn unwillingness of the two most ancient universities to get on the bandwagon of modernity. But in 1873 English was finally admitted into the Oxford "pass" examination for the final Schools—the tacit assumption being that students not bright enough to try for honors in the classics could somehow obtain adequate instruction in English from their college tutors. In 1877 an attempt was made to extend this gain by establishing an honors school of modern literature, including English, but it of course failed.

From 1854 to 1868 Friedrich Max Müller had been the second Taylorian professor of modern European languages at Oxford, but this new post, so widely unwelcome in the University, was abolished when he abandoned it to take the new chair of comparative philology. Here was the shape of things to come. The English Philological Society had been founded in 1842; the Cambridge and Oxford Philological Societies, in 1868 and 1870, respectively. Max Müller, who probably did more than any other man to popularize Germanic philology or linguistics in England, had published his two-volume *Science of Language* in 1861–63. When Oxford finally acquired a Merton Professor of English language and literature, he was to be another eminent philologist (A. S. Napier)—unhappily, as critics immediately complained, an expert on early English *language* with little or no interest in literature. In the United States the first professor of the English language and comparative philology was the scholarly Francis Andrew March, who was given this title by Lafayette

College in 1857 and held it until 1906. The title was highly significant; it spelled out the new field of linguistics that was eventually to give English studies solidity and respectability and influence at even the old, established universities. At Harvard, for example, that fine scholar, Francis James Child, who had been Boylston professor of rhetoric and oratory since 1851, and had actually been lecturing on English language and literature since about 1854, in 1876 became the first professor of English literature. English was now moving toward a new "image" or identity.

We need occasionally to remind ourselves of what English amounted to only eighty-three years ago, when a few leaders in the emerging profession felt it necessary to organize a *Modern* Language Association, joining forces with French and German to challenge the entrenched classical curriculum. In most of the colleges that had pioneered in teaching it, the place of English was still quite subordinate, both as to time allotted and results expected. The usual offering consisted of an hour or two of lectures for ten or twelve weeks by the professor of belles-lettres, who also taught such courses as history, logic, evidences of Christianity, moral philosophy, rhetoric, and oratory. The professor who taught *only* English was still a great rarity. The typical survey course was likely to be historical, biographical, and esthetic, with Chaucer, Spenser, and Shakespeare the most important figures. There was rarely any attempt to study the language historically or comparatively, for almost no English teachers had been trained to do this. The simple truth is that by 1883 almost no English teachers had been trained (period). The typical professor, as we have seen, was a doctor of divinity who spoke and wrote the mother tongue grammatically, had a general "society knowledge" of the literature, and had not specialized in this or any other academic subject.

But graduate education was, as everyone now knows, vigorously launched in the United States when the Johns Hopkins University opened in 1876, frankly setting out to import European (particularly German) ideals and methodology. It meant to naturalize, if possible, the spirit of specialization, the concept of the teacher as investigator and producing scholar, and, for our field, the "scientific" approach to literary and linguistic research. The fame of Paris and of the German universities had spread in this country for many decades, and so the stimulating example of Johns Hopkins was soon followed enthusiastically as other graduate schools sprang up in the institutions that could afford them. A new standard of post-baccalaureate work had been set. It was almost a symbolic act when English and German were combined into a single department at Johns Hopkins in 1882–83, with a future professor of German as head. Linguistically speaking, of course, this was not a strange marriage. Nor was it practically speaking, for if the young graduate student or recent

Ph.D. in English had something to publish (as was now expected of him), the logical place to send it before 1884 was either the *Englische Studien* or *Anglia,* both published in Germany and both devoted to English philology. No publication in any English-speaking country was yet exclusively devoted to the study of any of the modern languages.

Graduate work in English on the Johns Hopkins pattern meant rigorous training in linguistics and textual analysis. It also meant that little or nothing beyond seventeenth-century English literature was worthy of serious attention in graduate instruction; after all, there was the practical problem of time; with the now accepted need of mastering Anglo-Saxon, Middle English, old and modern French, old and modern German, and, preferably, several other Germanic languages or dialects, how could one possibly take graduate courses in recent English or American literature, even if they were offered? The linguistic emphasis of graduate training at Johns Hopkins—and subsequently at Harvard, Yale, and elsewhere—was to produce, during the next fifty years in America, a completely new kind of English professor, later to be rendered obsolete by the same educational revolution which had created him.

I must now repeat what I have had occasion to write elsewhere: the main objectives for which the MLA was founded would have been achieved during the next few decades whether or not the MLA had ever existed. From about 1883 onward, the classics declined in power and prestige, and the star of the modern languages rose. At least four factors in the decline and fall of the prescribed, classical curriculum are now quite clear. There were the impact of science, the American spirit of utilitarianism or pragmatism, and the exciting, new dream of democratic, popular education, an assumed corollary of which was the free elective system. A fourth factor may be described as a widespread mood of questioning and experimentation in education, a practical, revisionary spirit that challenged all traditions and accepted practices. Ironically, this attitude was later, in the third and fourth decades of the twentieth century, to disparage *all* foreign language study, but meanwhile it suffered the modern foreign languages to compete on equal terms with, and almost to supplant, the classical languages. English, on the other hand, was not to encounter the same reverses in favor; as we have seen, it was almost providentially prepared by recent events to be "scientific" and difficult in the most approved Germanic manner, but it was also, when provided with the means soon after 1883, quite willing to be utilitarian and popular. Since we still live with this paradox, and enjoy its precarious benefits, we had better understand it. It was the teaching of freshman composition that quickly entrenched English departments in the college and university structure—so much so that no one seemed to mind when professors of

English, once freed from this slave labor, became as remote from every-day affairs as the classicists had ever been. To the best of my knowledge, no one has ever shown why it is more "useful" to know Anglo-Saxon than to know Latin, or educationally more valuable to know English literature than to know Greek literature; and, in my considered judgment, either would be a very difficult case to make. But no one needs to persuade the American public that freshman composition is essential, despite the fact that it rarely accomplishes any of its announced objectives.

Surprising as the idea may first appear to you, there was, of course, no compelling reason at the outset why the teaching of *composition* should have been entrusted to teachers of the English language and literature. Teaching the language meant teaching it historically and comparatively, according to the latest methods of scientific philology. It was a far cry from this to freshman themes. As everyone knew in 1883, composition was a branch of rhetoric, a subject which had been a basic part of the college curriculum since medieval times. As everyone also knew in 1883, composition involved oratory in addition to writing intended only for silent reading. Another relevant fact was a matter of recent history: composition was now permitted in the mother tongue. But these facts do *not* add up to the conclusion that the professor of rhetoric and oratory should disappear, to be supplanted by the teacher of English language and literature. In 1876, when Francis Child became Harvard's first professor of English, his post as professor of rhetoric and oratory was immediately filled by someone else. And naturally so.

Chronology is the key to what finally happened; if "English" had been somewhat *later* in gaining academic recognition and respectability in the United States (as it actually was at Cambridge and Oxford, for example), it would probably never have been so strongly affected by the educational events of the 1880's and 1890's which we must now consider. This was a period in which the whole *structure* of higher education in America underwent profound changes, yielding to the pressures of new learning, the elective system, increased specialization, acceptance of the idea that practical or useful courses had a place in higher education, and, not least in importance, the actual *doubling* of college enrollments during the last quarter of the century. So long as there had been a narrow, prescribed curriculum and not too many students, departments of instruction had little or no administrative significance, and although the word "department" was sometimes used earlier, it was not really until the 1890's (at Harvard, for example, not until 1891; at my own university, not until 1893) that departments became important administrative units, pigeonholes into which one dropped all the elements of a rapidly expanding curriculum. Delegating responsibility, college officials looked to the various departments to judge the suitability of course offerings, the relationships of courses, prerequisites, and programs for majors and minors; to make recommendations for appointments, promotions, and salary increases; and to seek money or equipment or both. Perhaps inevitably, departments soon became competitive and ambitious, looking anxiously at any unoccupied territory between themselves and neighboring departments.

It was in this atmosphere that "English" in the United States, very recently became an accepted subject, grew to maturity, over-reached itself, and planted deeply the seeds of most of its subsequent troubles as an academic discipline. Early chairmen and early professors of English *literature* were willing if not eager to increase the prestige of their subject and the numbers of their students and course offerings by embracing, not only *linguistics* (including English grammar and the history of the language and even, whenever possible, comparative philology), but also *rhetoric,* which normally included, of course, oratory, elocution, and all forms of written composition. How this latter coup was possible I shall explain in a moment, but first let us remind ourselves of the full scope of the aggressiveness (some would say acquisitiveness) exhibited by departments of "English." They were later to embrace, just as greedily, journalism, business writing, creative writing, writing for engineers, play-writing, drama and theater, and American literature, and were eventually to be offering courses in contemporary literature, comparative literature, the Bible and world classics in translation, American civilization, the humanities, and "English for foreigners." In sum, English departments became the catchall for the work of teachers of extremely diverse interests and training, united theoretically but not actually by their common use of the mother tongue. Disintegration was therefore inevitable. Since there was no diminishing of the various forces that caused the original creation of departmental structure in colleges of arts and sciences, splintering of departments eventually ensued, often with great bitterness and an unhealthy increase in competitive spirit.

Let us pause a moment to recognize the practical implications of what I have been saying. Thanks first to its academic origins, and then to the spirit of competition and aggressiveness engendered by departmentalization, *"English" has never really defined itself as a discipline.* Before 1883, as we have seen, it was associated chaotically with rhetoric, logic, history, and many another definable subject. In 1885 Professor John McElroy of Pennsylvania was boasting to his MLA colleagues: "Today English is no longer, as it once was, every modern subject of the course except itself." *He* was a Professor of Rhetoric and the English Language, and his self-congratulations came just on the eve of history repeating itself. The typical English teacher in the 1890s and later no longer had a multi-title, but he belonged to a department that had multi-purposes, and normally his graduate training had almost nothing to do with what he found himself doing in the classroom. Having recently mastered Anglo-Saxon and the techniques of textual analysis, he began by teaching composition or speech, with perhaps an occasional survey course to lessen the pain. Much later, if he survived, he might be allowed to teach his specialty to graduate students who, in turn, would begin by teaching freshman composition.

How did it happen that newly created departments of English, with some variety of titles, were able at the close of the nineteenth century to preempt instruction in the skills of writing and speaking, to assume administrative control over the teaching of composition in any form? (This was not, to be sure, universal; at some few institutions, departments of rhetoric, oratory, or elocution developed alongside departments of English; but the prevailing administrative practice was to lump all these subjects under the rubric of "English.") As we have seen, historically the academic study of English literature was a protégé of the study of one of the oldest subjects in the curriculum, rhetoric, which during the later eighteenth and early nineteenth centuries, particularly in the Scottish universities, became increasingly identified with belles-lettres and literary criticism. But the Scottish school of rhetoric had also associated rhetoric with secular oratory. What probably changed this in the first half of the nineteenth century, and caused rhetoric to be more and more associated with belles-lettres, was the shift in attention from the written word to the voice and body control involved in the increasingly popular study of "elocution." Although taught in a number of American colleges during the nineteenth century, and required at some, elocution not only failed to achieve academic respectability; it caused a flight of teachers from oratory to imaginative literature (e.g., Hiram Corson at Cornell, or Bliss Perry at a later period), and it seriously damaged the once great prestige and importance of speech training. Elocution in the colleges was taught for the most part by specially trained itinerant teachers rather than by regular faculty members. In 1873 it ceased to be a required subject at Harvard. By 1900 the new School of Oratory at the University of Texas was carefully explaining that its purpose was *not* training in elocution. When the Speech Association of America was founded in 1914, it disdainfully dissociated itself from the "elocutionists" of the private schools. Perhaps in the hope of gaining academic respectability, elocution at the close of the nineteenth century associated itself more and more with literary criticism and appreciation, but this simply caused it to be swallowed up the more easily by English departments, which could then conveniently de-emphasize it.

To sum up: the ancient subject of rhetoric, which at first showed signs of adapting itself to changing times while preserving both its integrity and its vitality, in the nineteenth century lost both integrity and independent vitality by dispersing itself to academic thinness. It permitted oratory to become identified with elocution, and, as for written composition, it allowed this to become chiefly identified with that dismal, unflowering desert, freshman theme-writing. It is little wonder that speech and composition were readily accepted by administrators as appendices of English literature, especially when various events conspired to tie the knot tightly. In 1888, for example, the New England Commission for Colleges set a list of *books for reading* as preparation for college entrance examinations in English *composition.* In 1892 the "Committee of Ten" of the National Education Association formally recommended that literature and composition be unified in the high school course. That did it. Increasingly, thereafter, college entrance exams linked composition with literature, and, not unnaturally, linked high school work in "English" with beginning college work in composition. Speech training, once so important in education (as, indeed, it still is or should be), tended to get left out of this convenient combination, with results that should have been predictable.

And you know the sequel. Little by little English departments lost journalism, speech, and theater, and recently we have seen the development of separate undergraduate departments of comparative literature and linguistics. There have been polylingual grumblings from foreign language departments about the English department monopoly of courses in world literature. For a time there was a real threat of separate departments of "communication" (e.g., at Michigan State University), but "English" has somehow managed to hold on stubbornly to all written composition not intended for oral delivery—a subject which has always had a most tenuous connection with the academic study of language and literature, but which, not incidentally, from the outset has been a great secret of strength for "English" with both administrators and public, and latterly has made possible the frugal subsidizing of countless graduate students who cannot wait to escape it. Should our graduate students some day be subsidized instead by the Federal Government (as seems to me likely to happen eventually), it remains to be seen whether or not the nineteenth-century union of literature and composition was a true marriage or merely a marriage of convenience.

I have been tracing for you some not very ancient history, and I should like, finally, to draw some personal conclusions from it. They are rather drastic, and you may not be able to accept any of them. History teaches different things to different people, and some people believe that nothing can be learned from it. As I stated initially, I believe that we can learn a great deal. You may think me unfitted to be a chairman when I say, now, that the history of our profession inspires in me very little respect for departments of English; their story is one of acquisitiveness, expediency, and incredible stupidity. I care a lot about liberal education, and I care a lot about the study of literature in English, but it seems to me that English departments have cared much less about liberal education and their own integrity than they have about their administrative power and prosperity.

We cannot turn back the clock and bring speech back into English departments, but this realistic fact seems to me no justification for English abandoning all training in speech and oral composition for its majors—especially for those who intend to become teachers at any level of education, including the graduate level. English needs still to learn something from its mother.

And even more from its father. It strikes me as ironic and more than slightly ridiculous that we increasingly want "English" to mean the close reading of words while we steadily increase our ignorance of the nature and history of language in general and the English language in particular. Study of literature without more than casual or amateurish knowledge of language is destined, in my considered judgment, to share the fate of elocution. The penalty most fitting this crime would be to make us a sub-department of linguistics.

It also strikes me as ironic and more than slightly ludicrous that we take it on ourselves to teach, not only literature in English, but also world literature, in a monolingual vacuum. Our early associations with the classical languages and the modern foreign languages were meaningful and valuable; we have abandoned them at a high cost to our integrity and our common sense.

The history I have sketched for you shows "English" changing its character many times in the brief century of its academic existence, and these changes have of course continued in the past four decades, about which I have said nothing but am tempted to say a great deal, since they are the period in which I have been an active, conscious member of the profession. Let me say only that, so far as I know, few if any of the many changes have come about as a result of deliberate, long-range planning on the national level, despite the existence of the MLA and the NCTE. And that suggests my final thought: there will certainly be further changes in the years to come, but are we not now mature enough as a profession, and "hep" enough as historians, to frame our own future history, not for the benefit of English departments, but for the welfare of the young and the benefit of American education? I believe that we are, and I care about where English departments came from *only* because I care very deeply indeed about where they are going. Let me urge you to strike while the irony is hot.

JOHN C. GERBER

Suggestions for a Commonsense Reform of the English Curriculum

Let us start where all educational considerations should always start: with our contemporaries. Do we have a service to offer our contemporaries that is unique and essential for their well-being? The answer is *yes*. We have had such a service to offer ever since the beginning of our profession. And in one fashion or another, we *have* been offering it. But consciously or subconsciously over the years, we have taken pains to hide the fact from both the public and from ourselves. For the service is nothing more and nothing less than training our contemporaries to read and write.

By writing, I mean every type of written discourse from the simplest sentence wrestled over in writing laboratories to the most subtle kind of imaginative work produced in our creative-writing workshops. The term implies not only exposition but rhetoric, scientific and technical writing, business and professional writing, film and TV scenario writing, poetry and fiction writing, satire, and humor and burlesque, and whatever other modes are current and desired. By reading, I mean not attention to such concerns of the psychologist as eye-fixation and reading rate, but the reading of texts for pleasure and stimulation as well as understanding. Depending on the maturity of the students, the texts can vary from "Frankie and Johnny" to *Finnegan's Wake*.

As I intimated above, we have been at pains to cover up the fact that we are basically teachers of reading and writing, probably because we find it more assuaging to the ego to call ourselves Romanticists or Johnsonians than teachers of reading and writing. Writing we have called

From *College Composition and Communication*, 28 (December, 1977), 312–316. Reprinted by permission of the National Council of Teachers of English and John C. Gerber.

"composition," "rhetoric," or "exposition" and have assigned instruction in it largely to graduate assistants and staff members low on the scale of prestige. Reading we have dolled up by calling it "critical reading" or obscured it altogether by calling it "practical criticism." Yet we are teachers of reading, pure and simple, whether we have students practice Middle English pronunciation or explore the theme of *Hamlet* or determine the organization of *Tom Jones* or look for the movement in an Emersonian essay or examine *Mardi* as Melville's batting practice for *Moby-Dick* or compare *Tom Sawyer* with the young Sam Clemens. No matter what our approach, we are basically concerned with the accurate reading of texts.

True, you may be willing to say, but so what? There is a big "so what," because if we can conceive of our basic task as training our contemporaries to read and write, we have changed the context in which we think and work. We now have a context that brings us all together, Shakespearians and teachers of the fourth grade. We have a purpose that gives relation to all that we do. Whether we are historians, New Critics, or whatever, we are ultimately concerned with the same end: to help the students in reading a text to cut through the idiosyncrasies of the author, language, time, place, nationality, and literary form to the essential meaning. Seeing ourselves as teachers of reading and writing makes us a community again. Furthermore, we have a basic purpose that our contemporaries will accept as *unique*, since no other professional group is primarily concerned with it, and as *essential*, since regardless of the McLuhans, they recognize that the continuation of civilization depends upon the written word. Finally, and maybe most importantly of all, training our contemporaries to read and write is a basic purpose that *we* can see as necessary and vital. Who, we may well ask, performs a *more* necessary public service? Something like this, then, should be the opening sentence in our catalogue descriptions: The Department of English offers training in reading and writing in every mode and at every necessary level of difficulty.

The next question is: To whom do we offer this training in reading and writing? Since we are engaged in post-secondary education, the answer should be everybody from 17 to 97: young Penrod there in the first row in English 100 and his great grandmother in the nursing home across town. Without a doubt, we shall continue for some time to devote most of our effort to the young men and women who register for our classes, but increasingly our obligation should extend to those who have completed their professional training and who are now active in their professions or to those who simply seek further intellectual stimulation wherever they may wish to come together—in public libraries, churches, prisons, nursing homes, factories, or offices. For these serious and eager people, we cannot allow such instruction to be taken over by proprietary institutions, many of which are concerned only with the making of a fast buck. Except for some of our colleagues who teach in community colleges, we have hardly begun to tap the possibilities of adult education. Yet such education is clearly one of our responsibilities—and one of our practical opportunities, since adult education will require additional staff. I have seen one demographic study that concludes with the astonishing statement that "before the turn of the century the education of adults will become the principal purpose of American higher education." Here clearly is our best hope for improving our job market.

Now we come to the "oldie": what is our subject matter? In this broad context, the answer to this question should be equally broad: everything in writing is the product of the verbal imagination; that is, of the mind when it is seriously concerned with form and effect as well as content. This is a conclusion reached last year by the NCTE's Commission on Literature, and I happily borrow it here. If English and Speech were not separated, we could say *every* product of the verbal imagination—as they can say in departments of Communication or Language Arts in which the written and the spoken word are both matters of concern. But the written word in all its forms is enough of a challenge for most of us for the time being.

Thus we make for ourselves a context for admitting courses in literature and film, literature and TV, scenario writing, popular literature, and all the others that we have in fact admitted but been uneasy about. The real challenge will be to remain flexible enough to suit the material to the students and to build bridges between the popular and those works that we have traditionally most admired. Many of our colleagues in the community colleges have practiced this art for years. So now must we all, if we are to go public, so to speak, and train persons in reading and writing whoever they are and wherever they are. It will be instructive in more ways than one for a Shakespearian to deal with TV scenarios, for a Blake scholar to discuss hard-boiled realism with prison inmates, and for a distinguished poet to work with elderly ladies who want to write greeting card verses. But the experience will be good for our immortal souls, assuming that we have such, and it will make all of us much more human if not humane.

Still, for the foreseeable future, most of our activities will continue to occur in the conventional classroom, and thus we shall continue to have to deal with the problems of degree programs. What of them if our basic function is to teach reading and writing, and our subject matter includes every written product of the verbal imagination?

I have space to mention only a few of the implications of what I have said for our curricula. The undergraduate program, it seems to me, should be a liberal arts, non-professional program in which our primary concern is to train the students in the arts of reading and writing. Training in writing, as now, will probably have to begin with elementary composition, but above this level, there should be training in every mode and at every possible level of competence. There should be no distinction in these classes between majors and non-majors, though careful attempts should be made to adapt the type and level of writing to the needs and capabilities of the individual student. If we are to meet even the present demands for training in writing, we shall have to assign at least a third of our manpower to this field—this means a third of almost everyone's time, not a third of the department, meaning the youngest third.

Similarly, the training program in reading should result in a series of experiences that enable students to hone their reading skills, especially skill in reading English and American literature. There are many ways in which this program can be set up. I am particularly impressed with the idea of having the first level confined to the reading of individual texts and of having the higher levels require the student successively to read texts in larger and more complex contexts. That is, the first level could be designed to make reading as appealing and intellectually tantalizing as possible. The next higher levels could require reading works in the context of genres, in the context of literary and cultural periods, and finally in interdisciplinary contexts in which literature is related to art, science, social problems, myth, or whatever. At no level, however, should the literary work be presented as a cold artifact; at every level, the attempts should be to have the undergraduate read it as a personal message across time and space.

The graduate program I would make unabashedly professional. We have erred in my opinion in presuming that the undergraduate program should be primarily preparation for graduate training and that the graduate program in turn is nothing more than a continuation of the liberal-arts training for undergraduates. The vast majority of our undergraduates have no intention of going on for graduate work in English, and the vast majority of our graduate students are such because they want to be trained for vocations in English or related fields. Hence it seems to me only commonsense to base a graduate program on such propositions as these:

1. A graduate program is to prepare a student for an occupation.

2. It must therefore train students for the kinds of tasks that they will perform in their professional activities.

3. Most of the training, therefore, must be devoted to the acquisition of skills, not subject matter.

4. While subject matter is necessary, nothing like full coverage in any area is necessary, since coverage is a life-long, on-the-job responsibility.

5. Graduate programs in English should be broad enough and flexible enough to prepare students not only for teaching but for every kind of professional work requiring expertly trained readers, researchers, and writers.

As you can see from these five propositions, I would place the stress in our graduate training on the acquisition of skills rather than subject matter. Students should leave our graduate classrooms able to perform the tasks that they will be required to perform in their vocations.

First of all, they themselves should be able to write well. Thus, they need advanced training in rhetoric and stylistics and the theories of language and writing. More than that, they should have considerable training in writing itself, both critical and imaginative. In fact, I would be willing to make the writing of English prose one of the tool skills, substituting it for one of the foreign languages we now require. If nothing else, such a requirement might result in the injection of more liveliness into our solemn journals.

Second, our graduate students should be trained in reading, and not on the hit-and-miss basis that now obtains. They should have considerable work in critical theory and critical practice. For example, they should be schooled in the principles and methodology of such fields as phenomenology, structuralism, semiotics, and hermeneutics; and, if possible, they should have work in such allied fields as linguistics (including computer analysis), anthropology, aesthetics, and the psychology of learning. They should explore at length the special reading problems, not just the ideas, of English and American literature of every form and of selected literary periods.

Third, there should be more explicit and rigorous training in the techniques of research than we now offer in most departments. Research, it should be made clear, is a way of life in our profession, even for those who intend only to teach. For some quixotic reason, we call it "research" if we are working on scholarly books or articles, but we call it "preparation" if we are digging up material for a class lecture or discussion. The usual dichotomy between teaching and research is therefore a false one. The only dichotomy is the one between research that leads to oral publication in the classroom and research that leads to printed publication in books and journals. To repeat, the techniques of research are an essential part of every graduate student's training. And by techniques, I mean not just how to find a book in the local library or a government document in the Public Records Office but how to evaluate material found, how to draw conclusions and inferences from it, how to reason on the basis of it, how to assemble it and present it cogently to a variety of audiences. There should be basic courses in these techniques, and the techniques should be reinforced strongly in every graduate seminar.

Fourth, for the students planning to teach, there should be training in such arts as teaching, course organization, and testing at the college level. Already such training exists in many universities, many of the programs being very excellent indeed. Ideally, however, I would hope that there could be apprentice programs arranged whereby graduate students learn the rudiments of teaching not only in university classrooms but also in classrooms in two-year and four-year colleges. One of the reasons why community colleges don't want Ph.D.'s is that the Ph.D.'s seldom have any notion of the ambience of the two-year college, are not prepared for it, and in many cases quickly reject it.

It is only commonsense to have the doctoral examinations designed to disclose how well the candidate has mastered these skills, not simply how well he or she has achieved coverage in approved literary periods. Moreover, both the M.A. and the Ph.D. candidate should be encouraged to make writing, the theories of writing, and the theories of teaching writing an area of specialization. English M.A.'s have been surprisingly successful in finding positions when they can show that they have had intensive training in writing, and the last two MLA *Job Information Lists* indicate that those trained in the teaching of composition are in far greater demand than those specializing in any of the customary literary fields. The little moral of this fact should not go unnoticed by either graduate students or graduate faculties.

I see all of the changes I have recommended in this paper as based simply on commonsense. They are changes which can be brought into being in the coming year. Although they are admittedly not alterations that get at the basic problems of the power structure of American universities, they will have effects on the power structure in departments of English. The most valuable members of the department will no longer be those whose material is most esoteric and whose appeal is only to a small, elite group. Rather, the most valuable members will be those whose concern is with society as a whole and whose professional ambition is to train everyone who wishes such training to be clear writers and discerning and appreciative readers.

Do I foresee all such changes coming to pass in most departments in the near future? In a word, no. Most of us are too much the creatures of inertia, tradition, elitism, and sheer cussedness to be receptive to change, even such modest changes as I have outlined. The majority of our departments, I suspect, will be forced to make a few cosmetic alterations, adding a course in composition here, an adult-education class there. Mostly, I am afraid, they will continue to proceed on the assumption that old ways are best, on the assumption that the pendulum will eventually swing back to those allegedly splendid programs that existed when they were undergraduates and graduate students in English.

A few departments that are so opulent that they can continue to indulge themselves as they wish won't make *any* changes.

But there will be others, I hope, that will seriously ask themselves how they can best serve our contemporaries and that will reorder their work as best they can in order to do so. These in my opinion are the departments that will make it possible for our profession to survive.

Focus and Resolution

To freshmen we extol the virtues of focus in writing. "Narrow your topic," we say, "and ruthlessly cut out digression. Stick to your point." We divide a little in showing how Sterne or Lamb and their likes really had a point they were sticking to, but we are sure that somehow we can demonstrate that the unity exists so that we need not give up our advice to narrow the view. And see where it leads us.

Item. Recently the National Institute of Education sponsored an invitational conference on writing. About fifty people were invited to talk, and the group was suitably representative of males and females, of various ethnic groups. Departments of English, on the other hand, were only barely represented—some alleged as an afterthought—and no professional writers were included. The unstated assumption seemed to be that social scientists had focus and could define or narrow writing problems into sub-problems which are sufficiently restricted that they can be seriously studied. Sociologists, anthropologists, psychologists, ethnographers, and linguists abounded at the meeting. Writers DO writing and therefore could not be expected to talk about writing, perhaps because they try to keep all of the problems in mind at once.

Item. At the same conference the few literary people regularly brought up questions of purpose and value. No one quarreled about that, but neither would they discuss such issues. If literature was mentioned by the social scientists, it was either to damn "classic writers" or to cite the use of moral tales in the classroom as teaching devices. A number indicated that it was unrealistic to teach all students something about literary language, and no one among them cited or alluded to anything we might call

From *ADE Bulletin*, Number 57 (May, 1978), 8–12. Reprinted by permission of the Modern Language Association of America and Richard Lloyd-Jones.

literary. They also rarely used language we might recognize as literary. These very bright people simply found literary language unnecessary and uninteresting.

Item. Lest you think I am picking on NIE, which doubtless was trying to be helpful, let me tell you of two friends who were writing about fun with language as part of an introduction to a text for the freshman course. They wrote with literary wit, but their editor asked them to be solemnly pedestrian because English teachers would react to wit in a textbook as though it were a breech of decorum. I wish I thought the editor was wrong.

Item. Closer to home some directors of freshman English have formed an Organization of Writing Program Administrators. They did not find in MLA, NCTE, CCCC, ADE, or any of our other organizations a group which spoke to their needs as they saw fit. To be sure, we have new literary groups beyond count; often they deal with particular authors— Morris, Shaw, Disraeli, for example—and the composition people also have groups arguing special positions—"Writing as a Liberating Activity" or "Conference on Language Attitudes and Composition," for example. I note this one as a little different because it deals with the structure of departments. The writing directors, like the linguistics, and speech, and journalism people, bid to separate themselves from English in order to get focus and status.

Item. Enrollment in literature courses still declines and fewer students think a major in English has value. Probably the decline is leveling off, but our share of the totals predicted in polls of new freshmen do not encourage one to believe that we will be searching for new teachers to cope with additional students.

Item. Reliance on minimum competencies, behavioral objectives, and objective tests puts emphasis on knowledge of discrete bits of information as opposed to methods or heuristic approaches to knowledge. We have always tested students on their knowledge of texts by asking for factual detail, but we assumed that class discussion and paper writing ensured that students acquired a sense of how to read and evaluate at sophisticated levels. As the classroom paper becomes less common, as the classes get larger, as the methods of the sciences prevail, and as the goals of economic prosperity in an era of scarcity preoccupy the attention of the society, then we find the standardized test becomes the *only* source of knowledge about the student's work. It thus defines what the work is and makes insignificant the tacit knowledge we offer by classroom practice.

Item. Some departments, already tenured-in and fearful of more enrollment losses, worry more about protecting jobs than providing the needed education. Departments which just a few years ago were explaining why English should not be offering writing courses, now discover a crisis in literacy in order to get a few new sections. Often the people assigned to teach writing are the ones who are most defenseless in the organizational scheme rather than the most apt, but they fill classes. Assigning a writing class to each faculty member, a way of avoiding the invidious assigning of hard work only to the less prestigious of the faculty, merely guarantees that a number of the instructors will lack enthusiasm for the job—and often even the knowledge to do the job right. Some departments resist reviews of general education requirements in fear that they cannot make a proper case for literature and thus will lose even more sections. And if my inference is correct that literature is irrelevant to the lives of very bright, verbal, well-trained social scientists who are still interested enough in writing to study it, then our departments should be worried. Apparently in the past we have failed to convert some of the most likely candidates who now vote on general education requirements.

I might itemize some more, but it would just be depressing. Let me see whether I can draw lines between the itemized dots and get some whole picture to emerge.

Clearly we are on the defensive. No wonder, what with enrollments down, the humanities out of favor, and no obvious alternatives for employment, but perhaps defensive measures will just further erode our tight little island. Perhaps we have too much given in to fashion and too little asserted our own view of the world.

The present boredom with the humanities is probably not entirely of our own making, but we must live with it, so perhaps we should inquire why so many people consider us to be a fringe group to be pushed out with classics departments. Why did those bright social scientists turn off in school when you and I were turning on? As I recall we were exposed to two kinds of pedantry in our courses, but somehow we lived through it— or liked it so much we became pedants of the same kind. They quit.

One kind of pedant guided tours through stately literary monuments. We learned bodies of fact—all in isolation. I recall taking courses in which it was not necessary to read a single work of literature in order to pass. Yet the information we were examined on did not provide contexts, nor even especially good guidance in how to use the library. We did not see the past as a challenge to the present, nor even as especially interesting. Clearly those of us who survived found something out of the class pattern to make us want to survive, or didn't associate the class with what we considered literature to be, but it is easy to see why others did not. This was the world of the professors with yellowed notes and an arrogant delicacy of manner as they told you that you were boorish. Nevertheless, with a little labor one could pass the courses, so why complain?

I preferred the other kind of pedant, the one who milked a text. Because I thought of myself as a writer I had an appetite for devices and techniques. No internal relationship could bore me, and I took philosophy and psychology as well, so as to speculate on what the devices of language led to. Still, I noted that not all were so enthusiastic about dissecting texts, and I must admit we were fussy and we took a lot for granted. I can understand how other people thought we were playing in-games because we were clever at it, and I don't recall that we were much interested in the "mass" audience. The popularizers had gone out with journalism—or was it speech? Somehow we seemed to want literature without values, an artifact without an effect, perhaps even form without shape. And we despised "commercial" fiction or "writing for the movies."

Later when we became faculty, some of us, perhaps, were even parties to the rebellions against those kinds of pedantry. Some were so eager to be relevant, to go to the students where they were with what they had heard they wanted, that we threw out the solid old literary furniture for ill-built but gaudy, plastic fads. Some of the stuff we threw out really is dull; it served only to illustrate pedantic points. Some of what we added is good, undeservedly overlooked. Especially in teaching American literature it is important to go beyond those New Englanders with three names and include the less familiar excellences of American minorities—or even from various American regions. Social snobbery has caused us to devalue some important works and to give out to students some silly strictures about writing. Still, in our eagerness to correct a wrong we sometimes encouraged neglect of our important past, of views still powerful enough that we were reacting in opposition without really examining the value. We did, in fact, give up a large part of what makes the humanities important, and became pedants of another kind of trivia. Instead of enlarging the perspective by helping students feel at home in language of distant times and places we narrowed our focus to the faddish. When the National Endowment for the Humanities set up guidelines for grants for public funding of programs and said we should offer the views of the humanities on public issues, we saw no conflict. Why not read *King Lear* as a case study in gerontology? We let another discipline define our function. That is, we sold out.

At the same time, in reaction to dryasdust analysis we became sentimental in accepting good thoughts and sweet feelings. Recognizing that different ages and peoples have different needs and language does *not* mean that anything goes. We stopped requiring meaningful papers, cut reading lists, allowed bull sessions to replace systematic discussion or dialectic. I see no need to be grim about literature, but one must invest some work in order to get a return. One of the best arguments in favor of writing instead of speaking is that writing forces exactness despite the labor. People work hard when they see the value. No one says science is easy, or football, or even business management. People like work that satisfies their human needs. Surely what we offer contains the satisfaction which rewards work.

The confusing part of our error is that we now have all of these kinds of pedantry existing in single departments at the same time. Sometimes whole departments adopt just one kind, but on accreditation visits I have seen the complete mixture. The differences seem to cause only minor trouble in faculty meetings. In some instances, open requirements for the major mask the differences; the general education students take so few literature courses that the differences within a department don't show up to them. Even where requirements for the major are prescribed, the privacy of the classroom keeps secrets. Despite student opinionnaires and accountability we have managed, as Mina Shaughnessy says, to keep the classroom as private as the bedroom, and the people who come out the door brag equally of their spectacular successes. Still, we have reason to doubt.

Rather than blame our own attitudes toward literature and teaching, we prefer to blame the crass materialism of the time, and that is not wholly false. Better authentic Mammon than bogus humanism, as Mac-Niece said. We have seen in the last few decades large numbers of people drawn to college with the promise of larger incomes if they acquire a degree. Hardly ever do we hear education justified as essential to participation in self-government or even to human self-actualization. Private economic, not social, ends are stressed. We hear little about education as defining a good life as distinguished from a prosperous one. Freedom that results from understanding rather than from hedonism is hardly mentioned. In the last few years the public has chosen to measure the worth of education by its effectiveness in placing the young immediately into a specified slot in the economic machine. Our own departmental efforts to become bureaus of labor statistics, to control the number of graduates in relation to the number of jobs, tells just how much we are a part of the careerism we deplore. We can and should tell our Ph.D. candidates that English is a poor economic investment, but the society needs humanists more than it knows, and if the person enjoys the study enough to seek a doctorate with the prospect of being manager of a McDonald's, so be it. We have taught English as though it were a job skill rather than a compulsion, and those who come from a world of job-seeking can hardly be blamed for accepting our implicit admission that we have little else to offer.

I am not sure that I quite want to go back to Matthew Arnold and let literature substitute for religion, mostly because the preachers I've seen in the classroom seem to grow old and tedious so soon. In more stable times, perhaps one could ride a hobby horse for fifty years and not seem dull; nowadays even moralists have to stay alert to changes in society and scholarship or they end up preaching to the committed or to those who don't even recognize the issue. Polonius in his youth must have been a superbly practical court official, a Sam Rayburn or a Lyndon Johnson, but it is hard for us to see him in *Hamlet* as other than a windbag with his faults writ large.

If the temptation to devalue literature or to choose the model of science to present the message of literature has sapped our ability to be useful in society, our misvaluing of writing has been even more threatening. First we sent the most obviously transactional uses of language off to speech and journalism. We preferred to deal with high literary usage, and often pretended that it had no audience at all. The concern with what people in general might think was vulgar, probably tainted with social science. We narrowed our focus to deal with interpreting a limited range of discourse—often even a limited range of literary discourse. We dealt in completed texts and hoped to avoid the complex problems of teaching the verbal processes of relating to other humans. (We also got rid of remedial reading so we wouldn't have to think about the basic process of interpretation. We wanted only high intellectuality.)

Although we avoided most of the generative aspects of language, we did keep creative writing and to some extent the freshman course, although there is substantial evidence that we taught little writing in the freshman course. Some schools allowed courses in business and technical writing, and quite a number assigned some sort of advanced composition course to a crotchety person who did not quite fit into the department personnel plan. The courses have been popular, and thus embarrassing. The writing courses fill up, and the literature courses go begging. The natural response of those trained as readers has been to grumble about the expense and effort required for teaching writing, to jump all over the high schools for their malfeasance and pretend that we had nothing to do with the "literacy crisis." I suspect that the "crisis" is mostly a media event; the inability to write is chronic. Like most chronic diseases it should be treated, but probably the mad rush for quack treatments will cause as much harm as good. But that is another tale. The reaction of departments of English interests us now.

Talk of separating the freshman program from English is nothing new. Ours at Iowa has been separate for over thirty years, and that may be why it has worked so well. English has accepted a major responsibility for cooperating in its management, and we dared not to avoid paying attention or we'd have lost too much. Many community colleges offer "communication" or "humanities" or something else instead of English in recognition of the dormant function of the department. "English" has disappeared, as it did in elementary schools when the shift was made to "Language Arts." Many regret now the moves they made in the last decade to ditch the freshman program altogether, although one fears that the heart is laden with rue about the lost assistantships and credit hour production rather than about excessive narrowing of our view of ourselves. Still, departments join the propaganda about the crisis with a remarkable air of innocence. Suddenly there is federal money available for those who teach writing, programs spring up to train teachers of writing, remedial programs and skills centers are established (often outside of the English department with faculty rank independent of English), and writing teachers advocate a new organization for directors of freshman English, perhaps as part of ADE, but perhaps not. Separatism is a practical option.

By now it is apparent that I think that although it is an option, it is not one departments of English should like. Each time we've limited our definition of who we are, we have damaged our usefulness to higher education. Writing and reading are not truly reciprocal activities, but they are united in that they are concerned with language as it is experienced and valued. The linguists can be as scientific as they like—and their studies can be useful to us—but still we ought to engage both the practical and philosophic questions they declare out of their bounds. When we defined nonfiction out of literature and tried to restrict ourselves to teaching poetry and fiction, we distorted the nature of discourse as it exists and as it is important to a healthy society. The study of English should encompass all kinds of uses; our value to the academy and the society is that we study the mechanism which controls the perceptions of individual people and allows them to pool their experiences into a common understanding. Writing and reading in the full sense define humanity.

I am rejecting the notion that we encourage people to read, or write, or do scholarly work in our field primarily in order to increase their economic value. I accept the idea that the society ought to employ exceptionally good readers or writers to help it define itself and realize its own values. It may also want such people to teach. But I can imagine that the teaching can be trivialized—is often being trivialized under economic pressure—so we have to remind ourselves of our main purposes.

What do we need to do to serve our proper purposes? I think we need to find several balances among proper demands upon us, expecting to be harrassed by monomaniacs who want to define us all by what they are.

None of our purposes is new, but from decade to decade the over-compensation in one direction or another seems to change, so sometimes we have the illusion of stating new objectives.

First, we need to balance the contrasting needs to supply information about language and literature and to exemplify skills and processes of writing and reading. Essentially this was the issue between the first two sets of pedants I described. Clearly there is a tradition to be learned whether or not we equate it with the "Great Tradition." There are notable texts to be mastered, a common educational heritage upon which we all draw. We need information, but all of that information is practically unimportant unless we also know how to take a text apart, to discover meaning, to experience language in large segments.

Second, although we now have negotiated a relatively easy peace between scholars and critics about uses of knowledge, we still hear them battle over concerns with the text itself and the process by which a text is created. The concern is manifested in the battle between teachers of writing and reading, as well as between different camps on each side. In a practical sense, balancing writing and reading is *the* issue because most departments are heavily loaded with teachers of literature and have demands for teachers of writing, and (as I admitted) the operations are not reciprocal, and the teachers are not always ambidextrous. The writing teachers are expensive not because they draw remarkable salaries but because they can't teach many students at a time. Implicitly budget shifts are needed, and that is trouble.

Third, we still need to adjust the proportions of time devoted to old standards—to elitist works—and to popular culture. Even the terms are prejudicial. Much of the junk of the late 60s and early 70s has dropped out of print, and popular culture courses and cinema—often taught in American studies programs—have developed solid disciplinary bases. Revisionism in American literature has proceeded apace. Although we have moved out of the phase of wild claims and whimsical experiments, we still are working at the problems, and the general public often still doesn't know what is going on.

Fourth, we still must fight the battle between a liberal education and vocationalism, between servile and liberal ends. I have never quite been comfortable with Professor Orange's survey of employment opportunities for majors in English, although obviously the essay has seemed important to many people. I'd like to think it is self-evident that any person who is at home with language and who considers human values is potentially useful in any large organization of people. That the society, that English professors need to have it pointed out bothers me. But even more I am bothered by our acceptance of the notion that economic value is the principal value of education. Surely we do not offer physics or astronomy in general education or even in undergraduate majors for any practical value they have beyond that of satisfying human curiosity. The freshman psychology course merely exemplifies a way of knowing, and anyone who thinks it provides substantial material for therapy or product design is overreading the lessons. "If you're so smart, why ain't you rich" surely is intended as an ironical line. Our hope is that students will know the world in many ways, and from this knowledge wisdom will emerge.

Fifth, we need to reconsider how we treat the transactional functions of language in contrast to the formative ones. We are not likely to rejoin journalism and speech, but we can work jointly with them and make sure that our own expository courses or our general courses include language which is informative about something other than literary topics and persuasive in a variety of ways. To be sure, most of the techniques used to describe a poem are the same ones used to describe a single sideband transmitter, but the point needs to be made and illustrated, and the person in love with transmitters needs a chance to express that love in verbal language. Relating ideas to different kinds of audiences for different reasons is difficult for us all; neither do all professors of literature make good presentations for the local Lions Club. Even an occasional look at the mass media is good for us. We also need to consider the ways in which we become what we say. Efforts to help students find a voice, or a stance, or a set of values are implicit in learning to make language choices, and it involves us in complex moral relationships with our students. And the best of the formulators turn out to speak for the culture. A Thomas Jefferson may persuade us by using the best contemporary techniques of logical appeals as illustrated in the Rhetorics of his time, but he also found the language for a nation to live by; he provides the nation its values by phrasing the value.

I propose impossible tasks. How often does Strindberg say in *A Dream Play* that it is difficult to be human? Of course we will be out of balance. That is not the issue. The issue is that we should keep seeking a frame large enough to include the forces which are in opposition. Not only does the student need it to provide a sense of wholeness, we need it to keep ourselves active. There is no peace to be had by defining the opposition or ourselves out of the arena. The resolution of an image means that we bring sharper focus, but the resolution of issues means that we compound forces into a new, more powerful statement of reality. We have gone a long way toward inert isolation or narrow focus. We need to risk looking foolish and foolishly by trying to see with peripheral vision, by casting our eyes all about us so that we can better serve our functions as synthesizers in the academy.

WALTER J. ONG, S.J.

Literacy and Orality in Our Times

The English profession has always been concerned with how to create and interpret a written text. The past few years have seen a growth of interest, perhaps more theoretical than practical, in texts as such, in textuality, and a parallel growth of interest in readers as readers. But we know by contrast—an old philosophical principle long antedating modern phonemics and structuralism. Verbalization via texts and readers contrasts obviously with oral verbalization, the ancient and still basic form of verbalization. We have recently learned a great deal about the psychodynamics of orality, how oral verbalization, in pure preliterate form or in residual form within writing cultures, structures both thought processes and expression. But, strangely enough, those interested in writing and reading processes, either from a practical or a theoretical point of view, including the many and often brilliant structuralist and phenomenological analysts of textuality, have done little to enlarge understanding of these processes by contrasting writing and reading processes in depth with oral and oral-aural processes. This is what I propose to do here: to review the orality in our long cultural past in order to bring an understanding of it to bear on the present literary and para-literary situation.

Many people like to believe that today reading is on the wane. We have all heard the complaint that television is ruining the reading habits of children. This is a contrastive judgment: "ruining" implies that the time spent by today's children before television sets was all spent by yesterday's children with books. The implication appears at the very least naive. It is in fact very difficult to compare the present state of reading and writing skills or activity with those of the past because past student

From *ADE Bulletin*, Number 58 (September, 1978), 1–7. Reprinted by permission of the Modern Language Association of America and Walter J. Ong, S.J.

populations do not match those of the present. A few generations ago, there was no academic population with today's mix of family and cultural backgrounds, with the same assortment of entering abilities and disabilities, of skills and lack of skills, of desires and aims. Not long ago, America was largely rural. Now it is overwhelmingly urban or urbanized, even in rural areas, and educational expectations have correspondingly changed. Not long ago blacks were locked by law—illegal law—into a situation where even the most talented were denied upward mobility. And no one pointed a condemning finger at dropouts in any group because everyone took for granted that most boys and girls undergoing academic education of course dropped out, at least during college if they had not succeeded in dropping out earlier.

Even more importantly, the aims of literacy in the past were not quite the same as now. The McGuffey *Readers,* often cited in "back to basics" literature and talk, had objectives quite different from those commonly advanced today. They were in tune with our times in the sense that they were remedial texts—designed to improve the defective elementary and secondary education which William Holmes McGuffey blamed for the poor reading performance of his college students.[1] But "poor performance" meant largely poor oratorical performance: the McGuffey *Eclectic Readers* (so-called because they adroitly incorporated bits of often violently competing theories) introduced their readers to "sound-conscious" literature. "Reading" in McGuffey's world tended to mean training for public speaking and "elocution contests." In the process the McGuffey readers doubtless helped train writers, for, as Joseph Collignon has recently pointed out, the ability to write is closely connected with the ability to hear in one's imagination what a written text would sound like when read aloud.[2] But the McGuffey *Readers'* immediate aim was more directly oral.

McGuffey *Readers* touted in rotund periods heroic figures inherited from the old oral world. "Caesar was merciful, Scipio was continent, Hannibal was patient; but it was reserved for Washington to blend them all in one, and, like the lovely masterpiece of the Grecian artist, to exhibit in one glow of associated beauty, the pride of every model, and the perfection of every artist." This typical selection, from Lyman Beecher's "The Memory of Our Fathers" appears in McGuffey's *Rhetorical Guide, or Fifth Reader* (1844), p. 291.

As in Shakespeare's day and throughout earlier history in the West,

---

1. On the McGuffey *Readers* see Robert Wood Lynn, "Civil Catechetics in Mid-Victorian America: Some Notes about American Civil Religion, Past and Present," *Religious Education,* 68 (1973), 5–27.
2. Joseph Collignon, "Why Leroy Can't Write," *College English,* 39 (1978), 852–859.

literacy was still thought of in nineteenth-century America as somehow serving the needs of oratory, for education in the classical tradition had never been education in the "three R's"—which comes from post-classical, post-Renaissance schools training for commerce and domestic economy— but had been education for the oral performance of the man in public affairs. Little wonder that Charles Dickens' platform readings from his novels met with such wild success in McGuffey's *America*. Oratorical power and literary style tended to be somewhat synonymous. (The implications of this fact for the dynamics of Dickens' storytelling are little understood.)

But oratorical literacy was actually on the wane even in Dickens' day. The long-term history of the McGuffey *Readers* in fact registers the gradual demise of the tradition. Regularly revised between 1836 and 1920, the McGuffeys moved more and more away from oratorical to silent reading. Writing was subtly winning out everywhere over the old rhetorical public speaking ethos.

These reflections give some idea of the ways in which the oral and writing traditions have been interacting through not only our distant past but also our rather recent past. Throughout, scholars appear to have been quite unaware of the oral-literacy contrasts and of the gradual inroads of literacy upon orality. No one seems to have noticed as the teaching of rhetoric, which in its Greek original, *techne rhetorike*, means public speaking, imperceptibly became more and more, over the centuries, the teaching of writing. Earlier generations took their own residual orality for granted, so much so that they really had not even thought of orality explicitly at all as a state of culture or of consciousness.

I shall treat orality and literacy in two ways, first examining the ubiquitous and persistent problem of moving from oral expression to writing and then considering briefly some special approaches we might take in teaching writing today because of the new, secondary orality that surrounds us on radio and television. In both instances my remarks are intended to be provocative rather than inclusive. There is no way to treat this protean subject inclusively.

Although its founding fathers were steeped in a still strong oral and oratorical tradition, the United States was founded in literacy, as Denis Brogan liked to point out from his vantage point in England. Written documents—the *Declaration of Independence* and the *Constitution*—are crucial to our feeling for national identity in a way unmatched in any other nation through history, so far as I know. Most Americans, even those who write miserably, are so stubbornly literate in principle as to believe that what makes a word a real word is not its meaningful use in vocal exchange but rather its presence on the pages of a dictionary. We are so literate in ideology that we think writing comes naturally. We have to remind ourselves from time to time that writing is completely and irremediably artificial, and that what you find in a dictionary are not real words but coded marks for voicing real words, exteriorly or in imagination.

To point out that writing is artificial is not to deny that it is essential for the realization of fuller human potential and for the evolution of consciousness itself. Writing is an absolute necessity for the analytically sequential, linear organization of thought such as goes, for example, into an encyclopedia article. Without writing, as I have undertaken to explain in *The Presence of the Word* and in *Interfaces of the Word*, the mind simply cannot engage in this sort of thinking, which is unknown to primary oral cultures, where thought is exquisitely elaborated, not in analytic linearity, but in formulary fashion, through "rhapsodizing," that is, stitching together proverbs, antitheses, epithets, and other "commonplaces" or *loci* (*topoi*). Without writing, the mind cannot even generate concepts such as "history" or "analysis," just as without print, and the massive accumulation of detailed documented knowledge which print makes possible, the mind cannot generate portmanteau concepts such as "culture" or "civilization," not to mention "macroeconomics" or "polyethylene." The *New English Dictionary* entry for "civilization" notes Boswell's report of March 23, 1772, that Dr. Samuel Johnson would not permit the word "civilization" in his first *Dictionary*—it was too much of a neologism. Probably most of the words in our English lexicon today represent concepts which could not even be formed without writing and, often, without print.

In the world of the creative imagination, writing appears necessary to produce accounts of human life, that is, of what Aristotle calls "action," which are closely plotted in the sense in which Greek drama is closely plotted, with a steady rise of complex action to climax, peripeteia or reversal, and subsequent falling action and denouement. Oral genres of much length treating human "action" are typically not tightly organized in this fashion but are loose-knit and episodic. Greek drama, which first provides such tight plotting in the West, is the first verbal genre in the West to be controlled entirely by writing: staged plays were oral renditions of written compositions. Similarly, print, an extension and intensification of the visualized word produced by writing, appears absolutely, and somewhat mysteriously, necessary to produce tightly plotted narrative about the in-close human life world that we find in novels, which are the products of the deep interiorization of print achieved in the Romantic Age.

All this is to say that writing, and to a degree print, are absolutely essential not just for distributing knowledge but for performing the central noetic operations which a high-technology culture takes for granted.

But, however crucial for man to arrive at his present state of consciousness, writing is still totally artificial, a technology consciously and reflectively contrived. In this it contrasts with oral speech. In any and all cultures, every human being who is not physiologically or psychologically impaired, inevitably learns to speak. Speech wells up out of the unconscious, supported by unconsciously organized grammatical structures that even the most ardent structural and transformational grammarians now admit can never all be surfaced entirely into consciousness. Speech is structured through the entire fabric of the human person. Writing depends on consciously contrived rules.

Moreover, it depends on absences—which amount to the same thing as artificiality. I want to write a book which will be read by hundreds of thousands of people. So, please, everyone leave the room. I have to be alone to communicate. Let us face the utter factitiousness and fictitiousness of such a situation, which can in no way be considered natural or even normal.

To move from the entirely natural oral world into this artificial world of writing is bewildering and terrifying. How do I deal with persons who are not present to me and who never will be? For, except in the case of personal letters or their equivalents, writers commonly know almost none of their putative readers.

A recent article by a friend and former student of mine, Thomas Farrell, isolates nicely two of the basic problems a person has to face in moving from orality into the world of writing.[3] Everyone who teaches writing knows the common symptoms of the problems: students make assertions which are totally unsupported by reasons, or they make a series of statements which lack connections. Farrell notes that such performance is not necessarily an intellectual deficiency but only a chirographic deficiency. It is quite consistent with oral conversational situations. In conversation, if you omit reasons backing a statement and your hearer wants them, the normal response is to ask you for them, to challenge you. If the connections between the statements you make are not supplied by the concrete situation—which can supply connections of the most complex, multileveled sort, as students of enthnomethodology well know—your interlocutor can be expected to ask you to specify the connections. Generally speaking, in live oral communication the hearer will not need many "logical" connections, again because the concrete situation supplies a full context which makes articulation, and thus abstraction, at many points, superfluous.

3. Thomas J. Farrell, "Literacy, Basics, and All That Jazz," *College English*, 38 (1977), 443–459.

For the writer, the situation is totally different. No one is there to supply a real communicational context, to ask anything. There is no full context other than that which the writer can project. The writer has to provide all the back-up or fill-in. In the case of creative writing, the writer has to anticipate how much detail readers are willing and able to settle for. For there is no absolute measure of how much detail you have to supply in writing about anything. In the case of expository writing, the writer must anticipate all the different senses in which any statement can be interpreted and correspondingly clarify meaning, making sure to anticipate every objection that might be made and to cover it suitably. Every objection? Well, not quite. The situation is even worse than that. Select objections. The objections that the readers being addressed might think of. How is the writer to know what a particular group of imagined readers might think of? How do you imagine a group of readers anyway? For one thing, you have to read, read, read. There is no way to write unless you read, and read a lot. The writer's audience is always a fiction, and you have no way of fictionalizing your audience unless you know what some of the options for imagining audiences are—how audiences have been and are fictionalized.

The writer has also to anticipate all the connections which are needed by a particular audience of readers. In fictional or other narrative writing this is an exceedingly intricate and elusive business. In expository writing it is difficult, too. The writer has to learn to be "logical," to put matters together in a sequential, linear pattern so that anyone who comes along— or anyone of the group of readers being projected by the writer—can make complete sense of what is being written. There are no live persons facing the writer to clarify his thinking by their reactions. There is no feed-back. There are no auditors to look pleased or puzzled. This is a desperate world, a terrifying world, a lonely, unpeopled world, not at all the world of natural oral-aural exchange.

Everyone who writes must move at some point or points in his or her life from the world of oral exchange and thought processes into the curiously estranged and yet fantastically productive world of absent audiences that the writer deals with. Today, however, the orality away from which the writer moves is of two sorts. One kind, to use a terminology which I have developed in *Rhetoric, Romance, and Technology,* is "primary orality," the pristine orality of mankind untouched by writing or print which remains still more or less operative in areas sheltered to a greater or lesser degree from the full impact of literacy and which is vestigial to some degree in us all. The noetic processes of primary orality, as we have seen, are formulaic and rhapsodic rather than analytic. As in Homeric epic and to a great extent in classical oratory, particularly of the more orotund variety, this orality operates with the sort of commonplaces, formulary expressions, and clichés ordinarily despised by fully literate folk, for, without writing, an oral culture must maintain its knowledge by repeating it. Writing and, even more effectively, print store what is known outside the mind and downgrade repetitive styles. In lieu of more elaborate analytic categories, primary oral culture also tends to break down issues in simple polarities in terms of good and evil, "good guys" and "bad guys."

The other kind of orality we now live with I have called "secondary orality." This is the orality induced by radio and television, and it is by no means independent of writing and print but totally dependent on them. Without writing and print, electronic equipment cannot be manufactured and radio and television programming cannot be managed. (It should be noted here that, despite its name, television is in a fundamental way an oral-aural medium. It must have sound and, so far as I know, never uses purely visual devices: the weather map which you read without difficulty in the newspaper becomes a talk show on television, presided over by an articulate and attractive woman or an equally articulate and handsome man.)

The highly oral culture of our black urban ghettos as well as of certain isolated black and white rural areas is basically a primary oral culture in many ways, although it is more or less modified by contact with secondary orality today. The orality of nonghetto urban populations generally and of suburbia generally, white and black, is basically secondary orality. As Farrell has made clear in the article cited earlier, the problems of moving students out of the two kinds of orality are not the same.

A real incident will illustrate the way in which primary orality can manifest itself. It was reported to me a few years ago by a graduate student in a seminar of mine at Saint Louis University who was at the time teaching a class composed almost entirely of black inner-city students in a community college. It was the time of the Cambodia crisis in the Nixon administration. "What do you think of Nixon's action in Cambodia?" the instructor asked. A hand was raised. "Well?" "I wouldn't vote for that turkey. He raised his own salary."

Such an answer will raise the hackles of many teachers, who can find no sense in it at all. They find it purely emotional, not at all "logical," irrelevant to the question, and, in general, a blatant example of non-thought. However, some kind of basic understanding of thought processes in primary oral culture shows how this sort of response, in such a culture, is perfectly fitting as well as thoroughly intelligent and human.

The question put by the instructor called for some kind of intensive political analysis. In a primary oral culture, intensive analysis is not practiced, and not even thought of. The student was from a culture preserving much of primary orality. He was unconcerned with analysis, yet he recognized that the question was a question. The instructor was getting at something. What could it be? That is to say, into what commonplaces or *loci* or *topoi* could the issue be resolved? How could it be found to reinforce what everybody knew about the deeper issues of life? Selfishness and my reaction to selfishness might be what was at stake. So let's give that a try. "I wouldn't vote for that turkey. He raised his own salary." The reply had the added advantage for a primary oral culture of couching the issue in clearly polarized terms of good and evil. Was Nixon a good guy or a bad guy? Clearly, a bad guy.

Before we write off—and note the term "write off"—this response as naive at our present state of chirographic and typographic culture, let us reflect that, sensed in depth, the question, "Is Nixon a good guy or a bad guy?" was very likely what the instructor was really getting at anyway. Cambodia was just an example illustrating the instructor's real concern. Aristotle has said—or written? the exact mix of orality and chirography in Aristotle's works remains uncertain—that in rhetoric, which is fundamentally the art of public speaking or oratory, the example is the equivalent of induction in formal logical operations. Rhetorical examples and logical induction both move from individual instances to generalizations. The highly oral student handled the instructor's query as a rhetorical example, as a concrete instance referring to something at a higher, more generalized level of abstraction. It is rather unlikely that he had read Aristotle, but he was experientially familiar with the terrain of rhetoric. Orality sometimes provides nonanalytic short-cuts into the depths of human issues.

Let us take a second example. A couple of years ago, as a senior member of our Department of English, I was visiting the class of a graduate teaching assistant who was teaching writing. In one of the chairs sat a young man who, as I found subsequently, was from the highly oral inner-city black ghetto. He was very attentive, trying hard. But he had no textbook with him, and it was immediately apparent that he did not feel at all disadvantaged by this fact—even though the class was engaged in an analytic discussion of a text in the textbook with a view to a coming writing assignment. The student did not even try to look at the textbooks of any of the students near him. But he was clearly earnest, trying. Trying what? To be "with it"—just as, in his *Preface to Plato*, Eric Havelock has shown that the Greek boys in Plato's time had been trying to be "with it" as they got their Homer by heart. In a primary oral culture, education consists in identification, participation, getting into the act, feeling affinity with a culture's heroes, getting "with it"—not in analysis at all. This is what this freshman student thought the class was all about.

Plato's remedy for an educational tradition that operated simply to enable students to "get with it," to empathize with key figures in a given culture, rather than to analyze, was drastic, as Havelock has shown: Plato simply prescribed excluding all poets from his ideal republic so that genuine analytic thinking could get under way. He saw no other means of achieving what he felt was needed: a noetic *metanoia* or conversion, a complete turning around, a reversal of field—which we now know meant in effect a conversion from oral to chirographic thought. Forget empathy and face up to genuinely abstract questions: What makes a couch a couch? What is couchness?

In our literate culture, you can go too far with analysis, too. Reacting to the classroom situation I had observed, I was not at all inclined to throw out all the poets. But after class, I did try to bring home to the graduate teaching assistant the terrible injustice being done to this student of his if someone did not understand what the student's problem was and try to help him work through it. In my own experience, this is not an impossible thing at all. But you have to know where you are coming from.

Let us take a third example. Father Patrick Essien, an African diocesan priest of the diocese of Ikot-Ekpene, in South-East State in Nigeria, who has just finished a doctorate in educational administration at Saint Louis University, comes from a primary oral culture of a small village of the Annang, a tribe of some half million persons or more. In the curriculum vitae in his dissertation, which is about the present educational serviceability of proverbs, he proudly displays his oral credentials by noting explicitly that no one is sure of the date of his birth, and then produces complementary credentials as an experienced literate by carefully calculating what the most likely date is. Father Essien's father, now deceased, was a chief. Among the Annang, as among other peoples, this meant that he was also a judge. He used to sit in judgment over such things as property disputes: charges, for example, by a plaintiff that another was pasturing his cattle or planting his yams on the plaintiff's property. The judge-chief would listen to both sides of the case, take the matter under advisement for a while, then cite a saying or proverb, another proverb, perhaps a third and a fourth, and then deliver the verdict. Plaintiff and defendant would leave satisfied.

"But," Father Essien smiles, "you had better give voice to the proper proverbs or other sayings. Otherwise you are in deep trouble, for if you do not cite the ones that apply to the given case no one who hears the judgment is satisfied." The law is lodged in the proverbs or sayings of

Annang culture—or the law was, for Father Essien remarks sadly that it is getting harder and harder to find anyone with the skills that his father practiced so well. The law has become something written and does not work that way any more. Inevitably, Father Essien's feelings are mixed, and agonizing. The Annang must move into writing, for its advantages are incontestable. But writing entails losses of much that was good and true and beautiful in the old primary oral culture. You do what you can: Father Essien's dissertation will preserve some of the orality, but alas! only in writing.

A few months ago I was telling this story to another friend. "Sayings still work that way in the oral world of young children," he said. "Sayings settle disputes." He had had some young children in a car with him for a rather long drive a few days before, and there was a dispute when one wanted to preempt a window seat for the whole ride. "Turn about is fair play," my friend had said. And the dispute evaporated; the boy at the window yielded his seat to one of the others. My friend noted the psychodynamics of the episode: the saying saved the youngster's face. He was moved out of place not because he was weaker or less worthy or un-loved—considerations always urgent in the agonistically structured life-world of primary orality—but because "Turn about is fair play." This was something everybody knew, or should know, part of the common store of knowledge that a culture consists in. There is a deep humanity in the noetic processes of primary orality.

Settling a property dispute among adults, however, is a quite different matter from settling children's disputes. Not all have recognized this fact. Literates have had trouble understanding oral cultures precisely because in a highly literate culture experience of primary orality—or something close to primary orality—is likely to be limited to experience of the child's world. Hence persons from highly literate cultures have commonly been unable to react understandingly to adult, sophisticated levels of behavior in oral cultures but have tended to view the whole of "native"—that is, oral—populations as "child-like," including admirably adult men and women, middle-aged and older, who often have coped with life more adroitly and more successfully than their literate critics.

This defensive depreciatory interpretation of another culture by liter-ates is itself curiously childlike. It has forced literary scholars consciously or unconsciously espousing it to go through incredible intellectual con-tortions to make out the *Iliad* and *Odyssey* to be basically texts composed in writing instead of transcriptions of essentially oral performance, be-cause of the supposition that oral performance is not capable of the so-phistication these works manifest. Thanks to the work of Parry and Lord and Havelock and their now numerous epigoni, we should be beyond this today. We should know something of the psychodynamics of primary oral cultures, of primary oral noetics—how the mind works when it cannot rely directly or indirectly on writing and on the thought patterns that writing alone can initiate.

Once we know something about the psychodynamics of the oral mind, we can recognize that primary orality, at least in residual form, is still a factor in the thought habits of many of those to whom we are called upon to teach writing. Such recognition does not automatically solve our problems, but it at least enables us better to identify them. Our students from oral or residually oral cultures come not from an unorganized world, but from a world which is differently organized, in ways which can now be at least partly understood.

What of those students who come from the world of secondary oral culture? Does the oral world of radio and television drive all its denizens back from literate culture to the primary oral noetic economy? Of course not. If it did, that would be the end of radio and television. There is nothing on radio or television, however oral, not subject to some—and most often to utterly massive—chirographic and typographic control, which enters into program design, scripts, advertising, contractual agreements, diction, sentence structure, and countless other details. Primary orality cannot cope with electronic media. I recall talking to radio and television producers in Dakar a few years ago and speculating with them about how it would be to have a television series run by a *griot*, the West African singer of tales, oral purveyor of genealogies, crier of praises and taunts, custodian of the *loci* of the culture. An individual performance by a *griot* could prove interesting, the Senegalese media people knew, but would have to be carefully supervised, for the new kind of orality had made a world utterly different from the *griot's* world, using different techniques. There was no way for a *griot* to program a radio or television series.

But how about the audience? Does the oral world of radio and television reintroduce its viewers, as against its programmers or performers, to primary oral noetics? It appears not in any sophisticated way at all. Television viewers show no tendency, so far as I can discern, to organize their knowledge and express themselves the way the Nigerian villagers do in Chinua Achebe's novels. They have no such oral mastery of proverbial thinking at all. As I have noted in *Rhetoric, Romance, and Technology,* even relatively unsophisticated audiences in a high-technology culture feel they should scorn formulas or clichés as such, although they might not always succeed in avoiding them. Consequently, clichés addressed to audiences in a high-technology milieu tend to be accompanied by signals, verbal or other, that downgrade the clichés themselves. Archie Bunker's clichés are systematically debased by his malapropisms. The audience is encouraged and assisted to reject them and laugh at them. This is only some of the abundant evidence that popular culture is discernably under the influence of literacy today, and at many levels, even in its relatively unsophisticated members.

Secondary orality, in other words, is to varying degrees literate. In fact, a residual primary orality, literacy, and secondary orality are interacting vigorously with one another in confusing complex patterns in our secondarily oral world.

This situation does not automatically create sensitivity to literature or equip everyone with the ability to write well, but it can be made to work toward such goals. The world of secondary orality is a media-conscious world. In fact, this is the world which effectively brought about the discovery of the contrast between primary orality and literacy, and ultimately the contrast between both and secondary orality. Milman Parry and Albert Lord discovered the orality of ancient Homeric Greece not simply by studying texts but largely through sound recordings of twentieth-century Yugoslavian epic singers.

Because we live in a media-conscious world, we can make students aware of what this paper has attempted to sketch: what oral speech is and what writing is by contrast. This awareness can increase sensitivity to literature and to the problems of writing.

I am not suggesting here more courses in "the media." But I am suggesting that both those who teach writing and those who teach literature can in their teaching make a productive issue of the contrasts between the noetic and psychological milieu of primary orality, that of writing and of print, and that of secondary orality. Understanding these differences not in terms merely of slogans but circumstantially and in depth is itself a liberal education.

Perhaps I will be permitted to use another and final example from close to home. Last year, in a program at Saint Louis University on Man, Technology, and Society, funded by the National Endowment for the Humanities, we managed to give a course on "Technology and the Creation of Literature," which had to do with writing as a technology and its effects in producing literature in the full sense of the word: verbal communication actually composed in writing. This is what we are teaching when we teach writing. We are not teaching how to transcribe oral performance—as someone, we don't know who and we don't know how, transcribed the Homeric tales from the oral world and made them artificially for the first time into fixed texts, that henceforward had to be not retold but interpreted. We are teaching composing in writing, putting words together not with the help of a live and vocal interlocutor but with the help of an imagined audience and of something mute outside us. Like it or not, we are teaching a technology, for not only print, but also writing itself is a technology—a matter of tools outside us and seemingly foreign to us, which we nevertheless can interiorize and make human, transforming them and enhancing our own thinking and verbalizing activities in the process, much as a musician interiorizes the machine in the crook of his arm and shoulder that we call a violin.

I had treated this sort of subject earlier in graduate courses, but the course on "Technology and the Creation of Literature" had to be an undergraduate course by stipulation of the NEH grant. Somewhat to my surprise, it worked magnificently for undergraduate students. Their reception of the course showed conclusively that media-sensitive students today are fascinated by carefully worked out contrasts between primary oral performance and writing, and between both these and secondary orality, and that they are liberated by understanding what these contrasts are. The course was a demanding one. Readings included, besides secondary sources, books of the *Iliad* and the *Odyssey, The Mwindo Epic* of the Nyanga people in eastern Zaire, parts of Genesis, some Old Testament wisdom literature, Plato's *Crito, Everyman,* selections from *The Faerie Queene and Paradise Lost,* O. Henry's *The Gift of the Magi,* Poe's *The Gold Bug,* and James's *The Aspern Papers*—the whole gamut from complete primary orality (totally episodic—before the taping of *The Mwindo Epic* no one of the Banyanga had ever put together all the Mwindo stories in sequence) to all-pervasive literacy (the key to Poe's plotting in *The Gold Bug* is the reconstitution of a text and in *The Aspern Papers* the whole character of James's always absent protagonist lodges in his hidden writings, which finally go up in flames).

If undergraduate students can be sensitive to the differences between literacy and orality which this course explored, I am suggesting that it would help our understanding and our teaching of the writing craft for us to be sensitive to them, too.

ADDITIONAL READINGS

RONALD F. REID, "The Boylston Professorship of Rhetoric and Oratory, 1806–1904; A Case Study of Changing Concepts of Rhetoric and Pedagogy," *Quarterly Journal of Speech,* 45 (October, 1959), 239–257.

WALLACE DOUGLAS, "Rhetoric for the Meritocracy: The Creation of Composition at Harvard," Chapter 5 of Richard Ohmann's *English in America: A Radical View of the Profession* (New York: Oxford Univ. Press, 1976), pp. 97–132.

ROBERT M. GORRELL, "Freshman Composition," *The College Teaching of English,* ed. John C. Gerber (New York: Appleton-Century-Crofts, 1965), pp. 91–114.

LEONARD GREENBAUM, "The Tradition of Complaint," *College English,* 31 (November, 1969), 174–187.

WILLIAM E. COLES, JR., "Freshman Composition: The Circle of Unbelief," *College English,* 31 (November, 1969), 134–142.

RICHARD OHMANN, "Freshman Composition and Administered Thought," *English in America: A Radical View of the Profession* (New York: Oxford Univ. Press, 1976), pp. 133–171.

Theory

LEE ODELL

Teachers of Composition
and Needed Research in Discourse Theory

Whether by preference or by necessity, teachers of composition tend to be pragmatists. Our response to any new theory is most likely to be: What does it imply for our teaching? What specific classroom procedures does it suggest? Are these procedures practical? Will they work for the sort of students we have in our classes? Underlying these questions is at least one major assumption: our primary obligation is to have some influence on the way students compose, to make a difference in students' ability to use written language to give order and meaning to their experience.

As though this obligation were not demanding enough, I want to argue that we have at least one other responsibility. We must not only influence our students' writing, but also help refine and shape the discourse theory that will guide our work with students. In addition to being teachers, we should also function as discourse theorists and researchers. As we try to fulfill this new obligation, we will need to ask new kinds of questions. Is a given theory valid? Does it do justice to the complexities (and the simplicities) of the writing we see every day? Are the theory's assumptions borne out in writing done by our students?

It's tempting to avoid this sort of question by assuming that the work of highly skilled writers presents the most interesting test and the most dramatic illustration of discourse theory. And, of course, it would be foolish to overlook what such writers can help us discover about the composing process and the nature of effective writing. Yet if discourse theory is to make comprehensive descriptive statements about writing, theorists will have to test their assumptions against the actual performance of writers of quite diverse abilities. In our classrooms, we have unique access

From *College Composition and Communication*, 30 (February, 1979), 39–45. Reprinted by permission of the National Council of Teachers of English and Lee Odell.

to this diversity. The writing of our students represents a kind of information that is almost impossible to obtain in any context other than a course that is primarily concerned with students' writing. In the remainder of this article, I shall suggest ways we might use this source of information to examine and refine assumptions from current discourse theory. My suggestions will take the form of several research questions and some recommendations about how we might try to answer these questions.

One basic assumption in current discourse theory is expressed in James Kinneavy's claim that purpose in discourse is all important: "The aim of a discourse determines everything else in the process of discourse. What is talked about, the oral or written medium which is chosen, the words and grammatical patterns used—all of these are determined by the purpose of the discourse."[1] Kinneavy bases this assertion on the work of a number of theorists and on his analysis of pieces of written discourse. Yet Kinneavy's assertion is troublesome for two reasons. First, his statement about process is based primarily on an analysis of written products, rather than an analysis of the choices writers have made as their texts evolve through a succession of drafts. Second, in analyzing a written product, Kinneavy does not usually refer to the reasoning of the writer who actually produced the discourse. Granted, analyses of written products can let us make some inferences about the composing process. Furthermore, there is no simple, quick way to determine a writer's reasons for a given choice of language, syntax, etc. Yet we have, at present, no basis for assuming that analysis of products will let us find out everything we need to know about the writing process. Nor can we assume that writers' own insights will not be useful to us as we try to understand this process. Consequently, in our complex role of teacher/theorist/researcher we need to consider this sort of research question: What reasons do our students give for the choices they make in producing a piece of writing? Answers to this question should help us raise other questions, which I shall mention below.

To obtain information which would let us answer our first question, we might proceed in one of several ways. We might identify the sort of students Richard Beach calls "extensive revisers"[2] and ask them to let us see all the drafts they create for any given writing assignment. We could then identify the specific changes they make in these drafts and ask them to explain the reasoning that led them to make each change. Or we might follow one or both of the procedures Charles Cooper and I used in a re-

1. James L. Kinneavy, *A Theory of Discourse* (Englewood Cliffs, N.J.: Prentice Hall, 1971), p. 2.
2. Richard Beach, "Self-Evaluation Strategies of Extensive Revisers and Non-revisers," *CCC*, 27 (May, 1976), 160–164.

cent study of professional writers' composing process.[3] First, we could ask students to re-write a given assignment so as to achieve a different purpose and appeal to a different audience. We could then identify and ask questions about changes writers had made in their original drafts. A second procedure, one that might be especially useful with student writers who have little sense of the ways a piece of writing might be revised, would be for us to make changes in a draft students have already written. We might alter sentence length or complexity, or we might modify diction, perhaps replacing neutral words with emotive terms, general words with specific. In making such changes, we would have to assure students that we were not correcting or criticizing their work, that what we were interested in was their reasons for accepting or rejecting changes we had made.

In using any of the procedures I have mentioned, we would need to tape-record students' comments so that we could review them a number of times in order to categorize the reasons students gave for their choices. This process of devising categories for their reasons will probably be tedious. But Cooper and I found that it is possible to set up categories that another reader can use to make reliable judgments about the reasons writers give for their choices.

As we listen to students' comments, we might come up with answers to questions that do not bear directly on our central concern but that have important implications for our teaching:

> To what extent do students see composing as a process of making choices? How many of them are able to generate their own alternatives from which to choose?

> What proportion of our students are unable to articulate a reason—any sort of reason—for choices that they have made?

> Are certain kinds of choices (e.g., diction) easier for them to justify than are others?

We should also be able to answer other questions that bear directly on Kinneavy's assertion about the importance of purpose in the process of composition:

> Do students justify their choices by referring to their basic purpose in writing?

> Do they give other justifications for their choices?

3. Charles R. Cooper and Lee Odell, "Considerations of Sound in the Composing Process of Published Writers," *Research in the Teaching of English*, 10 (Fall, 1976), 103–115.

Do students give reasons that cannot be accounted for by reference to current discourse theory?

Do students' reasons vary according to the kind of writing task they're doing? (For example: Are there some kinds of tasks in which purpose seems a more important consideration than it does in other kinds of tasks?)

Do the kinds of reasons students give vary according to the skill of the writer?

Answers to these questions may lead us to revise discourse theory so as to accommodate new kinds of reasons students give for the choices they make in writing. Further, it may be that answers to our questions will help us re-define our job as teachers. As we understand the bases students presently use in making choices, we may be able to see how we could help them make even more effective choices.

A second major assumption in current discourse theory is that different writing tasks make quite different demands on writers. The writing strategies that are essential for success with one task may be relatively unimportant for another task. On the face of it, this assumption seems self-evidently true. A letter to a close, sympathetic friend would likely contain language and syntax that would almost never appear in, say, a formal report. Yet students (freshmen, upperclassmen, and graduate students) do not always make even the sort of gross distinctions suggested by my examples. Sometimes they approach different tasks with a single set of oversimplified rules ("Mr./Ms X taught us that we should *never* underline words for emphasis"). At other times, students use in a new context some device (a sarcastic phrase, a sentence fragment) that had previously proved appropriate for a different sort of task. In still other circumstances, students seem to be working toward contradictory purposes or establishing different speaker-audience relationships within what would appear to be a single writing task. This seeming disparity between student performance and discourse theory leads me to raise this question: Is it in fact true that different kinds of writing tasks elicit different kinds of writing performance from students? In the following discussion, I shall be concerned only with writing tasks that teachers assign. It might also be worth our while, however, to consider tasks that students assign themselves, e.g., self-initiated writings that students do outside of class.

To answer this question, we would need to assign students three different writing tasks—for example: (1) an expressive task, in which writers articulate their ideas and attitudes in a letter to a good friend; (2) a persuasive task, in which writers try not simply to express their own feelings but also to influence the feelings and actions of audiences that might appear to have little in common with the writers; (3) an explanatory task, in which writers convey information in a straightforward and reasonable manner.

In analyzing students' work on these different tasks, we might consider rather conventional matters such as diction, syntax, and organizational patterns. With diction, we might use the categories Edward Corbett mentioned in *Classical Rhetoric for the Modern Student*.[4] Our research question would become: Does one writing task elicit a greater number of abstract (or connotative or formal . . .) word choices than do the other tasks? In analyzing syntax, we could draw on the work of Charles Cooper and Barbara Rosenberg,[5] who found that certain features of syntax are most useful in making sharp distinctions between certain kinds of expository writing. We could re-phrase our basic question thus: Do different writing tasks lead students to use, on average, longer T-units (or more final free modifiers or more adjective modifiers . . .) than do other tasks? To investigate organizational patterns, we might draw upon two different procedures. We might look for students' use of transitional relationships identified by W. Ross Winterowd.[6] Or we might pursue Richard L. Larson's claim that within a given type of discourse, paragraphs are likely to perform a relatively small number of functions.[7] Thus we might ask: Do different tasks lead students to use different types of transitional relationships or to use paragraphs that fill different types of functions?

To refine our answers to the three questions I have just mentioned, we might have all the papers in our sample evaluated. We might ask several readers, working independently, to place each paper in one of three groups: most effective responses to the task; moderately effective responses to the task; least effective responses to the task. Then we could consider only the papers in the "most effective" and "least effective" groups and re-state our basic question thus: For students whose writing is rated most effective, can we say that different writing tasks elicit different writing performances? What about students whose work is rated least effective?

Implications of our answers to these questions become clear as we consider two further assumptions from current discourse theory. As a

4. Edward P. J. Corbett, *Classical Rhetoric for the Modern Student* (New York: Oxford University Press, 1965), pp. 408–409.
5. Charles R. Cooper and Barbara Rosenberg, "Indexes of Syntactic Maturity," Mimeograph. State University of New York at Buffalo, 1975. 25 pp.
6. W. Ross Winterowd, "Toward a Grammar of Coherence," in *Contemporary Rhetoric: Conceptual Background with Readings,* ed. W. Ross Winterowd (New York: Harcourt Brace Jovanovich, 1975).
7. Richard L. Larson, "Toward a Linear Rhetoric of the Essay," *CCC,* 22 (May, 1971), 140–146.

corollary to the premise that different demands made of writers elicit different performances from them, Richard Lloyd-Jones contends that (1) writing must not be judged by general criteria for "good" writing but by what Lloyd-Jones calls "primary traits," criteria that are uniquely suited to the specific task a writer is trying to perform; (2) people who are skillful with one sort of task may not be equally skillful with some other kind of task.[8]

In devising evaluation procedures for the National Assessment of Educational Progress, Lloyd-Jones has illustrated the former assumption; he has designed different scoring guides for each of several writing tasks used in the 1974 assessment. For example, to guide the scoring of one set of persuasive essays, Lloyd-Jones instructed judges to (1) determine the number of reasons students give in support of their arguments; (2) determine whether or not students elaborate on these reasons; (3) determine what kind(s) of authorities students refer to. For one set of expressive essays, Lloyd-Jones asked judges to decide whether students (1) entered into an imaginary role specified in the writing assignment; (2) elaborated upon that role by talking about the sort of details and feelings that established a distinct personality.

These scoring guides represent a significant departure from the customary practice of judging all expository writing by a single set of criteria, e.g., the categories found in an analytic scale. And this departure raises some problems for teachers and researchers. Whereas we once could use a single, widely agreed-upon procedure for evaluating all the writing done in a given mode, we may now have to use a variety of evaluation procedures, most of which we have to create for ourselves. Since Lloyd-Jones' evaluation procedures imply a substantial change in our evaluation of students' writing, we must consider two questions. Would different evaluation procedures lead us to make different judgments about a given student's writing performance? Is any one evaluation procedure especially helpful (or unhelpful) to students?

To answer the first question, we would need to examine one piece of writing from each of forty-five students. We would have each piece of writing judged according to several procedures such as the following:

1. Analytic scale (essays are judged on the basis of such general qualities as organization, clarity, etc.)

2. Primary traits (essays are judged on the basis of criteria that seem uniquely suited to the specific writing task. For example,

8. Richard Lloyd-Jones, "Primary Trait Scoring of Writing," in *Evaluating Writing: Describing, Measuring, Judging*, ed. Charles R. Cooper and Lee Odell (Urbana, Illinois: National Council of Teachers of English, 1977).

persuasive essays would not be judged on some general criterion such as organization but, rather, on some quality such as writers' ability to elaborate upon the reasons they give in support of their position.)

3. Analysis of specific qualities such as

   A. use of some of the transitions that Winterowd suggests are essential to "coherence";

   B. deviations from standard usage;

   C. syntactic complexity.

I mention these specific qualities with some reluctance. They probably should be included in an analytic scale. Yet each of these qualities is often treated independently as a significant feature of "good" writing. When our colleagues complain to us that we're not teaching students to write, they often mean that they're tired of seeing misspelled words and sentence fragments.

Each of the forty-five papers would have to be rated by using each of the five procedures (once using an analytic scale, once using a primary-trait scoring guide, once according to the number and kinds of transitions used . . .). After each rating, we would need to arrange the papers into three groups of equal size: superior, average, poor. Then we would be able to ask this question: As we vary the evaluation procedure, do the same papers keep appearing in the same groups? The answer would tell us whether different evaluation procedures result in different judgments about students' writing.

To determine whether any one evaluation procedure is especially helpful to students, we might consider how that procedure affects students' writing performance and how that procedure affects students' attitudes toward writing. To carry out this investigation, we would need ten or twelve classes of students, taught by five or six teachers. We would have to be sure that students were randomly assigned to these teachers and that each class would be conducted in the same way, that the only difference would be the evaluation procedure used. For an entire semester, students would be asked to write a rough draft of each essay, receive feedback on that draft, and use that feedback to revise their rough draft. In some classes, feedback would be guided by a teacher's use of an analytic scale. In others, it would be guided by a primary-trait scoring procedure. Our analysis would be based on students' first and last writing assignments of the semester. We could give judges a pair of essays from each student, a revised draft of the student's first essay of the term and a revised draft of the student's final essay of the semester. Our question for the judges would be: Which essay in each pair is the better essay? After we have judges' evaluations, we would be able to answer these questions: In each group of students (those whose instruction included evaluation by an analytic scale and those whose instruction included evaluation by primary-trait procedures) what proportion of the students showed improvement in their final essay of the term? Is this proportion substantially higher in one group than in the other?

Answers to these questions would let us determine whether one evaluation procedure was more useful than another. To find out whether one evaluation procedure had a greater effect on students' attitudes, we could use a relatively simple measure developed by John A. Daly and Michael D. Miller.[9] This measure asks students to indicate their reactions to twenty-six statements (e.g., I'm nervous about writing; People seem to enjoy what I write) about writing. We would need to ask students to respond to these statements at the beginning of the term and at the end of the term. We would then ask (1) how many students in each group showed a decrease in their apprehension about writing and (2) was the proportion of students showing a decrease in apprehension substantially greater in one group than in the other?

Once we feel reasonably confident about the sort of evaluation procedures we need to use, we could go on to ask whether students who are successful with one sort of writing task are equally successful with other kinds of writing tasks. To answer this question, we might be able to use as few as four classes of students—two from each of two teachers—but we would need at least four pieces of writing from each student. Two of these pieces of writing might ask students to perform a persuasive task; the other two might involve expressive tasks. After collecting these papers, we would need to remove students' names and ask judges to use a specific scoring procedure to group the responses to each assignment into three sets: most satisfactory, moderately satisfactory, unsatisfactory. Once all the papers had been rated, we could identify those students whose papers were most consistently rated superior for one kind of task. Then we would need to ask if those same students were consistently rated superior for the other sort of task.

If it is true that students are likely to be more successful with one sort of writing task than with others and if it is true that we must vary our evaluation procedure according to the specific writing task at hand, we may have to make substantial changes in the way we assign and evaluate writing. We will have to structure writing tasks much more carefully,

---

9. John A. Daly and Michael D. Miller, "The Empirical Development of an Instrument to Measure Writing Apprehension," *Research in the Teaching of English,* 9 (Winter, 1975) 242–249.

being sure that we don't equate tasks that make substantially different demands on student writers. If different kinds of tasks really do make different demands/require different skills, it seems a little unfair to treat writing performance globally, either judging all expositions by the same criterion or averaging an A in expression with a C in persuasion to produce a meaningless B that reflects neither ability.

Studies proposed in this article are relatively simple. They can be carried out by a single teacher or by a few colleagues in a single composition program. Because of their limited scope, it seems unlikely that any of these studies will be definitive. Considered individually, none will enable us to generalize about all composition students in all circumstances; none will, once and for all, refute or confirm basic assumptions in discourse theory. Yet as a number of us begin to ask the same sort of questions and pursue related studies, we should be able to obtain information that will be useful in several ways. At the very least, our work should help us insure that discourse theory does not become a procrustean bed for our own students. By testing theory against the real world of student writing, we can insure that our assumptions are reasonable, that they do justice to our students' writing. In addition, we may find that this process of testing helps us refine, or at least raise useful questions about, the assumptions of a discipline that is still in its formative stages. And finally, this testing may give us more insight into our students' writing and, consequently, into our job as teachers. If our studies do not lead us to certainty, they should enable us to fulfill our multiple roles of researchers, theorists, and teachers. Our students and our discipline can only benefit.

Diving In: An Introduction to Basic Writing

Basic writing, alias remedial, developmental, pre-baccalaureate, or even handicapped English, is commonly thought of as a writing course for young men and women who have many things wrong with them. Not only do medical metaphors dominate the pedagogy (*remedial, clinic, lab, diagnosis,* and so on), but teachers and administrators tend to discuss basic-writing students much as doctors tend to discuss their patients, without being tinged by mortality themselves and with certainly no expectations that questions will be raised about the state of *their* health.

Yet such is the nature of instruction in writing that teachers and students cannot easily escape one another's maladies. Unlike other courses, where exchanges between teacher and student can be reduced to as little as one or two objective tests a semester, the writing course requires students to write things down regularly, usually once a week, and requires teachers to read what is written and then write things back and every so often even talk directly with individual students about the way they write.

This system of exchange between teacher and student has so far yielded much more information about what is wrong with students than about what is wrong with teachers, reinforcing the notion that students, not teachers, are the people in education who must do the changing. The phrase "catching up," so often used to describe the progress of BW students, is illuminating here, suggesting as it does that the only person who must move in the teaching situation is the student. As a result of this view, we are much more likely in talking about teaching to talk about students, to theorize about *their* needs and attitudes or to chart *their* development and ignore the possibility that teachers also change in response

From *College Composition and Communication,* 27 (October, 1976), 234–239. Reprinted by permission of the National Council of Teachers of English.

to students, that there may in fact be important connections between the changes teachers undergo and the progress of their students.

I would like, at any rate, to suggest that this is so, and since it is common these days to "place" students on developmental scales, saying they are eighth-graders or fifth-graders when they read and even younger when they write or that they are stalled some place on Piaget's scale without formal propositions, I would further like to propose a developmental scale for teachers, admittedly an impressionistic one, but one that fits the observations I have made over the years as I have watched traditionally prepared English teachers, including myself, learning to teach in the open-admissions classroom.

My scale has four stages, each of which I will name with a familiar metaphor intended to suggest what lies at the center of the teacher's emotional energy during that stage. Thus I have chosen to name the first stage of my developmental scale GUARDING THE TOWER, because during this stage the teacher is in one way or another concentrating on protecting the academy (including himself) from the outsiders, those who do not seem to belong in the community of learners. The grounds for exclusion are various. The mores of the times inhibit anyone's openly ascribing the exclusion to genetic inferiority, but a few teachers doubtless still hold to this view.

More often, however, the teacher comes to the basic-writing class with every intention of preparing his students to write for college courses, only to discover, with the first batch of essays, that the students are so alarmingly and incredibly behind any students he has taught before that the idea of their ever learning to write acceptably for college, let alone learning to do so in one or two semesters, seems utterly pretentious. Whatever the sources of their incompetence—whether rooted in the limits they were born with or those that were imposed upon them by the world they grew up in—the fact seems stunningly, depressingly obvious: they will never "make it" in college unless someone radically lowers the standards.

The first pedagogical question the teacher asks at this stage is therefore not "How do I teach these students?" but "What are the consequences of flunking an entire class?" It is a question that threatens to turn the class into a contest, a peculiar and demoralizing contest for both student and teacher, since neither expects to win. The student, already conditioned to the idea that there is something wrong with his English and that writing is a device for magnifying and exposing this deficiency, risks as little as possible on the page, often straining with what he does write to approximate the academic style and producing in the process what might better be called "written Anguish" rather than English—sentences whose subjects are crowded out by such phrases as "it is my conviction that" or "on the contrary to my opinion," inflections that belong to no variety of English, standard or non-standard, but grow out of the writer's attempt to be correct, or words whose idiosyncratic spellings reveal not simply an increase in the number of conventional misspellings but new orders of difficulty with the correspondences between spoken and written English. Meanwhile, the teacher assumes that he must not only hold out for the same product he held out for in the past but teach unflinchingly in the same way as before, as if any pedagogical adjustment to the needs of students were a kind of cheating. Obliged because of the exigencies brought on by open admissions to serve his time in the defense of the academy, he does if not his best, at least his duty, setting forth the material to be mastered, as if he expected students to learn it, but feeling grateful when a national holiday happens to fall on a basic-writing day and looking always for ways of evading conscription next semester.

But gradually, student and teacher are drawn into closer range. They are obliged, like emissaries from opposing camps, to send messages back and forth. They meet to consider each other's words and separate to study them in private. Slowly, the teacher's preconceptions of his students begin to give way here and there. It now appears that, in some instances at least, their writing, with its rudimentary errors and labored style has belied their intelligence and individuality. Examined at a closer range, the class now appears to have at least some members in it who might, with hard work, eventually "catch up." And it is the intent of reaching these students that moves the teacher into the second stage of development—which I will name CONVERTING THE NATIVES.

As the image suggests, the teacher has now admitted at least some to the community of the educable. These learners are perceived, however, as empty vessels, ready to be filled with new knowledge. Learning is thought of not so much as a constant and often troubling reformulation of the world so as to encompass new knowledge but as a steady flow of truth into a void. Whether the truth is delivered in lectures or modules, cassettes or computers, circles or squares, the teacher's purpose is the same: to carry the technology of advanced literacy to the inhabitants of an underdeveloped country. And so confident is he of the reasonableness and allure of what he is presenting, it does not occur to him to consider the competing logics and values and habits that may be influencing his students, often in ways that they themselves are unaware of.

Sensing no need to relate what he is teaching to what his students know, to stop to explore the contexts within which the conventions of academic discourse have developed, and to view these conventions in patterns large enough to encompass what students do know about language already, the teacher becomes a mechanic of the sentence, the paragraph, and the essay. Drawing usually upon the rules and formulas that were part of his training in composition, he conscientiously presents to his students flawless schemes for achieving order and grammaticality and anatomizes model passages of English prose to uncover, beneath brilliant, unique surfaces, the skeletons of ordinary paragraphs.

Yet too often the schemes, however well meant, do not seem to work. Like other simplistic prescriptions, they illuminate for the moment and then disappear in the melee of real situations, where paradigms frequently break down and thoughts will not be regimented. S's keep reappearing or disappearing in the wrong places; regular verbs shed their inflections and irregular verbs acquire them; tenses collide; sentences derail; and whole essays idle at one level of generalization.

Baffled, the teacher asks, "How is it that these young men and women whom I have personally admitted to the community of learners cannot learn these simple things?" Until one day, it occurs to him that perhaps these simple things—so transparent and compelling to him—are not in fact simple at all, that they only appear simple to those who already know them, that the grammar and rhetoric of formal written English have been shaped by the irrationalities of history and habit and by the peculiar restrictions and rituals that come from putting words on paper instead of into the air, that the sense and nonsense of written English must often collide with the spoken English that has been serving students in their negotiations with the world for many years. The insight leads our teacher to the third stage of his development, which I will name SOUNDING THE DEPTHS, for he turns now to the careful observation not only of his students and their writing but of himself as writer and teacher, seeking a deeper understanding of the behavior called writing and of the special difficulties his students have in mastering the skill. Let us imagine, for the sake of illustration, that the teacher now begins to look more carefully at two common problems among basic writers—the problem of grammatical errors and the problem of undeveloped paragraphs.

Should he begin in his exploration of error not only to count and name errors but to search for patterns and pose hypotheses that might explain them, he will begin to see that while his lessons in the past may have been "simple," the sources of the error he was trying to correct were often complex. The insight leads not inevitably or finally to a rejection of all rules and standards, but to a more careful look at error, to the formulation of what might be called a "logic" of errors that serves to mark a pedagogical path for teacher and student to follow.

Let us consider in this connection the "simple" *s* inflection on the verb, the source of a variety of grammatical errors in BW papers. It is, first, an alien form to many students whose mother tongues inflect the verb differently or not at all. Uniformly called for, however, in all verbs in the third person singular present indicative of standard English, it would seem to be a highly predictable or stable form and therefore one easily remembered. But note the grammatical concepts the student must grasp before he can apply the rule: the concepts of person, tense, number, and mood. Note that the *s* inflection is an atypical inflection within the modern English verb system. Note too how often it must seem to the student that he hears the stem form of the verb after third person singular subjects in what sounds like the present, as he does for example whenever he hears questions like "Does *she want* to go?" or "Can the *subway stop?*" In such sentences, the standard language itself reinforces the student's own resistance to the inflection.

And then, beyond these apparent unpredictabilities within the standard system, there is the influence of the student's own language or dialect, which urges him to ignore a troublesome form that brings no commensurate increase in meaning. Indeed, the very *s* he struggles with here may shift in a moment to signify plurality simply by being attached to a noun instead of a verb. No wonder then that students of formal English throughout the world find this inflection difficult, not because they lack intelligence or care but because they think analogically and are linguistically efficient. The issue is not the capacity of students finally to master this and the many other forms of written English that go against the grain of their instincts and experience but the priority this kind of problem ought to have in the larger scheme of learning to write and the willingness of students to mobilize themselves to master such forms at the initial stages of instruction.

Somewhere between the folly of pretending that errors don't matter and the rigidity of insisting that they matter more than anything, the teacher must find his answer, searching always under pressure for short cuts that will not ultimately restrict the intellectual power of his students. But as yet, we lack models for the maturation of the writing skill among young, native-born adults and can only theorize about the adaptability of other models for these students. We cannot say with certainty just what progress in writing ought to look like for basic-writing students, and more particularly how the elimination of error is related to their over-all improvement.

Should the teacher then turn from problems of error to his students' difficulties with the paragraphs of academic essays, new complexities emerge. Why, he wonders, do they reach such instant closure on their ideas, seldom moving into even one subordinate level of qualification but either moving on to a new topic sentence or drifting off into reverie and anecdote until the point of the essay has been dissolved? Where is that attitude of "suspended conclusion" that Dewey called thinking, and what can one infer about their intellectual competence from such behavior?

Before consigning his students to some earlier stage of mental development, the teacher at this stage begins to look more closely at the task he is asking students to perform. Are they aware, for example, after years of right/wrong testing, after the ACT's and the GED's and the OAT's, after straining to memorize what they read but never learning to doubt it, after "psyching out" answers rather than discovering them, are they aware that the rules have changed and that the rewards now go to those who can sustain a play of mind upon ideas—teasing out the contradictions and ambiguities and frailties of statements?

Or again, are the students sensitive to the ways in which the conventions of talk differ from those of academic discourse? Committed to extending the boundaries of what is known, the scholar proposes generalizations that cover the greatest possible number of instances and then sets about supporting his case according to the rules of evidence and sound reasoning that govern his subject. The spoken language, looping back and forth between speakers, offering chances for groping and backing up and even hiding, leaving room for the language of hands and faces, of pitch and pauses, is by comparison generous and inviting. The speaker is not responsible for the advancement of formal learning. He is free to assert opinions without a display of evidence or recount experiences without explaining what they "mean." His movements from one level of generality to another are more often brought on by shifts in the winds of conversation rather than by some decision of his to be more specific or to sum things up. For him the injunction to "be more specific" is difficult to carry out because the conditions that lead to specificity are usually missing. He may not have acquired the habit of questioning his propositions, as a listener might, in order to locate the points that require amplification or evidence. Or he may be marooned with a proposition he cannot defend for lack of information or for want of practice in retrieving the history of an idea as it developed in his own mind.

Similarly, the query "What is your point?" may be difficult to answer because the conditions under which the student is writing have not allowed for the slow generation of an orienting conviction, that underlying sense of the direction he wants his thinking to take. Yet without this conviction, he cannot judge the relevance of what comes to his mind, as one sentence branches out into another or one idea engenders another, gradually crowding from his memory the direction he initially set for himself.

Or finally, the writer may lack the vocabulary that would enable him to move more easily up the ladder of abstraction and must instead forge out of a nonanalytical vocabulary a way of discussing thoughts about thoughts, a task so formidable as to discourage him, as travelers in a foreign land are discouraged, from venturing far beyond bread-and-butter matters.

From such soundings, our teacher begins to see that teaching at the remedial level is not a matter of being simpler but of being more profound, of not only starting from "scratch" but also determining where "scratch" is. The experience of studenthood is the experience of being just so far over one's head that it is both realistic and essential to work at surviving. But by underestimating the sophistication of our students and by ignoring the complexity of the tasks we set before them, we have failed to locate in precise ways where to begin and what follows what.

But I have created a fourth stage in my developmental scheme, which I am calling DIVING IN in order to suggest that the teacher who has come this far must now make a decision that demands professional courage—the decision to remediate himself, to become a student of new disciplines and of his students themselves in order to perceive both their difficulties and their incipient excellence. "Always assume," wrote Leo Strauss, to the teacher, "that there is one silent student in your class who is by far superior to you in head and in heart." This assumption, as I have been trying to suggest, does not come easily or naturally when the teacher is a college teacher and the young men and women in his class are labeled remedial. But as we come to know these students better, we begin to see that the greatest barrier to our work with them is our ignorance of them and of the very subject we have contracted to teach. We see that we must grope our ways into the turbulent disciplines of semantics and linguistics for fuller, more accurate data about words and sentences; we must pursue more rigorously the design of developmental models, basing our schemes less upon loose comparisons with children and more open case studies and developmental research of the sort that produced William Perry's impressive study of the intellectual development of Harvard students; we need finally to examine more closely the nature of speaking and writing and divine the subtle ways in which these forms of language both support and undo each other.

The work is waiting for us. And so irrevocable now is the tide that brings the new students into the nation's college classrooms that it is no longer within our power, as perhaps it once was, to refuse to accept them into the community of the educable. They are here. DIVING IN is simply deciding that teaching them to write well is not only suitable but challenging work for those who would be teachers and scholars in a democracy.

Writing as a Mode of Learning

Writing represents a unique mode of learning—not merely valuable, not merely special, but unique. That will be my contention in this paper. The thesis is straightforward. Writing serves learning uniquely because writing as process-and-product possesses a cluster of attributes that correspond uniquely to certain powerful learning strategies.

Although the notion is clearly debatable, it is scarcely a private belief. Some of the most distinguished contemporary psychologists have at least implied such a role for writing as heuristic. Lev Vygotsky, A. R. Luria, and Jerome Bruner, for example, have all pointed out that higher cognitive functions, such as analysis and synthesis, seem to develop most fully only with the support system of verbal language—particularly, it seems, of written language.[1] Some of their arguments and evidence will be incorporated here.

Here I have a prior purpose: to describe as tellingly as possible *how* writing uniquely corresponds to certain powerful learning strategies. Making such a case for the uniqueness of writing should logically and theoretically involve establishing many contrasts, distinctions between (1) writing and all other verbal languaging processes—listening, reading, and especially talking; (2) writing and all other forms of composing, such

From *College Composition and Communications*, 28 (May, 1977), 122–128. Reprinted by permission of the National Council of Teachers of English and Janet Emig.

1. Lev S. Vygotsky, *Thought and Language*, trans. Eugenia Hanfmann and Gertrude Vakar (Cambridge: The M.I.T. Press, 1962); A. R. Luria and F. Ia. Yudovich, *Speech and the Development of Mental Processes in the Child*, ed. Joan Simon (Baltimore: Penguin, 1971); Jerome S. Bruner, *The Relevance of Education* (New York: W. W. Norton and Co., 1971).

sing a painting, a symphony, a dance, a film, a building; and omposing in words and composing in the two other major graphic mbol systems of mathematical equations and scientific formulae. For the purpose of this paper, the task is simpler, since most students are not permitted by most curricula to discover the values of composing, say, in dance, or even in film; and most students are not sophisticated enough to create, to originate formulations, using the highly abstruse symbol system of equations and formulae. Verbal language represents the most *available* medium for composing; in fact, the significance of sheer availability in its selection as a mode for learning can probably not be overstressed. But the uniqueness of writing among the verbal languaging processes does need to be established and supported if only because so many curricula and courses in English still consist almost exclusively of reading and listening.

WRITING AS A UNIQUE LANGUAGING PROCESS

Traditionally, the four languaging processes of listening, talking, reading, and writing are paired in either of two ways. The more informative seems to be the division many linguists make between first-order and second-order processes, with talking and listening characterized as first-order processes; reading and writing, as second-order. First-order processes are acquired without formal or systematic instruction; the second-order processes of reading and writing tend to be learned initially only with the aid of formal and systematic instruction.

The less useful distinction is that between listening and reading as receptive functions and talking and writing as productive functions. Critics of these terms like Louise Rosenblatt rightfully point out that the connotation of passivity too often accompanies the notion of receptivity when reading, like listening, is a vital, construing act.

An additional distinction, so simple it may have been previously overlooked, resides in two criteria: the matters of origination and of graphic recording. Writing is originating and creating a unique verbal construct that is graphically recorded. Reading is creating or re-creating *but not* originating a verbal construct that is graphically recorded. Listening is creating or re-creating but not originating a verbal construct that is *not* graphically recorded. Talking is creating *and* originating a verbal construct that is *not* graphically recorded (except for the circuitous routing of a transcribed tape). Note that a distinction is being made between creating and originating, separable processes.

For talking, the nearest languaging process, additional distinctions should probably be made. (What follows is not a denigration of talk as a valuable mode of learning.) A silent classroom or one filled only with the teacher's voice is anathema to learning. For evidence of the cognitive value of talk, one can look to some of the persuasive monographs coming from the London Schools Council project on writing: *From Information to Understanding* by Nancy Martin or *From Talking to Writing* by Peter Medway.[2] We also know that for some of us, talking is a valuable, even necessary, form of pre-writing. In his curriculum, James Moffett makes the value of such talk quite explicit.

But to say that talking is a valuable form of pre-writing is not to say that writing is talk recorded, an inaccuracy appearing in far too many composition texts. Rather, a number of contemporary trans-disciplinary sources suggest that talking and writing may emanate from different organic sources and represent quite different, possibly distinct, language functions. In *Thought and Language*, Vygotsky notes that "written speech is a separate linguistic function, differing from oral speech in both structure and mode of functioning."[3] The sociolinguist Dell Hymes, in a valuable issue of *Daedalus*, "Language as a Human Problem," makes a comparable point: "That speech and writing are not simply interchangeable, and have developed historically in ways at least partly autonomous, is obvious."[4] At the first session of the Buffalo Conference on Researching Composition (4–5 October 1975), the first point of unanimity among the participant-speakers with interests in developmental psychology, media, dreams and aphasia was that talking and writing were markedly different functions.[5] Some of us who work rather steadily with writing research agree. We also believe that there are hazards, conceptually and pedagogically, in creating too complete an analogy between talking and writing, in blurring the very real differences between the two.

What are these differences?

1. Writing is learned behavior; talking is natural, even irrepressible, behavior.

2. Writing then is an artificial process; talking is not.

3. Writing is a technological device—not the wheel, but early

2. Nancy Martin, *From Information to Understanding* (London: Schools Council Project Writing Across the Curriculum, 11–13, 1973); Peter Medway, *From Talking to Writing* (London: Schools Council Project Writing Across the Curriculum, 11–13, 1973).

3. Vygotsky, p. 98.

4. Dell Hymes, "On the Origins and Foundations of Inequality Among Speakers," *Daedalus*, 102 (Summer, 1973), 69.

5. Participant-speakers were Loren Barrett, University of Michigan; Gerald O'Grady, SUNY/Buffalo; Hollis Frampton, SUNY/Buffalo; and Janet Emig, Rutgers.

enough to qualify as primary technology; talking is organic, natural, earlier.

4. Most writing is slower than most talking.

5. Writing is stark, barren, even naked as a medium; talking is rich, luxuriant, inherently redundant.

6. Talk leans on the environment; writing must provide its own context.

7. With writing, the audience is usually absent; with talking, the listener is usually present.

8. Writing usually results in a visible graphic product; talking usually does not.

9. Perhaps because there is a product involved, writing tends to be a more responsible and committed act than talking.

10. It can be said that throughout history, an aura, an ambience, a mystique has usually encircled the written word; the spoken word has for the most part proved ephemeral and treated mundanely (ignore, please, our recent national history).

11. Because writing is often our representation of the world made visible, embodying both process and product, writing is more readily a form and source of learning than talking.

UNIQUE CORRESPONDENCES BETWEEN LEARNING AND WRITING

What then are some *unique* correspondences between learning and writing? To begin with some definitions: Learning can be defined in many ways, according to one's predilections and training, with all statements about learning of course hypothetical. Definitions range from the chemophysiological ("Learning is changed patterns of protein synthesis in relevant portions of the cortex")[6] to transactive views drawn from both philosophy and psychology (John Dewey, Jean Piaget) that learning is the re-organization or confirmation of a cognitive scheme in light of an experience.[7] What the speculations seem to share is consensus about certain

---

6. George Steiner, *After Babel: Aspects of Language and Translation* (New York: Oxford University Press, 1975), p. 287.
7. John Dewey, *Experience and Education* (New York: Macmillan, 1938); Jean Piaget, *Biology and Knowledge: An Essay on the Relations between Organic Regulations and Cognitive Processes* (Chicago: University of Chicago Press, 1971).

features and strategies that characterize successful learning. These include the importance of the classic attributes of re-inforcement and feedback. In most hypotheses, successful learning is also connective and selective. Additionally, it makes use of propositions, hypotheses, and other elegant summarizers. Finally, it is active, engaged, personal—more specifically, self-rhythmed—in nature.

Jerome Bruner, like Jean Piaget, through a comparable set of categories, posits three major ways in which we represent and deal with actuality: (1) enactive—we learn "by doing"; (2) iconic—we learn "by depiction in an image"; and (3) representational or symbolic—we learn "by restatement in words."[8] To overstate the matter, in enactive learning, the hand predominates; in iconic, the eye; and in symbolic, the brain.

What is striking about writing as a process is that, by its very nature, all three ways of dealing with actuality are simultaneously or almost simultaneously deployed. That is, the symbolic transformation of experience through the specific symbol system of verbal language is shaped into an icon (the graphic product by the enactive hand. If the most efficacious learning occurs when learning is re-inforced, then writing through its inherent re-inforcing cycle involving hand, eye, and brain marks a uniquely powerful multi-representational mode for learning.

Writing is also integrative in perhaps the most basic possible sense: the organic, the functional. Writing involves the fullest possible functioning of the brain, which entails the active participation in the process of both the left and the right hemispheres. Writing is markedly bispheral, although in some popular accounts, writing is inaccurately presented as a chiefly left-hemisphere activity, perhaps because the linear written product is somehow regarded as analogue for the process that created it; and the left hemisphere seems to process material linearly.

The right hemisphere, however, seems to make at least three, perhaps four, major contributions to the writing process—probably, to the creative process generically. First, several researchers, such as Geschwind and Snyder of Harvard and Zaidal of Cal Tech, through markedly different experiments, have very tentatively suggested that the right hemisphere is the sphere, even the *seat*, of emotions.[9] Second—or perhaps as an illustration of the first—Howard Gardner, in his important study of the brain-damaged, notes that our sense of emotional appropriateness in discourse may reside in the right sphere:

8. Bruner, pp. 7–8.
9. Boyce Rensberger, "Language Ability Found in Right Side of Brain," *New York Times*, 1 August 1975, p. 14.

Emotional appropriateness, in sum—being related not only to *what* is said, but to how it is said and to what is *not* said, as well—is crucially dependent on right hemisphere intactness.[10]

Third, the right hemisphere seems to be the source of intuition, of sudden gestalts, of flashes of images, of abstractions occurring as visual or spatial wholes, as the initiating metaphors in the creative process. A familiar example: William Faulkner noted in his *Paris Review* interview that *The Sound and the Fury* began as the image of a little girl's muddy drawers as she sat in a tree watching her grandmother's funeral.[11]

Also, a unique form of feedback, as well as reinforcement, exists with writing, because information from the *process* is immediately and visibly available as that portion of the *product* already written. The importance for learning of a product in a familiar and available medium for immediate, literal (that is, visual) re-scanning and review cannot perhaps be overstated. In his remarkable study of purportedly blind sculptors, Géza Révész found that without sight, persons cannot move beyond a literal transcription of elements into any manner of symbolic transformation—by definition, the central requirement for reformulation and re-interpretation, i.e., revision, that most aptly named process.[12]

As noted in the second paragraph, Vygotsky and Luria, like Bruner, have written importantly about the connections between learning and writing. In his essay "The Psychobiology of Psychology," Bruner lists as one of six axioms regarding learning: "We are connective."[13] Another correspondence then between learning and writing: in *Thought and Language*, Vygotsky notes that writing makes a unique demand in that the writer must engage in "deliberate semantics"—in Vygotsky's elegant phrase, "deliberate structuring of the web of meaning."[14] Such structuring is required because, for Vygotsky, writing centrally represents an expansion of inner speech, that mode whereby we talk to ourselves, which is "maximally compact" and "almost entirely predicative"; written speech is a mode which is "maximally detailed" and which requires explicitly supplied subjects and topics. The medium then of written verbal language requires the establishment of systematic connections and relationships. Clear writing by definition is that writing which signals without ambigu-

10. Howard Gardner, *The Shattered Mind: The Person After Brain Damage* (New York: Alfred A. Knopf, 1975), p. 372.
11. William Faulkner, *Writers at Work: The Paris Review Interviews*, ed. Malcolm Cowley (New York: The Viking Press, 1959), p. 130.
12. Géza Révész, *Psychology and Art of the Blind*, trans. H. A. Wolff (London: Longmans-Green, 1950).
13. Bruner, p. 126.
14. Vygotsky, p. 100.

ity the nature of conceptual relationships, whether they be coordinate, subordinate, superordinate, causal, or something other.

Successful learning is also engaged, committed, personal learning. Indeed, impersonal learning may be an anomalous concept, like the very notion of objectivism itself. As Michael Polanyi states simply at the beginning of *Personal Knowledge:* "the ideal of strict objectivism is absurd." (How many courses and curricula in English, science, and all else does that one sentence reduce to rubble?) Indeed, the theme of *Personal Knowledge* is that

> into every act of knowing there enters a passionate contribution of the person knowing what is being known, . . . this coefficient is no mere imperfection but a vital component of his knowledge.[15]

In *Zen and the Art of Motorcycle Maintenance,* Robert Pirsig states a comparable theme:

> The Quality which creates the world emerges as *a relationship* between man and his experience. He is a *participant* in the creation of all things.[16]

Finally, the psychologist George Kelly has as the central notion in his subtle and compelling theory of personal constructs man as a scientist steadily and actively engaged in making and re-making his hypotheses about the nature of the universe.[17]

We are acquiring as well some empirical confirmation about the importance of engagement in, as well as self-selection of, a subject for the student learning to write and writing to learn. The recent Sanders and Littlefield study, reported in *Research in the Teaching of English,* is persuasive evidence on this point, as well as being a model for a certain type of research.[18]

As Luria implies in the quotation above, writing is self-rhythmed. One writes best as one learns best, at one's own pace. Or to connect the two processes, writing can sponsor learning because it can match its pace. Support for the importance of self-pacing to learning can be found in

---

15. Michael Polanyi, *Personal Knowledge: Toward a Post-Critical Philosophy* (Chicago: University of Chicago Press, 1958), p. viii.

16. Robert Pirsig, *Zen and the Art of Motorcycle Maintenance* (New York: William Morrow and Co., Inc., 1974), p. 212.

17. George Kelly, *A Theory of Personality: The Psychology of Personal Constructs* (New York: W. W. Norton and Co., 1963).

18. Sara E. Sanders and John H. Littlefield, "Perhaps Test Essays Can Reflect Significant Improvement in Freshman Composition: Report on a Successful Attempt," *RTE,* 9 (Fall, 1975), 145–153.

Benjamin Bloom's important study "Time and Learning."[19] Evidence for the significance of self-pacing to writing can be found in the reason Jean-Paul Sartre gave last summer for not using the tape-recorder when he announced that blindness in his second eye had forced him to give up writing:

> I think there is an enormous difference between speaking and writing. One rereads what one rewrites. But one can read slowly or quickly: in other words, you do not know how long you will have to take deliberating over a sentence. . . . If I listen to a tape recorder, the listening speed is determined by the speed at which the tape turns and not by my own needs. Therefore I will always be either lagging behind or running ahead of the machine.[20]

Writing is connective as a process in a more subtle and perhaps more significant way, as Luria points out in what may be the most powerful paragraph of rationale ever supplied for writing as heuristic:

> Written speech is bound up with the inhibition of immediate synpractical connections. It assumes a much slower, repeated mediating process of analysis and synthesis, which makes it possible not only to develop the required thought, but even to revert to its earlier stages, thus transforming the sequential chain of connections in a simultaneous, self-reviewing structure. Written speech thus represents a new and powerful instrument of thought.[21]

But first to explicate: writing inhibits "immediate synpractical connections." Luria defines *synpraxis* as "concrete-active" situations in which language does not exist independently but as a "fragment" of an ongoing action "outside of which it is incomprehensible."[22] In *Language and Learning*, James Britton defines it succinctly as "speech-cum-action."[23] Writing, unlike talking, restrains dependence upon the actual situation. Writing as a mode is inherently more self-reliant than speaking. Moreover, as Bruner states in explicating Vygotsky, "Writing virtually forces a remoteness of reference on the language user."[24]

Luria notes what has already been noted above: that writing, typically, is a "much slower" process than talking. But then he points out the relation of this slower pace to learning: this slower pace allows for—indeed,

19. Benjamin Bloom, "Time and Learning," *American Psychologist,* 29 (September, 1974), 682–688.
20. Jean-Paul Sartre, "Sartre at Seventy: An Interview," with Michael Contat, *New York Review of Books,* 7 August 1975.
21. Luria, p. 118.
22. Luria, p. 50.
23. James Britton, *Language and Learning* (Baltimore: Penguin, 1971), pp. 10–11.
24. Bruner, p. 47.

encourages—the shuttling among past, present, and future. Writing, in other words, connects the three major tenses of our experience to make meaning. And the two major modes by which these three aspects are united are the processes of analysis and synthesis: analysis, the breaking of entities into their constituent parts; and synthesis, combining or fusing these, often into fresh arrangements or amalgams.

Finally, writing is epigenetic, with the complex evolutionary development of thought steadily and graphically visible and available throughout as a record of the journey, from jottings and notes to full discursive formulations.

For a summary of the correspondences stressed here between certain learning strategies and certain attributes of writing see Figure 1.

This essay represents a first effort to make a certain kind of case for writing—specifically, to show its unique value for learning. It is at once over-elaborate and under-specific. Too much of the formulation is in the off-putting jargon of the learning theorist, when my own predilection

FIGURE 1. Unique cluster of correspondences between certain learning strategies and certain attributes of writing

Selected characteristics of successful learning strategies	Selected attributes of writing, process and product
(1) Profits from multi-representational and integrative re-inforcement	(1) Represents process uniquely multi-representational and integrative
(2) Seeks self-provided feedback:	(2) Represents powerful instance of self-provided feedback:
(a) immediate	(a) provides product uniquely available for *immediate* feedback (review and re-evaluation)
(b) long-term	(b) provides record of evolution of thought since writing is epigenetic as process-and-product
(3) Is connective:	(3) Provides connections:
(a) makes generative conceptual groupings, synthetic and analytic	(a) establishes explicit and systematic conceptual groupings through lexical, syntactic, and rhetorical devices
(b) proceeds from propositions, hypotheses, and other elegant summarizers	(b) represents most available means (verbal language) for economic recording of abstract formulations
(4) Is active, engaged, personal—notably, self-rhythmed	(4) Is active, engaged, personal—notably, self-rhythmed

would have been to emulate George Kelly and to avoid terms like *rein-forcement* and *feedback* since their use implies that I live inside a certain paradigm about learning I don't truly inhabit. Yet I hope that the essay will start a crucial line of inquiry; for unless the losses to learners of not writing are compellingly described and substantiated by experimental and speculative research, writing itself as a central academic process may not long endure.

ADDITIONAL READINGS

RICHARD BRADDOCK, RICHARD LLOYD-JONES, and LOWELL SCHOER, "The State of Knowledge about Composition," *Research in Written Composition* (Champaign, Ill.: National Council of Teachers of English, 1963), pp. 29–53.

MARTHA L. KING, "Research in Composition: A Need for Theory," *Research in the Teaching of English*, 12 (October, 1978), 193–202.

NANCY I. SOMMERS, "The Need for Theory in Composition Research," *College Composition and Communication*, 30 (February, 1979), 46–49.

ANDREA A. LUNSFORD, "What We Know—and Don't Know—About Remedial Writing," *College Composition and Communication*, 29 (February, 1978), 47–52.

WILLIAM F. IRMSCHER, "Writing as a Way of Learning and Developing," *College Composition and Communication*, 30 (October, 1979), 240–244.

DEAN MEMERING, "The Reading/Writing Heresy," *College Composition and Communication*, 28 (October, 1977), 223–226.

GEORGE E. YOOS, "An Identity of Roles in Writing and Reading," *College Composition and Communication*, 30 (October, 1979), 245–251.

FRANK J. D'ANGELO

The Search for Intelligible Structure
in the Teaching of Composition

It has been a little over a decade since George B. Leonard, writing in *Look* magazine, contended,

> Writing is the disgrace of American education. Millions of our boys and girls are graduating from high school—and thousands from college—unable to write 500 sensible words on a single subject. Teachers of composition have grown accustomed to working under "impossible" conditions. The best of them do huge labors and get little thanks. The worst of them—probably a majority—know next to nothing about teaching writing and can barely tell good writing from bad.[1]

This point of view has been amply documented by teachers and scholars in the field. For example, George Stade writes that the teaching of composition "is in a bad way. Everyone says so, even people who are responsible for its being as it is . . . it has suddenly become as embarrassing and superfluous as it is difficult to part with."[2] Virginia Burke emphasizes this point even more forcefully: "There is chaos today in the teaching of composition because since the turn of the century, composition has lacked an informing discipline, without which no field can maintain its proper dimensions, the balance and proportion of its various parts, or its very integrity. Consequently, the practice of composition has shrunk, has lost important elements, has become a victim of all manner of distortion."[3]

From *College Composition and Communication*, 27 (May, 1976), 142–147. Reprinted by permission of the National Council of Teachers of English and Frank D'Angelo.

1. George B. Leonard, "Why Johnny Can't Write," *Look*, 20 June 1961, p. 103.
2. George Stade, "Hydrants into Elephants: The Theory and Practice of College Composition," *College English*, 31 (November, 1969), 143.
3. Virginia M. Burke, "The Composition-Rhetoric Pyramid," *CCC*, 16 (February, 1965), 5.

More recently, Malcolm Scully, in *The Chronicle of Higher Education,* reports that a recent survey of English department chairman in colleges and universities reveals that students entering college today are just as deficient in basic writing skills as their counterparts in the early 60's and that even the more verbally gifted students can't express their thoughts in writing. Many entering students are in fact "functionally illiterate."[4] As a result, many major state universities are offering remedial composition courses. In view of this latest "crisis" in composition, few teachers today would take seriously Warner Rice's proposal, made in 1960, that freshman composition be abolished.[5]

Many reasons have been given for our failure to teach writing adequately: heavy class loads; inadequate or nonexistent teacher-preparation programs in composition; the lack of clear goals; the lack of any discernible structure or logical sequence in the composition program; the dearth of good composition texts; the neglect of teaching composition in favor of teaching literature, media, or some other related subject area; poor student motivation; poor teaching; inappropriate course content, and counter-influences in society which are beyond the control of the teacher. But *one* of the most important reasons for our inability to teach composition adequately is that we have failed to identify the most significant principles and concepts in the field which will make intelligible everything we do. As Virginia Burke puts it,

> The power of a discipline to identify and maintain a field and to energize practice in it should be self-evident. *Without a discipline,* arbitrary decisions to add or drop a composition course, to write a theme a week or a theme a month, to use this text-book or that, to feature one kind of writing or one kind of reading over another, to evaluate papers chiefly for content or for organization or for mechanics—all such arbitrary decisions are without rationale; no decision at all may do as well as a decision one way or the other. *With a discipline,* some reasonable sequence, moving *from* something identifiable *toward* something identifiable, is clearly suggested; and the scope of concerns within the discipline must be explicitly taken into account. *Without a discipline,* undergraduate and graduate offerings in advanced composition and rhetoric can continue slight or nonexistent; and the preparation of teachers of high school and college composition can be treated in familiar, cavalier fashion; *with a discipline,* we must confront the peculiarities and gaps

---

4. Malcolm G. Scully, "Crisis in English Writing," *The Chronicle of Higher Education,* 9 (Septeber 23, 1974), 1, 6.
5. Warner G. Rice, "A Proposal for the Abolition of Freshman English, As It is Now Commonly Taught, from the College Curriculum," *College English,* 21 (April, 1960), 361–367.

in our undergraduate and graduate offerings as well as our whole approach to English studies.[6]

Unfortunately, there have been few attempts by teachers and scholars to try to identify the underlying principles that constitute the discipline in composition. To add to the confusion, there appears to be a semantic muddle in our use of terms in trying to come to grips with the problem. For example, composition has been described as both a content and a content-less subject in the field of English studies. Those who view it as having a content describe that content as variously being literature, the humanities, communication skills, the students' own writing, grammar, linguistics, semantics, logic, and so forth. Those who view it as being content-less argue that there is no specific subject matter that must be covered in order for the teacher to achieve his objectives, that in fact we don't even know the relationship between the wide variety of content found in composition courses and the development of writing skills.

This multiplication and confusion of terms, goals, and means has obscured our ability to see our field of inquiry clearly and to see it whole. According to James Moffett, our approach to composition has been "far too substantive. . . . The failure to distinguish *kinds* and *orders* of knowledge amounts to a crippling epistemological error built into the very heart of the overall curriculum. The classification by 'subject matters' into English, history, math, science, French, etc., implies that they are all merely contents that differ only in what they are about."[7]

My thesis is that composition does have an underlying structure which gives unity and coherence to the field, that that structure can be conceived of in terms of principles and forms (akin to those found in music or painting, for example), and that these principles and forms need to be taught in an orderly sequence.[8] In the remainder of this paper, therefore, I would like to delineate a few of the most important of these principles and forms and to discuss their implications for the teaching of composition.

I would like to begin my exposition of the structure of composition by presenting some tentative concepts in the following diagrammatic form:

6. Burke, p. 6.
7. James Moffett, "A Structural Curriculum in English," *Harvard Educational Review,* 36 (Winter, 1966), 20, 21.
8. This division of composition or rhetoric into principles and forms is hinted at by Quintilian who argues that invention, arrangement and style belong to the "art" of rhetoric and that the "kinds" of oratory are part of the "material" of rhetoric. Each kind (i.e. mode) "requires invention, arrangement, expression, memory, and delivery," contends Quintilian. *The Institutio Oratoria of Marcus Fabius Quintilianus,* with an English Summary and Concordance by Charles Edgar Little (Nashville: George Peabody College for Teachers, 1951), 116.

THE STRUCTURE OF COMPOSITION

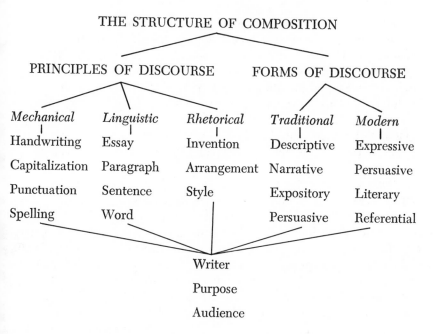

PRINCIPLES OF DISCOURSE   FORMS OF DISCOURSE

Mechanical	*Linguistic*	*Rhetorical*	*Traditional*	*Modern*
Handwriting	Essay	Invention	Descriptive	Expressive
Capitalization	Paragraph	Arrangement	Narrative	Persuasive
Punctuation	Sentence	Style	Expository	Literary
Spelling	Word		Persuasive	Referential

Writer

Purpose

Audience

The principles of discourse pertain to the fundamental laws, rules, and conventions of discourse. These principles are the basic principles determining the intrinsic nature of discourse.[9] They can be found in all forms of discourse; consequently, they can be said to inform the modes of discourse. The forms of discourse refer to the different modes of existence of a discourse. They are concerned with the shape and structure, the overall plan or design or configuration of particular kinds of discourse. These modes are extrinsic in relation to the nature of discourse. Thus, for example, a specific kind of expository writing may be said to be a form of discourse. It in turn may be informed by the linguistic principles of coordination and subordination or by the rhetorical principles of cause and effect. This fundamental distinction between principles and forms should become clearer as we go along. Suffice it to say at this point that writing ability consists in the ability to use these underlying principles and basic forms.

The mechanical principles are basically four: handwriting, capitalization, punctuation, and spelling. The use of the term "mechanical" is not

9. It is not my purpose to argue how these principles are derived but to identify and place into a coherent system a few that I feel are self-evident. Clearly some of these principles (or laws) are assumptions, some are self-evident, some are based on the observation of repeated events, and some are derived from theory.

to be taken in a pejorative sense, but it is clear that these principles are not as central to the composition process as are the linguistic principles and the rhetorical principles. One might argue, however, that the principles involved in some of the mechanical skills, punctuation, for example, are inextricably tied in with the other principles, that punctuation is tied in with the linguistic principles of stress, pitch, and juncture, for instance. Nevertheless, it is more useful to consider these principles as being peripheral rather than central to the composition process.

The linguistic principles may be divided into four basic categories: the principles of the essay, the paragraph, the sentence, and the word. The linguistic principles are those that are delineated in the major grammatical texts. These principles are syntactic, morphological, phonological, or graphological, and semantic. They are exemplified by such concepts as coordination and subordination, embedding, negation, relativization, nominalization, compounding, clipping, blending, derivation, functional shift, and the like. These principles may also be found in the major composition texts as well as scattered throughout the journals. There has been so much done with the grammar of the sentence and of the word that extensive discussion of the underlying principles is not necessary. Less familiar perhaps is the work being done with the grammar of the paragraph or of the essay. I might mention as typical examples Alton Becker's tagmemic approach to paragraph analysis, Francis Christensen's generative rhetoric of the paragraph, Paul Rodger's discourse-centered rhetoric of the paragraph, Zellig Harris's discourse analysis, Willis Pitkin's discourse blocs, Michael Grady's conceptual rhetoric of the composition, and my own work with discourse structure. Quite obviously, much more work needs to be done in this important area.

The rhetorical principles are those which are ordinarily found in composition and rhetoric books and those derived from rhetorical theory.[10] I have listed the major principles as being those of invention, arrangement, and style. The principles of invention are exemplified in rhetoric texts by the topics: categories such as analysis, definition, comparison, and cause and effect which suggest questions that a student can use to probe any subject, to discover ideas before he begins to write. The principles of internal arrangement are exemplified by such concepts as analysis, classification, comparison, thesis and support, induction, deduction, and so forth. The schemes and tropes of classical rhetoric are directly concerned with rhetorical principles of style on the sentence level. (Some typical examples of these are parallelism, inversion, various schemes of repetition such as anaphora, metaphor, metonymy, and various kinds of puns.) The prin-

10. See, for example, my discussion of rhetorical principles in *A Conceptual Theory of Rhetoric* (Cambridge, Mass.: Winthrop Publishers, Inc., 1975).

ciples of diction, as a part of style, are usually approached in terms of paired opposites: general/particular; abstract/concrete; literal/figurative; formal/informal; Anglo-Saxon/Latinate, and so forth.

These concepts do not exhaust the principles of discourse that we ought to be concerned with in the study of composition, but they do suggest that with a little time and effort, we can identify some of the most important principles which are fundamental to the discipline. Clearly, we need to identify and explicate many more.

I had previously mentioned that the principles of discourse are the basic elements that determine the intrinsic nature of discourse. The forms or modes of discourse determine the extrinsic nature of discourse. The modal approach is based on the idea that all writing can be classified on the basis of form. As far as can be determined, Alexander Bain was the first to establish the classification of the four modes of discourse (description, narration, exposition, and argumentation) found in many textbooks today. Bain's categories, however, included poetry as a fifth mode. According to Bain, the forms of discourse are the kinds of composition which relate to the faculties of the mind (the understading, the will, and feelings), to the aims of discourse (to inform, to persuade, and to please), and more generally to the laws of thought. Thus narration, description, and exposition relate to the faculty of understanding; persuasion relates to the will; and poetry relates to the feelings.

Since Alexander Bain, many other scholars have been interested in the forms-of-discourse approach to writing.[11] One of the most significant of the new approaches to the modes of discourse has been articulated by James L. Kinneavy in his book *A Theory of Discourse*. Following Alexander Bain, Kinneavy contends that each mode of discourse corresponds to a different kind of thinking and to a different view of reality. Furthermore, the reason for the existence of these modes can be found in the human uses of language and the purpose to which this language is put. Thus Kinneavy is as much concerned with the "aims" of discourse as he is with the "modes" of discourse.

11. Alexander Bain, *English Composition and Rhetoric*, rev. American ed. (New York: D. Appleton and Co., 1890); George R. Bramer, "Like It Is: Discourse Analysis for a New Generation," *CCC*, 21 (December, 1970), 347–355; James L. Kinneavy, *A Theory of Discourse* (Englewood Cliffs, N.J.: Prentice-Hall, Inc., 1971); Carol Kupendall, "Sequence Without Structure," *English Journal*, 61 (May, 1972), 715–722; James Moffett, *A Student-Centered Language Arts Curriculum, Grades K–13: A Handbook for Teachers* (Boston: Houghton Mifflin, 1968); James Moffett, *Teaching the Universe of Discourse* (Boston: Houghton Mifflin, 1968); Leo Rockas, *Modes of Rhetoric* (New York: St. Martin's Press, 1964); Martin Stevens, "Modes of Utterance," *CCC*, 14 (May, 1963), 65–72; Joshua Whatmough, *Poetic, Scientific, and Other Forms of Discourse* (Berkeley, Calif.: University of California Press, 1956).

Although Kinneavy's theory of modes derives in part from the aims of discourse, it owes part of its theoretical justification to communications theory. The aims of discourse are based on the four elements of the communication triangle: the encoder (the speaker or writer), the decoder (the audience or reader), the reality (the outer world), and the message (the work itself). The following scheme depicts the relationships that obtain among these four modes:

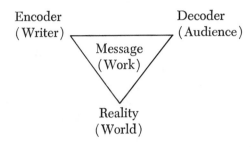

The aims of discourse and the modes of discourse are closely connected. If the writer's aim is self-expression, then the emphasis is on the writer or speaker himself (the encoder), and the result is expressive discourse. If the writer's aim is to convince or persuade, then the stress is on the audience (the decoder), the reader or listener, and the result is persuasive discourse. If the writer's aim is to convey reality, then the emphasis is on that reality (the world), and the result is referential discourse. Finally, if the writer is concerned with the text itself (the message), and the stress is on the internal ordering of the formal characteristics of the text, then the result is literary discourse. These four modes (the expressive, the persuasive, the referential, and the literary) constitute the basic forms of discourse.

Expressive discourse includes such forms as diaries, journals, conversations, protests, gripe sessions, and the like. Referential discourse includes news stories, articles, textbooks, summaries, histories, interviews, theories, taxonomic classifications, descriptive analyses, and so forth. Persuasive discourse comprises advertising, propaganda, oratory, political speeches, sermons, and editorials. Literary discourse embraces the genres of literature, songs, puns, the limerick, jokes, and the T. V. drama.

The reader will notice that an emphasis on the forms of discourse necessarily brings into play a consideration of the writer, his purpose, and his audience. A modal approach to the discourse forces us to consider the interrelationships that exist between the writer and his audience, the writer and the text, and the writer and the world, or between the audience and the world, or the world and the text. Thus the writer, the writer's purpose, the writer's audience, the text, and the rhetorical context (perhaps best exemplified by Kenneth Burke's Pentad: Act, Scene, Agent, Means, Purpose), are principles that are fundamental to the study of composition.

What are the implications of emphasizing the structure of a discipline, of identifying the fundamental principles of a field? The first implication is that a knowledge of the basic ideas of a subject will enable us to use them effectively in developing new curricula. Curricula in composition must be organized around the most fundamental principles of the discipline if they are to be meaningful. Clearly, some sense of progression, some sense of sequence, some kind of connection among various activities is needed in individual courses and from course to course. The second implication is that a knowledge of fundamental principles will help us delineate general goals and specific objectives. How can teachers set up behavioral objectives for composition (as many are increasingly called upon to do) unless they have some basic understanding of the underlying principles of the field? Such objectives can only end up being either idiosyncratic or impressionistic at best. The third implication is that a grasp of basic principles is a necessary precondition for effective teaching. Course "content," teaching techniques, approaches to evaluation, and the choice of the best available texts are just a few things related to effective teaching that depend upon a knowledge of underlying principles and concepts. A fourth implication is that teacher preparation programs in composition might be substantially improved. If a knowledge of linguistic and rhetorical principles and forms is necessary for good composition teaching, then surely teacher-preparation programs should include some knowledge of linguistics, of new grammars, of semantics, of classical and modern rhetoric, of rhetorical theory, and of new approaches to the teaching of composition. A final implication is that a knowledge of basic principles will help us to identify the gaps in our knowledge and as a consequence encourage us to generate new research. Unfortunately, in some areas, composition does not have the same kind of relevant research to draw upon as other related disciplines.

Identifying the underlying structure or structures of the discipline is not a panacea for all of our composition ills. It is, however, an important first step in bringing a new unity and order to the field. The vast proliferation of knowledge and the lack of simplifying ideas is a grave embarrassment in the field of composition today. The next major advance in composition can come about only as we begin to discover the underlying principles that will inform everything we do. Our task is not merely to identify these fundamental principles and concepts, but to see them as simple. If there exists a simple order in the universe, then clearly the universe of discourse must reflect that order. The call then is for articulate structure in the teaching of composition. As teachers and scholars, we can have no greater goal.

The Basic Aims of Discourse

INTRODUCTION

Most of us make implicit assumptions about the aims of discourse when we loosely distinguish expository writing from literature or creative writing, and, no doubt, there is some validity to the distinction. Many college composition textbooks often assume a similar distinction and address themselves to the province of expository writing. But it may be that this simple distinction is too simple and that other aims of discourse ought to be given some consideration. It is this question which I would like to investigate in this paper.

First, at least one working definition. I am concerned with complete discourse, not individual sentences or even paragraphs. It is often impossible to determine the aim of an individual sentence or paragraph without its full context. The same sentence or even paragraph in another context may have a very different aim. "Discourse" here means the full text, oral or written, delivered at a specific time and place or delivered at several instances. A discourse may be a single sentence, "Fire," screamed from a hotel window, or a joke, or a sonnet, or a three-hour talk, or a tragedy, or Toynbee's twelve volumes of *A Study of History*. Sometimes the determination of text is difficult: a conversation may trail off into another one; a novel like *Sanctuary* may pick up years later in *Requiem for a Nun;* there are trilogies in drama and novel, etc.; but usually the determination of text is a fairly simple matter.

From *College Composition and Communication,* 20 (December, 1969), 297–304. Reprinted by permission of the National Council of Teachers of English and James L. Kinneavy.

By aim of discourse is meant the effect that the discourse is oriented to achieve in the average listener or reader for whom it is intended. It is the intent as embodied in the discourse, the intent of the work, as traditional philosophy called it. Is the work intended to delight or to persuade or to inform or to demonstrate the logical proof of a position? These would be typical aims.

The determination of the basic aims of discourse and some working agreement in this area among rhetoricians would be a landmark in the field of composition. For it is to the achievement of these aims that all our efforts as teachers of composition are directed.

Yet a classification of diverse aims of discourse must not be interpreted as the establishing of a set of iron-clad categories which do not overlap. Such an exercise must be looked upon as any scientific exercise—an abstraction from certain aspects of reality in order to focus attention on and carefully analyze the characteristics of some feature of reality in a scientific vacuum, as it were. The scientist who is attempting to formulate the law of gravity isolates the gravitational forces from air resistance, from surface variations, from electric attraction, etc., and hopefully postulates a principle of gravity. The re-insertion into real situations wherein wind, surface variations, electricity and other forces intervene come later. Similarly, an attempt to formulate the nature of information, as such, must operate in a discourse vacuum which momentarily abstracts from the fact that information can be used in propaganda or be a component of a literary discourse. In actual practice such pure discourses as information devoid of persuasion, or persuasion devoid of information, or literature without some personal expression, and so forth, are almost non-existent or as rare as the laboratory concept of gravitation. But that does not destroy the validity of the classifications.

THE DETERMINATION
OF THE AIMS OF DISCOURSE

Some negative and some external norms. There are some useful cautions about determination of aims made in literary theory by W. K. Wimsatt and Monroe Beardsley which can be extended to discourse theory. It is dangerous in literature (and even more in persuasion) to assume that what the author says he is trying to do is actually what the work really accomplishes. To determine the aim by author intent is to run the risk of the "intentional fallacy." A parallel danger is to assume that the reaction of a given reader is an accurate indication of purpose. This fallacy has been termed the "affective fallacy" by Wimsatt and Beardsley.[1] The stated intentions of the author and the reactions of a given reader are useful markers that can point to significant evidence in the discourse itself, as the linguist Michael Riffaterre points out;[2] for this reason they should not be disregarded. Similarly, many authors advise us to take into account the cultural conventions of the genre employed; anthropologists like Malinowski warn of the importance of the immediate historical context; McLuhan emphasizes the significance of the medium used; Kenneth Burke writes a whole book on the influence of the semantic range, the grammar he calls it, of the motivational field; and even the grammatical choices offered by the language can restrict and modify the aim, as Sapir and Whorf caution us. All of these, external to the discourse, are nonetheless weighty determinants of aim and are so many arguments against the mythical autonomy of the text.

Internal norms of aim. Among the writers who have sought to establish the aims of discourse by norms internal to the discourse there is considerable variation in the kind of norm singled out. Yet there is a surprising measure of agreement among the analysts on so fundamental an issue. In Figure 1, I have attempted to show some of these various approaches, together with the principle of division and the resulting classifications of aims of discourse. The parallel classifications of the various systems are indicated in the horizontal rows. All of the authorities whom I have analyzed could not be presented on a single page, so I have only indicated typical representatives of various approaches.

The eldest and most persistent approach in western civilization is that beginning in Plato, codified by Aristotle, continued by the medieval Arab philosophers Averröes and Avicenna, Aquinas and Albertus Magnus, and passed on to modern times by the classical tradition and some comparative philologists, like Joshua Whatmough. Aristotle and Aquinas distinguish a *scientific* use of language achieving certainty, a *dialectical* use of language operating in the area of probability, a *rhetorical* or persuasive use of language based on seeming probability, and a *poetic* use of language incorporating a rigid but internal probability. The principle of division is obviously a scale of diminishing probability.[3]

1. For the treatment of both fallacies, see W. K. Wimsatt and Monroe Beardsley, *The Verbal Icon* (Lexington, Kentucky, 1965), pp. 3–18, 21–39.
2. "Criteria for Style Analysis," in *Essays on the Language of Literature*, eds. Seymour Chatman and Samuel R. Levin (Boston, Massachusetts, 1967), pp. 419 ff.
3. For a historical survey of this school, see J. Craig La Drière, "Rhetoric and 'Merely Verbal' Art," in *English Institute Essays, 1948*, ed. D. A. Robertson (New York, 1949), pp. 123–153.

FIGURE 1. A comparison of some systems of aims of discourse

School / Principle of division	Aristotle and Aquinas	Cassirer	Morris	Miller	Russell	Reichenbach	Richards	Bühler, Jakobson, Kinneavy
	Level of probability	Historical sequence in Greece	Behavioral reactions of animals to stimuli	Socio-psych. motives for communications	Grammar (kinds of sentences)	Faculty addressed to	Proportions of reference and emotion	Component of communication process stressed
	Scientific —certain	Metaphysical —representative of the world	Informative	Informative —to increase uniformity of information	Informative —declarative	Communicative (thoughts to be believed)	Scientific (pure reference)	Reference Informative; Scientific Exploratory
	Dialectical —probable		Valuative	Opinion —to increase uniformity of opinions	Questioning —interrogative			
	Rhetorical —seemingly probable	Pragmatic —practical use by sophists	Incitive	Status change	Imperative —imperative	Promotive (actions to be accomplished)	Rhetorical (mixed reference and emotion)	Persuasive
	Poetic —internally probable	Mythological —expressive of aspirations; Interjectional	Systemic	Emotive	Expressive (of emotion) —exclamatory	Suggestive (emotions to be aroused)	Poetic (pure emotion)	Literary; Expressive

Ernst Cassirer, examining the historical sequence of Greek views on the functions of language, sees first a *mythological* view of language as a medium for expressing the aspirations of early Greek society. This partially (though not at all totally) corresponds to Aristotle's poetic function. This was followed by a period in which it was felt by the philosophers that language was admirably suited to mirror or represent the universe. This *metaphysical* period, as he calls it, corresponds to Aristotle's scientific use of language. The practical or *pragmatic* use of language by the sophists and rhetoricians came next. Finally, Democritus pointed to a basic and initial *interjectional* or emotive use of language—to which Aristotle has no direct parallel.[4]

In the next column of Figure 1, C. W. Morris, the semiotician, bases his aims of discourse on a behavioral analysis of how animals react to stimuli. The animal first *informs* itself of the features of its environment, then *evaluates* the seemingly useful features, then responds to these as *incitive* "stimuli," and finally *systematizes* his signs in order to achieve the purpose for which he engaged in this expressive activity. There is a rough approximation here to Aristotle's scientific, dialectic, and rhetorical functions. Morris' systemic has some affinity with the expressive function of the others on the chart.[5]

George Miller, a communication theorist, establishes his distinctions on the socio-psychological motives for the communications which are revealed in the discourse. The *informative* use of language attempts to increase uniformity of fact and information in the community; the *opinion* use of language attempts to increase uniformity of the probable in the society; the *status change* use of language is oriented to improve one's societal position; and the *emotive* use is oriented to individual satisfaction in an expressive use of language. The similarities to the preceding systems are fairly obvious.[6]

In an interesting chapter on "The Uses of Language" in *Human Knowledge, Its Scope and Limits*, Bertrand Russell takes issue with the dominant logical positivist view of a simple dichotomy of referential and emotive uses of language and distinguishes the informative, the questioning, the promotive and the emotional uses of language. These correspond quite naturally to the kinds of rhetorical sentences in the language: declarative, interrogative, imperative, and exclamatory. These *image* quite

4. See Ernst Cassirer, *An Essay on Man* (New Haven, 1944), pp. 109 ff.
5. See C. W. Morris, *Signs, Language and Behavior* (Englewood Cliffs, New Jersey, 1946), pp. 96 ff.
6. See George A. Miller, *Language and Communications* (New York, 1951), p. 253.

closely Miller's, Morris' and Aristotle's categories, though the principle of division is different in each.[7]

Hans Reichenbach, a logical positivist, in a brief introduction to his book on symbolic logic, differentiates functions of language by the faculty appealed to in the discourse. He therefore distinguishes a communicative use emphasizing thoughts to be believed by the intellect, from a promotive use directed to actions to be accomplished, from a suggestive use oriented to emotions to be aroused.[8]

Both Reichenbach and Richards take the logical positivist position as their springboard. Richards emphasizes the kind of reference found in the discourse. In his various books, Richards suggests various categories of discourse. I have followed here the distinctions to be found in *How to Read a Page* and *Principles of Literary Criticism* rather than some of his other works. Discourses exist in a continuum with decreasing referential and increasing emotive affirmations. Pure reference discourse is scientific, pure emotive discourse is poetic. Any appreciable mixture of the two is rhetoric. Further subdivisions of the mixed area (rhetoric) are generally useless.[9]

The equating of poetry with emotive discourse in Richards is a common phenomenon among these classificatory systems—a fact the figure illustrates. Sometimes poetry is subsumed under emotive, sometimes poetry is equated to the emotive (as in Richards). Sometimes there is no provision for one or the other—thus Aristotle makes no room for expressive discourse as such, though emotion is important for his concept of catharsis in poetry and in the whole second book of his *Rhetoric*.

The last column of the figure distinguishes aims by the focus on the component of the communication process which is stressed in a given discourse. At one time I thought that this principle of classification was original with me, but I later found that Karl Bühler, a German psychologist, had used it in depth in the 1930's and that Roman Jakobson, acknowledging Bühler as his source, had also used it to classify aims of discourse in the early 1960's. The beginnings of this norm can be found in Aristotle who calls science language directed to things and rhetoric language directed to persons. Alan Gardiner, the linguist, had also suggested this principle of classification in the 1950's.[10]

7. See Bertrand Russell, *Human Knowledge, Its Scope and Limits* (New York, 1948), pp. 58 ff.
8. See Hans Reichenbach, *Introduction to Symbolic Logic* (New York, 1947), pp. 17 ff.
9. See I. A. Richards, *How to Read a Page* (London, 1943), p. 100; and *Principles of Literary Criticism* (London, 1925), p. 261.
10. See Roman Jakobson, "Linguistics and Poetics," in *Essays on the Language of Literature*, eds. Seymour Chapman and Samuel R. Levin (Boston, 1967), pp. 299 ff.

This principle can be seen illustrated in Figure 2. If one represents the components of the communication process as a triangle composed of an encoder (writer or speaker), a decoder (reader or listener), a signal (the linguistic product), and a reality (that part of the universe to which the linguistic product refers), then a focus on one of these tends to produce a specific kind of discourse. Discourse dominated by subject matter (reality talked about) is called referential discourse. There are three kinds of referential discourse: exploratory, informative, and scientific. These correspond to elements in the first and second rows across Figure 1. Here, however, it seems important to distinguish the merely informative kind of writing (such as news stories in journalism, simple encyclopedia or textbook presentations) from the strictly scientific, though few authorities make the distinction. Aristotle, for example, has no theory of information, though he has one of science. And Miller has provision for informative, though he has no specific provision for the scientific. And it is equally important to distinguish a kind of discourse which asks a question (exploratory, dialectical, interrogative in some formulations) from discourse which answers it (informative) and proves the answer (scientific). Yet all three of these kinds of discourse are subject-matter or reference dominated. Examples of all three are given in Figure 2. These subdistinctions of reference discourse are my own and differ somewhat from Jakobson's.

Secondly, as Bühler, Jakobson and Aristotle point out, discourse which focusses on eliciting a specific reaction from the decoder and is dominated by this request for reaction emerges as persuasion or rhetoric. In this use, the encoder may purposely disguise his own personality and purposely distort the picture of reality which language can paint in order to get the decoder to do something or believe something (as in dishonest advertising or some political propaganda). These distortions are not essential to persuasion, however. What is essential is that encoder, reality, and language itself all become instrumental to the achievement of some practical effect in the decoder. Obvious examples of such aims of discourse are given in the last column of Figure 2.

Thirdly, when the language product is dominated by the clear design of the writer or speaker to discharge his emotions or achieve his own individuality or embody his personal or group aspirations in a discourse, then the discourse tends to be expressive. The expressor or encoder here dominates the communication process. Sometimes in such uses the decoder and the referential components even become negligible—as with curse words uttered in private. But often such uses carry strong subcomponents of information and persuasion, as in the *Declaration of Independence*. Some examples of such uses are given in the first column of the figure we have been analyzing.

FIGURE 2. The basic purposes of composition

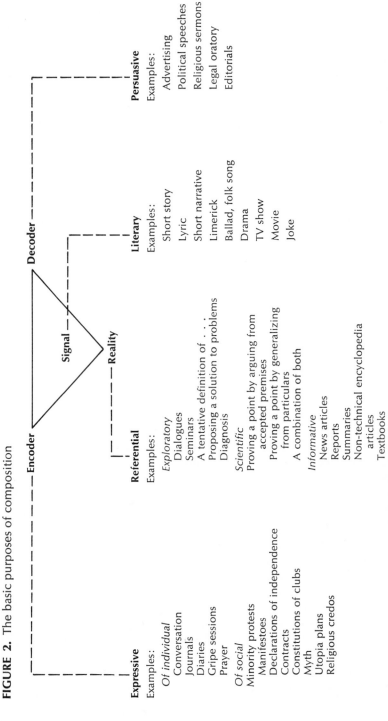

Expressive

Examples:

Of individual
Conversation
Journals
Diaries
Gripe sessions
Prayer

Of social
Minority protests
Manifestoes
Declarations of independence
Contracts
Constitutions of clubs
Myth
Utopia plans
Religious credos

Referential

Examples:

Exploratory
Dialogues
Seminars
A tentative definition of . . .
Proposing a solution to problems
Diagnosis

Scientific
Proving a point by arguing from accepted premises
Proving a point by generalizing from particulars
A combination of both

Informative
News articles
Reports
Summaries
Non-technical encyclopedia articles
Textbooks

Literary

Examples:
Short story
Lyric
Short narrative
Limerick
Ballad, folk song
Drama
TV show
Movie
Joke

Persuasive

Examples:
Advertising
Political speeches
Religious sermons
Legal oratory
Editorials

Encoder ——— Decoder

Signal

Reality

Finally, the product or text or work itself may be the focus of the process as an object worthy of being appreciated in its own right. Such appreciation gives pleasure to the beholder. In this use of language, language calls attention to itself, to its own structures, not as references to reality or as expressions of personal aspirations or as instruments of persuasion, but as structures worthy of contemplation in their own right. Of course, reference, author personality, and persuasion may and usually are involved. But they are not rigidly relevant as primary foci. Indeed the reality may be fictional or very distorted; the author may be hidden under dramatic projections; and the persuasions involved may be quite trivial on occasion. This last use of language is called literature. It appears in such varied forms as the pun, the salacious joke, the sonnet, the novel, the TV drama, the epic, etc.

If a comparison may be drawn, it could be said that language is like a windowpane. I may throw bricks at it to vent my feelings about something; I may use a chunk of it to chase away an intruder; I may use it to mirror or explore reality; and I may use a stained-glass window to call attention to itself as an object of beauty. Windows, like language, can be used expressively, persuasively, referentially, and esthetically.

SOME CONCLUSIONS ABOUT AIMS OF DISCOURSE

I have not included in Figure 1 many of the other approaches to aims of discourse, most of which are fairly symmetrical to those given here. These would include the several groups interested in the functions of language at its origin (was it imitative of reality, the bow-wow theory, was it a utilitarian rhetorical tool, the yo-he-ho theory, was it an expressive emotional theory, the ah-ah, pooh-pooh theory, or did language begin in play and poetry, the ding-dong theory). These theories, like the child function theories, do parallel the four functions arrived at. Some anthropologists, like Malinowski and Doob, have examined primitive societies and isolated the functions of language found there (they do not find a literary or play use, I might add, though Lévi-Strauss did). Nor have I mentioned the semanticists; Hayakawa's four uses of language also parallel the model sketched here. The uses of language, established by the Nebraska high school composition program and drawn heavily from the ordinary language philosophers, also closely parallel these distinctions.

The important lesson to be drawn from this almost fearful symmetry is that no composition program can afford to neglect any of these basic aims of discourse. There have been periods in the history of the teaching of composition, whether in the elementary or secondary or college level, when one or the other has been unduly prominent and others slighted or entirely neglected. The results have usually been educationally disastrous. In speech departments where persuasion was, for too long a time, too prominent, two cancerous effects have often followed: first, expository or reference discourse is assimilated into and made equivalent to persuasion and Aristotelian rhetorical proofs are extended to all discourse; secondly, even literature is reduced to persuasion, and some modern theories of oral interpretation now speak of the oral interpreter's function as one of coercing the audience into a desired emotional attitude. At the elementary and secondary school during the Deweyite progressive period, the reduction of all language to self-expression destroyed alike any objective scientific or literary norms. At the college level, in English departments during the period immediately preceding the present, the restriction of composition to expository writing and the reading of literary texts has had two equally dangerous consequences. First, the neglect of expressionism, as a reaction to progressive education, has stifled self-expression in the student and partially, at least, is a cause of the unorthodox and extreme forms of deviant self-expression now indulged in by college students on many campuses today. Secondly, the neglect of persuasion has often caused persuasion to be assimilated and absorbed into literature in many cases. Expressionism has often been similarly absorbed so that literature has become prostituted to propaganda or the most weird forms of formless self-expression. In philosophy, with the logical positivists, interested solely in scientific statements, the ignoring of other uses of discourse has caused all of them to be lumped into the general category of nonsensical or meaningless. None of these situations is healthy. It is to the good of each of the aims of discourse to be studied in conjunction with the others.

The reason for this is to be seen in the various principles of classification used in the establishing of the aims by various writers. Scientific discourse is generally different in its logic, its level of probability, from the other aims of discourse. In fact, each aim of discourse has its own logic, its own kind of references, its own communication framework, its own patterns of organization, and its own stylistic norms. Sometimes these logics and stylistic principles even contradict each other. Overlaps certainly occur but the ultimate conflation and confusion of any of the aims of discourse with any other is pedagogically disastrous.

The study of these distinct aims of discourses is only a continuation of the basic liberal arts tradition. That tradition, coalesced into the trivium of grammar, rhetoric, and logic or dialectic, simply meant the study of literature, the study of persuasion, and the study of scientific and exploratory discourse. When the English departments presided over the dissolution of the liberal arts tradition in the early 1900's by exiling persuasion to speech departments and by exiling logic to philosophy departments, only literature (grammar) remained, and literature, as such, had never been the only basis of the liberal arts. My plea is simply for a preservation of the liberal arts tradition with composition as the foundation stone.

CAROLINE D. ECKHARDT
DAVID H. STEWART

Towards a Functional Taxonomy
of Composition

Writing, like anything else, can be divided into manageable segments in order to be comprehended. Nobody teaches simply "writing"; everyone who teaches writing fashions a series of compositional experiences, dividing the larger subject into meaningful and manageable parts. The problem of how best to divide and conquer writing, which by its very nature as personal expression may come in as many types as there are examples, has been addressed in many different ways. We intend here not to survey them all, because histories of rhetorical approaches abound, but to discuss two basically different responses to the challenge. One we shall call the *approach through techniques;* the other, *the approach through purposes.* As these terms imply, one emphasizes *means;* the other, *ends.* Most teachers of composition in American colleges and universities probably stress the first, while teachers of speech communication stress the second. Walter C. Ong has analyzed the origin and consequences of this unfortunate split in "Literacy and Orality in Our Times," *ADE Bulletin* (September, 1978).

The use of techniques, with its emphasis on how things are done, corresponds to many other social and pedagogical approaches in a society increasingly preoccupied with technique in general and with its partner, technology (the science of technique). It responds to the fundamental human need to use tools of every sort, including language, to manipulate our surroundings, including other people. In the broadest sense, perhaps, it is a way of coping. In an increasingly mechanized society, people require highly diverse coping skills. We routinely use dozens of machines

From *College Composition and Communication*, 30 (December, 1979), 338–342. Reprinted by permission of the National Council of Teachers of English and Caroline D. Eckhardt and David H. Stewart.

100

each day. We employ many different tactics in dealing with other people, as the behavioral scientists point out. We share an apprehensiveness, in fact, that if we do not learn the relevant technique, then other people and a multitude of machines and gadgets, acting as if self-propelled, will manage us.

Preoccupation with technique, then, has excellent social justifications and explanations. In recent years, however, various "holistic" philosophies have reminded us of another basic human need. *People perceive and re-member information, not as isolated bits but as sets, "structures," which are in some way applicable to their other personal concerns.* We naturally seek *meaning and purpose* in the mass of information available to us. The need to recognize purpose is as fundamental as the need to manipulate; the question "Why?" is as inherent to our natures as the question "How?" In fact, questions of connection (Why?) are psychologically and ration-ally prior to questions of implementation (How?).

The importance of this principle to the question of writing is to re-mind us that to give precedence to means per se is contrary to natural human modes of thought. It may be convenient, but it is abnormal, to concentrate on how to measure things without knowing why. It may be convenient, but it is abnormal, to concentrate on the comparison-and-contrast method of structuring a paper without knowing why one is en-gaged in that activity at all. As this last example suggests, the way that we teach writing often reflects an approach through means, but an ap-proach through ends may more nearly correspond to the natural way in which the mind assimilates information.

A great many composition courses now follow a pattern that derives from the classical "forms of discourse," of which there were four: Descrip-tion, Exposition, Narration, and Argumentation. These forms have been further divided so that in many textbooks there are six or seven, or even more, such divisions: definition, description, narration, process analysis, comparison and contrast, division and classification, analogy, and so forth. To these divisions some textbooks add other techniques: metaphor, per-sonification, induction, and deduction. All of these categories, and others like them, represent ways of achieving something else, yet they are often taught as if they themselves were the achievement. "A student should know how to write a comparison-and-contrast paper." Yet in the non-academic world there is no such thing as a comparison-and-contrast paper. No employer says, "Go write a 500-word comparison-and-contrast report for next Wednesday"; no tax return states, "Using analogy, clarify the nature of your occupation"; no local expert on Afghanistan is asked by the Lions Club, "Come talk to us by means of division and classification." An employer asks for an evaluation of three proposed sites for a factory;

a tax return requires that the source of "other" income be identified; the Lions Club invites the local expert to talk about life in Afghanistan.

The point is that the traditional forms of discourse and their contemporary counterparts are, in themselves, merely techniques; they are means to an end. In isolation, they are conveniences that obstruct, as often as they facilitate, good writing. Any composition course that takes techniques themselves as its structure and its goal is, in so doing, responding to one form of human need while doing violence to another: hence the boredom of freshmen who dutifully write one technique-paper after another, not knowing why (except to get a grade); hence the alienation often felt by the teacher, who cannot in conscience claim that to know half a dozen such techniques is to know much about making writing serve real needs; hence the frustration, even panic, felt by the teacher when a member of the class challenges this approach by bringing in a newspaper, a magazine, or other samples of published writing and seeking in vain for pure examples of the textbook categories. The *Ding an sich* in the non-academic world will not answer to its name; and, as Lewis Carroll's caterpillar asked Alice, what's the good of having names for things if the things do not answer to their names?

Some composition teachers seek an answer to this problem or, more properly, a way of sidestepping it by searching for ever more refined taxonomies of technique. One recent textbook adds "Texture" and "Climax" to its rhetorical categories. (Who ever saw a real piece of writing that fit those labels?) Composition staffs debate whether division and classification should be taught as one category or as two. Teachers struggle in the classroom to explain where analogy leaves off and metaphor begins. The basic approach remains unchanged: in whatever guise, with better or worse terminologies, it is an approach that responds to the human need to practice technique but not to the human need to recognize and fulfill purpose. And nothing is gained if one says that comparison-and-contrast (etc.) *is* the purpose; the claim is merely absurd.

In the classical forms of discourse, from which the difficulty stems, also lies the beginning of a solution. The four modes suggest a hybridization of two concepts. The modes called Exposition, Description, and Narration represent primarily ways of arranging language. (We ignore here *fictive* narration, whether mimetic or didactic, because we are concerned with referential discourse.) On the other hand, the form called Argumentation represents a strong intention or purpose: argumentation is the effort to convince somebody of the validity of a viewpoint. Exposition, Description, and Narration imply technique; Argumentation implies purpose too. Since the four terms do not derive wholly from the same taxonomic system, as a group they are neither complete nor mutually exclusive. As

Plato amply demonstrated in the *Republic,* narration is an excellent means of argumentation. The New Testament's parables serve the same purpose. Like Plato's "myths," their function is to argue for the rightness of an interpretation.

Let us turn now to the approach through purposes, represented by the last-named of the classical forms. Argumentation is surely one of the most widely shared purposes for writing (or speaking). It can use, as befits the occasion, one or more techniques: narration, definition, description, process analysis, comparison and contrast, division and classification, induction and deduction, analogy, metaphor, even that odd fellow "climax," which presumably has something to do with emphasis and with pacing. The purpose of the piece of writing becomes paramount; and the writer selects whatever tools, instruments, and tactics seem most functional to that purpose, given the writer's sense of style, and subject-matter, and the audience.

Assuming the priority of ends over means, of purpose over technique, what categories should be used in teaching writing? In our experience, there are only four basic purposes for writing.

1. To clarify what the subject is (to define a word, to explain a concept, to report evidence);

2. To substantiate a thesis about the subject (to demonstrate that an inference or conclusion about it is valid);

3. To evaluate the subject (to judge it as good or bad with reference to utilitarian, ethical, or aesthetic standards);

4. To recommend that something be done about the subject (to persuade people to think or act differently about it).

Virtually all occasions for composition writing, we would submit, fall into one of these four categories, which we call Definition, Substantiation, Evaluation, and Recommendation (see Figure 1). (Even the all but forgotten epideictic or demonstrative form can be subsumed here.) These terms are the names of *purposes:* of ends, not of means. The categories themselves are incremental. Definition or clarification, while sometimes sufficient in itself, often functions as part of a piece of writing whose larger purpose is to substantiate a thesis, to evaluate, or to recommend; similarly, the substantiation of a thesis, while sometimes sufficient in itself, often functions as part of a piece of writing whose larger purpose is to evaluate or to recommend; and evaluation, while sometimes sufficient in itself, often functions as part of a piece of writing whose larger purpose is to recommend.

FIGURE 1.

Definition	*Substantiation* Definition
Evaluation Substantiation Definition	*Recommendation* Evaluation Substantiation Definition

Each purpose builds upon the one preceding it. Recommendation, the final category, embodies a cumulative purpose that is likely to involve the other three. A student who wants to convince his or her parents to support a year's study in England, for example, may need to define exactly what the academic program at the London School of Economics consists of, substantiate the claim that this program is more advanced or complete (or whatever) than the programs available in the United States, and establish the value of education abroad. These functions would form part of the larger purpose of making the proposal (the recommendation "Support me for a year in England") as persuasive as possible.

The approach through purposes incorporates, rather than cancels, the approach through technique. Techniques are presented as potentially useful in all four categories of writing, as, in fact, they are: one can use comparison-and-contrast to define (clarify); to substantiate a thesis; to evaluate; to recommend. For instance, one can compare turtles and tortoises to clarify the nature of both; one can compare the heights of American children in 1968 and 1978 to substantiate a thesis about growth patterns; one can compare two novels to evaluate the quality of characterization, using one as a standard of comparison against which to judge the other; one can compare the projected results of buying and renting houses to recommend that people in certain financial circumstances buy (or rent). Seen in the context of purpose, technique has meaning. Technique is a means to an end.

Teaching writing on the basis of purposes has certain advantages. The primary advantage is the greater resemblance to "real writing." Most students' papers are apprentice work, as the students themselves know, but it is far easier to point to non-academic analogues of the categories of purpose than it is to point to examples of the techniques standing alone. An advertisement or editorial recommends that we accept a specified product, political viewpoint, or action. A film review evaluates this week's release. A magazine article substantiates the claim that ESP is (or is not) reliable; another magazine article defines and clarifies a new type of stereo component. Where more than one purpose seems to be present, this situation can be regarded as quite natural, since the purposes are often cooperative and incremental. The film reviewer needs to define a technical innovation in order for us to understand the judgment that the film is technically brilliant (or bungled).

A second advantage of the approach through purposes is that it permits students to see progress in their knowledge of rhetoric. When a course moves from narration to description to comparison and contrast to induction and deduction (or a similar sequence), there is no necessary connection, between one category and the next. The course becomes fragmented—two weeks on narration, two weeks on description, two weeks on comparison and contrast (or however much time the syllabus permits); the technique, once learned, is perhaps never used again. The structure seems arbitrary; and in fact it *is* arbitrary, since one might just as well begin at some other point in the series. Writing by means of techniques does not embody a rhetorical progression. Writing in accordance with purposes, however, does. The class can begin with definition and will continue to use definition as it moves into substantiation; it will continue to use both definition and substantiation as it moves into evaluation; it will continue to use definition, substantiation, and evaluation as it moves into recommendation. The repertory of techniques is introduced at once, and briefly; the emphasis is on the growth of the writer's sense of purpose. The sense of incremental progress is strong and steady.

A corollary benefit to this approach is that it provides designations for models that students read, and joining reading with writing can be expected to enhance both skills. Instead of combing through essays to locate a "negative detail" paragraph or an analogy (that is not a metaphor) or a comparison (that is not a contrast), teachers and students alike can readily identify entire essays or parts in terms of purpose. Then they can examine the technique used to achieve the purpose.

The two major advantages—a greater degree of resemblance to writing as practiced outside the classroom and a much stronger sense of incremental progress—would in themselves make the approach through purposes preferable. However, there is a third, although indirect, advantage to this approach.

The concentration on *means* (methods, processes, procedures, and so forth), which this paper began by discussing, has been part of our culture's flight from values. As long as our attention is engaged wholly in the details of the functioning of the activity, we are not likely to ask what the value or goal of the activity as a whole might be. It is ultimately dangerous, we submit, to teach expertise in technique apart from the question of what the technique is being used to accomplish. This is not the place for a general discussion of the political potential of language, but we would like simply to reiterate that rhetoric is a powerful and value-laden—not neutral—tool.

The educated person should be more than a technician, an expert in the practice of technique. The educated person should also be aware of the purposes and effects of technique. The approach through purposes returns our emphasis, in the teaching of composition, to first principles. *What* you want to accomplish surely claims priority over *how* to go about it. In bringing purpose to the fore, this approach also brings value-implications to the fore. Once the goal is stated, its appropriateness can be addressed.

A corollary to this foregrounding of purpose is that it moves writing and speaking closer together. To be sure, "edited language" in print will always differ radically from speech. But students learn quickly that a "speech act" fails to achieve its purpose if it violates either grammatical or social conventions. We make lexical, syntactic, and tonal shifts in terms of our purpose and audience, and this continuous choice of means makes speech vital and dramatic. Awareness of this fact about speaking can sensitize students to similar possibilities in reading and writing. (That is why English teachers once upon a time required students to memorize the funeral speeches of Brutus and Antony.)

At this point, someone may ask, "Isn't teaching through purpose still a *means* that neglects questions about why a student should write at all?" Our answer is that the usual responses (success in a career, survival in college, discovery of self, or acquisition of control over our increasingly verbal environment) are themselves statements of purpose. Motivation to write becomes inseparable from the procedure that we recommend.

"Today we have naming of parts," wrote the poet Henry Reed, describing each element of a soldier's rifle. His purpose was to express bitterness and frustration at the way he was taught to kill by merely learning component parts: today this, tomorrow that, the next day something else—a rhetoric of means, without consideration of ends. If we permit technique to become predominant, we are not only making our task as teachers of writing harder by choosing an incomplete and unrealistic approach but also presenting the activity of writing in a way that discourages the asking of important questions of purpose and value.

ADDITIONAL READINGS

RICHARD L. LARSON, "Structure and Form in Non-Fiction Prose," *Teaching Composition: 10 Bibliographical Essays,* ed. Gary Tate (Fort Worth: Texas Christian University Press, 1976), pp. 45–71.

FRANK J. D'ANGELO, "Modes of Discourse," *Teaching Composition: 10 Bibliographical Essays,* ed. Gary Tate (Fort Worth: Texas Christian University Press, 1976), pp. 111–135.

RICHARD FULKERSON, "Four Philosophies of Composition," *College Composition and Communication,* 30 (December, 1979), 343–348.

GLENN MATOTT, "In Search of a Philosophical Context for Teaching Composition," *College Composition and Communication,* 27 (February, 1976), 25–31.

ANN E. BERTHOFF, "From Problem-Solving to a Theory of Imagination," *College English,* 33 (March, 1972), 636–649.

MICHAEL GRADY, "A Conceptual Rhetoric of the Composition," *College Composition and Communication,* 22 (December, 1971), 348–354.

The Rhetorical Stance

Last fall I had an advanced graduate student, bright, energetic, well-informed, whose papers were almost unreadable. He managed to be pretentious, dull, and disorganized in his paper on *Emma,* and pretentious, dull, and disorganized on *Madame Bovary.* On *The Golden Bowl* he was all these and obscure as well. Then one day, toward the end of term, he cornered me after class and said, "You know, I think you were all wrong about Robbe-Grillet's *Jealousy* today." We didn't have time to discuss it, so I suggested that he write me a note about it. Five hours later I found in my faculty box a four-page polemic, unpretentious, stimulating, organized, convincing. Here was a man who had taught freshman composition for several years and who was incapable of committing any of the more obvious errors that we think of as characteristic of bad writing. Yet he could not write a decent sentence, paragraph, or paper until his rhetorical problem was solved—until, that is, he had found a definition of his audience, his argument, and his own proper tone of voice.

The word "rhetoric" is one of those catch-all terms that can easily raise trouble when our backs are turned. As it regains a popularity that it once seemed permanently to have lost, its meanings seem to range all the way from something like "the whole art of writing on any subject," as in Kenneth Burke's *The Rhetoric of Religion,* through "the special arts of persuasion," on down to fairly narrow notions about rhetorical figures and devices. And of course we still have with us the meaning of "empty bombast," as in the phrase "merely rhetorical."

I suppose that the question of the role of rhetoric in the English course

From *College Composition and Communication,* 14 (October, 1963), 139–145. Reprinted by permission of the National Council of Teachers of English and Wayne C. Booth.

is meaningless if we think of rhetoric in either its broadest or its narrowest meanings. No English course could avoid dealing with rhetoric in Burke's sense, under whatever name, and on the other hand nobody would ever advocate anything so questionable as teaching "mere rhetoric." But if we settle on the following, traditional, definition, some real questions are raised: "Rhetoric is the art of finding and employing the most effective means of persuasion on any subject, considered independently of intellectual mastery of that subject." As the students say, "Prof. X knows his stuff but he doesn't know how to put it across." If rhetoric is thought of as the art of "putting it across," considered as quite distinct from mastering an "it" in the first place, we are immediately landed in a bramble bush of controversy. Is there such an art? If so, what does it consist of? Does it have a content of its own? Can it be taught? Should it be taught? If it should, how do we go about it, head on or obliquely?

Obviously it would be foolish to try to deal with many of these issues in twenty minutes. But I wish that there were more signs of our taking all of them seriously. I wish that along with our new passion for structural linguistics, for example, we could point to the development of a rhetorical theory that would show just how knowledge of structural linguistics can be useful to anyone interested in the art of persuasion. I wish there were more freshman texts that related every principle and every rule to functional principles of rhetoric, or, where this proves impossible, I wish one found more systematic discussion of why it is impossible. But for today, I must content myself with a brief look at the charge that there is nothing distinctive and teachable about the art of rhetoric.

The case against the isolability and teachability of rhetoric may look at first like a good one. Nobody writes rhetoric, just as nobody ever writes writing. What we write and speak is always *this* discussion of the decline of railroading and *that* discussion of Pope's couplets and the other argument for abolishing the poll-tax or for getting rhetoric back into English studies.

We can also admit that like all the arts, the art of rhetoric is at best very chancy, only partly amenable to systematic teaching; as we are all painfully aware when our 1:00 section goes miserably and our 2:00 section of the same course is a delight, our own rhetoric is not entirely under control. Successful rhetoricians are to some extent like poets, born, not made. They are also dependent on years of practice and experience. And we can finally admit that even the firmest of principles about writing cannot be taught in the same sense that elementary logic or arithmetic or French can be taught. In my first year of teaching, I had a student who started his first two essays with a swear word. When I suggested that perhaps the third paper ought to start with something else, he protested that his high school teacher had taught him always to catch the reader's attention. Now the teacher was right, but the application of even such a firm principle requires reserves of tact that were somewhat beyond my freshman.

But with all of the reservations made, surely the charge that the art of persuasion cannot in any sense be taught is baseless. I cannot think that anyone who has ever read Aristotle's *Rhetoric* or, say, Whateley's *Elements of Rhetoric* could seriously make the charge. There is more than enough in these and the other traditional rhetorics to provide structure and content for a year-long course. I believe that such a course, when planned and carried through with intelligence and flexibility, can be one of the most important of all educational experiences. But it seems obvious that the arts of persuasion cannot be learned in one year, that a good teacher will continue to teach them regardless of his subject matter, and that we as English teachers have a special responsibility at all levels to get certain basic rhetorical principles into all of our writing assignments. When I think back over the experiences which have had any actual effect on my writing, I find the great good fortune of a splendid freshman course, taught by a man who believed in what he was doing, but I also find a collection of other experiences quite unconnected with a specific writing course. I remember the instructor in psychology who penciled one word after a peculiarly pretentious paper of mine: *bull.* I remember the day when P. A. Christensen talked with me about my Chaucer paper, and made me understand that my failure to use effective transitions was not simply a technical fault but a fundamental block in my effort to get him to see my meaning. His off-the-cuff pronouncement that I should never let myself write a sentence that was not in some way explicitly attached to preceding and following sentences meant far more to me at that moment, when I had something I wanted to say, than it could have meant as part of a pattern of such rules offered in a writing course. Similarly, I can remember the devastating lessons about my bad writing that Ronald Crane could teach with a simple question mark on a graduate seminar paper, or a penciled "Evidence for this?" or "Why this section here?" or "Everybody says so. Is it true?"

Such experiences are not, I like to think, simply the result of my being a late bloomer. At least I find my colleagues saying such things as "I didn't learn to write until I became a newspaper reporter." or "The most important training in writing I had was doing a dissertation under old *Blank.*" Sometimes they go on to say that the freshman course was useless; sometimes they say that it was an indispensable preparation for the later experience. The diversity of such replies is so great as to suggest that before we try to reorganize the freshman course, with or without explicit confrontations with rhetorical categories, we ought to look for whatever there is in common among our experiences, both of good writing and of good writing instruction. Whatever we discover in such an enterprise ought to be useful to us at any level of our teaching. It will not, presumably, decide once and for all what should be the content of the freshman course, if there should be such a course. But it might serve as a guideline for the development of widely different programs in the widely differing institutional circumstances in which we must work.

The common ingredient that I find in all of the writing I admire—excluding for now novels, plays and poems—is something that I shall reluctantly call the rhetorical stance, a stance which depends on discovering and maintaining in any writing situation a proper balance among the three elements that are at work in any communicative effort: the available arguments about the subject itself, the interests and peculiarities of the audience, and the voice, the implied character, of the speaker. I should like to suggest that it is this balance, this rhetorical stance, difficult as it is to describe, that is our main goal as teachers of rhetoric. Our ideal graduate will strike this balance automatically in any writing that he considers finished. Though he may never come to the point of finding the balance easily, he will know that it is what makes the difference between effective communication and mere wasted effort.

What I mean by the true rhetorician's stance can perhaps best be seen by contrasting it with two or three corruptions, unbalanced stances often assumed by people who think they are practicing the arts of persuasion.

The first I'll call the pedant's stance; it consists of ignoring or underplaying the personal relationship of speaker and audience and depending entirely on statements about a subject—that is, the notion of a job to be done for a particular audience is left out. It is a virtue, of course, to respect the bare truth of one's subject, and there may even be some subjects which in their very nature define an audience and a rhetorical purpose so that adequacy to the subject can be the whole art of presentation. For example, an article on "The relation of the ontological and teleological proofs," in a recent *Journal of Religion*, requires a minimum of adaptation of argument to audience. But most subjects do not in themselves imply in any necessary way a purpose and an audience and hence a speaker's tone. The writer who assumes that it is enough merely to write an exposition of what he happens to know on the subject will produce the kind of essay that soils our scholarly journals, written not for readers but for bibliographies.

In my first year of teaching I taught a whole unit on "exposition" without ever suggesting, so far as I can remember, that the students ask themselves what their expositions were *for*. So they wrote expositions like this one—I've saved it, to teach me toleration of my colleagues: the title is "Family relations in More's *Utopia*." "In this theme I would like to discuss some of the relationships with the family which Thomas More elaborates and sets forth in his book, *Utopia*. The first thing that I would like to discuss about family relations is that overpopulation, according to More, is a just cause of war." And so on. Can you hear that student sneering at me, in this opening? What he is saying is something like "you ask for a meaningless paper, I give you a meaningless paper." He knows that he has no audience except me. He knows that I don't want to read his summary of family relations in *Utopia*, and he knows that I know that he therefore has no rhetorical purpose. Because he had not been led to see a question which he considers worth answering, or an audience that could possibly care one way or the other, the paper is worse than no paper at all, even though it has no grammatical or spelling errors and is organized right down the line, one, two, three.

An extreme case, you may say. Most of us would never allow ourselves that kind of empty fencing? Perhaps. But if some carefree foundation is willing to finance a statistical study, I'm willing to wager a month's salary that we'd find at least half of the suggested topics in our freshman texts as pointless as mine was. And we'd find a good deal more than half of the discussions of grammar, punctuation, spelling, and style totally divorced from any notion that rhetorical purpose to some degree controls all such matters. We can offer objective descriptions of levels of usage from now until graduation, but unless the student discovers a desire to say something to somebody and learns to control his diction for a purpose, we've gained very little. I once gave an assignment asking students to describe the same classroom in three different statements, one for each level of usage. They were obedient, but the only ones who got anything from the assignment were those who intuitively imported the rhetorical instructions I had overlooked—such purposes as "Make fun of your scholarly surroundings by describing this classroom in extremely elevated style," or "Imagine a kid from the slums accidentally trapped in these surroundings and forced to write a description of this room." A little thought might have shown me how to give the whole assignment some human point, and therefore some educative value.

Just how confused we can allow ourselves to be about such matters is shown in a recent publication of the Educational Testing Service, called "Factors in Judgments of Writing Ability." In order to isolate those factors which affect differences in grading standards, ETS set six groups of readers—business men, writers and editors, lawyers, and teachers of English, social science and natural science—to reading the same batch of papers. Then ETS did a hundred-page "factor analysis" of the amount of agreement and disagreement, and of the elements which different kinds of graders emphasized. The authors of the report express a certain amount of shock at the discovery that the median correlation was only .31 and that 94 per cent of the papers received either 7, 8, or 9 of the 9 possible grades.

But what *could* they have expected? In the first place, the students were given no purpose and no audience when the essays were assigned. And then all these editors and business men and academics were asked to judge the papers in a complete vacuum, using only whatever intuitive standards they cared to use. I'm surprised that there was any correlation at all. Lacking instructions, some of the students undoubtedly wrote polemical essays, suitable for the popular press; others no doubt imagined an audience, say, of *Reader's Digest* readers, and others wrote with the English teachers as implied audience; an occasional student with real philosophical bent would no doubt do a careful analysis of the pros and cons of the case. This would be graded low, of course, by the magazine editors, even though they would have graded it high if asked to judge it as a speculative contribution to the analysis of the problem. Similarly, a creative student who has been getting A's for his personal essays will write an amusing colorful piece, failed by all the social scientists present, though they would have graded it high if asked to judge it for what it was. I find it shocking that tens of thousands of dollars and endless hours should have been spent by students, graders, and professional testers analyzing essays and grading results totally abstracted from any notion of purposeful human communication. Did nobody protest? One might as well assemble a group of citizens to judge students' capacity to throw balls, say, without telling the students or the graders whether altitude, speed, accuracy or form was to be judged. The judges would be drawn from football coaches, jai-alai experts, lawyers, and English teachers, and asked to apply whatever standards they intuitively apply to ball throwing. Then we could express astonishment that the judgments did not correlate very well, and we could do a factor analysis to discover, lo and behold, that some readers concentrated on altitude, some on speed, some on accuracy, some on form—and the English teachers were simply confused.

One effective way to combat the pedantic stance is to arrange for weekly confrontations of groups of students over their own papers. We have done far too little experimenting with arrangements for providing a genuine audience in this way. Short of such developments, it remains true that a good teacher can convince his students that he is a true audience, if his comments on the papers show that some sort of dialogue is taking place. As Jacques Barzun says in *Teacher in America*, students should be made to feel that unless they have said something to someone, they have failed; to bore the teacher is a worse form of failure than to anger him. From this point of view we can see that the charts of grading symbols that mar even the best freshman texts are not the innocent time savers that we pretend. Plausible as it may seem to arrange for more corrections with less time, they inevitably reduce the student's sense of purpose in writing. When he sees innumerable W13's and P19's in the margin, he cannot possibly feel that the art of persuasion is as important to his instructor as when he reads personal comments, however few.

This first perversion, then, springs from ignoring the audience or over-reliance on the pure subject. The second, which might be called the advertiser's stance, comes from *under*valuing the subject and overvaluing pure effect: how to win friends and influence people.

Some of our best freshman texts—Sheridan Baker's *The Practical Stylist,* for example—allow themselves on occasion to suggest that to be controversial or argumentative, to stir up an audience is an end in itself. Sharpen the controversial edge, one of them says, and the clear implication is that one should do so even if the truth of the subject is honed off in the process. This perversion is probably in the long run a more serious threat in our society than the danger of ignoring the audience. In the time of audience-reaction meters and pre-tested plays and novels, it is not easy to convince students of the old Platonic truth that good persuasion is honest persuasion, or even of the old Aristotelian truth that the good rhetorician must be master of his subject, no matter how dishonest he may decide ultimately to be. Having told them that good writers always to some degree accommodate their arguments to the audience, it is hard to explain the difference between justified accommodation—say changing *point one* to the final position—and the kind of accommodation that fills our popular magazines, in which the very substance of what is said is accommodated to some preconception of what will sell. "The publication of *Eros* [magazine] represents a major breakthrough in the battle for the liberation of the human spirit."

At a dinner about a month ago I sat between the wife of a famous civil rights lawyer and an advertising consultant. "I saw the article on your book yesterday in the Daily News," she said, "but I didn't even finish it. The title of your book scared me off. Why did you ever choose such a terrible title? Nobody would buy a book with a title like that." The man on my right, whom I'll call Mr. Kinches, overhearing my feeble reply, plunged into a conversation with her, over my torn and bleeding corpse. "Now with my *last* book," he said, "I listed 20 possible titles and then tested them out on 400 businessmen. The one I chose was voted for by 90 per cent of the businessmen." "That's what I was just saying to Mr. Booth," she said. "A book title ought to grab you, and *rhetoric* is not going to grab anybody." "Right," he said. "My *last* book sold 50,000 copies already; I don't know how this one will do, but I polled 200 businessmen on the table of contents, and . . ."

At one point I did manage to ask him whether the title he chose really fit the book. "Not quite as well as one or two of the others," he admitted, "but that doesn't matter, you know. If the book is designed right, so that the first chapter pulls them in, and you *keep* 'em in, who's going to gripe about a little inaccuracy in the title?"

Well, rhetoric is the art of persuading, not the art seeming to persuade by giving everything away at the start. It presupposes that one has a purpose concerning a subject which itself cannot be fundamentally modified by the desire to persuade. If Edmund Burke had decided that he could win more votes in Parliament by choosing the other side—as he most certainly could have done—we would hardly hail this party-switch as a master stroke of rhetoric. If Churchill had offered the British "peace in our time," with some laughs thrown in, because opinion polls had shown that more Britishers were "grabbed" by these than by blood, sweat, and tears, we could hardly call his decision a sign of rhetorical skill.

One could easily discover other perversions of the rhetorician's balance—most obviously what might be called the entertainer's stance—the willingness to sacrifice substance to personality and charm. I admire Walker Gibson's efforts to startle us out of dry pedantry, but I know from experience that his exhortations to find and develop the speaker's voice can lead to empty colorfulness. A student once said to me, complaining about a colleague, "I soon learned that all I had to do to get an A was imitate Thurber."

But perhaps this is more than enough about the perversions of the rhetorical stance. Balance itself is always harder to describe than the clumsy poses that result when it is destroyed. But we all experience the balance whenever we find an author who succeeds in changing our minds. He can do so only if he knows more about the subject than we do, and if he then engages us in the process of thinking—and feeling—it through. What makes the rhetoric of Milton and Burke and Churchill great is that each presents us with the spectacle of a man passionately involved in thinking an important question through, in the company of an audience. Though each of them did everything in his power to make his point persuasive, including a pervasive use of the many emotional appeals that have been falsely scorned by many a freshman composition text, none would have allowed himself the advertiser's stance; none would have polled the audience in advance to discover which position would get the votes. Nor is the highly individual personality that springs out at us from their speeches and essays present for the sake of selling itself. The rhetorical balance among speakers, audience, and argument is with all three men habitual, as we see if we look at their non-political writings. Burke's work on the Sublime and Beautiful is a relatively unimpassioned philosophical treatise, but one finds there again a delicate balance: though the implied author of this work is a far different person, far less obtrusive, far more objective, than the man who later cried *sursum corda* to the British Parliament, he permeates with his philosophical personality his philosophical work. And though the signs of his awareness of his audience are far more subdued, they are still here: every effort is made to involve the *proper* audience, the audience of philosophical minds, in a fundamentally interesting inquiry, and to lead them through to the end. In short, because he was a man engaged with men in the effort to solve a human problem, one could never call what he wrote dull, however difficult or abstruse.

Now obviously the habit of seeking this balance is not the only thing we have to teach under the heading of rhetoric. But I think that everything worth teaching under that heading finds its justification finally in that balance. Much of what is now considered irrelevant or dull can, in fact, be brought to life when teachers and students know what they are seeking. Churchill reports that the most valuable training he ever received in rhetoric was in the diagraming of sentences. Think of it! Yet the diagraming of a sentence, regardless of the grammatical system, can be a live subject as soon as one asks not simply "How is this sentence put together," but rather "Why is it put together in this way?" or "Could the rhetorical balance and hence the desired persuasion be better achieved by writing it differently?"

As a nation we are reputed to write very badly. As a nation, I would say, we are more inclined to the perversions of rhetoric than to the rhetorical balance. Regardless of what we do about this or that course in the curriculum, our mandate would seem to be, then, to lead more of our students than we now do to care about and practice the true arts of persuasion.

ROBERT GORRELL

Not by Nature: Approaches to Rhetoric

Dogberry in *Much Ado* displays his learning by informing the Watch that

> To be a well-favored man is the gift of fortune; but to write and read comes by nature.

Dogberry, of course, with the usual perversity of his mind, was neatly mixing matters, reversing the attitude of his day. We often seem to play Dogberry the unfair trick of taking him literally. Because we do not really know how "to write and read comes," we behave comfortably as if we believe that writing and reading come by nature. That is, we manage to teach everything we can think of except writing—literary biography, telephone manners, how to choose a vocation, for examples—and hope that somehow or other writing will flourish. We behave in this way partly because we realize that teaching writing is difficult, and we are not quite sure how to do it. The faith healing often works; I suppose that to write and read does come partly by nature.

But often it does not. I think that when it does not, we need not despair. There is a subject matter that can be called *composition* and can be both respectable and profitable. A subject called *rhetoric* exists and has been a recognized academic discipline for 2,500 years. It is a central business for those of us who teach English. I am aware that rhetoric is *in* this year, that the word *rhetoric* carries some of the magic inspired by hope or desperation. I do not want to look on rhetoric as trickery or as a panacea for the illiteracies that plague students. I want to look on it rather as a difficult and demanding subject, one that we know too little about, but one that by its very inclusiveness is important.

There is, of course, a great tradition of rhetorical discussion available,

From *English Journal,* 55 (April, 1966), 409–416, 449. Reprinted by permission of the National Council of Teachers of English and Robert Gorrell.

117

both theoretical and practical, much of it highly useful. But I do not propose to rehearse the tradition here. I want rather to submit three principles, partly because they seem to me to describe accurately what happens in writing but more significantly because they seem to me to provide some practical approaches to writing and the teaching of writing. These are simply three different ways of looking at the same phenomena, often the same constructions. They do not exhaust the subject, nor do they provide anything like a comprehensive rhetorical theory. Furthermore, they overlap; they do not provide a logical analysis of the problems of rhetoric. I am proposing them as approaches, as ways of thinking about writing which seem to me fruitful. I am calling them the principles of addition, continuity, and selection.

Writing can be considered as a process of addition, of adding comments to topics. The approach is so fundamental that it seems obvious; and in a way it is, based on the observation that writing is saying something about something. It is, for instance, a rather over-simplified way of describing notionally what happens in a sentence. But the implications of the approach are perhaps not obvious, or at least not obviously observed. For one thing, the process of addition may produce a two-word sentence or an extended composition, depending on how much comment we wish to add. The topic *birds* may have as its comment a single word *sing*, or it may have a volume on ornithology. Consider the following paragraph, which may illustrate rather too neatly:

> (1) Some English words have a negative, but no positive. (2) Anything which is *indelible* cannot be erased, but there is no *delible*. (3) An *uncouth, unkempt* person is crude and untidy, but even if he should reform his ways, he would not be *couth* and *kempt*. (4) We can speak with *impunity*, but not with *punity*, be *immune* to disease, but not *mune*. (5) All these words, and others, were originally formed from a negative prefix and a positive word. (6) In some cases the positive word was never taken into our language, but only the combined form with a negative meaning; in other cases the positive word eventually dropped out and only the negative combination remained. (7) *Unkempt*, for instance, is from English *un-*, not, and *kempt*, a dialect form of *combed*. (8) We no longer use *kempt*, but have kept *unkempt*, which from the original meaning of "uncombed" came to mean "generally untidy." (9) *Indelible* is from Latin *in-*, not, and *delibilis*, perishable. (10) We adopted the Latin word *indelibilis*—but not *delibilis*—and changed it to *indelible*. Helene and Charlton Laird, *The Tree of Language* (World, 1957).

The paragraph contains about 175 words arranged in ten varied sentences to convey a good deal of information. It has the complexity of any piece of prose, and thorough examination of every aspect of this group of words might involve a volume of linguistic analysis. But the paragraph can also be considered as very simple, as an extended comment on a single topic, *words*. The basic comment is contained in a few key words, *have negative but no positive*. All the remaining words in the paragraph continue and elaborate the comment about *words*. They attach to the basic framework in various ways. To begin with, *Some English* restricts the group of words being considered. And then nine sentences augment and clarify the opening statement, as in the following diagram:

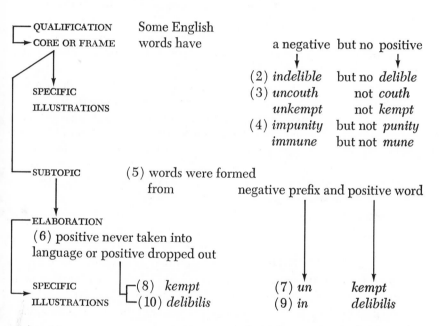

As the diagram shows, sentences 2, 3 and 4 add specific examples of the key assertion. Then sentence 5 varies the comment of the opening sentence explaining why the words have a negative but no positive by telling how the *words were formed;* and sentence 6 adds elaboration to 5. Then, just as 2, 3, and 4 illustrate 1, sentences 7, 8, 9, and 10 illustrate 5 and 6.

The principle of addition, of course, does not explain the psychological generation of a sentence. A writer does not produce a simple sentence like *The ash tray fell on the floor* by choosing a topic like *ash tray* and then casting about for a comment to make on it. Obviously, it is the comment which motivates the utterance; the writer observes what happens to the ash tray, and therefore the comment suggests the topic. And it is the comment that gives any unit of writing its individuality.

The paragraph above, for example, in the book from which it is taken, serves as only part of a series of comments on the topic *words*. The opening framework, *words have negative but no positive*, is one of several comments on the general topic of this section of the book. This comment, however, becomes a topic on which the next three sentences comment. And 5 and 6 are part of the comment on 1 as well as the presentation of a new topic for additional comment in the final four sentences. Patterns interlock, carrying the reader step by step through a composition by specifying and clarifying the relationships between topic and comment.

Complex as thoughts may get, these basic relationships between topic and comment can be considered as only four. Two of them, predication and linkage, are basic in the development of the English sentence. Two others, coordination and subordination, are important within the sentence but also in the structure of larger units.

Predication. Although basic in grammatical structure of the English sentence, the relationship of subject to verb and sometimes to objects—which I am calling predication—is difficult to describe. Grammatically the relationship is expressed in the kernel sentences of English and their main transforms. It can sometimes be described as the relation of actor to action to goal. Or it can be described as the relationship among ideas in which something does or affects something else. It is, of course, the relationship revealed in the key words of the opening sentence above, *words have negative but no positive*. It is perhaps the most common way of making a comment on a topic. Word order usually reveals the relationship.

Linkage. Although the patterns expressing the relationship I am calling linkage look like predication patterns, they express a quite different relationship. Like predication, linkage produces kernel sentences, but in linkage patterns the topic is regularly coupled with something else. A subject is joined by *be* or a linking verb to a noun or a modifier. The relationship might be described as identification, or sometimes almost of equation. That is, something is or is like something else. Sentence 3 in the paragraph above is an example; *person* is linked by *is* to the modifiers *crude* and *untidy*.

Coordination. Coordination may relate individual words or other units within a sentence, sentences within a paragraph, or paragraphs or other longer units in a longer composition. Coordination describes the relationship between items similar in status; coordinate elements have the same function in their contexts. The relationship is sometimes expressed by putting the coordinate items in parallel form, sometimes by placing them in parallel positions in their contexts, and sometimes by joining them with words like *and* or *or*. In the opening sentence of the paragraph above, *a negative* and *no positive* are related as coordinates within the sentence. Moreover, sentences 2, 3, and 4 are coordinate sentences in the paragraph, all of them bearing the same status in relation to the opening sentence.

Subordination. Subordination is one of the most common processes of addition, and one of the most difficult to describe. By subordination, secondary characteristics of a word or a full statement or a developed idea can be added. Most commonly, subordination is modification of some sort. That is, subordinate additions qualify or clarify or illustrate. In the first sentence of the paragraph above, *some English* is an addition subordinated to *words,* modifying *words* within the sentence. Less obviously, sentences 2, 3, and 4—which are coordinate with each other—are subordinate to the opening, providing concrete examples.

These devices of addition—predication, linkage, coordination, and subordination—are obviously basic to all writing. The writer needs to learn what the devices do so that he can use them wisely. And the devices will not work on the basis of rules or dogma attempting to define what must appear in structures. For instance, predication cannot be managed simply by some such formula as "Always make the most important idea the subject." The choice of subject depends on what the writer wants the sentence to do. Neither will a rule like "Put ideas of equal importance in parallel form" hold. The design or purpose of the whole guides the writer in framing ideas to show the relationships he wishes to emphasize. Coordination or subordination is not necessarily inherent in the ideas themselves—in their importance or any other characteristic. The writer coordinates ideas, because he wants to present them in this relationship. Similarly, the common injunction to subordinate less important ideas is misleading, the result of taking too literally a grammatical term which developed by analogy. In the paragraph about words, the first sentence is not in itself "more important" than the next three. It is more general, which may be important, as I shall suggest later.

My first principle, then, the principle of addition, is simple enough in outline. It is that by predication, linkage, coordination, and subordination we can add the comments to topics to produce composition. Filling in the details of the outline would add complexities and puzzles, but the principle provides one way of imposing some order on the complexities.

A second principle is that writing can be considered as continuity, as a series of commitments and responses. That is, the patterns which reveal the relationships of addition described above can also be looked at as a flow or a sequence. Within the sentence, for instance, every predication or linkage pattern takes form partly because every word the writer chooses commits him in some way to what is to follow—limits him, sometimes quite narrowly, to the words—the responses—which may follow. When, for instance, the writer chooses a sentence subject, he commits himself in several ways to certain types of responses. If he chooses to begin with an abstraction like *his insistence* or *the reason,* he limits possibilities for following verbs. He eliminates action verbs like *jump* or *grumble;* he increases considerably the likelihood that his verb will be *is* or *was.* If he does select *is* or *was,* he is again committed, grammatically at least, to a modifier or subject complement as a response.

The principle is more significant, however, as an approach to longer units than sentences—as a way of looking at the development or generation of prose as a sequence of ideas. Consider the beginning of the paragraph above about words. The opening sentence

Some English words have a negative, but no positive.

makes a commitment; that is, it limits the possibilities that can follow. As a relatively general assertion, it creates an expectation in the reader; the reader expects in the following sentence to get further enlightenment about what the opening sentence means. The sentence commits the writer to saying more explicitly what he means—to illustrating, explaining, justifying, elaborating his opening assertion. Sentence 2 responds with a concrete, specific illustration, which clarifies the assertion of sentence 1. But sentence 2 also makes a commitment, and sentence 3 responds by citing another example. Sentence 4 responds to 3—and, of course, both 3 and 4 also respond to 1—with two more illustrations. One could go on through any segment of prose, analyzing various elements—words, sentences, parts of sentences, parts of paragraphs—as sequences of commitments and responses.

But I am interested in the concept less as a device for the analysis of existing prose than as a guide for the generation of prose—as a way of thinking about composition. The application of the principle to writing is obvious: every unit of composition must be conceived and tested both as a commitment to what follows and a response to what precedes. The implications of the principle are perhaps less obvious and are certainly far-reaching; they encompass much of practical rhetoric. They direct the writer—and of course the teacher of writing—to two basic considerations:

1. *Commitment.* Any unit of continuing prose makes a commitment, but it is convenient here to consider sentences. The writer must be aware of the kind of commitment each sentence makes. The opening sentence of the above paragraph might have been cast in many different ways, but any change would change the commitment. For example, the writers of the paragraph might have begun:

Some English words offer variations which seem illogical and inconsistent.

The commitment here is much less restricting than in the original. The paragraph might go on to talk about spelling variations, about unusual semantic changes—or about negatives without positives. The sentence offers less help than the original. If the sentence were still broader,

Some English words present very interesting problems.

it would be almost useless as an opening for the paragraph, because it commits the writer so extensively that he can respond only in a book. On the other hand, a generalization as broad as this—though hopefully less vague and more meaningful—might serve usefully as an opening, making a commitment to several paragraphs or chapters. Because commitments vary in scope, a sentence may make a commitment to only the sentence following it, to three or four sentences—as does the opening sentence of the original—or to a whole book. If the writers had omitted the opening sentence, begun the paragraph with sentence 2, a different sort of problem would have existed: the opening sentence would have limited the possibilities of what could follow but would not have extended its influence so widely over the entire paragraph.

Such speculation about alternatives suggests obvious broad precepts, mostly variations on don't bite off more than you can chew, but bite off something. That is, at each stage in his composition the writer is making commitments—in form and in content. The commitment must not be so great that no sensible response is possible; a generalization must not include everything, but it must say something.

2. *Response.* Although obviously an unlimited number of specific sentences may follow any other, the types of likely responses to any commitment seem to me surprisingly few. In general, the writer seems to me committed to one of the following: a. Specification, b. Repetition, c. Diversion.

a. *Specification.* Probably the most common response to a commitment is an illustration, an example, an explanation. In the paragraph above, sentence 2 obviously responds to sentence 1 in this way. Or, in the following three sentences, William James moves to one level of increased specificity and then goes to examples:

But, with all this beating and tacking on my part,
I fear you take me to be reaching a confused result.
   I seem to be just taking things up and dropping them again.
      First I took up Chautauqua, and dropped that; then Tolstoi and

the heroism of common toil, and dropped them; finally, I took up
ideals, and seem now almost dropping those.
The Will to Believe and Other Essays (Reynolds, 1897).

The second sentence turns the paragraph to discussion of the first part of
the first sentence, sharpening the focus. The third responds to the second
with examples. In the following, the second sentence specifies somewhat
differently.

Because it is small, the small firm has one potential advantage over the
big one. It can't afford big research teams to administrate or interlocking committees to work up programs, and it doesn't have a crystallized
company "family" to adjust to.
William H. Whyte, Jr.,
The Organization Man (Simon and Schuster, 1956).

The first sentence asserts that the small firm has an advantage which is its
very smallness. Then the second lists two or three specific aspects of this
advantage of smallness.

Often the specification moves farther, selecting only part of a preceding sentence as its commitment and providing a specific emphasis for
what is to follow. The second sentence of the paragraph above on words,
for example, might have gone something like this:

These words seldom cause difficulty, but they could provide temptations
for anyone who likes to play games with words.

This kind of sentence would turn the generalization of the opening in a
new direction, establishing a new kind of commitment. A third sentence,
then would have to be something like:

They might stimulate someone to praise the convenience of *delible* ink,
to come to an *evitable* conclusion, and to speak with *punity*.

The paragraph could go on, although it would be moving in a different
way. The following illustrates the same sort of variation:

If the essence of history is the memory of things said and done, then it
is obvious that every normal person, Mr. Everyman, knows some history.
Of course we do what we can to conceal this invidious truth.
Carl Becker,
"Everyman His Own Historian,"
American Historical Review (January 1932).

The second sentence responds to only part of the assertion of the first,
turning the direction enough that it might be considered a deviation as
well as specification. As might be expected, the third sentence offers specification for sentence 2, for how we "conceal this invidious truth":

> Assuming a professional manner, we say that so and so knows no history, when we mean no more than that he failed to pass the examinations set for a higher degree; and simple-minded persons, undergraduates, and others, taken in by academic classifications of knowledge, think they know no history because they have never taken a course in history in college, or have never read Gibbon's *Decline and Fall of the Roman Empire.*

Interestingly, however, the paragraph after another sentence or two moves back to respond more directly to the opening sentence, providing specific support for the statement that Mr. Everyman knows some history.

b. *Repetition.* It is also common to follow a sentence with another of the same sort, in effect paralleling or repeating a response to an earlier commitment. In the paragraph about words, sentence 3 responds to 2 by repeating on the same level of specificity adding a parallel example, and sentence 4 follows 3 in the same way. Or notice the sentence that follows those quoted above from William H. Whyte, Jr.:

> Because it hasn't caught up yet with modern management, to put it another way, it provides an absence of the controls that make the scientist restive.

The sentence may move slightly toward greater specificity than the one preceding it, but essentially it is a parallel, putting it another way.

c. *Deviation.* Often a writer achieves movement of his ideas by using one sentence as the basis for a shift in a direction in a following one. That is, a possible response to a commitment may be a deviation, which turns the course of discourse, even reverses it. A possible second sentence for the paragraph on words might have shifted direction:

> Most English negatives, however, have a corresponding positive.

Such a sentence would seem to commit the third to respond with examples of pair: *intangible* and *tangible, invisible* and *visible,* and so on. Or, the second sentence might have gone even farther afield:

> This suggests that English speakers generally have taken a pessimistic view toward life.

Obviously, such a turn does not provide a very promising way to continue. A response which provides a deviation occurs most frequently along in the middle of a paragraph as a way of providing a kind of subtopic, as in the following:

> By temperament I lean to the side that considers composing in our community as a natural force—something to be taken for granted—rather than the freakish occupation of a very small minority of our citizens.

And yet, judging the situation dispassionately, I can see that we ought
not to take it for granted.
>   Aaron Copland,
>   *Music and Imagination* (Harvard University Press, 1952).

The paragraph continues with specification to develop the second sentence.

I have used examples of sentences in pairs to emphasize the continuity from sentence to sentence, but variations should be pointed out. Sometimes a response is made to an earlier commitment, as discourse breaks into units longer than a single sentence. In the paragraph above, for instance, sentence 5 is actually a response to the commitment of sentence 1, starting a new sequence in which 6 specifies 5, and the remaining sentences are parallel specifications of 6. On the other hand, a single sentence may present not only the commitment and response involved in the basic predication but also illustrative specification:

> Scholars have introduced learned spellings in many words,
>   e.g., *debt, doubt,* on account of Latin *debita, dubito,* formerly written
>   as in French *dette, doute;*
>   *victuals,* formerly *vittles.*
>   Otto Jespersen,
>   *Essentials of English Grammar* (Allen and Unwin, 1933).

And, of course, responses do not necessarily fit neatly into the categories I have listed but frequently combine; a diversion often specifies, for example.

My third observation is that writing can be looked at as selection, as a series of choices among alternatives. In one sense, I am using selection to describe the practical problems of addition and continuity, to include, I suppose, most of rhetoric. That is, for the writer or the teacher of writing, notions like the principles of addition or continuity are useful mainly as they direct choices of words or structures. A topic is chosen because the writer wants to comment on it; the topic directs the choice of comments. A phrasing for a commitment is selected because of what it requires in a response, and the response is limited by its obligations to the commitment. But there are many other influences on selection, of which I shall mention only two or three.

Grammar. Anyone writing obviously uses the grammatical patterns of his language, and his selections are partly determined by them. That is, the writer does not say "The dog me bited" or "Rapidity artichoked filigree," because they are not grammatical. He also, however, has the problem of making choices among the grammatical patterns that are available, and this can be more difficult and often more important. For example, he may need to decide whether to use a basic kernel pattern or a transform of it, whether to say "The children broke the record" or "The record was broken by the children." Or, to look from another direction, he may need to know how to choose the grammatical structure which will reinforce the relationship of a response to a commitment.

Semantic Compatibility. Questions of grammaticalness are not always simple, are often bound up closely with questions of meaning. I can black my shoes but not brown them. It is possible to tar and feather a person but not to egg him. Although many combinations are possible if a meaning is discernible, selection depends frequently on customs which place certain words in certain contexts. We are likely to *deliver* a lecture or *make* a speech but not to *make* a lecture. The writer selects words which work in meaning with the words around them.

Usage. All of the many questions of usage influence selection. Whether to use *contact* as a verb or *type* as a modifier is one kind of selection problem, with the writer's decision depending on his assessment of the consequences of using alternatives.

Tone and Purpose. In a broader sense, selection is constantly influenced by the writer's commitment to his audience and his attitude to his subject. These are obviously subjects too complicated for treatment here, but they are fundamental to most questions of selection.

I am not sure that the principles I have mentioned are of much significance for a theory of rhetoric, but I am interested in them as practical approaches to writing. Practically, I think they are useful, because they provide ways of getting at important writing problems, of thinking about writing as a composing process, of thinking of choices made for reasons more meaningful than an arbitrary rule. For the teacher, such approaches offer almost unlimited opportunities for both criticism of student writing and productive practice in writing problems. Various kinds of exercises are possible with sentences or longer sequences, and I shall simply mention a few at random.

1. Students might be asked to think of a comment on a topic, a comment that seems to them worth making. They then might list additional comments, as many as possible. Then they might be guided in putting the additions into a sentence or sentences.

2. Or working from the other direction students might be given a subject, topic, or an actual sentence and then a list of all the additions. Their task would be to construct a sentence, and their results could be compared with the original sentence.

3. Students might be given a sentence, possibly the topic sentence of a paragraph, asked to analyze the commitment it makes and then asked to frame possible responses. Such an exercise could be handled effectively with an overhead projector with the teacher offering alternative responses as well as the one actually in the paragraph.

Obviously various kinds of exercises, for analysis of existing writing or for development of new writing, could be devised.

These principles will not solve all writing problems nor create a new generation of highly literate students. But I think that Dogberry was probably wrong—at least for most students—and I think that there are things about writing that can be taught and that should be taught.

RICHARD E. YOUNG
ALTON L. BECKER

Toward a Modern Theory of Rhetoric:
A Tagmemic Contribution[1]

> Our discussion will be adequate if it has as much clearness as the sub-
> ject-matter admits of, for precision is not to be sought for alike in all
> discussions. . . . We must be content . . . in speaking of such sub-
> jects and with such premises to indicate the truth roughly and in out-
> line, and in speaking about things which are only for the most part true
> and with premises of the same kind to reach conclusions that are no
> better. In the same spirit, therefore, should each type of statement be
> *received;* for it is the mark of an educated man to look for precision in
> each class of things just so far as the nature of the subject admits; it is
> evidently equally foolish to accept probable reasoning from a mathema-
> tician and to demand from a rhetorician scientific proofs.

> Aristotle
> *Nichomachean Ethics*, i.3.1094b 12–28
> Trans. W. D. Ross

I

Years ago, the heart of a liberal education was the trivium of grammar,
logic, and rhetoric. Modern linguistics has come to encompass more and
more of this trivium, and has in the process become transformed. Tradi-

From *Harvard Educational Review*, 35 (Fall, 1965), 450–468. Reprinted by permission of the *Harvard Educational Review* and Richard E. Young and Alton L. Becker.

1. This article was in part supported by the Center for Research on Language and
Language Behavior, University of Michigan, under Contract OE 5-14036, U.S. Office
of Education.

129

tional grammar is no longer anathema to the linguist, and linguistic description has adopted many of the techniques of logical analysis. Furthermore, linguistics is becoming increasingly interested in the analysis and description of verbal structures beyond the sentence, traditionally a rhetorical concern. It seems fitting, therefore, to explore the relationships of linguistics and rhetoric—discovering, hopefully, just what contributions a theory of language can make to a modern theory of rhetoric.

As Aristotle states in the quotation given above, the nature of the subject matter imposes some constraints on the statements we make about it. It is our intention, therefore, to define the subject matter of rhetoric as it has been understood traditionally, and then to illustrate how aspects of one modern linguistic theory—tagmemics—can form the basis for a new approach to rhetorical problems. The field is broad and there are many points of contact between linguistics and rhetoric which will be passed over here. Nor can we hope to consider all linguistic points of view, each with important contributions to make. We will limit ourselves to a description of three traditional stages in the rhetorical process—invention, arrangement, and style—and then approach the problems of each stage via tagmemic theory.

There are four rhetorical traditions which, taken together, constitute the history of rhetoric. There is sophistic rhetoric, which has as its goal the effective manipulation of language without regard to truth and logic. This tradition continues in modern propaganda and in advertising techniques. There is Platonic anti-rhetoric, which stresses not the art of writing but the quality of the writer in his adherence to truth and virtue: a good writer is a good man writing. There is the rhetoric of literary criticism, which applies the categories and techniques of rhetoric to the analysis and evaluation of poetry, drama, and narration. And finally, there is Aristotelian rhetoric, which had its origins in the law courts of early Greece and which was expanded, systematized, and given a philosophic foundation by Aristotle. After being brought to perfection by Cicero and Quintilian, it constituted a basic, and at times *the* basic, discipline in Western education for fifteen hundred years. It survives today, but with greatly diminished influence. Because this is still the most complete rhetoric ever developed and because it best defines what traditionally has been the scope of rhetoric, we shall focus our attention almost exclusively on the Aristotelian tradition.

For Aristotle, rhetoric was "the faculty of observing in any given case the available means of persuasion."[2] Its immediate end was to persuade a popular audience of what is true and just; its ultimate end was to se-

2. Aristotle, *Rhetoric*, i.2.1355b 26–27, trans. W. D. Ross, in *The Basic Works of Aristotle*, ed. Richard McKeon (New York: Random House, 1941), p. 1329.

cure the cooperation necessary for a civilized society. The classical art of rhetoric consisted of five separate arts which together embraced the entire process of developing and presenting a persuasive discourse: invention, arrangement, style, memory, and delivery. As the last two concern speaking rather than writing (which has become the principal concern of modern rhetoric), we shall consider only the first three: invention, arrangement, and style.

"Invention," wrote Cicero, "is the discovery of valid or seemingly valid arguments to render one's cause plausible."[3] Rhetoricians distinguished two kinds of arguments: extrinsic arguments, which came ready-made to the writer (e.g., eyewitness testimony, documents, confessions), and intrinsic arguments. The latter were of special interest to rhetoricians because they were subject to discovery by means of a system of topics. These topics were a kind of checklist of mental acts one could use when investigating and collecting arguments on a subject (e.g., definition by genus and differentia, comparison and contrast, cause and effect). Certain of these topics—the "common" topics—were appropriate to all types of speech; others—the "special" topics—were appropriate to only one of the three types of speech studied in the classical system: forensic, political, or ceremonial.

Use of the topics presupposed wide learning since they were primarily a method for putting the writer in contact with knowledge which already existed. Edward Corbett has remarked that Mortimer Adler's *Syntopicon* of Great Ideas of the Western World would have been an ideal reference work for the ancient rhetorician.[4] It was the art of invention which made rhetoric the core of humanistic education until the late Renaissance.

During the Renaissance, under the influence of Bacon and Descartes, logic increasingly came to be seen not as the art of learned discourse, as it had been since Greek times, but as an instrument of inquiry. Rhetoric gradually enlarged its boundaries to include the arts of both learned and popular discourse. The process was finally completed in the nineteenth century in the work of John Stuart Mill; commenting on the proper domains of logic and rhetoric, Mill remarked that

> the sole object of Logic is the guidance of one's own thoughts: the communication of those thoughts to others falls under the consideration of Rhetoric, in the large sense in which that art was conceived by the ancients. . . .[5]

3. Quoted in Wilbur S. Howell, *Logic and Rhetoric in England, 1500–1700* (Princeton, N.J.: Princeton University Press, 1956), p. 66.
4. Edward P. J. Corbett, *Classical Rhetoric for the Modern Student* (New York: Oxford University Press, 1965), p. 171.
5. Quoted in Howell, p. 350.

This spirit of modern science which was modifying the nature of logic and the scope of rhetoric also had its effect on the art of invention. Since the seventeenth century, we have increasingly regarded facts and experimental evidence as the basis for sound argument, rather than relying—as did our ancestors—on the wisdom of the past. That is, we have increasingly put our faith in extrinsic arguments. We have become much more interested in techniques for discovering what is unknown than in techniques for bringing old beliefs to bear on new problems. Thus the classical art of invention has diminished in importance while the modern art of experimental inquiry has expanded immensely. But this art of inquiry is no longer a part of modern rhetoric—each academic discipline having developed its own discovery procedures. The strength and worth of rhetoric seem, however, to be tied to the art of invention; rhetoric tends to become a superficial and marginal concern when it is separated from systematic methods of inquiry and problems of content.

The second art in classical rhetoric was that of arrangement. Rhetoricians developed persuasive patterns for organizing their materials—flexible systems of slots into which appropriate categories of subject matter were fitted. One common arrangement, the Ciceronian, had six slots: the exordium; the narrative, or exposition of the problem's history; the proposition; the demonstration; the refutation of alternative propositions; and the peroration. The functions and structures of each of these slots were systematically developed and described. Arrangement was the art of distributing within this pattern the subject matter gathered in the process of invention; arrangement also involved modifying the pattern by expanding, omitting, or reorganizing the various steps to meet the needs of the audience, speaker, and subject matter. The pattern was employed in all three types of speech: forensic, political, and ceremonial.

Since rhetoric was the art of persuasion, patterns for other modes of discourse (e.g., description, exposition) were given little attention. In the seventeenth century, however, developments in science led to an increasing interest in expository prose, a movement which parallels the shift from intrinsic to extrinsic argument. Other developments, such as the decline in the power of the aristocracy and the growing importance of evangelical religion, led to a rejection of elaborate patterning and the development of simpler, more manageable rhetorical forms, though none was described in the same detail as were the classical patterns.

Implicit in classical theory was a dualistic conception of discourse. Form was treated as independent of both the subject matter and the writer. Since the Renaissance, there has been a tendency to see form as the product of a particular mind or as discoverable within the subject matter itself. In the latter case, the form of a discourse is not separable from the content—the discourse is seen as having an organic unity. In either case, the form of a work is not predictable. If form is a personal matter, or is implicit in the subject matter, the rhetorician can make fewer generalizations about arrangement. Classical rhetoric was a rhetoric of precept; in modern times it has become, for the most part, a rhetoric of practice.

Style, the third of the rhetorical arts in classical rhetoric, was largely the technique of framing effective sentences. Its function was to give clarity, force, and beauty to ideas. Although grammar was its foundation, style was clearly a separate art, concerned with the effective use of language rather than simply with the correct use. Both, however, were concerned with language at the sentence level.

Aristotle justified the study of style on practical grounds. Ideally, rational argument alone should be sufficient to persuade. Since experience suggests that this is often not sufficient, the art of style must be employed if wisdom is to be persuasive. The art of style tended, however, to become an end in itself, at times preempting the entire field of rhetoric, possibly—as in the classical conception of arrangement—because of a dualistic view in which content and style were separable.

In the classical tradition, good style was a deliberate departure from the speech of everyday life. Renaissance classicists ingeniously isolated and systematized figures of speech. Henry Peacham's *Garden of Eloquence* (1577), for example, lists 184 schemes and tropes—artistic departures from ordinary syntax and word meanings. Clarity and appropriateness became less frequent constraints than elegance and ingenuity. As a result, "rhetoric" gained its pejorative connotation of elegant but empty verbosity.

As with the other rhetorical arts, there was a reaction against this concept of style; rhetoricians now sought a norm closer to the speech of everyday life. In the eighteenth century, the dualistic conception of style and content began to compete with monistic conceptions. Style came to mean either the characteristic expression of a particular personality (*Le style c'est l'homme même*) or the mode of expression organically a part of the subject matter itself.

Since the eighteenth century, the analysis of style has become almost exclusively the concern of literary criticism. In rhetoric courses today, style is still seen by and large as the art of framing effective sentences; but the art is much simpler, less systematic, and considerably more intuitive than it was in classical rhetoric.

The classical art of rhetoric has a number of weaknesses which make it inadequate for our time. Without involving ourselves directly in a criticism of the philosophical assumptions upon which classical rhetoric is based, we can note, in general, four major problems. First, the classical art of invention stresses authoritative confirmation of present beliefs, while modern modes of inquiry stress imaginative discovery of new facts and relationships. Second, the art of arrangement includes only patterns of persuasion, and neglects considerations of form in other important rhetorical modes such as description, narration, and exposition. Third, both the art of arrangement and the art of style divorce form from content, failing to consider the importance of the act of discovery in the shaping of form. And finally, the art of style is concerned primarily with embellishing, clarifying, and giving point to sentences, an approach which neglects both the deeper personal roots of style and the ways in which style is manifested in patterns beyond the sentences.

In recent years, numerous rhetoricians have been seeking a new rhetoric which would be as effective on a practical level and as stimulating and coherent on a theoretical level as is classical rhetoric. As Daniel Fogarty puts it, there are numerous "roots for a new rhetoric."[6] While other members of the trivium have changed greatly from their earlier forms (witness the revolution in Mill's *System of Logic,* the later changes in symbolic logic, and the recent revolution in grammatical theory), there has as yet been no comparable change in rhetoric. That is, there has been no change which includes both a complete theory and an explicit practical method. Rhetoric is still in the midst of a chaotic transition period. I. A. Richards is right, unfortunately, when he describes the general state of rhetoric today as

> the dreariest and least profitable part of the waste that the unfortunate travel through in Freshman English! So low has Rhetoric sunk that we would do better just to dismiss it to Limbo than to trouble ourselves with it—unless we can find reason for believing that it can become a study that will minister successfully to important needs.[7]

II

The tagmemic approach to language analysis and description, developed primarily by Kenneth L. Pike and his associates in the Summer Institute

6. Daniel Fogarty, *Roots for a New Rhetoric* (New York: Bureau of Publications, Teachers College, Columbia University, 1959).

7. I. A. Richards, *The Philosophy of Rhetoric* (New York: Oxford University Press, 1936), p. 3. Kenneth Burke and S. I. Hayakawa have both developed extremely interesting theories of rhetoric and must be mentioned, along with Richards, as having made notable contributions to the development of a new rhetoric.

of Linguistics,[8] has for many years been concerned with problems which have traditionally been within the scope of rhetoric. This concern results, in part, from the strong motivation which such a model gives for moving beyond the specification of well-made sentences. In tagmemic theory, any linguistic unit is assumed to be well defined only when three aspects of the unit are specified: its contrastive features, its range of variation, and its distribution in sequence and ordered classes. This constraint on grammatical description (defined as a description necessary and sufficient to include all relevant aspects of any linguistic unit) has meant that a complete description of sentences, for example, should include a specification of their distribution in paragraphs and other larger units of discourse.

This concern with problems which traditionally have been a part of rhetoric also results from the desire of many who use the tagmemic model to provide a means for producing extended discourse, primarily biblical translation. Translators frequently encounter instances of grammatical constraints extending beyond the sentence. In some Philippine languages, for example, there is a system of focus somewhat like active and passive voice in English though vastly more complex. To produce understandable discourse in these languages apparently requires a marked correlation between situational roles (actor, goal, instrument, setting, etc.) and grammatical roles (subject, predicate, object, locative, etc.) in a sequence of sentences.[9]

As the linguist moves beyond the sentence, he finds himself asking questions which have long concerned rhetoricians. The description of the structure of a sentence and the description of the structure of an expository paragraph, extended argument, or novel are not sharply different kinds of activity, for all involve selecting and ordering language in a significant way. The traditional separation of grammar, logic, rhetoric, and poetics begins to break down.

Selecting and ordering language, however, has two aspects. One sort of inquiry into the selection and ordering of language leads us deeply into the mental activity of the writer and into questions which are difficult, perhaps impossible, to answer except intuitively. Can we specify in

8. The basic source of tagmemic theory is Kenneth L. Pike, *Language* (*in Relation to a Unified Theory of the Structure of Human Behavior*) (Glendale, Calif.: Summer Institute of Linguistics, Part I, 1951; Part II, 1955; Part III, 1960). A new edition, to be published by Mouton, is in preparation. Pike applies tagmemic theory to problems of rhetoric in "Beyond the Sentence," *College Composition and Communication*, XV, No. 3 (October, 1964), and "Discourse Analysis and Tagmeme Matrices," *Oceanic Linguistics* (April, 1965).

9. Kenneth L. Pike, "A Syntactic Paradigm," *Language*, XXXIX (April–June, 1963), 216–30. See also "Discourse Analysis and Tagmeme Matrices," footnote 8.

detail why a writer chooses to write "John loves Mary" rather than "John is in love with Mary"? Probably not; we can only describe the choices he does make, the characteristic features of his style. Another sort of inquiry, however, leads us to the conventions which constrain the writer. We can specify the reasons why "Love John is Mary in" does not make sense to us except in rather farfetched ways. In the same way, we believe we can specify why the following sequence of sentences does not make sense:

> The trees are budding. Coal is a form of carbon. He has been singing for three hours now. The world used to be round. It seems enough.

If we were to prod the reader, insisting that the above "sentence" and "paragraph" do have meaning, he could probably find some sense in them, as many have in Chomsky's "Colorless green ideas sleep furiously." In each case one "discovers" meaning by imposing conventional formal patterns on the deviant sequences.

Both the process of imposing pattern on (or discovering pattern in) apparently meaningless utterances and the process of describing the conventions of language are important to the linguist. In the former process, he uses some sort of discovery procedure; in the latter, he employs a descriptive model which specifies the structures of conventional utterances. Although the act of discovery is in part intuitive, the model does provide both a method for finding significant linguistic patterns and a taxonomy of the sort of patterns the analyst is likely to find—the still tentative universals of language. Discovery procedures are not mechanical; there is as yet no completely systematic way of analyzing a language, just as there is no algorithm for planning an effective literary composition. But there are important guides to the processes: one can learn to analyze a language, and he can learn a great deal about how to write an essay or a novel.

We believe that the procedures the linguist uses in analyzing and describing a language are in some important ways like the procedures a writer uses in planning and writing a composition, and hence the tagmemic theory can provide the basis for a new approach to rhetoric. Tagmemic discovery procedures can provide a heuristic comparable to the Aristotelian system of invention; the tagmemic descriptive model can give us a vehicle for describing conventional rhetorical patterns. If our beliefs are sound, this approach will provide a bridge between the traditionally separate disciplines of grammar and rhetoric.

A heuristic is a method of solving problems, a series of steps or questions which are likely to lead an intelligent analyst to a reasonable solution of a problem. There are two different (though related) kinds of heuristic: a taxonomy of the sorts of solutions that have been found in the past; and an epistemological heuristic, a method of inquiry based on assumptions about how we come to know something. Bacon's statement of the distinction is worth quoting:

> The invention of speech or argument is not properly an invention: for to invent is to discover that we know not, and not to recover or resummon that which we already know; and the use of this invention is no other but *out of the knowledge whereof our mind is already possessed, to draw forth or call before us that which may be pertinent to the purpose which we take into our consideration.* So as, to speak truly, it is no *Invention,* but a *Remembrance* or *Suggestion,* with an application; which is the cause why the schools do place it after judgment, as subsequent and not precedent. Nevertheless, because we do account it a Chase as well of deer in an inclosed park as in a forest at large, and that it hath already obtained the name, let it be called invention: so as it be perceived and discerned, that the scope and end of this invention is readiness and present use of our knowledge, and not addition or amplification thereof.[10]

Aristotelian rhetoric provides a taxonomy of effective rhetorical arguments which a speaker can use to attain specific ends with specific audiences. Tagmemic theory, on the other hand, provides an epistemological heuristic.

Tagmemic epistemology is based largely on two principles, though other principles are necessary for a complete statement of the theory. These two principles emphasize the active role of the observer in discovering pattern, and hence meaning, in the world around him. The first principle contrasts external and internal views of human behavior—in tagmemic jargon, *etic* and *emic* views. This distinction can be seen in the differences between phonetic and phonemic contrasts in linguistic phonology. A phonetic inventory provides a systematic statement of the overt phonological distinctions which occur in various human languages, while a phonemic description provides a systematic statement of the *significant* phonological distinctions in a particular language. A distinction is judged significant, and hence phonemic, if it signals a difference in the lexical meaning of linguistic units. Though there is much controversy about how phonological signals are to be described, the basic distinction remains valid: the contrast, for example, between aspirated and unaspirated consonants is lexically significant for a native speaker of Hindi or Burmese but not for a native speaker of English, who has difficulty in learning to hear this contrast.

The distinction is especially important when two emic systems come in contact, as when the speaker of English is learning to speak Hindi and

10. Quoted in Howell, p. 367.

is forced to recognize that his native distinctions are emic and not necessarily universal. Likewise, one who finds himself in a different culture must learn to distinguish universals of human behavior from particular customs and mores which taken together comprise the emic distinctions of a culture. The ways of treating time and space, for example, vary throughout the world, and one must learn these ways if he wishes to communicate and cooperate outside his own culture.

Though it is interesting to envision a universal etics of rhetoric—an orderly classification of the rhetorical forms found throughout the world— our present concern must be with the writer of English who is writing for readers of English. Even with this restriction one confronts frequent clashes of emic systems, for if a writer has anything new to say, his image of the world must be in some way different from that of his reader. It is at this point of difference that his message lies. He may seek to expand or clarify some feature of the reader's image, thus making it more nearly like his own, or he may seek to replace some feature of the reader's image. In the first instance he would be informing; in the second, persuading.

Before developing this discussion of rhetorical intention further, we must introduce the second major principle in tagmemic epistemology. This principle asserts that a complete analysis of a problem necessitates a trimodal perspective. After the trimodal principle had been worked out in tagmemic theory and the so-called *feature, manifestation,* and *distribution* modes had been defined, Pike noted a striking similarity between these modes and the triple perspective of modern physics—the complementary views of physical phenomena as involving particles, waves, and fields; as a consequence, Pike decided to adopt this second set of terms for his behavioral model.[11]

Language phenomena—and presumably all human behavior—can be viewed in terms of particles (discrete contrastive bits), waves (unsegmentable physical continua), or fields (orderly systems of relationships). For example, a sentence can be viewed as a sequence of separate words or morphemes; as a physical continuum consisting of acoustic waveforms; or as a system of interrelationships manifesting the grammatical, lexical, and phonological rules of English. Tagmemic theory asserts that only by this complementarity of perspectives is a complete analysis of language structure possible.

The principle of trimodalism gives the analyst both a procedure for approaching new problems and a safeguard against a too limited view of the data. Only when he has described his data from all three perspectives can he be reasonably sure that his analysis is complete. The writer, like-

11. Kenneth L. Pike, "Language as Particle, Wave, and Field," *The Texas Quarterly,* II (Summer, 1959), pp. 37–54.

wise, can use the principle as an aid in discovering a wide range of features in his topic. Though a writer often emphasizes one mode in a particular work, he should be aware of the other possibilities, particularly if his readers customarily emphasize a different mode. Let us consider a simple example. A particle description of a flower emphasizes those features which make it distinctive from other flowers. A wave description emphasizes the flower as a moment in a process from seed to final decay (even this is only a peak in a larger wave) or as merging into a scene. A field description may partition a flower into its functional parts or classify it in a taxonomical system. The flower may also be seen metaphorically or symbolically, in which case it is conceived as part of a new conceptual field (religious, say, or geometric), where certain of its features (its beauty or its shape) are hypostatized, allowing it to manifest a category in a new field. One can view any topic trimodally and soon discovers a wide range of significant perspectives.[12] The process is broad, flexible, and intuitive, though the intuition is guided by what has proved to be a very fruitful principle. It is especially useful since it is not limited to a particular subject matter. In this sense, it is similar to the "common" topics of classical rhetoric. A generally applicable approach helps to free us from the built-in limitations of a conventional, specialized approach. Thus the discovery procedure has a corrective function also.

This heuristic procedure—based on the emic-etic distinction and trimodal perspective—both helps the writer explore his topic and generates a set of questions which he can use to analyze his reader's preconceptions, that is, his reader's emic system:

1. What are the distinctive features of the reader's conception of the topic? What characteristics does it have that lead him to contrast it with similar things? (Particle view)

2. How are the reader's views on this topic part of a mental process, a phase in the continual development of his system of values and assumptions? (Wave view)

3. How does the reader partition the topic? What are its functional elements for him? How does he classify it? (Field view)

The answers to these questions provide criteria for selecting and ordering the writer's subject matter as he develops his discourse.

The missionary linguist in the field seeks to translate his message into the language and cultural conventions of the people, not to teach them

12. For further illustrations of the use of tagmemic discovery procedures in rhetorical invention, see Hubert English, "Linguistics as an Aid to Invention," *College Composition and Communication*, XV, No. 3 (October, 1964).

English and his own emic conventions. He does not seek to replace their emic system with his own, but to modify their image after finding within it their motivations for receiving his message.[13] For he realizes that change is most effective and enduring when it occurs within the emic system of those he is trying to convince. Unlike traditional rhetoric which sought to persuade people by confirming authoritative attitudes, modern rhetoric, we believe, must seek identification. That is, the writer must seek to have his readers identify his message with their emic system.

Because it seeks identification rather than persuasion, and because this assumption often leads the writer to modify his own position, modern rhetoric—still in the process of development—is characterized by Kenneth Burke and others as "discussion rhetoric." The basis for a rhetoric of this sort has been developed by Anatol Rapaport in his book *Fights, Games, and Debates,* where it is called Rogerian debate—its assumptions having been derived from the methods of the psychotherapist Carl Rogers.[14] This principle of identification of the writer with his audience points toward a rhetoric not of opposition but of mutual respect.

A comparison of emic systems—different systems of selecting and grouping followed by writer and reader—leads the writer to find what he shares with his reader in his conception of the topic and what he does not share. One of the assumptions of tagmemics is that change can occur only over the bridge of a shared element. There can be no action at a distance. The key to understanding language change, for example, is the identification of the shared features of the initial state and the subsequent altered state. The writer's message is an unshared item in the comparison, while the shared items, insofar as they are relevant to the message, provide the means by which the reader can identify—and identify with—the message. Shared items are the potential bridges over which change can take place. These bridges may be broad cultural conventions or more specific things such as common social roles, problems, or philosophical assumptions. Among the most important of these shared items is a common language— a common set of patterns and rules governing selection and grouping of words or morphemes within a sentence, and of sentences and paragraphs within still larger units of discourse. It is here that the linguist can make his unique contribution to a new theory of rhetoric, especially as he broadens his focus to include units larger than the sentence.

So far we have dealt chiefly with what might be called prewriting

13. Our conception of the image here is drawn in large part from Kenneth Boulding, *The Image* (Ann Arbor: University of Michigan Press, 1956), and from William Angus Sinclair, *Conditions of Knowing* (London: Routledge and Kegan Paul, 1951). 14. Anatol Rapaport, *Fights, Games, and Debates* (Ann Arbor: University of Michigan Press, 1961).

problems, problems of discovery. We believe, as did Aristotle and Cicero, that a complete theory of rhetoric must include the entire sequence of acts which result in the finished discourse, beginning with the initial act of mental exploration. We have offered two principles of tagmemic heuristic as an indication, hardly an exhaustive one, of how linguistics can contribute to this aspect of rhetorical theory. We now turn to a description of rhetorical patterns beyond the sentence, extending techniques which have been used in the past in the description of lower-level patterns.

Early tagmemics was essentially, but not entirely, a slot-and-substitution grammar, describing linguistic patterns as sequences of functional slots which are filled, or manifested, by a class of fillers. These slots are seen as functional parts of a pattern and may be stated in a formula such as the following simplified formula for an English transitive sentence.

+ Subject + Verb + Object ± Manner ± Locative ± Temporal

(He walked the dog slowly around the block yesterday.) Some of these slots are obligatory (+), some optional (±). Each may be manifested by one of a set of filler constructions; thus the subject slot can be filled by a noun phrase, a pronoun, an adjective phrase, a verbal phrase, a clause, etc. More fully represented, the subject slot in the formula above would be:

+ Subject: np,p,ap,vp, . . . c

Tagmemics assumes that language is composed of interlocking lexical, phonological, and grammatical hierarchies. Here, the internal surface structure of the fillers of the subject slot of the sentence are described at the clause, phrase, word, and morpheme levels of the grammatical hierarchy.

In at least two important ways, however, recent tagmemic grammar goes beyond the surface-level descriptions of other slot-and-substitution grammars.[15] First, tagmemic grammars go on to represent the filler class of a functional slot as a multidimensionally ordered set, or, in tagmemic jargon, a matrix. The categories of these ordered sets indicate relationships of concord between one tagmeme and another; thus, the filler class of the subject tagmeme is ordered into categories such as singular-plural and human-nonhuman in concord with these same categories in the predicate, so that, for example, a singular, nonhuman subject specifies the selection of a singular, nonhuman verb, preventing such collocations as "the tree jump fences."

15. A full description of tagmemic grammatical theory can be found in Robert Longacre, *Grammar Discovery Procedures* (The Hague: Mouton, 1964). Tagmemics is contrasted with transformational and other models in Longacre, "Some Fundamental Insights of Tagmemics," *Language*, XLI, No. 1 (January–March, 1965), pp. 65–76.

Second, and more important for our present discussion, tagmemic grammars specify in addition to the surface structure of patterns an ordered set of operations to be carried out on the patterns. These include ordered reading rules by which all possible readings of a formula are generated. Then each reading is reordered according to permutation rules. Finally, in each reading and its permuted variants, the tagmeme symbols are replaced by each of the possible filler constructions according to a set of exponence rules. These operations are carried out repeatedly until only morphemes or symbols for morpheme classes manifest the formulas, which are then terminal grammatical strings, not yet sentences until phonological and lexical specifications have been met.

Though a description of English will not specify sentences such as the one mentioned earlier, "Love John is Mary in," it so far contains no constraints to prevent it from accepting a sequence of this type:

> The trees are budding. Coal is a form of carbon. He has been singing for three hours now. The world used to be round. It seems enough.

This is not a paragraph because there is no formal connection between the sentences. We can discern no conventional pattern relating them, as we can, for example, in this pair of sentences:

What is John doing?
He's washing his face.

This second sequence manifests a conventional rhetorical pattern—Question-Answer. The question is marked by three formal features: the word order, the question word *what,* and (in writing) the punctuation. The second sentence is recognized as an answer to the question by: the pronoun reference (*he* has to be a substitute for *John* here); the parallel grammatical structure, in which the functional slots of the question words in the first sentence (What . . . doing) are filled in the second (washing his face); the parallelism of verb form (is—ing); the fact that *washing* is a possible lexical equivalent for *doing;* and (in writing) the period. Question-Answer is a formal pattern illustrating a number of formal constraints which extend beyond the sentence.

The relationship of these two sentences can be described in numerous ways (probably most simply by seeing the first as a permutation of the second), but the sentences can only be described as a *sequence* by positing the larger Question-Answer pattern, and by specifying the formal ways in which the two functional slots in this larger pattern are related, just as we specify the relationship between subject and predicate in a sentence. A number of these relatively simple two-part patterns can be described, including greetings, cause and result (hypothesis), topic and illustration, topic and partition, disjunction, and so forth. These patterns can be manifested by a single sentence or by two or more sentences. A large number of higher-level units of discourse can be described as chains of these simple two-part patterns.

As we move on to larger rhetorical patterns, the complexity increases. Formal signals become redundant: for example, we can identify the Answer in the Question-Answer pattern above by five of its contrastive features. Further, lexical and semantic features become increasingly important in recognizing patterns: in the example above we recognize *washing* as a lexical equivalent of *doing*. Lexical equivalence chains are probably the most important markers of higher-level patterns.[16] We can illustrate some of this complexity by attempting to describe the paragraph as a formal structure, limiting ourselves here to only one rather simple pattern.

We believe that written paragraphs are emically definable units—not just groups of sentences isolated by rather arbitrary indentations—and that this fact can be demonstrated. We are presently carrying out controlled testing of the recognition of these units in collaboration with psychologists at the Center for Research on Language and Language Behavior, University of Michigan. Informal investigation has shown that readers, given a text in which all paragraph indentations have been removed, can successfully mark paragraph breaks, with only limited indeterminacy at predictable points. In addition, the readers are able to recognize a number of recurring paragraph patterns and to partition these patterns in predictable ways.

One of the most common of these patterns is the one we have labelled TRI (topic-restriction-illustration) or more formally,

$$+ T^2 \pm R + I^n.$$

(The raised numbers indicate that in reading the formula, T may be read twice; R, once; and I, n number of times recursively.) This is the Topic-Illustration pattern with an optional intermediary slot in which the topic is restricted in some way (e.g., by definition, classification, or partition). The following paragraph illustrates this pattern:

> (T) The English Constitution—that indescribable entity—is a living thing, growing with the growth of men, and assuming ever-varying forms in accordance with the subtle and complex laws of human character. (T) It is the child of wisdom and chance. (I) The wise men of 1688 moulded it into the shape we know, but the chance that George I could not speak English gave it one of its essential peculiarities—the system of a Cabinet independent of the Crown and subordinate to the

16. The concept of lexical equivalence chains is derived in large part from Zellig S. Harris, *Discourse Analysis Reprints* (The Hague: Mouton, 1963), pp. 7–10.

Prime Minister. The wisdom of Lord Grey saved it from petrification and set it upon the path of democracy. Then chance intervened once more. A female sovereign happened to marry an able and pertinacious man, and it seemed likely that an element which had been quiescent within it for years—the element of irresponsible administrative power— was about to become its predominant characteristic and change completely the direction of its growth. But what chance gave, chance took away. The Consort perished in his prime, and the English Constitution, dropping the dead limb with hardly a tremor, continued its mysterious life as if he had never been.[17]

The slots in this tripartite pattern are marked by lexical equivalence classes, two of which have extended domains: 1) English Constitution, indescribable entity, living thing, It, child, . . . English Constitution; 2) men, human character, wise men of 1688, George I, Lord Grey, . . . Consort. Note that the domain of the first chain is the entire paragraph, while that of the second chain is the I slot. Chains can thereby be ranked as head and attribute chains, each paragraph including a head chain and one or more attribute chains.

The slots are also marked by: grammatical parallelism (first and second sentences, third and fourth sentences); tense shift (shift to past in the I slot); pronoun domains; determiners; and transitional function words (then, but).

The TRI pattern has a number of variant forms which can be specified by the reading, permutation, and exponence rules. Only a few of these variants will be illustrated. Since R is optional, the pattern can be read as: + T + I. For example, a paragraph by Marchette Chute:

> (T) The only safe way to study contemporary testimony is to bear constantly in mind this possibility of prejudice and to put almost as much attention on the writer himself as on what he has written. (I) For instance, Sir Anthony Weldon's description of the Court of King James is lively enough and often used as source material; but a note from the publisher admits that the pamphlet was issued as a warning to anyone who wished to "side with this bloody house" of Stuart. The publisher, at any rate, did not consider Weldon an impartial witness. At about the same time Arthur Wilson published his history of Great Britain, which contained an irresistibly vivid account of the agonized death of the Countess of Somerset. Wilson sounds reasonably impartial; but his patron was the Earl of Essex, who had good reason to hate that particu-

17. Lytton Strachey, *Queen Victoria* (New York: Harcourt, Brace, 1921), pp. 300–301.

lar countess, and there is evidence that he invented the whole scene to gratify his patron.[18]

If I is read a number of times, the pattern may be broken by indentation into more than one paragraph, although it remains a single emic unit. Indentation, like line ends in poetry, can either correspond to formal junctures or, for various reasons, can interrupt the structure in a way somewhat similar to poetic enjambment.

The TRI pattern can be permuted to IRT, producing the so-called funnel effect or inductive structure. This is comparable to such permutations at the sentence level as "Home is the sailor" from "The sailor is home." Another illustration by Marchette Chute:

> (I) The reason Alice had so much trouble with her flamingo is that the average flamingo does not wish to be used as a croquet mallet. It has other purposes in view. The same thing is true of a fact, which can be just as self-willed as a flamingo and has its own kind of stubborn integrity. (R) To try to force a series of facts into a previously desired arrangement is a form of misuse to which no self-respecting fact will willingly submit itself. (T) The best and only way to treat it is to leave it alone and be willing to follow where it leads, rather than to press your own wishes upon it.[19]

This permutation is frequently used to begin or end discourse, probably because it imparts a greater sense of closure than the more open-ended TRI order.

Other permutations include TIRI, ITR, and TRIT, to list only the most common. Following exponence rules, slots in paragraph patterns may be filled by other rhetorical patterns. In the following example by Bernard Iddings Bell, the Answer slot in the Question-Answer pattern which we discussed earlier is filled by a TRI pattern, producing a compound paragraph structure:

> (Q) Is the United States a nation composed chiefly of people who have not grown up, who think and act with the impulsiveness of adolescents? (A-T) Many shrewd observers of the American scene, both abroad and here at home, are saying that this is indeed the case. (R) They intentionally disturb our patriotic complacency. (I) They bid us view with alarm cultural immaturity revealed by current trends in journalism, by the radio, by the motion picture, by magazines and best-selling books, by mass response to emotionalized propaganda—political

18. Marchette Chute, "Getting at the Truth," *The Saturday Review*, Sept. 19, 1953, p. 12.
19. *Ibid.*, p. 44.

and otherwise; by a patent decay of good manners, by the spread of divorce and by other manifestations of parental irresponsibility; by all the various aspects of behavior which indicate to a student of human affairs the health or sickness of a civilization.[20]

Tagmemic matrix theory provides further insight into another traditional problem of rhetoric. We said earlier that form and idea are seen by many as organically unified, a view that we share. The literary statement contains within itself its own dimensions of development. It constitutes a semantic field which is clearly perceived when we try to extend it. The relevant categories of the English Constitution paragraph discussed above can be displayed in the rows and columns of an emic paragraph matrix (see Table 1).

If we were to extend the paragraph, we would be obliged to supply a still more recent illustration of the effect of wisdom on the Constitution. It should be possible from a study of a large number of paragraph matrices to generalize further about various types of paragraph development. The investigation of paragraphs as semantic fields is as yet only beginning.

A writer's style, we believe, is the characteristic route he takes through all the choices presented in both the writing and prewriting stages. It is the manifestation of his conception of the topic, modified by his audience, situation, and intention—what we might call his "universe of discourse." These variables directly affect selecting and grouping in all three linguistic hierarchies: grammatical, phonological, and lexical. An analysis and description of styles involves the specification of the writer's characteristic choices at all points in the writing process, although usually only the final choices are directly accessible to the analyst.

The classical conception of style has a number of limitations. To see style as an addition to the message, an affective layer imposed on conventional language, ignores the close connection between language and idea. Seeing it as essentially a matter of sentences ignores stylistic patterns beyond the sentence. In addition, the theory grew out of a very specialized sort of practice—formal public speaking in the courts and legislatures and at ceremonial gatherings. As a result it has a limited range of applicability. Seventeenth-century critics were right in saying that its generalizations were inappropriate to a wide range of important topics, audiences, and situations. Finally, the highly normative approach of classical rhetoric tends to ignore the individuality of the writer, describing *a style* rather than *style* itself.

To consider style, however (as do some modern rhetoricians), to be

20. Bernard Iddings Bell, "We Are Indicted for 'Immaturity'," *New York Times Magazine*, July 20, 1947, p. 8.

TABLE 1.

Forces shaping the English Constitution Historical manifestations	Wisdom	Chance
(1688)	The wise men . . . molded it into the shape we know.	
(1714)		George I . . . gave it . . . the system of a Cabinet independent of the Crown and subordinate to the Prime Minister.
(1832)	Lord Grey saved it from petrification and set it upon the path of democracy.	
(1840)		[Victoria's marriage made it seem likely that a quiescent element] was about to become its predominant characteristic and change . . . the direction of its growth.
(1861)		[With the death of the Consort] the English Constitution . . . continued its mysterious life as if he had never been.
( )		

the expression of a particular personality lays too much stress on one variable in the universe of discourse and too little on the others. Some stylistic features of a work inevitably remain unexplained if one commits himself to this definition strictly. To see style as a vision of the topic also has limitations; it ignores the influence of situation and audience on choice. It assumes that the act of writing is essentially expressive, not communicative. Both of these views inhibit systematic theorizing about style; when style is seen as something highly personal, generalization becomes difficult.

To see style in the way many linguists do today—as deviation from conventional language—leads to the difficulty of defining conventional language. Somehow, the deviations must be separated from the corpus, perhaps by measuring the frequencies of patterns. However it is done, it leaves conventional language as a styleless language. This view, like the classical view, tends to conceive of style as an embellishment, an added affective layer. Though very unconventional styles can be identified as linguistic deviations, there are "conventional" styles which this approach does not explain. These include the different styles we all use in various situations, with various audiences, and in writing with various intents on various topics.

It seems to us that a full discussion of style must include the prewriting process if it is to interpret the formal manifestations on the written page—the purely linguistic choices that the writer has made. Without the context of a linguistic unit—the universe of discourse—we are able to describe stylistic features only in a fairly trivial way. With the context provided, there is the possibility of explaining the writer's choices. In a complete theory, then, a particular style is a characteristic series of choices throughout the entire process of writing, including both discovery (invention) and linguistic selection and grouping (arrangement).

We have presented what we believe to be the traditional problems of rhetoric and have suggested how a linguistic model which includes both a discovery procedure and a descriptive technique may provide the base for a new approach to rhetoric, a bridge between the humanities and the sciences. A tagmemic rhetoric stands somewhere between the· rigorous theories of science and the almost purely intuitive theories of the humanities. We see no reason to reject the insights of either the former or the latter, believing that all new knowledge—like the process of writing itself—involves both intuitive analogy and formal precision.

ADDITIONAL READINGS

JIM W. CORDER, "Rhetorical Analysis of Writing," *Teaching Composition: 10 Bibliographical Essays,* ed. Gary Tate (Fort Worth: Texas Christian University Press, 1976), pp. 223–240.

DONALD C. BRYANT, "Rhetoric: Its Function and Its Scope," *Quarterly Journal of Speech,* 39 (December, 1953), 401–424.

JAMES M. McCRIMMON, "Will the New Rhetorics Produce New Emphases in the Composition Class?" *College Composition and Communication,* 20 (May, 1969), 124–130.

BARRY ULANOV, "The Relevance of Rhetoric," *English Journal,* 55 (April, 1966), 403–408.

JOHN WARNOCK, "New Rhetoric and the Grammar of Pedagogy," *Freshman English News,* 5 (Fall, 1976), 1–4, 12–22.

HANS GUTH, "The Politics of Rhetoric," *College Composition and Communication,* 23 (February, 1972), 30–42.

Practice

RICHARD C. GEBHARDT

Balancing Theory with Practice in the Training of Writing Teachers

A title such as mine may sound innocuous—who, after all, would want to split theory from practice completely? It may also sound pretentious—who can explain in a few pages just what a comprehensive balance of theory and practice of composition teaching might be? But "Balancing Theory with Practice in the Training of Writing Teachers" does indicate my thesis: that students preparing to teach writing in public school or college should understand important conceptual underpinnings of composition and the teaching of writing and should test them out in practice. So without being too innocuous or too pretentious, I will try to outline four kinds of theoretical or conceptual information that I think should be included in teaching-of-writing programs, and then I will try to illustrate briefly what I mean by a balance between theory and practice.

FOUR KINDS OF KNOWLEDGE FOR THE WRITING TEACHER

Ideally, the student preparing to teach writing would master a world of knowledge that runs from transactional analysis to neat handwriting, from conventions of the sonnet to the pyramid structure of the news story, from the most venerated ideals of Aristotle to the most voguish ideas of the latest educational trend. But no writing program can do everything, and it seems to me that four kinds of knowledge are especially important for future teachers of writing.

From *College Composition and Communication*, 28 (May, 1977), 134–140. Reprinted by permission of the National Council of Teachers of English and Richard C. Gebhardt.

First, writing teachers need to have an understanding of the *structure and history of the English language* sound enough to let them apply their knowledge to the teaching of revision, style, dialect differences, and the like. The program Francis Christensen outlined in his article, "The Course in Advanced Composition for Teachers"[1] is a good example of this sort of knowledge. Christensen wrote that the future teacher should move through a sequence of courses beginning with grammar, progressing to language history, and ending in composition. The goal of this sequential program, Christensen made clear, is thoroughness of preparation: an understanding of grammar complete enough that students can apply it in practical situations; an understanding of language history that reinforces grammatical principles learned in the earlier course; and a sense of usage that rests on a clear understanding of how the language has developed. Something like this language program is essential in the training of writing teachers.

The second kind of knowledge that writing teachers need to have is a solid understanding of *rhetoric*. The range of such knowledge is illustrated in Donald Nemanich's article "Preparing the Composition Teacher." Nemanich writes that he has his students "read such books as Dudley Bailey's *Essays on Rhetoric* or Ross Winterowd's *Rhetoric: A Synthesis* or Edward P. J. Corbett's *Classical Rhetoric for the Modern Student* for some kind of historical perspective." And Nemanich continues this way:

> I expect students in my classes to know something of Aristotle and what he had to say about the art of persuasion. In addition, I want my students to know of recent work in rhetoric and composition, especially Ken Macrorie's "free writing," Francis Christensen's "generative rhetoric," and Robert Zoellner's "talk-write" pedagogy. . . . I hope that some time during the course, we would also talk about the work of Wallace Douglas, Janet Emig, James Moffett, and Edward Jenkinson, and Donald Seybold—among others.[2]

The sheer mass of possible information about rhetoric that is implied by this list of titles and names may suggest that the training of writing teachers must involve considerable technical understanding of rhetoric. A highly technical grounding in rhetoric is not absolutely necessary, as the NCTE book, *What Every English Teacher Should Know*, implies when it distinguishes between "good" and "superior" writing teachers. The latter, the book indicates, should have "a detailed knowledge of theories and history of rhetoric," though the "good" teacher need only be

1. *College Composition and Communication,* 24 (May, 1973), 166–167.
2. *College Composition and Communication,* 25 (February, 1974), 47.

able to recognize "such characteristics of good writing as substantial and relevant content; organization; clarity; appropriateness of tone."[3] Similarly, in an article in *The Journal of Teacher Education*, Richard Larson denies that future writing teachers need "extended study of rhetorical theory" but argues that they should understand fundamentals of rhetoric. And what does Larson mean by fundamentals of rhetoric? This is how he puts it:

> . . . future teachers should recognize that writing is a series of choices among alternatives and that a good writer must shape his discourse carefully to make it reach its intended audience effectively and accomplish its intended purpose. This view of rhetoric . . . encourages teachers to approach their writing and that of their students with such questions as these: Whom am I addressing? On what occasion am I addressing him? What is my purpose in speaking? What is my relationship to him? What tone of voice ought I assume in this discourse? What kinds of language will best enable me to achieve my purpose in addressing this audience?[4]

An intelligent understanding of—and ability to use—such questions is, I think, the second essential part of the training of writing teachers.

The third kind of knowledge that composition teachers need to master is some *theoretical framework* with which to sort through the ideas, methodologies, and conflicting claims of texts, journal articles, and convention addresses. Writing teachers face a confusing abundance of theories and approaches. They may pick up an essay, such as Wallace Douglas's chapter in *How Porcupines Make Love*, and read that effective writing classes must be flexible and fairly unstructured, since good writing instructions requires freedom, spontaneity, and a lucky combination of events and feelings.[5] But as they read, they may remember this claim from a text on sentence exercises:

> Writing is a skill, and like playing the violin or throwing a discus, it may be learned by observing how others do it—by trying to imitate, carefully and thoughtfully, the way it was done. In writing, we can "observe" by copying sentences and paragraphs written by master stylists. And we can imitate these sentences and paragraphs in our own writing, making them a part of our basic repertoire.[6]

3. J. N. Hook, Paul Jacobs, and Raymond Crisp, *What Every English Teacher Should Know* (Urbana: NCTE, 1970), p. 18.
4. "A Special Course in Advanced Composition for Prospective Teachers," *Journal of Teacher Education*, 20 (Summer, 1969), 173.
5. "Peak Experiences and the Skill of Writing," *How Porcupines Make Love*, ed. Alan Purves (Lexington, MA: Xerox, 1972), pp. 165–180.
6. Winston Weathers and Otis Winchester, *Copy and Compose*, (Englewood Cliffs, N.J.: Prentice Hall, 1969), p. 1.

Writing teachers need to be able to make some sense out of the obvious differences in emphasis—if not outright contradictions—between such approaches. Similarly, they need to be able to find their way through the jungle Donald Stewart outlines in *Freshman English Shop Talk:*

> We teach beginnings, middles, and ends; topic sentences and development; the word, the sentence, the paragraph, the theme; narration, description, exposition, and argument; definition, classification, comparison and contrast, analysis, theme indivisible, or strategy unlimited. If we are linguists, we work on their syntax; if we are perceptionists, we improve their powers of observation; if we are pre-writers, we help them get their concepts manipulable before they begin to write; if we are behaviorists, we get them behaving and then proceed to modify that behavior on the spot; if we are rhetoricians, we make them aware of the subject, speaker/writer, and audience triangle and the way they must mediate between these entities.[7]

Part of the preparation of writing teachers, then, is some theoretical framework against which writing teachers can test new materials and ideas in order to find effective and compatible approaches for their classes. Three overlapping frameworks that I suggest are these: *Classical/ Existential, Thinking/Writing,* and *Product/Process.*

The first of these three pairs of concepts contrasts assumptions of objective truth, reality, and value that often are called "classical" with the more subjective tendencies of existential thought. The conceptual difference is one that Richard Ohmann implied when he contrasted the older rhetorical assumption "that the speaker or writer knows in advance what is true" with the more contemporary rhetorical "pursuit—and not simply the transmission—of truth and right."[8] When students understand the possibilities of the Classical/Existential framework, they are better able to draw useful and coherent distinctions between teaching approaches as different as Douglas's interest in freedom and flexibility and Weathers and Winchester's system of imitating the work of masterful stylists or approaches as far apart as Lou Kelly's "open" writing class[9] and Elizabeth Oggel's idea that students should be "furnished with a set of standards" so that they can see how their writing "measures up to these standards."[10]

The second pairing of concepts, Thinking/Writing, recognizes that behavioral psychology is making changes in the concept of the writing process but that, at the same time, many teachers and materials follow an

7. "Tips for the Freshman," *Freshman English Shop Talk,* 1. No. 2, [p. 5].
8. "In Lieu of a New Rhetoric," *College English,* 26 (October, 1961), 19.
9. "Toward Competence and Creativity in an Open Class," *College English,* 34 (February, 1973), 646.
10. *Thoughts Into Themes,* 3rd ed. (New York: Holt, 1957), p. v.

older idea of the writing process. Recognizing differences in approaches and materials that stem from basic differences in the psychology of writing lets future teachers find their way to consistent materials through the storm of contradictions suggested by two statements by Ray Kytle and Peter Elbow. First, there is this statement from *Composition: Discovery and Communication:*

> Composition of an essay does not begin when you put pen to paper . . . an essential part of the total process of composition takes place before that first word is written. For before you can begin to write on a subject, you must discover what you want to say about it.[11]

And just as convinced that writing precedes ideas as Kytle is that thought precedes composition, Peter Elbow writes this in *Writing Without Teachers:*

> Instead of a two-step transaction of meaning-into-language, think of writing as an organic, developmental process in which you start writing at the very beginning—before you know your meaning at all—and encourage your words gradually to change and evolve. . . . Meaning is not what you start out with but what you end up with.[12]

The third pair of concepts. Product/Process, lets future teachers decide whether teaching approaches and materials place more emphasis on the written artifact produced by the student or on the process that leads toward this product. Obviously, product and process are both important to the writing teacher, and neither can be put aside without seriously oversimplifying the writing process. But differences in emphasis do result in different methodologies. Product-centered teaching tends to work by applying standards—marking papers, grading, and the like. Process-centered teaching tends to keep instruction in grammar, structure, usage, punctuation, and organization within the highly individualized context of the writer writing. Future writing teachers should understand these distinctions so that they can more intelligently develop their own teaching styles and select compatible teaching materials.

Besides knowledge of the history of the English language, of rhetoric, and of some theoretical frameworks with which to understand the wide range of approaches and materials available to them, future writing teachers need a broad awareness of *reliable, productive methods* to help students learn to write. I think, for instance, that prospective teachers should understand the ideas summarized in the dozen and a half points in the 1974 Position Statement of the NCTE's Commission on Composition.[13]

11. (New York: Random House, 1970), p. 2.
12. (New York: Oxford, 1973), p. 15.
13. *College English,* 36 (October, 1974), 219–220.

Even more specifically, I think every would-be writing teacher should understand these five ideas:

1. The importance of *writing* in the composition class and the value of what James Moffett calls "Learning to Write by Writing."[14]

2. The importance of *audience* in any writing situation and the pedagogical usefulness of writing for groups of students and for audiences other than the teacher.

3. The importance of seeing writing as a *process* that moves and grows so that initial ideas and sentences become more coherent, complex, and clear. Whether students conceive of this process as starting with thoughts or with physical behavior seems less important than that they know that writing is not a static thing. Indeed, teachers should understand the logic, usefulness, and limitations of pre-writing and behavioral approaches so that they will be able to modify their teaching to fit the individuals they will teach.

4. The importance of *positive instruction by teachers experienced in the agonies of trying to write.*

5. The importance of *helping students take responsibility for their own writing so that they become their own best editors and teachers.*

BALANCED PREPARATION FOR WRITING TEACHERS

Teachers of writing, then, need to know quite a lot about concepts of composition teaching, about rhetoric, about the English language. But they should not just know these subjects, in the sense of being able to pass multiple-choice tests on them. Instead, they need to know information *and* the principles behind the information. They need to know the "what" of composition teaching; but they also need to know the "how" and the "why." In fact, Richard Larson feels that writing teachers have a greater need to know "why" than "how," since the teacher "must be able to reveal to his students the choices that confront them as they write and the possible consequences of those choices, and enough about how words work and thoughts connect so that he can set tasks before his students in the order and against the background that will help them perform at their best" ("A Special Course," p. 172).

14. *Teaching the Universe of Discourse* (Boston: Houghton Mifflin, 1968), pp. 188–200.

Of course, it is one thing to read such words as these and quite another to make good on them. And the question faced by anyone developing a training program for future writing teachers is, essentially, how can the student learn the necessary *what's* and *how's* and *why's?* Courses in grammar, linguistic history, and rhetorical theory, on the one hand, may teach students much useful information (*what*) without helping them internalize the information enough to understand the all-important underlying principles. Advanced composition courses, on the other hand, may emphasize the *how* of writing to such an extent that they do not adequately help students toward *why's* of words, thoughts, and choices so important to the writing teacher.[15] Clearly, what is needed is a synthesis of some sort: a way to guarantee that students do not merely learn facts of grammar, rhetoric, or pedagogy but that they think about what they learn, relate the facts to each other, examine the underlying principles behind the facts, and use the information in the kind of practical context that can give it genuine meaning for the students.

Such a synthesis requires, first of all, the information that comes in courses in The Structure of the English Language, The History of the English Language, and Advanced Composition and Rhetoric. Beyond these courses comes the real balancing of knowledge with experience. The Teaching of Writing program should include a special course in Writing for Teachers of Writing. It should provide practical work in tutoring, editing, and grading, both within the Writing for Teachers of Writing course and in supervised programs within a campus writing-center or writing-laboratory. And it should provide, for students seeking certification as public school teachers, student-teaching placements that emphasize work in writing.

The Writing for Teachers of Writing course should be, first of all, a writing course in which students continue to develop their skills as writers and become more self-consciously familiar with the frustrations, dead-ends, and pitfalls that their students will encounter. In *A Writer Teaches Writing*, Donald Murray writes that "the most inexperienced student writer shares with the most experienced writer the terror of the blank pages."[16] The Writing for Teachers of Writing course should exploit this fact and try to help students realize how their writing experiences in the course—especially their frustrating and exhausting ones—are helping them become good teachers. Secondly, the course should press home to students the necessity, as a natural pre-requisite of their chosen profession,

15. It was this second limitation that led Larson to conclude that the prospective English teacher "needs a special course in advanced writing, in most cases different from the one open to all students in a university." "A Special Course," p. 168.
16. (Boston: Houghton Mifflin, 1968), p. 70.

of their being writers. In *What Every English Teacher Should Know,* J. N. Hook, Paul Jacobs, and Raymond Crisp make the point that writing teachers must be writers: "Can a golf coach who never swings a club be successful? Can a shop foreman who never operates a machine do a good job? Can a writing teacher who never writes teach writing well? Probably not." They go on to say that this does not mean that every writing teacher must be a professional, but that every writing teacher "should be able to make ideas hang together in prose, should know how to make each sentence express a clear idea clearly, should have a precise knowledge of mechanics." And they say, later, that this writing should be given up to sharp criticism, since the teacher "who has experienced candid, constructive criticism can often become a more constructive critic" (p. 35). This matter of criticism is a third general feature of the Writing for Teachers of Writing course. The course should provide opportunity for students to serve as critics of other students' papers—and, of course, to have their papers examined by sharp-eyed students as well. It should do this in a friendly, constructive, but serious climate. And students should see that such activity is necessary, again as a pre-requisite of their chosen profession.

The Writing for Teachers of Writing course, then, is a writing course informed by the general spirit of Pope's lines from *An Essay on Criticism:*

Let such teach others who themselves excell,
And censure freely [well, not *too* freely] who have written well.

But in order that students learn specific information—*what, how,* and *why*—about the teaching of composition, the Writing for Teachers of Writing course should ask students to write *about* the teaching of writing. And to provide material about which to write, it should use readings, guest speakers, lectures, and discussions to direct students to a wide range of approaches and materials.

My own approach is to organize readings and materials into these areas:

1. *What is a writing teacher?* Donald Murray has a good deal of intelligent information about this in *A Writer Teaches Writing.* I also direct students to *What Every English Teacher Should Know,* to English methods texts, and to articles in *English Journal, College Composition and Communication, College English,* and other sources.

2. *What's wrong with writing teaching today?* This may sound like a negative topic, but my aim is to focus on problems that students will confront when they start to teach their classes and

also to use these problems as springboards to talk about productive solutions. Here, students read Eugene Smith's *Teacher Preparation in Composition* and other materials and hear presentations by a number of classroom teachers.

3. *What are the elements of effective writing instruction?* This huge area is prevented by the brevity of the academic term from ever being complete enough. Typically, I ask students to become well versed in four topics:

   a. The "Learning to Write by Writing" Concept in James Moffett's *Teaching the Universe of Discourse.*

   b. Students as Their Own Editors and Teachers—an idea deriving from Moffett and Murray, from Kenneth Bruffee's "Collaborative Learning" (*College English,* Feb. 1973), and from my own forthcoming text, *Teamwork: Collaborative Strategies for the College Writer.*

   c. Evaluating Student Writing. I draw on a wide range of materials here—from the CCCC Language Statement (*CCC,* Fall 1974), to methods texts, to Barrett Mandel's "Teaching Without Judging" (*College English,* Feb. 1973), to R. W. Reising's "Controlling the Bleeding" (*CCC,* Feb. 1973).

   d. Holding Student Conferences. Here, again, I use Murray, as well as Lou Kelly's "Is Competent Copy-reading a Violation of the Students' Right to Their Own Language?" (*CCC,* Oct. 1974), and a variety of other materials.

In addition to these four subjects, I have students read material and hear presentations on a range of other topics: Motivating Students, "Publishing" Student Writing, Creating Interesting Assignments, Developing Lesson Plans, Writing Behavioral Objectives, and The Students' Right to Their Own Language.

Since what I am recommending is a *writing* course, readings over such important topics as these cannot be allowed to become ends in themselves. They are grist for the writers' mills; they are substance for papers. To guarantee that students think of their reading as a prelude to writing, I ask them to maintain a looseleaf notebook with sections for "Writing Tips," "Teaching Tips," and "Reactions." I also ask students to write papers—such as an examination of the causes of poor writing instruction, a definition of a "good" writing teacher, and an argument on behalf of some specific approach to writing instruction—that require them to develop their own perspectives on ideas contained in the readings.

And, to help blend theory and practice even further, I have students work on these papers in small writing-workshop groups where they practice the concepts of feedback, diagnosis, and prescription about which they are reading. In these groups, students learn about audience definition and audience response, and about how it feels to have a key point missed by readers interested in little but well-placed commas. In these groups, students come to understand the importance of cooperation, the power of peer pressure, the difficulty of opening up to a critic, the bitterness of a writer under attack. And all of these things reinforce what the students are reading and writing about and thereby help students prepare to be effective writing teachers.

JIM W. CORDER

What I Learned at School

When fall comes and the school year begins, I'm sometimes plagued by a temporary friskiness that tends to cause me some trouble before it subsides. This friskiness, I think, rises from two sources: part of it is left over from the summer when for a moment or two I'm led to think that I can really be a teacher, chiefly because there are not any committee meetings in the summer; part of it is left over from old times when I thought September 1 was New Year's Day because soon school would start and the Sears Roebuck catalogue would come.

At any rate, I am sometimes troubled by this coltish vigor before it wanes to be replaced by the decrepitude that is my more normal wont. This year, it led me to make a special mess of things. In an excess of zeal during the first meeting of my freshman composition class, I vowed that I would write an essay every time they did and that I would turn my essays over to them as they turned theirs in to me. Once I had said that, I was led by fear, desperation, and a smidgin of honor to do what I had said I would do. Now, nine essays and some short written exercises later, the term has ended, and I am blurred and fuzzy around the edges. Still, I want to do two things: I want to report what I think I learned while I was writing essays with my students, and I want to exhibit the last of these essays as one way of thinking about a composition class.

When I try to tally the things I learned while writing essays, the total is not impressive, but what's there is sufficiently troublesome, perplexing, confusing, instructive, and vexatious to bring me up short and to cast doubt upon certain assumptions about freshman composition.

From *College Composition and Communication,* 26 (December, 1975), 330–334. Reprinted by permission of the National Council of Teachers of English and Jim W. Corder.

1. I learned that writing out one's own assignments is a marvelous corrective to any tendency one might have for using merely habitual assignments or for witlessly making thoughtless or stupid assignments.

2. With some of the arguments and assumptions that undergird freshman composition I am familiar. I know that "the ability to write a literate essay is the hallmark of the educated person." I know that "a competent student ought to be able to produce a decent piece of writing on call." But I also learned that to write nine essays in a semester of fourteen weeks (I'm leaving out holiday weeks and the like) is a task very nearly not doable. I thought for a while that I would have to give myself an "I" for the course. I'll return to this item a bit later.

3. I learned that I often did precisely what I urged my students not to do: I hurried; I waited until the last moment, because that was the only moment there was; I accepted available subjects that came easily to mind; I wrote some "nice" essays and some "acceptable" essays; once or twice I turned in rough drafts as if they were finished papers. Perhaps I should add that I did usually get semicolons in the right place.

4. I need to say more about items 2 and 3 in order to tell what I really learned, to tell why writing nine essays is a task very nearly not doable. Perhaps what I really learned is that I have not learned enough. Or perhaps what I really learned is that part of what I know *about* writing (though right enough in its way) is not germane or immediate or companionable when one is *doing* the writing. Perhaps I shall be thought merely naive, but as I was writing the nine essays I found myself being shocked and surprised and stunned. (I'd not want anyone to think I was in a state of heightened sensibilities all of the time—a good part of the time I was simply stuporous.) The things that kept disturbing me can be suggested best, I think, under two headings: Problems in the inventive capacities given by a semester, and problems in establishing occasions for writing.

I know some of the hopes and goals associated with invention or "prewriting" and some of the methods developed to foster rich and generative invention. But a term has markedly little time in it. Last semester when I was writing the nine essays, I was busy (and I'd like to stop and sing a sad song or two about that), but that's no great matter: every person's life is usually busy to the level that can be tolerated. Students in the class, who also had to write nine essays, were in this sense as busy as I was. A semester affords precious little time for genuine invention, exploration, and discovery. I found that I frequently was unable to do what I often advised my students to do in searching out subjects and finding ways to be with the subject and an audience in a paper. Actually, in class I was pretty reckless in recommending ways of thinking into subjects: I proposed that my students use journals and write existential sentences; we tackled the topics; I recommended the series of exploratory questions offered by Richard E. Larson (in *College English*, October, 1968); we practiced using problem-solving systems for locating the materials of a paper; we hungered after various heuristic models for discovery; we looked at this, that, and the other thing as particles, waves, and fields. We even tried the TUTO rhythmic method (and I'll be glad to answer letters inquiring after the TUTO mysteries).

But the sorry truth is that, whatever the students were able to do as they were writing, I was almost never able to think a paper out ahead of time; I was never able to write a draft and let it alone awhile before I revised it for final copy; I was never able to try portions of the essays from different perspectives and in different styles. I was never able to take a possible subject, hold it in my hand, look at it in this way and that way, and scout its possibilities. What I actually did was to cash in ideas I *already* had for writing, threshing around among scraps of paper, notebooks, and lists of things to do that were piled on my desk, finding subjects and sketched designs for writing that I wanted to do some time. A dark thought struck me one night: What if I didn't have these notations collected to cash in? That dark thought was followed by another: What if I were not in the habit of writing, of expecting to write, of saving notes against the time when I would write? In other words, I finally thought, what if I were in the same fix that most of the students in my class were in?

But the perturbation I felt went further. I found myself continually troubled by the character of what I'll call the occasions for writing. I remember sitting at my desk one evening when I *had* to get an essay written to give to my students the next morning. I remember the moment clearly. I was sitting there looking at the assignment I had given to my students, when another dark thought came: "I *know* how to write this thing," I remember saying to myself, "but why in hell would anybody *want* to?"

What I am trying to get at here is that the occasion is wrong. The occasion contains no immediacy; it offers no genuine need that must be genuinely answered. I mean to suggest that even some of our best assignments—imaginative and thoughtful as they may be—do not elicit a driving need to write. I mean to suggest that some of our best assignments do not elicit the students' investment of themselves in the work.

Perhaps I should learn not to worry. Perhaps I should learn to accept the freshman composition course as a place for the acquisition of tools and for practice in using them skillfully in finger exercises. There'd be no shame in that—indeed, nothing but good. But I think I won't learn that, because I keep learning something else at school, every term. I can best begin to say what that is, I believe, by exhibiting the last essay I wrote with the students in my class.

Half Thoughts on a Whole Semester

I was ruminating last night over certain features of English 1203, sensing a weight that some of its parts carry. Ruminating, I should say, is an activity, better still a condition, I assign high priority to. Given the choice, I'll ruminate anytime rather than turn the compost pile or paint the dining-room or grade papers or fix the shelf that's been waiting for five and a half years or work on the manuscript that's due March 1. At any rate, I was ruminating, turning the semester's topics this way and that to see how they looked from the under side and what consequence they had.

But I can only speak of consequence in certain ways. I'd not presume to declare that topics of my devising had this, that, or the other specific consequence for students. I'm generally inclined to think that all courses are failures: there's always more to be said than can be said in a given moment, always more reaches of thought to be in than one can be in at a given moment. So if I speak of consequences, I am not speaking of consequences of the course, but of consequences, weights, significances carried by the topics of concern themselves. The topics, the issues, the practices carry meaning, I think, even if it is not presently realized in us. The subject makes its own assertions, to which we're seldom equal.

On the first day of the term, I remember remarking that I wanted to conceive of the work we might do not as the work of a single term, but as the work of a two-term, nine-month period. I said then, I recall, that as I was presently able to understand the work before us, it could be seen in three stages: the practice of *invention,* the shaping of *structure,* and the tuning of *styles.* As I recollect the occasion, I noted that I expected the end of the fall term to come between the second and third of these.

Since that day much has happened, though often without notice. Miss Puckitt has always come early, usually followed by Miss Ramsey. Miss Daniel and Miss Cesarotti have always been punctual—two minutes late. Miss Pugh and Miss FitzSimmon have walked down the hall together. Mr. Ragsdale has written an essay about toothpaste. Mr. White has been quiet in the back, though his essays are not quiet alone but forceful. Miss Steinberg has seen to it that I remembered to be humble. Miss Stamper has found sonata form in Stegner's essay. Miss Westbrook has mediated on epistolary ills. Mr. Spleth from a "Bad Beginning" has surged toward who knows what ending. Miss Fouch has found a way to talk about intravenous tubes and cats in the same essay. Mr. Haney has embarked upon a series of essays that may come at last to seventeen volumes and be studied by freshmen. Miss Bachman has told a strange Thanksgiving narrative in which much depended on a word heard out of context. Mr. Hayes has vowed his distaste for hickory nuts. Mr. Posselt, lately arrived from the north, has encountered a street evangelist. Mr. Sherwood has found in empathy a way of distinguishing among teachers. Miss Lawson has almost learned to be decisive. Mr. Whitney has celebrated his home town's virtues, though we both hope that the actual text of the celebration is not to be published abroad in Tyler. And Mr. Steimel has slept as well as could be reasonably expected, though of late he has taken to staying awake and disturbing the class.

Meanwhile, with various fanfares, flourishes, and fallings-down, I like to imagine that I have been talking about *invention* and *structure*. What I think I said (as distinct from what you may have heard, distracted by 372 pipe lightings) arranged itself in something like this order:

INVENTION (the exploration that precedes and leads to writing)
   —where you find subjects if you don't have one, or what to do with a
      subject that someone else hands you
   —taking a subject over, making it into something of your own
   —seeing the fullness of a subject, learning its potential
   —ways of thinking through subjects
   —relationships among writer, subject, and audience, and the dis-
      tances between them
   —using the resources that you need to deal with a subject
   —logical development and emotional appeals
   —learning to be real with an audience

STRUCTURE (design, organization, shape in writing)
   —some practice in describing structures
   —some talk about structural transfers from one medium or art form
      to another
   —using structures that others use
   —some talk about the relation of structure and meaning

A little earlier, you may recall, I was talking about the consequences such topics have, trying to establish that the consequences I am talking about are not those of the course, but the weights, values, meanings the topics themselves carry. I can illustrate what I mean, I think by referring to the list just above. For example, we talked at various times about using the resources that are available to you, including research, and about taking over and using a structure that other writers have used. Those two notions, whether I managed to say it fully or not, whether you managed to hear it fully or not, can carry an import in their own right, an import and significance not limited to freshman composition. They give us a way of knowing that we are, after all, together with each other, that we are in community if we wish to be, that others have striven and learned, and that we may learn from them with less strife, that we are not alone, though we can be if we wish. In some way or another, I think each of the items arranged above carries such meaning.

But I have been thinking from the start not about the signification of each topic raised, but about the meaning carried by invention itself, by structure itself, and by the order in which they appeared. Such meaning —and it is of course not complete—stretches out, it seems to me, from English composition to everything, but can at the moment best be expressed in the context and language of a composition class, as I have tried to do below. I herewith advance to you certain propositions intended to suggest what is learnable from composition study and practice (though it's also nice if you learn where to put semicolons). If you find the numbering system below a bit strange, you will understand from it, I think, that there are yet other propositions I have not found.

Ninth law of composition: Everything comes from somewhere and goes some place. You touch other people, and they enter your world, coming from another. You read a book and capture its author into your world. Both come from somewhere and move elsewhere, into your thoughts, giving texture to the universe you live in, becoming finally the words you speak.

Eleventh law of composition: Some things precede other things. Invention precedes structure. Thinking and feeling and being precede writing. Structure made without invention are false or superficial. There probably is a fit sequencing of things, even if we don't always see it.

Eighteenth law of composition: You are always standing somewhere when you say something. You are in a world, you have thoughts, you've made choices (whether or not consciously) any time you say anything. If you are in a position whenever you say anything, it's probably best to know what the position is.

Twenty-fifth law of composition: Invention is an invitation to openness. It asks of you that you open yourself to the ways other people think, to the knowledge that already exists, to the intricacies and whims of your own beings. It asks of you that you therefore be tentative a while, consider alternatives a while, be in process a while.

Twenty-sixth law of composition: But structure is a closure. You can't organize an essay or a sonata unless you have ruled out other organizations. When structure begins to be made, you are no longer open: you have made choices.

Twenty-seventh law of composition: Invention and structure, then, represent a way of being in the world. They exert certain demands upon you, and they afford you certain pleasures. Invention invites you to be open to a creation filled with copious wonders, trivialities, sorrows, and amazements. Structure requires that you close. You are asked to be open and always closing.

Thirty-second law of composition: What follows feeds, enlarges, and enriches what precedes. Invention precedes and is open. Structure follows and closes. That may seem a narrowing disappointment, a ruling out of possibilities. It needn't be. Every choice, every decision, every structure has the potential of being another entry in the inventive world you live in, modifying it, punching it in here, pooching it out there, giving color to it yonder. Invention precedes, structure follows, but invention does not cease thereby. The structure we make today may give grace to tomorrow's invention. That means that if today we fail to be wise and generous and good, tomorrow we may succeed, and if not, we may fail at a higher level.

I should report, in closing, that when the students in my class examined my papers, as I examined theirs, they concluded that I was given to rambling.

DONALD M. MURRAY

Write Before Writing

We command our students to write and grow frustrated when our "bad" students hesitate, stare out the window, dawdle over blank paper, give up and say, "I can't write," while the "good" students smugly pass their papers in before the end of the period.

When publishing writers visit such classrooms, however, they are astonished at students who can write on command, ejaculating correct little essays without thought, for writers have to write before writing.

The writers were the students who dawdled, stared out windows, and, more often than we like to admit, didn't do well in English—or in school.

One reason may be that few teachers have ever allowed adequate time for prewriting, that essential stage in the writing process which precedes a completed first draft. And even the curricula plans and textbooks which attempt to deal with prewriting usually pass over it rather quickly, referring only to the techniques of outlining, note-taking, or journal-making, not revealing the complicated process writers work through to get to the first draft.

Writing teachers, however, should give careful attention to what happens between the moment the writer receives an idea or an assignment and the moment the first completed draft is begun. We need to understand, as well as we can, the complicated and intertwining processes of perception and conception through language.

In actual practice, of course, these stages overlap and interact with one another, but to understand what goes on we must separate them and look at them artificially, the way we break down any skill to study it.

From *College Composition and Communication,* 29 (December, 1978), 375–381. Reprinted by permission of the National Council of Teachers of English and Donald M. Murray.

170

First of all, we must get out of the stands where we observe the process of writing from a distance—and after the fact—and get on the field where we can understand the pressures under which the writer operates. On the field, we will discover there is one principal negative force which keeps the writer from writing and four positive forces which help the writer move forward to a completed draft.

RESISTANCE TO WRITING

The negative force is *resistance* to writing, one of the great natural forces of nature. It may be called The Law of Delay: that writing which can be delayed, will be. Teachers and writers too often consider resistance to writing evil, when, in fact, it is necessary.

When I get an idea for a poem or an article or a talk or a short story, I feel myself consciously draw away from it. I seek procrastination and delay. There must be time for the seed of the idea to be nurtured in the mind. Far better writers than I have felt the same way. Over his writing desk Franz Kafka had one word, "Wait." William Wordsworth talked of the writer's "wise passiveness." Naturalist Annie Dillard recently said, "I'm waiting. I usually get my ideas in November, and I start writing in January. I'm waiting." Denise Levertov says, "If . . . somewhere in the vicinity there is a poem then, no, I don't do anything about it, I wait."

Even the most productive writers are expert dawdlers, doers of unnecessary errands, seekers of interruptions—trials to their wives or husbands, friends, associates, and themselves. They sharpen well-pointed pencils and go out to buy more blank paper, rearrange offices, wander through libraries and bookstores, chop wood, walk, drive, make unecessary calls, nap, daydream, and try not "consciously" to think about what they are going to write so they can think subconsciously about it.

Writers fear this delay, for they can name colleagues who have made a career of delay, whose great unwritten books will never be written, but, somehow, those writers who write must have the faith to sustain themselves through the necessity of delay.

FORCES FOR WRITING

In addition to that faith, writers feel four pressures that move them forward towards the first draft.

The first is *increasing information* about the subject. Once a writer decides on a subject or accepts an assignment, information about the subject seems to attach itself to the writer. The writer's perception apparatus finds significance in what the writer observes or overhears or reads or thinks or remembers. The writer becomes a magnet for specific details, insights, anecdotes, statistics, connecting thoughts, references. The subject itself seems to take hold of the writer's experience, turning everything that happens to the writer into material. And this inventory of information creates pressure that moves the writer forward towards the first draft.

Usually the writer feels an *increasing concern* for the subject. The more a writer knows about the subject, the more the writer begins to feel about the subject. The writer cares that the subject be ordered and shared. The concern, which at first is a vague interest in the writer's mind, often becomes an obsession until it is communicated. Winston Churchill said, "Writing a book was an adventure. To begin with, it was a toy, and amusement; then it became a mistress, and then a master. And then a tyrant."

The writer becomes aware of a *waiting audience,* potential readers who want or need to know what the writer has to say. Writing is an act of arrogance and communication. The writer rarely writes just for himself or herself, but for others who may be informed, entertained, or persuaded by what the writer has to say.

And perhaps most important of all, is the *approaching deadline,* which moves closer day by day at a terrifying and accelerating rate. Few writers publish without deadlines, which are imposed by others or by themselves. The deadline is real, absolute, stern, and commanding.

REHEARSAL FOR WRITING

What the writer does under the pressure not to write and the four countervailing pressures to write is best described by the word *rehearsal,* which I first heard used by Dr. Donald Graves of the University of New Hampshire to describe what he saw young children doing as they began to write. He watched them draw what they would write and heard them, as we all have, speaking aloud what they might say on the page before they wrote. If you walk through editorial offices or a newspaper city-room you will see lips moving and hear expert professionals muttering and whispering to themselves as they write. Rehearsal is a normal part of the writing process, but it took a trained observer, such as Dr. Graves, to identify its significance.

Rehearsal covers much more than the muttering of struggling writers.

As Dr. Graves points out, productive writers are "in a state of rehearsal all the time." Rehearsal usually begins with an unwritten dialogue within the writer's mind. "All of a sudden I discover what I have been thinking about a play," says Edward Albee. "This is usually between six months and a year before I actually sit down and begin typing it out." The writer thinks about characters or arguments, about plot or structure, about words and lines. The writer usually hears something which is similar to what Wallace Stevens must have heard as he walked through his insurance office working out poems in his head.

What the writer hears in his or her head usually evolves into note-taking. This may be simple brainstorming, the jotting down of random bits of information which may connect themselves into a pattern later on, or it may be journal-writing, a written dialogue between the writer and the subject. It may even become research recorded in a formal structure of note-taking.

Sometimes the writer not only talks to himself or herself, but to others —collaborators, editors, teachers, friends—working out the piece of writing in oral language with someone else who can enter into the process of discovery with the writer.

For most writers, the informal notes turn into lists, outlines, titles, leads, ordered fragments, all sketches of what later may be written, devices to catch a possible order that exists in the chaos of the subject.

In the final stage of rehearsal, the writer produces test drafts, written or unwritten. Sometimes they are called discovery drafts or trial runs or false starts that the writer doesn't think will be false. All writing is experimental, and the writer must come to the point where drafts are attempted in the writer's head and on paper.

Some writers seem to work more in their head, and others more on paper. Susan Sowars, a researcher at the University of New Hampshire, examining the writing processes of a group of graduate students found

> a division . . . between those who make most discoveries during pre-writing and those who make most discoveries during writing and revision. The discoveries include the whole range from insights into personal issues to task-related organizational and content insight. The earlier the stage at which insights occur, the greater the drudgery associated with the writing-rewriting tasks. It may be that we resemble the young reflective and reactive writers. The less developmentally mature reactive writers enjoy writing more than reflective writers. They may use writing as a rehearsal for thinking just as young, reactive writers draw to rehearse writing. The younger and older reflective writers do not need to rehearse by drawing to write or by writing to think clearly or to discover new relationships and significant content.

This concept deserves more investigation. We need to know about both the reflective and reactive prewriting mode. We need to see if there are developmental changes in students, if they move from one mode to another as they mature, and we need to see if one mode is more important in certain writing tasks than others. We must, in every way possible, explore the significant writing stage of rehearsal which has rarely been described in the literature on the writing process.

THE SIGNALS WHICH SAY "WRITE"

During the rehearsal process, the experienced writer sees signals which tell the writer how to control the subject and produce a working first draft. The writer, Rebecca Rule, points out that in some cases when the subject is found, the way to deal with it is inherent in the subject. The subject itself is the signal. Most writers have experienced this quick passing through of the prewriting process. The line is given and the poem is clear; a character gets up and walks the writer through the story; the newspaperman attends a press conference, hears a quote, sees the lead and the entire structure of the article instantly. But many times the process is far less clear. The writer is assigned a subject or chooses one and then is lost.

E. B. White testifies, "I never knew in the morning how the day was going to develop. I was like a hunter, hoping to catch sight of a rabbit." Denise Levertov says, "You can smell the poem before you see it." Most writers know these feelings, but students who have never seen a rabbit dart across their writing desks or smelled a poem need to know the signals which tell them that a piece of writing is near.

What does the writer recognize which gives a sense of closure, a way of handling a diffuse and overwhelming subject? There seem to be eight principal signals to which writers respond.

One signal is *genre*. Most writers view the world as a fiction writer, a reporter, a poet, or an historian. The writer sees experience as a plot or a lyric poem or a news story or a chronicle. The writer uses such literary traditions to see and understand life.

"Ideas come to a writer because he has trained his mind to seek them out," says Brian Garfield. "Thus when he observes or reads or is exposed to a character or event, his mind sees the story possibilities in it and he begins to compose a dramatic structure in his mind. This process is incessant. Now and then it leads to something that will become a novel. But it's mainly an attitude: a way of looking at things; a habit of examining everything one perceives as potential material for a story."

Genre is a powerful but dangerous lens. It both clarifies and limits. The writer and the student must be careful not to see life merely in the stereotype form with which he or she is most familiar but to look at life with all of the possibilities of the genre in mind and to attempt to look at life through different genre.

Another signal the writer looks for is a *point of view*. This can be an opinion towards the subject or a position from which the writer—and the reader—studies the subject.

A tenement fire could inspire the writer to speak out against tenements, dangerous space-heating systems, a fire-department budget cut. The fire might also be seen from the point of view of the people who were the victims or who escaped or who came home to find their home gone. It may be told from the point of view of a fireman, an arsonist, an insurance investigator, a fire-safety engineer, a real-estate planner, a housing inspector, a landlord, a spectator, as well as the victim. The list could go on.

Still another way the writer sees the subject is through *voice*. As the writer rehearses, in the writer's head and on paper, the writer listens to the sound of the language as a clue to the meaning in the subject and the writer's attitude toward that meaning. Voice is often the force which drives a piece of writing forward, which illuminates the subject for the writer and the reader.

A writer may, for example, start to write a test draft with detached unconcern and find that the language appearing on the page reveals anger or passionate concern. The writer who starts to write a solemn report of a meeting may hear a smile and then a laugh in his own words and go on to produce a humorous column.

News is an important signal for many writers who ask what the reader needs to know or would like to know. Those prolific authors of nature books, Lorus and Margery Milne, organize their books and each chapter in the books around what is new in the field. Between assignment and draft they are constantly looking for the latest news they can pass along to their readers. When they find what is new, then they know how to organize their writing.

Writers constantly wait for the *line* which is given. For most writers, there is an enormous difference between a thesis or an idea or a concept and an actual line, for the line itself has resonance. A single line can imply a voice, a tone, a pace, a whole way of treating a subject. Joseph Heller tells about the signal which produced his novel *Something Happened*:

> I begin with a first sentence that is independent of any conscious preparation. Most often nothing comes out of it: a sentence will come to

mind that doesn't lead to a second sentence. Sometimes it will lead to thirty sentences which then come to a dead end. I was alone on the deck. As I sat there worrying and wondering what to do, one of those first lines suddenly came to mind: "In the office in which I work, there are four people of whom I am afraid. Each of these four people is afraid of five people." Immediately the lines presented a whole explosion of possibilities and choices—characters (working in a corporation) a tone, a mood of anxiety, or of insecurity. In the first hour (before someone came along and asked me to go to the beach) I knew the beginning, the ending, most of the middle, the whole scene of that particular "something" that was going to happen; I knew about the brain-damaged child, and especially, of course, about Bob Slocum, my protagonist, and what frightened him, that he wanted to be liked, that his immediate hope was to be allowed to make a three-minute speech at the company convention. Many of the actual lines throughout the book came to me—the entire "something happened" scene with those solar plexus lines (beginning with the doctor's statement and ending with "Don't tell my wife" and the rest of them) all coming to me in that first hour on that Fire Island deck. Eventually I found a different opening chapter with a different first line ("I get the willies when I see closed doors") but I kept the original, which had spurred everything, to start off the second section.

Newspapermen are able to write quickly and effectively under pressure because they become skillful at identifying a lead, that first line—or two or three—which will inform and entice the reader and which, of course, also gives the writer control over the subject. As an editorial writer, I found that finding the title first gave me control over the subject. Each title became, in effect, a pre-draft, so that in listing potential titles I would come to one which would be a signal as to how the whole editorial could be written.

Poets and fiction writers often receive their signals in terms of an *image.* Sometimes this image is static; other times it is a moving picture in the writer's mind. When Gabriel Garcia Marquez was asked what the starting point of his novels was, he answered, "A completely visual image . . . the starting point of *Leaf Storm* is an old man taking his grandson to a funeral, in *No One Writes to the Colonel,* it's an old man waiting, and in *One Hundred Years,* an old man taking his grandson to the fair to find out what ice is." William Faulkner was quoted as saying, "It begins with a character, usually, and once he stands up on his feet and begins to move, all I do is trot along behind him with a paper and pencil trying to keep up long enough to put down what he says and does." It's a comment which seems facetious—if you're not a fiction writer. Joyce Carol Oates adds, "I visualize the characters completely; I have heard their dialogue, I know how they speak, what they want, who they are, nearly everything about them."

Although image has been testified to mostly by imaginative writers, where it is obviously most appropriate, I think research would show that nonfiction writers often see an image as the signal. The person, for example, writing a memo about a manufacturing procedure may see the assembly line in his or her mind. The politician arguing for a pension law may see a person robbed of a pension, and by seeing that person know how to organize a speech or the draft of a new law.

Many writers know they are ready to write when they see a *pattern* in a subject. This pattern is usually quite different from what we think of as an outline, which is linear and goes from beginning to end. Usually the writer sees something which might be called a gestalt, which is, in the words of the dictionary, "a unified physical, psychological, or symbolic configuration having properties that cannot be derived from its parts." The writer usually in a moment sees the entire piece of writing as a shape, a form, something that is more than all of its parts, something that is entire and is represented in his or her mind, and probably on paper, by a shape.

Marge Piercy says, "I think that the beginning of fiction, of the story, has to do with the perception of pattern in event." Leonard Gardner, in talking of his fine novel *Fat City*, said, "I had a definite design in mind, I had a sense of circle . . . of closing the circle at the end." John Updike says, "I really begin with some kind of solid, coherent image, some notion of the shape of the book and even of its texture. *The Poorhouse Fair* was meant to have a sort of wide shape. *Rabbit, Run* was kind of zigzag. *The Centaur* was sort of a sandwich."

We have interviews with imaginative writers about the writing process, but rarely interviews with science writers, business writers, political writers, journalists, ghost writers, legal writers, medical writers—examples of effective writers who use language to inform and persuade. I am convinced that such research would reveal that they also see pattern or gestalts which carry them from idea to draft.

"It's not the answer that enlightens but the question," says Ionesco. This insight into what the writer is looking for is one of the most significant considerations in trying to understand the freewriting process. A most significant book based on more than ten years of study of art students, *The Creative Vision, A Longitudinal Study of Problem-Finding in Art,* by Jacob W. Getzels and Mihaly Csikszentmihalyi, has documented how the most creative students are those who come up with the *problem* to be solved rather than a quick answer. The signal to the creative person may well be the problem, which will be solved through the writing.

We need to take all the concepts of invention from classical rhetoric and combine them with what we know from modern psychology, from studies of creativity, from writers' testimony about the prewriting process. Most of all, we need to observe successful students and writers during the prewriting process, and to debrief them to find out what they do when they move effectively from assignment or idea to completed first draft. Most of all, we need to move from failure-centered research to research which defines what happens when the writing goes well, just what is the process followed by effective student and professional writers. We know far too little about the writing process.

IMPLICATIONS FOR TEACHING WRITING

Our speculations make it clear that there are significant implications for the teaching of writing in a close examination of what happens between receiving an assignment or finding a subject and beginning a completed first draft. We may need, for example, to reconsider our attitude towards those who delay writing. We may, in fact, need to force many of our glib, hair-trigger student writers to slow down, to daydream, to waste time, but not to avoid a reasonable deadline.

We certainly should allow time within the curriculum for prewriting, and we should work with our students to help them understand the process of rehearsal, to allow them the experience of rehearsing what they will write in their minds, on the paper, and with collaborators.

We should also make our students familiar with the signals they may see during the rehearsal process which will tell them that they are ready to write, that they have a way of dealing with their subject.

The prewriting process is largely invisible; it takes place within the writer's head or on scraps of paper that are rarely published. But we must understand that such a process takes place, that it is significant, and that it can be made clear to our students. Students who are not writing, or not writing well, may have a second chance if they are able to experience the writers' counsel to write before writing.

ADDITIONAL READINGS

RICHARD L. LARSON, "In-Service Training for the English Composition Teacher," *The Bulletin of the National Association of Secondary School Principals,* 52 (February, 1968), 29–47.

"Guidelines for the Preparation of Teachers of English," *English Journal,* 57 (April, 1968). Three-fourths of this issue is devoted to this subject.

ROBERT ZOELLNER, "Talk-Write: A Behavioral Pedagogy for Composition," *College English,* 30 (January, 1969), 267–320.

WALKER GIBSON, "The Writing Teacher as a Dumb Reader," *College Composition and Communication,* 30 (May, 1979), 192–195.

PAUL B. DIEDERICH, "How to Measure Growth in Writing Ability," *English Journal,* 55 (April, 1966), 435–449.

EUGENE H. SMITH, "Composition Evaluation: A Problem of Voice," *English Journal,* 56 (November, 1967), 1189–1194.

RICHARD L. LARSON, "Training New Teachers of Composition in the Writing of Comments on Themes," *College Composition and Communication,* 17 (October, 1966), 152–155.

DONALD C. STEWART

Composition Textbooks
and the Assault on Tradition

During the past two or three years, article after article has appeared in the popular press advocating a return to the basics in the teaching of English composition. For example, *Newsweek's* December, 1975, issue decorated its cover with "Why Johnny Can't Write" and then proceeded to explain *why,* in terms which were, for those of us who try to keep abreast of work in composition theory and practice, simplistic and out-dated. How ironic that the writer of the *Newsweek* article was reaching an audience of millions, while Richard Young of Michigan, one of this country's truly knowledgeable people in composition theory and practice, was reaching only a few hundred with a paper delivered at the 1975 Buffalo Conference on the Composing Process. In that paper, still unpublished, Young says that current composition theory and practice are dominated by a paradigm which Daniel Fogarty has called "current-traditional rhetoric" (See *Roots for a New Rhetoric* [New York: Teacher's College, Columbia Univ., 1959], p. 118). Young uses *paradigm* here to mean a "disciplinary matrix," a term he derives from Thomas Kuhn's *Structure of Scientific Revolutions* (Chicago: Univ. of Chicago Press, 2nd ed. 1970). It describes "a system of widely shared values, beliefs and methods which determines the nature and conduct of [a] discipline. A paradigm determines, among other things, what is included in the discipline and what is excluded from it, what is taught and not taught, what problems are regarded as important and unimportant and, by implication, what research is regarded as valuable in developing the discipline. . . . For those working within a discipline a paradigm is an eye to see with" (Young, pp. 1, 2).

Although superficial variations in the current-traditional composition

From *College Composition and Communication,* 29 (May, 1978), 171–176. Reprinted by permission of the National Council of Teachers of English and Donald C. Stewart.

paradigm do exist, says Young, its principal features are quite obvious: "Emphasis on the composed product rather than the composing process; the analysis of discourse into words, sentences, and paragraphs; the classification of discourse into description, narration, exposition, and argument; the strong concern with usage (syntax, spelling, punctuation) and with style (economy, clarity, emphasis); the preoccupation with the informal essay and the research paper; etc." He argues further, that vitalist assumptions, inherited from the nineteenth-century Romantics, underlie many of the features of the current-traditional paradigm. "Vitalism," Young says, "with its stress on the natural powers of the mind and the uniqueness of the creative act, leads to a repudiation of the possibility of teaching the composing process. Hence the tendency of current-traditional rhetoric to become a critical study of the products of composing and an art of editing." Of even greater interest to him are those things, once included in the discipline, which are now excluded because of these vitalist assumptions, most noticeably, the art of invention. The reasons traditionally given for excluding invention, he says, are (1) that rhetoric is primarily the art of presenting ideas and information, not generating them, as the primary subject disciplines do, and (2) "that creative processes, which include the composing process, are not susceptible to conscious control by formal procedures."

Now there is nothing wrong with a paradigm dominating and giving stability to a discipline, so long as the paradigm articulates and generates solutions to the problems which occur in the discipline. The question, then, is whether or not the current-traditional paradigm in rhetoric and composition still serves that function. I think it does not. It has been under assault from several directions for the last fifteen years, primarily for its failure to deal adequately with the composing process. Young identifies four theories of invention which have attempted to respond to the current-traditional paradigm's inadequacies in dealing with composing: (1) a revival of interest in invention as presented in classical rhetoric, best exemplified in a text like Edward P. J. Corbett's *Classical Rhetoric for the Modern Student;* (2) the development of pre-writing techniques by Gordon Rohman and Albert Wlecke of Michigan State; (3) Kenneth Burke's dramatistic method, characterized by the pentad of *act, agency, actor, scene,* and *purpose;* and (4) Kenneth Pike's tagmemic theories, which, according to Young, combine the best features of prewriting and classical invention. My own judgment is that of the four, the topics of classical rhetoric and Burke's pentad are the heuristic systems most familiar to those textbook writers and teachers who are concerned with providing students with help in the invention process. But I find virtually no evidence that the authors of most textbooks which now include sections on pre-writing are at all familiar with Rohman and Wlecke's report of their work, a document entitled *The Construction and Application of Models for Concept Formation* (Cooperative Research Project No. 2174, HEW, East Lansing, 1964). There is no question, however, that these men were addressing the inadequacies which Young identifies in the current-traditional paradigm: "A failure to make a useful distinction between thinking-as-discovery and writing has led to a fundamental misconception which undermines many of our best efforts to teach writing: that if we train students how to recognize an example of good prose (the rhetoric of the finished word), we have given them a basis on which to build their own writing abilities. All we have done, in fact, is to give them standards to judge the goodness or badness of their finished effort. *We have not really taught them how to make that effort.* . . . Whereas the classical practice of imitation held up the finished masterpiece for emulation, we sought ways for our students to imitate the creative principle of discovery itself which makes possible a finished work" (p. 17).

Equally difficult to find is any evidence that Pike's tagmemic theory has been either widely understood or adopted. The only text which presents it fully is *Rhetoric: Discovery and Change* (New York: Harcourt, Brace, and World, 1970) by Young, Becker, and Pike. As far as I am aware, the book has not been widely adopted, and its theories have scarcely been incorporated into even a small minority of texts now on the market.

In addition to these assaults on the failure of the current-traditional paradigm to deal with the composing process, there have been even more sharp and dramatic assaults launched against other aspects of it. One thinks immediately of Robert Zoellner's "Talk-Write" A Behavioral Pedagogy for Composition" in the January, 1969, issue of *College English*. In a sense, Zoellner was also attacking deficiences in the current-traditional paradigm's presentation of the composing process, but his approach had little in common with the four already cited. Whereas they attempted to deal with aspects of cognition, Zoellner introduced a new dimension, physical behavior, into the writing process. Teachers were not ready then, as some still are not, to believe that writing difficulties, particularly in the work of remedial students, have less to do with the way their minds work and more to do with the way their muscles have been conditioned. There is evidence in some textbooks now, however, that some teachers are finally and grudgingly beginning to admit that composition is a heavily conditioned responsive process and that while they may object violently to an English teacher who tells them that principles of operant conditioning will be useful in the composition class, they had better test his hypothesis before dismissing it as so much scientific hogwash illicitly invading the traditional territory of humanistic studies. But Zoellner's approach is still so original and so fundamental and so far beyond the boundaries of the current-traditional paradigm that most English teachers still regard it with intense hostility. Significantly, Zoellner was the first to recognize that problems with a dominant paradigm underlay resistance to his hypothesis.

A still newer and equally dramatic assault against the current-traditional paradigms treatment of arrangement and style comes from Winston Weathers's "Grammars of Style: New Options in Composition," in *Freshman English News,* Winter, 1976. Some selected quotations from this remarkable essay will give one a sense of his concerns:

> What I've been taught to construct is: the well-made box. I have been taught to put "what I have to say" into a container that is always re-markably the same, that—in spite of varying decorations—keeps to a basically conventional form: a solid bottom, four upright sides, a fine-fitting lid. Indeed, I may be free to put "what I have to say" in the plain box or in the ornate box, in the large box or the small box, in the fragile box or in the sturdy box. But always *the box*—squarish or rectangular. And I begin to wonder if there isn't somewhere a round box or oval box or tubular box, if somewhere there isn't some sort of container (1) that will allow me to package "what I have to say" without trimming my "con-tents" to fit into a particular compositional mode, (2) that will actually encourage me to discover new "things to say" because of the very op-portunity a newly shaped container gives me, (3) that will be more suitable perhaps to my own mental processes, and (4) that will provide me with a greater rhetorical flexibility, allowing me to package what I have to say in more ways than one and thus reach more audiences than one. (p. 1)

Weathers wants no part of the dichotomy between "expository" and "creative" writing. "I'm asking simply to be exposed to, and informed about, the full range of compositional possibilities. That I be introduced to all the tools, right now, and not be asked to wait for years and years until I have mastered right-handed affairs before I learn anything about left-handed affairs. That, rather, I be introduced to all the grammars/ve-hicles/tools, compositional possibilities *now* so that even as I 'learn to write' I will have before me as many resources as possible. That all the 'ways of writing' be spread out before me and that my education be de-voted to learning how to use them" (p. 1).

But composition teachers have not offered their students a number of different "boxes." "Our assumption," says Weathers—"regardless of liber-ality so far as diversity of styles is concerned—is that every composition must be well-organized and unified, must demonstrate logic, must contain well-developed paragraphs; that its structure will manifest a beginning, middle, and end; that the composition will reveal identifiable types of order; that so far as the composition deals with time it will reveal a general diachronicity; etc. Our teaching and texts will be concerned, almost without exception, with 'subject and thesis,' 'classification and order,' 'beginning and ending,' 'expansion,' 'continuity,' 'emphasis,' and the like. All remains, in other words, within a particular grammar of style that leads to compositions that 'make sense' " (p. 2).

In contrast to this, Weathers offers an alternate grammar of style, which he argues has been present in Anglo-American writing for some time, in the works of Laurence Sterne, William Blake, D. H. Lawrence, James Joyce, Virginia Woolf, John Barth, Donald Barthelme, Tom Wolfe, and others. It is not primarily rational, logical, or ordered. Instead, it is often the very opposite. Its principal features are the crot, "an autonomous unit, characterized by the absence of any transitional devices that might relate it to preceding or subsequent crots," labyrinthine sentences and sentence fragments, lists, double-voices, repetitions/repetends/refrains, synchronicity (particularly noticeable in Joyce's or Virginia Woolf's work where linear prose is shaped to produce an effect of vertical time), and collage/montage."

Weathers does not argue that his new grammar should replace the old one; he sees it as a means of enriching our rhetorical options in discourse: "If we'd spend less time trying to 'protect' the language from 'misuse,' and spend more time opening our own minds to all the things language can do and is doing, we'd be better off. . . . The art of composition finally does have something to do with the art of life. Our verbal compositions become emblematic of and analogous to our social and political 'compositions.' If we come to composition with options, openmindedness, adaptability we not only fulfill ourselves the more but we obviously are capable of giving more to others" (p. 18).

Question: To what extent have these assaults upon prominent features of the current-traditional paradigm in rhetoric and composition been reflected in widely used composition textbooks? Early this year I asked twenty-eight well-known publishers if they could give me the titles of textbooks which had sales exceeding 100,000 copies. I made the point that I did not intend to pry into their financial affairs. I merely wanted to identify textbooks that were either widely adopted or extensively used in parts of the country. Twenty-two replied, of whom only two said that such information was so confidential that their companies would not release it. Most were quick to respond and were very generous in giving me the information and books I requested.

The list I compiled contained 52 titles, but I reviewed only 34 in preparing this paper. Of the 34, 15 were handbooks, 9 rhetorics, and 10 readers. All have gone through several editions, so I examined the latest edition of each book. Twenty-three were published in 1975, 1976, or 1977. The other eleven, which I suppose should be called "oldies but goodies," were published between 1970 and 1974. The point is that all have been revised recently enough to have been touched by the work I have mentioned, except for Weathers's essay, and the 1977 titles, of which there were eleven, could even have responded to that.

I carefully searched appropriate sections of each book for indications that their authors were at least aware of the new approaches to the composing process, writing behavior, and stylistic options which I have been citing. Regrettably, only seven of the 34 contained any appreciable awareness of the work of people like Corbett, Rohman, Burke, Pike, Zoellner, or Weathers. The other 27, and some are the products of people with enormous reputations as literary scholars, were strictly current-traditional in their discussions of invention, arrangement, and style.

As I worked my way through these books, I became aware of a very simple test for determining whether or not they had been touched by the leading edge of composition research over the past decade and one half. One had only to look at the names of authors and of people in the acknowledgments. When I saw Ed Corbett, Greg Cowan, Wilma Ebbitt, Robert Gorrell, William Irmscher, Richard Lloyd-Jones, James Kinneavy, Charlton Laird, Richard Larson, Elisabeth McPherson, James Sledd, Ross Winterowd, or Richard Young on the cover or in the acknowledgments, I knew that an attempt had been made, at least, to incorporate or to get an author to incorporate some recent material into his or her text. Sometimes some of the attempts were more successful than others.

What, then, is one to make of this situation? What, for example, can one think of an advertisement in the Spring of 1977 for a "complete NEW guide for your composition courses" which contains narration, description, exposition, argument, the research paper—in short, all of the features of the current-traditional paradigm which had its origin in late nineteenth-century rhetorical theory. New? Certainly not. An advertising huckster's work. Useful in my composition course? Not a chance, since it either ignores or does not know of most of the important work in composition theory and practice since 1960. But there are 27 books much like it on the market now which have already had sales exceeding 100,000 copies. Are English teachers to fault the publishers for keeping them in their comfortable rut? I think not. My experiences with publishers have been very good. They have been enthusiastic about good projects, generous with their books, quick to respond to my requests for information, and, in this project, astonishingly open with their figures. After all, they *serve* English teachers and their students. Publishers do not exist to lose money, however. They have to make it, and in our market system, they make it by selling the consumer what he/she wants.

I have been careless with my pronouns. They do not, for the most part, sell *me* what *I* want. But I am obviously atypical. Who buys these books with outdated theory? English teachers do. English teachers whose knowledge of composition history and theory is not up-to-date. In many cases, it has never existed. Why? Because the professional training of the English teacher has been in literature. And in literary history, theory, and criticism, most English teachers know their stuff. I have known English teachers whose sophistication in literary criticism and theory was equalled only by their ignorance of composition history and theory. This lack of knowledge and hence preparation for teaching composition is the theme of numbers of articles which have appeared in English professional journals within the last twelve months. (See, for example, Richard Lloyd-Jones. "The Silver Lining's Dark Cloud," *Kansas English,* Dec., 1976; George Bramer, "Comp. Vs. Lit—What's the Score?", *College Composition and Communication,* Feb., 1977; and Karl Klaus, "Public Opinion and Professional Belief," *College Composition and Communication,* December, 1976.) But let us be blunt. Until very recently, composition research and teaching have not been considered intellectually respectable by those in power in college English departments in this country. For many, they still aren't.

The war on this kind of snobbery and ignorance is being fought at the University of Southern California, Ross Winterowd's base, the University of Iowa, and Tulsa, the only institutions I know of which offer Ph.D.'s in rhetoric, and by such persons as Jim Kinneavy at Texas, Tommy Boley at Texas El Paso, Gary Tate at Texas Christian, Ed Corbett at Ohio State, Janice Lauer at Detroit, and Richard Young at Michigan. And I am happy to report that my school, Kansas State, is on the verge of implementing an M.A. option with an emphasis in composition and rhetoric.

But isolated programs are not enough. Until courses in composition history and theory (and I include supporting courses in linguistics and psychology) are a requirement in the program of every English major at every level, graduate and undergraduate, English teachers are going to continue to perpetuate the current-traditional paradigm, no matter how outdated it becomes, with no more success than they have had, and they will receive a continuing barrage of complaints about their inability to teach all the Johnnies and Janies to write well. But you will not find me sustaining the status quo. I'm crusading for alternatives to the current-traditional paradigm and will continue to do so until either my vocal chords, or my pen, or both, give out.

DAVID V. HARRINGTON
PHILIP M. KEITH
CHARLES W. KNEUPPER
JANICE A. TRIPP
WILLIAM F. WOODS

A Critical Survey of Resources
for Teaching Rhetorical Invention:
A Review-Essay

One of the more important changes in the teaching of writing during the last decade or so has been a slow shift of attention away from arrangement—the structure and development of discourse—and a growing interest in invention, in the process of discovering the subject matter of discourse. As teachers of writing we have become as much concerned with what students have to say as with their methods of organizing it, and if the many journal articles, or the sections on invention, pre-writing and heuristic devices at the national conventions are any indication, a much greater part of the average composition course is now devoted to showing students how to discover ordering principles in their subject matter, how to locate and define convincing evidence, how to focus on the subject in ways that simplify the reader's task of comprehension.

The theoretical base for teaching invention consists of writings in support of four main theories of invention that Richard Young, in his well-known "Invention: A Topographical Survey" (*Teaching Composition: 10 Bibliographical Essays,* ed. Gary Tate [Fort Worth: Texas Christian University Press, 1976], pp. 1–43), has called Neo-Classical Invention, Pre-Writing, Tagmemic Invention, and the Dramatistic Method. Neo-

From *College English,* 40 (February, 1979) 641–661. Reprinted by permission of the National Council of Teachers of English and David V. Harrington *et al.*

Classical Invention refers to current attempts to teach the classical invention of Aristotle, Cicero, and Quintilian, or to adapt its essential principles for use in the modern classroom. Pre-Writing, which got its start in the 1960s, has close ties with Jerome Bruner's writings on creativity, and is best known for its emphasis on the self-actualization of the writer. Tagmemic invention is rooted in Kenneth Pike's tagmemic linguistic theory, but its true development must be sought in the work of Alton Becker and Richard Young, culminating in a textbook, *Rhetoric: Discovery and Change* (1970). Kenneth Burke's dramatistic method of invention is mainly to be found in his *Grammar of Motives* (1945) and *Rhetoric of Motives* (1950), but it has also been assimilated by a scattering of recent commentaries and textbooks.

Since Young's bibliographic survey appeared in 1976, teachers have had no difficulty finding information about the various methods of rhetorical invention. Yet despite the availability of scholarship, the teacher who wants to stress the importance of invention in a writing course still has the problem of finding a textbook that will support this aim. As Donald Stewart pointed out recently in "Composition Textbooks and the Assault on Tradition" (*College Composition and Communication,* 29 [1978], 171–6), the great majority of current writing texts have little to offer but the stale conventional wisdom of years past—"the current-traditional paradigm." Textbooks that reflect the new work being done in the field are uncommon. To correct that deficiency, we reviewed the available textbooks, as well as some other resources for teaching the four methods of invention, hoping to facilitate teachers' efforts to discover texts useful to them. This review is designed to complement Young's survey, but with emphasis on textbooks and with the addition of a fifth category, Resources in Speech Communication. We particularly call attention to this discussion because, although this field is neglected by most English teachers, it offers much that is helpful for the teaching of writing, and invention in particular.

NEO-CLASSICAL INVENTION

If "Neo-Classical Invention" calls forth the image of dusty tomes not to be found in the bookstore or in the modern classroom, what then do we make of a short, slick paperback like Steward La Casce and Terry Belanger's *The Art of Persuasion: How to Write Effectively About Almost Anything* (New York: Scribner's, 1972), which is not a primer of advertising style, or even the new sophistry, but essentially an Aristotelian rhetoric, scaled down and streamlined to sell as a trade book. This "Art" contains sections on arrangement and style, but the heart of the book is devoted to invention—three readable chapters on the ethical appeal, the appeal to emotion, and the appeal to reason. In short, the main features of classical invention are covered by this pragmatic text, whose cover bears an accolade from none other than Gary Tate.

The Art of Persuasion points to an interest in classical rhetoric which has been developing since the 1950s, when Cleanth Brooks and Robert Penn Warren's *Modern Rhetoric,* 3rd ed. (New York: Harcourt Brace Jovanovich, 1970) and Richard M. Weaver's *A Rhetoric and Composition Handbook,* 2nd ed. (New York: William Morrow, 1974) first appeared, offering a vigorous dose of classical rhetorical theory. After more than twenty years these are still composition classics, despite certain dubious features from a prior tradition like the division of invention into the four modes of discourse (description, narration, exposition, argumentation). As we might expect, Brooks and Warren offer superb units on description and narration, and indeed the whole book has a literary flavor supplied by the many prose passages used as illustrations. Yet the sections on the topics of invention, the three kinds of rhetorical appeals, and logic are solid, even elaborate, shot through with diagrams and intermittent brief exercises. A cluttered text, it still repays close study. In contrast, Weaver makes little effort to capture the reader with sub-headings and exercises, but thanks to his clarity and control of the subject, the units on exposition (definition, analysis) and argumentation (the topics, logic) are among the best discussions available. Weaver does not treat the appeal to emotion or the ethical appeal, perhaps because of his central concern with logical analysis.

The renaissance of classical rhetoric was not fairly begun, however, until 1965, when Edward P. J. Corbett's *Classical Rhetoric for the Modern Student,* 2nd ed. (New York: Oxford, 1971) made its first appearance. Corbett displays classical invention in full dress, taking pains to show how formulating a thesis leads to a consideration of the three modes of appeal (logical, pathetic, ethical), which in turn condition one's use of the various topics of intention. But fortunately, the book retains its practical emphasis. After opening with sample analyses of two passages (one ancient, one modern), Corbett also includes several full-length readings for each major section of the book (invention, arrangement, style), and again provides sample analyses as guides. The resulting text, drawing upon the full range of classical theory and free of accretions like the four modes of discourse, has been called the most uncompromising of the classical revivals. For capable students, and especially for writing classes beyond the sophomore level, this clearly written book is among the few appropriate choices; as a reference text, it is simply without peer.

Reacting, perhaps, to Corbett's attempt at combining classical theory and modern application, subsequent authors have produced books that are essentially (1) discussions of classical rhetorical theory, (2) adaptations of classical rhetoric for the purpose of teaching writing, or (3) composition texts in which features of classical rhetoric are assimilated but still recognizable. Representative of the first group is Richard E. Hughes and P. Albert Duhamel's *Principles of Rhetoric* (Englewood Cliffs, N.J.: Prentice-Hall, 1966). This text first appeared in 1962 as *Rhetoric: Principles and Usage,* but the combination of rhetorical theory and composition handbook proved unwieldy, and the 1966 version was pared down to eleven compact chapters on invention, arrangement, and style. As in Weaver's text, we find the four modes of discourse; yet unlike Weaver, the authors include few illustrative passages, no exercises, and fewer readings than any book previously described. Nonetheless, the section on invention is interesting and contains original features such as the treatment of propositions as "presentations of the writer's judgment." John Mackin's *Classical Rhetoric for Modern Discourse* (New York: Free Press, 1969) is that rare entity, a textbook with a thesis—an argument for the utility of Socratic, as opposed to Aristotelian, rhetoric. Some teachers do not find this a practical book, perhaps because the longer illustrative passages are drawn from speeches in the plays of Shakespeare, and it is currently out of print. The long chapter on Invention ("Logos") is worth reading, though, because it leads one through the process of defining an idea, forming a hypothesis about it, and finally exploring it through use of the topics.

When Thomas W. Benson and Michael H. Prosser's *Readings in Classical Rhetoric* (Bloomington: Indiana University Press, 1972) came out, it was hailed as a breakthrough—a selection of readings from the ancient rhetorics that would be useful for teaching specific rhetorical principles. The readings on invention are drawn from Aristotle, Quintilian, Cicero, and Augustine. Occasionally the selections overlap in their coverage, but herein lies a virtue: a comparison of analogous passages brings out significant variations in emphasis and intent, a reminder that classical invention was not a doctrine but a living theory.

A second category of books are those that adapt principles of classical rhetoric for the teaching of writing. One of the newest of these is Corbett's *The Little Rhetoric* (New York: Wiley, 1977), not a short version of *Classical Rhetoric for the Modern Student,* but a kind of annotated index to rhetorical devices, both classical and modern. Along with the inventional topics, for instance, we find brief explanations of brainstorming, meditation, the journalistic formula, Burke's "Pentad," and problem solving. This book provides a helpful overview of the principles of invention, even though one desires more indication of how these devices work in practice.

A striking adaptation of classical invention is Jacqueline Berke's *Twenty Questions for the Writer: A Rhetoric with Readings* (New York: Harcourt Brace Jovanovich, 1976). Richard Larson once suggested that the topics could be "revitalized" by putting them as direct questions (see "Discovery Through Questioning: A Plan for Teaching Rhetorical Invention," *College English*, 30 [1968], 126–34), and indeed, here are twenty chapters, each demonstrating the use of one key question, e.g., "What is the essential function of X?" This book succeeds admirably in showing how topical questions can be used to analyze subject matter. It is less effective in suggesting how one *combines* such questions to explore an issue or develop an argument about it; each question seems rather to imply a separate kind of essay. Another text responding to Larson's article is W. Ross Winterowd's *The Contemporary Writer: A Practical Rhetoric* (New York: Harcourt Brace Jovanovich, 1975), which reprints Larson's entire list of questions but still does not show how these questions might be applied.

A more sustained attempt to adapt rhetoric for the teaching of writing is Maxine Hairston's *A Contemporary Rhetoric* (Boston: Houghton Mifflin, 1974), which devotes four chapters to Invention. Wisely, Hairston presents the topic ("Modes of Argument") as resources for constructing arguments, rather than as paradigms for organizing essays, and this important principle is reinforced by workable exercises at the chapter's end. In short, Hairston has achieved that difficult synthesis, a solid exposition of rhetorical principles carefully adapted to the needs of freshman English.

The third, and by far the largest, category of newer texts are those in which principles of invention (usually the topics and inductive and deductive logic) have been transmuted into devices for paragraph and essay development. A good example is A. M. Tibbetts and Charlene Tibbetts' *Strategies of Rhetoric*, revised ed. (Glenview, Ill.: Scott, Foresman, 1974). The chapter on the topics ("Developing Themes: Seven Strategies") offers various practical ideas for writing classification themes, etc., but there are few suggestions on how these "strategies" can work together as a system. Harry H. Crosby and George F. Estey's *Just Rhetoric* (New York: Harper and Row, 1968) teems with cartoons, graphics, and quotes from modish contemporary authors, yet even here, invention survives, lurking in a chapter on "Development" which contains units on the ladder of abstraction, the paragraph, the sentence, facts, and finally, "methods of development" (the topics). Enno Klammer's *Paragraph Sense: A Basic Rhetoric* (New York: Harcourt Brace Jovanovich, 1978) shows how the topics and some principles of logic can be used to construct outlines for writing paragraphs and themes. Klammer does not discuss rhetorical invention as such, but it is heartening to see the essential ideas at work in this clear, incisive remedial writing text.

A final resource for teaching classical invention is a rhetoric reader like Randall E. Decker's well-known *Patterns of Exposition 6*, 6th ed. (Boston: Little, Brown, 1978), which contains essays reflecting the standard topics of invention. Gerald Levin's *Short Essays: Models for Composition* (New York: Harcourt Brace Jovanovich, 1977) adds sections on Argument and Persuasion, and the essays are indeed short, inviting close analysis. Forrest D. Burt and E. Cleve Want's *Invention and Design: A Rhetoric Reader*, 2nd ed. (New York: Random House, 1978) represents a better variety of inventional devices, and some attempt is made to show the flexibility of certain topics (e.g., simple, extended, and complex comparison/contrast). "Argument" is a pleasant surprise, with sections on the appeals to reason and emotion. These features, along with the substantial discussions introducing each topic, make this a good supplementary text for teaching rhetorical invention.

THE PRE-WRITING SCHOOL

The word "pre-writing" could be thought of as a synonym for invention. But in its history and influence, pre-writing more commonly indicates a special approach to the teaching of rhetorical invention observable in a number of successful textbooks published in the late 1960s and early 1970s. D. Gordon Rohman of Michigan State University can properly be credited with popularizing the term and originating several of its most distinctive features, though Rohman himself never wrote a textbook. The genesis of the pre-writing movement appears in a report by Rohman and Albert O. Wlecke, *Pre-Writing: The Construction and Application of Models for Concept Formation in Writing* (East Lansing: Michigan State University, U.S. Office of Education Cooperative Research Project No. 2174, 1964). In briefer form, these ideas reappear in "Pre-Writing: The Stage of Discovery in the Writing Process," *CCC*, 16 (1965), 106–112. At a time when few textbooks paid attention to invention, Rohman urged primary emphasis on the process of finding ideas in teaching composition. He also advocated three major techniques for generating ideas—keeping a journal, practicing meditation, and using analogy—techniques which frequently reappear in textbooks making use of the term pre-writing. But a more significant principle that dominates the textbooks growing out of this movement is a statement of purpose in teaching composition: the teacher's goal is the self-actualization of the writer, to make the student more aware of the power of creative discovery within her or him. Subsequent authors of pre-writing texts recommend other discovery techniques such as brainstorming, free-association, and free-writing, but all focus primarily on the self-realization of the student or on the writer's exploring his or her own humanity. They are student-centered texts.

The earliest text in this tradition was written by another Michigan State professor, Clinton S. Burhans. *The Would-Be Writer,* now in its third edition (Lexington, Mass.: Xerox College Publishing, 1971), is one of the few attempts to tie pre-writing in with the total writing process. Burhans recommends postponing training in "grammar, mechanics, logic, rhetoric, and exposition," as do all the authors of textbooks referred to here, until the student has learned to discover aspects of individual experience and knowledge worth writing about. Burhans' pre-writing techniques are keeping a journal, free-association, the categorical list, and the existential sentence. There are sections on "Writing" and "Re-Writing" and a collection of essays. Burhans writes well, but his coverage of all stages is sketchy.

Ray Kytle's *Prewriting: Strategies for Exploration and Discovery* (New York: Random House, 1972) is even thinner, but cheaper. Kytle recommends analysis, analogy, brainstorming, and systematic inquiry as methods of pre-writing. Each of these methods needs much fuller development to be instructive. Michael Paull and Jack Kligerman have also written a small text entitled *Invention: A Course in Pre-Writing and Composition* (Cambridge, Mass.: Winthrop, 1973). Their methods include the journal, happenings, meditation, and non-representational forms. Like Kytle's book, this one gives more space to illustrations, visual as well as verbal, than to advice or instructions on writing; and the instruction seems limited primarily to helping writers discover "the uniqueness of their own perceptions."

Probably the best pre-writing textbook is Donald C. Stewart's *The Authentic Voice: A Pre-Writing Approach to Student Writing* (Dubuque, Iowa: William C. Brown, 1972), which embodies all the key principles suggested so far. Stewart's text is carefully written and fully developed, placing the teaching emphasis on the process of writing, rather than on analysis of the product. Stewart encourages self-discovery and recommends such now familiar techniques as the journal, meditation, analogy, and the existential sentence.

Two lively and entertaining textbooks by Ken Macrorie, *Telling Writing,* 2nd ed. (Rochelle Park, N.J.: Hayden, 1976), and *Writing to be Read,* 2nd ed. (Rochelle Park, N.J.: Hayden, 1976), relate to pre-writing in that Macrorie wants students to write about themselves in original and creative language. Macrorie's major efforts are to help students rid themselves of conventional, predictable, insincere language ("Engfish"), and to express themselves directly and honestly. He gives us abundant quotations from student writings to show desirable results. He also advocates "free-writing," a writing exercise in which the student regularly writes rapidly for a short period of time knowing that what he or she has written will be neither corrected nor criticized.

The emphasis by Macrorie on genuineness and on free-writing shows itself also in Peter Elbow's *Writing Without Teachers* (New York: Oxford, 1973). Elbow develops the free-writing method more fully and persuasively, and like many of the authors working in this tradition, explains metaphorically, with reference to "growing" and "cooking," how a person generates new ideas or improves upon or corrects old ones while in the very process of writing. Elbow and Macrorie share another trait in denigrating traditional rhetorical approaches, especially authoritarian teaching.

Two very different textbooks, which nonetheless have principles in common with other books in the pre-writing school, are *Word, Self, Reality: The Rhetoric of Imagination* by James E. Miller, Jr. (New York: Dodd, Mead, 1972), and *Composing: Writing as a Self-Creating Process* by William E. Coles, Jr. (Rochelle Park, N.J.: Hayden, 1974). Miller's purpose is to spin the reader "out of his own orbit into other orbits—intellectual, imaginative, linguistic—for deeper exploration and personal discovery." Throughout his text he intersperses quotations from interesting people—William James, Norman O. Brown, Susanne K. Langer, T. S. Eliot—to inspire students to write more creatively about their own lives and values. The book depends heavily upon free association. Coles' book, however, seems based upon a more deeply pondered study of what a person tries to do when writing. The emphasis, as in the other books, is on the individual finding her own voice, his own values; and there is, if anything, an overemphasis on avoiding clearly defined goals in a writing assignment. But Coles adds another dimension in urging students to discover themselves as language-using individuals. The emphasis is on writing about teaching and learning, but really on writing about writing. Writers should become as conscious as possible of what they do when writing. Thus the course in writing will not become a course on something other than writing. This could be a difficult text to work with successfully, but Coles' ideas about writing deserve serious study.

The various books cited above share certain strengths in common. They concern themselves with intention, with the need to develop fluency in expression, with creative self-expression, with greater consciousness of the individual voice and personal values, with the process of writing, and with mysterious gains in substance and style that grow out of the very act of writing. These are positive values, substantial enough to justify continuation, revision, and further development of these texts.

But, if there are revised editions of these books, certain needs for an ideal textbook should be taken into account. The pre-writing books profit from, indeed capitalize upon, the mood of individualism, rebellion against authority, disdain for conventions and standards of the late 1960s and early 1970s. They need rewriting to get rid of what are now painful clichés, an outmoded or at least exaggerated state of mind. More important, however, the emphasis on pre-writing needs redefining to go beyond just the personal essay to tie in with more traditional goals of expository of persuasive writing. In making that transfer, the authors need to relate pre-writing techniques to other inventive techniques more suitable for presentation of subject matter: the selection and rejection of data, evaluation and effective presentation of evidence, consideration of alternative hypotheses, and scrupulous testing or verification of conclusions.

TAGMEMIC INVENTION AND LINGUISTIC THEORY

The "linguistic revolution" has been accompanied by a quieter reformation in the ranks of the trivium—a revival of the study of invention in compositional rhetoric, a movement which has often drawn major theoretical support from linguistics itself. The following discussion traces the influence of linguistics in the treatment of invention in a handful of texts. The review is too brief to be comprehensive, but it does attempt to survey major trends through a selection of representative texts.

Frank Flowers' *Practical Linguistics for Composition* (Indianapolis, Ind.: Odyssey Press, 1968) contains no explicit mention of invention, but Flowers' system of "practical linguistics" rests on the assumption that "generative" operations in linguistic theory are relevant to the teaching of composition—"not in the narrow sense of some modern grammarians," he writes, "but in the larger sense of productivity, or creativity" (p. 5). In particular, he believes that the transformation principle of the new grammar can be a fruitful source for a new—and needed—instructional component in a writing class: the "logical extension of thought" through recognition of the "extensional possibilities" in a sentence. To this end, Flowers wishes to move "beyond grammar"—beyond the sentence, that is, to address thinking and connected discourse. He notes that certain categories of meaning, such as agent, action, and place, recur in sentences; these abstractions, he believes, are the "parts of thought," and the grammatical unit they comprise is a "kernel idea." He catalogues and discusses purely descriptive patterns of arrangement such as comparison/contrast and definition as "patterns of thought." With a classification of the "parts and patterns of thought" in hand, a student, Flowers believes, is provided the means of generating content for writing—given that he or she can discover evidence of and potential for "linguistic" transformations in a "sentence thought." For, despite his intent to move beyond the limits of traditional language study, Flowers' focus remains on the sentence. Writers, in Flowers' view, apparently analyze sentences, not problems or issues or topics. Flowers does indeed take up discourse structures: the student is told that discourse is simply a "higher linguistic level" than the sentence, and that understanding is "a level of linguistic classification higher than the grammatical" (p. 41). He treats writing, in short, as a "practical" branch of linguistics, and invention as an exercise in recognizing past and potential transformations in a sentence. Flowers perhaps gets "beyond" grammar in the sense of dipping into other branches of linguistics. But he never gets beyond language.

Joseph M. Williams' 1970 text, *The New English: Structure/Form/ Style* (New York: The Free Press), asserts a close relationship between language study and rhetoric even in its format; the text begins with a transformational grammar, ends with a rhetoric, and contains an interplay between the two in each. Williams treats invention within the familiar rhetorical trivium, and his versions of audience and intention are likewise traditional. For that portion of invention concerned with "discovering the 'structure' of a subject," however, he presents the student with a complex of eight categories in a matrix format—categories which, along with their use as means of systematic discovery, are derived from tagmemic linguistics, Kenneth Pike's theory of language, and language behavior.

The terms of the Williams heuristic (modified from the original, technical tagmemic terminology) are familiar: state and process, internal and external, part and kind and phase. The greater part of Williams' discussion of invention, however, goes to explaining their meaning in this context. For they are being used operationally, as terms descriptive of the mind's activity. A student must learn to associate terms like "internal" and "external" with something she does, and as a portion of the stance she can assume in regard to a subject. She learns to view linguistic product as structurally determined by mental process. This brief catalogue of mental processes or operations is conflated in the matrix and arranged so that the student may view them as alternatives, as the grounds for choice. The assumptions underlying the categories are inverted and, as series of questions accompany individual boxes of the matrix, become a means of eliciting information. Only if a student considers his subject from all eight points of view specified by the heuristic, Williams writes, will he raise to the level of consciousness the "best ideas and insights" he has. The heuristic procedure is, then, an elaborate retrieval system, and taps the memory as a kind of data bank which will only yield its riches if it is moved to do so in this way. At the same time, the heuristic is a means of encouraging a "fresh" analysis of experience; a writer may, by means of it, be able to break out of the "conventional categories" of language to think of something original. It is a means of encouraging creativity.

Williams' treatment of invention is congenial with the system known as "tagmemic invention," a system developed by Pike himself along with Richard Young and Alton Becker. *Rhetoric: Discovery and Change* (New York: Harcourt, Brace and World, 1970), however, devotes ten chapters (more than half the text) to invention in the most highly developed and complete version available in a compositional rhetoric. Several fundamentals of tagmemic linguistics are presented discursively as "maxims," such as "People conceive of the world in terms of repeatable units" (p. 26). The material presented in some of the maxims provides students with a set of assumptions about language behavior which they will eventually make use of in a new format: the tagmemic matrix devised by Young, Becker, and Pike. But the maxims also implicitly define the scope and purpose of rhetoric, and thus invention, in the tagmemic view. There is no need, for example, to consider the means by which change can be achieved (Maxim 5: "Change between units can occur only over a bridge of shared features") unless rhetoric includes community and its problems among its concerns (p. 172).

Tagmemic invention also presents students with a generalized description of their typical behavior in situations calling for the exercise of inventional skills: this sequence of four roughly isolable stages (preparation, incubation, illumination, and verification) is called the "process of inquiry." Invention as a process has, of course, been implicit in the other systems of invention we have discussed. But it has received no emphasis. It has played no functional role. In *Rhetoric: Discovery and Change,* the whole system for invention is directed to invention as a process. Tagmemic invention offers the student three heuristics addressed to those stages in the process of inquiry which are susceptible to direct manipulation for improvement. Each heuristic is designed to make a student's effort in a particular task deliberate and strategic rather than random. It introduces system to activity which would otherwise be "haphazard." The three strategies—a heuristic for problem statement, the tagmemic matrix for exploration of a subject, and informal tests for the validity of a thesis—could all be said to have their heuristic value only as a student can understand and use them within the framework of the process of inquiry. Thus from this perspective, students can deliberately and methodically improve inventional skills because they can see the means of improvement—the heuristic strategies—as variations on what they already do.

Both the tagmemic maxims—the "theoretical core" of the rhetoric—and invention treated as process thus ground tagmemic invention in personal experience. Where the fundamental unit of Flowers' system, for instance, is the sentence, the fundamental unit of Young, Becker, and Pike treatment of invention is, to borrow their terminology, a "unit of experience."

The tagmemic heuristic for subject exploration is the only heuristic explicitly drawn from linguistic theory. It combines a cluster of maxims already discussed in the text—in particular, maxims which postulate a series of "perspectives and unit characteristics": particle, wave, and field (levels of focus, or alternate perspectives); and contrast, variation, and distribution ("characteristics of a unit that must be known if it is to be understood" [p. 128]). In use as a set of instructions for investigating a subject, these categories are displayed in a nine-cell matrix, with each cell supplemented by questions specifying the operational meaning of the term—what questions a student needs to ask to investigate the subject from a given perspective. Young, Becker, and Pike believe that the "perspectives in the chart supplement one another," so that exploration of a subject from the full range of these perspectives "gives us some assurance that we are thinking well, that we have not overlooked important data" (p. 130). By using the matrix as a guide to inquiry, sutdents will discover what they do and do not know about a subject. And, viewed as a phase in the process of inquiry, the exploration of a subject "prepares the mind" to discover a thesis. The terms of the matrix, drawn directly from tagmemic principles, stand at some distance from the human thought processes they are being used to designate in the discovery procedure. They retain their hold on the fields from which they are derived, as vocabulary appropriate to their "universe of discourse." Nonspecialists, for example, do not conceive of perspectives as particle, wave, and field; physicists do. The Young, Becker, and Pike tagmemic matrix thus retains the sense of an interdisciplinary hybrid while functioning as a paradigm for mental experience—a difficulty not present, say, in Williams' matrix, although the terms Williams uses, of course, also need to be explained in light of their special functioning.

Frank D'Angelo's *Process and Thought in Composition* (Cambridge, Mass.: Winthrop, 1977) does not borrow from linguistics. D'Angelo's own "conceptual theory of rhetoric" stands as the text's theoretical base. Like the authors previously discussed, however, D'Angelo is interested in exploiting the heuristic potential in the relationship between discourse theory and thought processes, so his text is compatible with the range of texts we are surveying. D'Angelo tells the student that "patterns [of arrangement] are not simply static conventional forms. They represent, rather, *dynamic organizational processes*" (p. 73). And on this assumption—that thought processes are operational equivalents of discourse patterns—D'Angelo bases his treatment of invention. In a sense, he collapses what has traditionally been treated separately as invention and arrangement by appropriating the discourse structures of arrangement as heuristic tools. The student is to use these patterns as means of exploring ideas systematically since "Compositional categories such as analysis, classification, and comparison and contrast, besides being principles of thought, are categories that suggest questions that can be used in exploring ideas for writing" (p. 31).

So with D'Angelo's treatment of invention, as with Flowers', we again have a focus on structure, a "form consciousness" which concentrates on what one might call the "relics" of choice—relics because, in contrast with the categories of the tagmemic matrices, or even Flowers' semantic categories, the patterns to which D'Angelo draws a student's attention are abstracted from already-written connected discourse. They are relevant to choice, but they represent the result or aftermath of choice, not the terms of the choice itself. The tagmemic matrix can be justly said to guide systematic inquiry because it surveys the range of perspectives we can assume on a subject; it is in this sense a model of the mind. A writer explores systematically when looking into a subject methodically from all angles. Discourse structures, however, cannot be delimited in this way, and systematic exploration as guided by some comprehensive set of them is impossible. Discourse patterns, like sentences, go on *ad infinitum*.

It may well be true that, as D'Angelo asserts, patterns of arrangement are the linguistic correlates of thought processes. But it does not follow of a certainty that the two are reversible or reciprocal in some way. Such a theory of invention implies that one can discover material for a composition by more or less filling in the blanks of an empty structure, what we might call a "coloring-book" technique for generating ideas. Finding an argument, however—and finding something about which to argue in the first place—pertains to a different world than that of formal structures. It pertains to *our* world, the one in which we live and perceive and act, rather than the subterranean, purely theorized world of language processes. It involves the intuition of a problem or an aspect of experience to be investigated, the forming of a thesis about this, substages of these stages, and so on. It involves, in short, a process that culminates rather than begins in the discovery of appropriate structure. D'Angelo's use of discourse structures as strategies for invention suggests that his process can be inverted or ignored.

Some of our texts have placed invention in a context larger than language. They have assimilated aspects of linguistics to the study of invention while retaining, even significantly enriching, a rhetorical frame for the teaching of writing. Others have suggested that the constructs of linguistics or discourse theory define the limits of the art, that the study and manipulation of discourse is sufficient to guide and stimulate invention. If composition is viewed as a process or activity, however—as a complex of things we experience and do, including but not limited to verbal behavior—composition texts which begin and end and never move their treatments of invention beyond considerations of language will be found inadequate to the complexity of the task. For if theory of language is taught for its own sake, if the horizon of the composition class shrinks to theoretical descriptions of language and mind, then purpose in verbal activity vanishes and so does rhetoric.

THE DRAMATISTIC METHODS: KENNETH BURKE AND COMPOSITION MATERIALS

The rhetorician and dialectician Kenneth Burke has been recognized for some time as having interesting and important things to say related to composition pedagogy. But his writings are addressed to a diffusion of contexts and concerns, and his topics of reference are so wide-ranging that his influence to date has been largely piecemeal, operating through the borrowings of isolated concepts rather than through the synthetic body of knowledge and insight he has developed in his well over half-century in harness. Furthermore, Burke's works themselves are not really teachable to college freshmen, but require extensive and imaginative translation or transformation to become effective pedagogical models. Yet Burke's ideas are a richly suggestive source for penetrating insights into the nature and processes of discourse beyond strictly formal and grammatical levels—an area where present pedagogical methods seem particularly thin. In short, while one should not expect to substitute *A Grammar of Motives* for *The Borzoi Reader*, Burke will increasingly carry weight in professional courses for teachers of composition and rhetoric.

In the body of texts and pedagogical materials that use or shadow Burke, we can distinguish two basic approaches, one sophistic and one dialectic. The two approaches are most clearly delineated in two recent companion articles in *Freshman English News*, John Warnock's "New Rhetoric and the Grammar of Pedagogy," (Fall, 1976), and Ann Berthoff's critique of that article, "Towards a Pedagogy of Knowing," (Spring, 1978). For Warnock, composition pedagogy should consist of a set of discrete concepts that are "generalizable potencies applicable regardless of the conceptual framework in which they are applied." The student learns topics, questions, models and so forth, which she can then apply to other problems. Warnock uses Burke's pentad—the heuristic terms: Act, Scene, Agent, Agency, and Purpose—to structure his essay and provide a global perspective on the problem of what we should teach in composition courses; he specifically cites Burke as a thinker who is focusing on such potencies rather than on ideologies. Berthoff responds that it is a fiction to assume that such potencies are generalizable in this way; rather, they are simply part of a dialectic that allows a writer to broaden and transform his perspective. She accuses Warnock of thinking that any terms for order can be neutral, and she cites Burke on her side to the effect that any set of terms will embody a trained incapacity to see broadly enough.

For Burke, the pentad is simply an elaborate dialectical device, and he has gone on public record at a recent MLA conference as being critical of uses of the pentad as an isolated inventional model rather than as an instrument for analyzing and transforming discourse in order to avoid the embarrassments of narrow perspectives. However, the sophist can argue, as Professor Charles Kneupper did at a recent CCC conference seminar, that Burke's perspective as a literary critic and discourse analyst has become a trained incapacity for seeing the value and importance of the pentad as a broadly systematic device for the invention of arguments.

The concepts from Burke that are sophistically isolated in texts and other pedagogical materials are his notion of identification as the ground of persuasion, his notion of form or arrangement as involving the creation and satisfaction of reader expectations, and, of course, the inventional use of the pentad to generate ideas. The only language-arts text making extensive use of Burke focuses on identification—Byker and Anderson's speech text, *Communication as Identification* (New York: Harper and Row, 1975). In the third edition of Brooks and Warren's *Modern Rhetoric* (New York: Harcourt, Brace and World, 1970), the authors added a new chapter on persuasion (as distinct from argumentation) grounded in Burkean analyses of sublogical appeals through identification.

The other conceptions concerning form and the pentad are most broadly developed in pedagogical terms by Ross Winterowd in his two writing texts, *Rhetoric and Writing* (Boston: Allyn and Bacon, 1965) and *The Contemporary Writer* (New York: Harcourt Brace Jovanovich, 1975), and in his theoretical study, *Rhetoric: a Synthesis* (New York: Holt, Rinehart and Winston, 1968). Winterowd's *Rhetoric and Writing*, which seems to be intended for advanced rhetoric and composition classes, draws widely on Burke, and balances sophistic methodology with dialectical injunctions against sacrificing the ends of truth to the means of persuasion. In *Rhetoric: a Synthesis*, Winterowd's discussions of form and metaphor also take him into issues of dialectics, but in *The Contemporary Writer,* such conceptually complex matters are ignored in order to provide reduced models for uninitiated students to manipulate. In so shifting his ground, Winterowd moves more strictly into the sophistic camp. William Irmscher has used Burke's pentad as the basis for his discussion of prewriting in *The Holt Guide to English,* 2nd ed. (New York: Holt, Rinehart and Winston, 1976). Like Winterowd's *The Contemporary Writer,* Irmscher's text presents a scaled-down version of the pentad as an interpretive device. The sources of Burke's concepts of identification, form, and invention (via the pentad) are his first critical book, *Counterstatement* (reissued, Berkeley: University of California Press, 1968), and the Introduction to *A Grammar of Motives* (reissued, Berkeley: University of California Press, 1969).

The materials dealing with the dialectical version of Burke are the above mentioned article by Ann Berthoff and her recent textbook, *Forming, Thinking, Writing: the Composing Imagination* (Rochelle Park, N.J.: Hayden, 1978), and Philip Keith's "Burke for the Composition Class," *CCC,* 28 (1977) 348–51. Berthoff does not produce models from Burke for students to use, but she endorses his idea of writing as a process of dialectical transformation in language. Her dialectical heuristic model, *HDWDWW* (How Did, Who Did, Where, When), is closer to Aristotle's four causes than to Burke's pentad since she leaves out the scenic perspective (for reasons worth speculating about). Keith's essay offers a collection of Burkean terms as a teacher's instrument to help lead students dialictically through re-seeings and revisions of their papers. Finally, two sets of writing assignments that are dialectically structured and thus related to Burkean perspectives, if not directly influenced by Burke, are Walker Gibson's *Seeing and Writing* (New York: David McKay, 1973) and William E. Coles, Jr., *Composing* (Rochelle Park, N.J.: Hayden, 1974).

Of Burke's own writings, those which have special relevance for the teaching of invention are: *Permanence and Change* (reissued, New York: Bobbs-Merrill, 1965), in particular the section on interpretation; *A Grammar of Motives,* particularly the sections on "Ways of Placement" and "Dialectic in General"; and *Language as Symbolic Action* (Berkeley: University of California Press, 1968). The student of composition pedagogy would also find it useful to look at some of Burke's fairly recent brief attempts to summarize and clarify his views in "Linguistic Approaches to Problems of Education," *Modern Philosophies of Education,* Nelson B. Henry, ed. (Chicago: University of Chicago Press, 1955), pp. 259–303, and "Dramatism," *International Encyclopedia of the Social Sciences* (New York: Macmillan and Free Press, 1968), vol. 7, 445–52.

Burke is a crucial thinker for composition pedagogy because his double focus on rhetoric and dialectic offers methods for getting beyond our present almost obsessive concern with style and surface in most writing courses and programs. Through Burkean concepts and constructs, composition methods can give more emphasis to developing powers of conceptual manipulation and nimbleness, and can come into close methodological sympathy both with the tradition of classical rhetoric and with the dialectically oriented ways of thinking about writing that are now common in Europe and other parts of the world.

RESOURCES IN SPEECH COMMUNICATION

Among the potential resources containing theory and pedagogy with direct applications for the teaching of composition is a substantial portion of literature in Speech Communication. Rhetorical theory can be directly applied to both oral and written composition with only minor modifications to adjust for differences attributable to change of media. At least four areas of Speech Communication should be of special interest to the composition instructor: public speaking, argumentation and debate, persuasion, and rhetorical theory and criticism. Each of these areas has produced a literature too voluminous to be comprehensively reviewed. We will try only to identify the present concerns and highlight some of the outstanding texts in each of these areas. ·

Public speaking. Speech communication pedagogy and fundamentals of public speaking are best characterized as dominated by the classical rhetorical tradition. Most texts explicitly treat the canons of invention, arrangement, style, and delivery. The treatment of invention tends to be predominantly neo-Aristotelian with emphasis on argument, rational persuasion, ethos-pathos-logos, and the types of inartistic proofs (facts, statistics, testimony, law, maxims). Comparatively little or no treatment of artistic proofs or heuristic procedures will be found in most public speaking texts.

Typical examples of this dominant genre of public speaking texts are: John F. Wilson and Carroll C. Arnold, *Public Speaking as a Liberal Art* (Boston: Allyn and Bacon, 1974); Roderick P. Hart, Gustav W. Friedrick, and William D. Brooks, *Public Communication* (New York: Harper and Row, 1975); and Eugene E. White, *Practical Public Speaking* (New York: Macmillan, 1978). A slightly more implicit treatment of the canons is apparent in texts such as: Otis M. Walter and Robert L. Scott, *Thinking and Speaking* (New York: Macmillan, 1973); and Walter's *Speaking Intelligently* (New York: Macmillan, 1976). Some significant, though partial, deviations are present in texts such as Alan H. Monroe, *Principles and Types of Speech* (New York: Scott, Foresman, 1949). Although generally consistent with the classical rhetorical tradition, Monroe's motivated sequence provides a new and useful organizational procedure for constructing persuasive messages. Texts such as James McCrosky, *An Introduction to Rhetorical Communication* (Englewood Cliffs, N.J.: Prentice-Hall, 1972) and Bert E. Bradley, *Fundamentals of Speech Communication* (Dubuque, Iowa: William C. Brown, 1974) represent attempts to synthesize and integrate traditional theory with the growing body of experimental research findings. Finally, Donald Byker and Loren J. Anderson, *Communication as Identification* (New York: Harper and Row, 1973), provide a first attempt at applying Burkean concepts to speech communication pedagogy.

Argumentation and debate. Although most argumentation texts give passing attention to matters of organization, style, and delivery, they are predominantly concerned with rhetorical invention. The emphasis is clearly on extrinsic sources of evidence, logical prerequisites for a *prima facie* case, and policy argument. Methods of artistic invention, if treated, will usually be variants of the *topoi,* and various case-types (need, advantage, criteria, or comparative) are used as organizational heuristics. Typical examples of the traditional argumentation text include: James H. Mc-Burney, James M. O'Neill, and Glen E. Mills, *Argumentation and Debate* (New York: Macmillan, 1961); Wayne N. Thompson, *Modern Argumentation and Debate* (New York: Harper and Row, 1971); Austin J. Freeley, *Argumentation and Debate: Rational Decision Making* (Belmont, Calif.: Wadsworth, 1976); and Douglas Ehninger and Wayne Brockriede, *Decision by Debate* (New York: Harper and Row, 1978).

A number of recent texts have made significant contributions to argumentation theory. Stephen Toulmin, *The Uses of Argument* (Cambridge: University Press, 1964) develops a diagramatic model of practical argument. Although technically a philosophy text, Toulmin's model has been widely used in speech communication as a substitute for syllogistic logic. Richard R. Newman and Dale R. Newman, *Evidence* (New York: Houghton Mifflin, 1969) is a thorough examination of the sources and methods of evaluating extrinsic evidence. Textbooks incorporating other contemporary developments include Bernard L. Brock, James W. Chesbro, John F. Cragan, and James F. Klump, *Public Policy Decision Making: Systems Analysis and Comparative Advantages Debate* (New York: Harper and Row, 1973), which develops the implications of general systems theory to policy analysis; and Richard D. Rieke and Malcolm O. Sillars, *Argu-*

mentation and the Decision Making Process (New York: John Wiley, 1975), which develops an untypically strong sense of the role of audience in argument and provides an excellent treatment of value systems.

Persuasion. Textbooks in persuasion can be loosely divided into two camps. One camp accounts for persuasive effects and primarily reflects empirical research findings. Such texts include Carl I. Hovland, Irving L. Janis, and Harold A. Kelley, *Communication and Persuasion* (New Haven: Yale University Press, 1953), and Philip Zimbardo and Ebbe B. Ebbesen, *Influencing Attitudes and Changing Behavior* (Reading, Mass.: Addison-Wesley, 1969). These texts present attitude theory and research with implications for the production of discourse, but they are not oriented directly to consider the construction of oral or written messages. Such persuasion texts come primarily from social psychology research. The second camp covers both attitude theory and research and a practical consideration of methods of message construction and presentation. Texts of this style include Winston L. Brembeck and Wilbur Samuel Howell, *Persuasion: A Means of Social Control* (Englewood Cliffs, N.J.: Prentice-Hall, 1952); Kenneth E. Anderson, *Persuasion: Theory and Practice* (Boston: Allyn and Bacon, 1971); Erwin P. Bettinghaus, *Persuasive Communication* (New York: Holt, Rinehart, and Winston, 1973); and Herbert W. Simons, *Persuasion: Understanding, Practice and Analysis* (Reading, Mass.: Addison-Wesley, 1976). A slight variation is Charles U. Larson, *Persuasion: Reception and Responsibility* (New York: Holt, Rinehart and Winston, 1973), which emphasizes the receiver role in persuasion and in part attempts to produce critical consumers. The persuasion literature is especially noteworthy for its blend of scientific and traditional theories and strong consideration of audience.

Rhetorical theory and criticism. Rhetorical theory guides rhetorical criticism. When the composition instructor criticizes an essay on matters other than spelling, grammar, and punctuation, that criticism is necessarily rhetorical. The neo-Aristotelian approach dominated speech criticism until the early 1960s. This critical approach is reflected in texts such as Marie Hochmuth Nichols, *Rhetoric and Criticism* (Baton Rouge: Louisiana State University Press, 1963); Anthony Hilbruner, *Critical Dimensions: The Art of Public Address Criticism* (New York: Random House, 1966); Lester Thonssen, A. Craig Baiard, and Waldo W. Braden, *Speech Criticism* (New York: The Ronald Press, 1970); and Carroll C. Arnold, *Criticism of Oral Rhetoric* (Columbus, Ohio: Charles E. Merrill, 1974). Of these dominantly neo-Aristotelian texts, Arnold is distinctive for his incorporation of the concept of the rhetorical situation and discussion of implied content. Nichols also provides an introductory treatment of Burke and Richards, but is not hostile toward the classical tradition.

Attacks on neo-Aristotelian theory and criticism and attempts at new theoretical development characterize such texts as Edwin Black, *Rhetorical Criticism* (New York: Macmillan, 1965), which proposes a "genre" approach to criticism; Karl R. Wallace, *Understanding Discourse* (Baton Rouge: Louisiana State University Press, 1970), which applies developments in speech act analysis from the philosophy of language to rhetorical theory; Karlyn Kohrs Campbell, *Critiques of Contemporary Rhetoric* (Belmont, Calif.: Wadsworth, 1972), which suggests that Aristotelian theory is not appropriate for some modern discourse and encourages dramatistic and genre approaches; and Robert L. Scott and Bernard L. Brock, eds., *Methods of Rhetorical Criticism: A 20th-Century Perspective* (New York: Harper and Row, 1972), which surveys traditional, experiential, and new critical approaches while editorially encouraging a pluralistic approach to rhetorical criticism.

ADDITIONAL READINGS

RICHARD YOUNG, "Invention: A Topographical Survey," *Teaching Composition: 10 Bibliographical Essays*, ed. Gary Tate (Fort Worth: Texas Christian University Press, 1976), pp. 1–43.

PAUL T. BRYANT, "A Brand New World Every Morning," *College Composition and Communication*, 25 (February, 1974), 30–33.

JANICE M. LAUER, "Toward a Metatheory of Heuristic Procedures," *College Composition and Communication*, 30 (October, 1979), 268–269.

JAMES KINNEY, "Classifying Heuristics," *College Composition and Communication*, 30 (December, 1979), 351–356.

D. GORDON ROHMAN, "Pre-Writing: The Stage of Discovery in the Writing Process," *College Composition and Communication*, 16 (May, 1965), 106–112.

SUSAN WELLS, "Classroom Heuristics and Empiricism, *College English*, 39 (December, 1977), 467–476.

RICHARD L. LARSON

Teaching Before We Judge:
Planning Assignments in Composition

Many published discussions of the teaching of composition today still focus on the grading of themes as if it were the central activity in all instruction about writing. The young teacher of composition has at his disposal an abundance of articles, pamphlets, and books that seek to help him in the handling of his students' themes. If he wants to test his grading standards against those of his professional peers, he can find published collections of graded themes written by students in the grade he teaches, in which the basis for the editor's grade on each theme is carefully set forth. If he wishes guidance in writing comments on his students' papers, he can turn to published compilations of themes fully annotated with marginal and general comments. Often the editors of these compilations accompany the comments they would address to the writer of each theme with a paragraph to the teacher, explaining the strategy of their comments. Most of these model comments are exemplary in the friendly constructiveness of their advice to students, and the example these models set for the teacher, if demanding, is often worthy of emulation.

What one misses in many discussions of how to annotate and evaluate themes, however, is attention to the theme assignment itself. Many compilations of themes, despite the thoroughness of the comments on what the students wrote, contain only cursory descriptions of the assignment to which the student was responding, and say little about the instructions and advice to students before they wrote. For all that the young teacher can tell, it makes no difference how carefully or how carelessly a theme assignment is made, so long as the theme submitted by the student is

From *The Leaflet,* 66, No. 1 (1967), 3–15. Reprinted by permission of the New England Association of Teachers of English and Richard L. Larson.

dealt with thoroughly. To judge from many of these compilations, moreover, the instruction in writing that preceded an assignment is of no consequence; each assignment, the teacher is free to infer, can be treated as an isolated task.

Now it is, of course, somewhat unfair to censure the compilers of graded themes for failing to describe elaborately the assignments themselves and the preceding instruction. The compilations promise no more than to offer a range of student responses to a representative group of assignments. They deal, as their titles imply, with the *evaluating* of themes, not with the assigning of them.

But even recent books on the teaching of English give relatively little attention to what a teacher ought to consider in planning a specific theme assignment. These books often describe general goals for the program in composition, and make numerous suggestions about the kinds of writing that students in various grades should practice. Occasionally they enumerate subjects that have proven useful or might prove useful for student writing, although the value of these subjects and the problems they would present for students who attempted them are not often discussed in much detail. These texts also offer much advice about annotating and judging themes.

I am convinced that these discussions do not explore in sufficient depth the responsibilities of the teacher in presenting theme assignments to students. For a theme assignment ought not to be given simply to evoke an essay that can be judged. Its purpose should be to teach, to give students an experience in composing (selecting, arranging, and expressing thoughts) from which he can learn as much as he can from the reactions of his teacher to his essay. The very act of writing the assignment should help the student think a little more incisively, reason a little more soundly, and write a little more effectively than he did before encountering it. If it is to give the student this help, a theme assignment cannot be presented haphazardly. Nor can it be made without regard to what the student has been taught about thinking and writing before attempting it, for the student's paper will inevitably be affected by the instructions he has received, even more than by the comments made on earlier papers. Although good comments teach (and teach eloquently), the important work of teaching composition ought to begin at the moment the course is designed and continue with the planning and presenting of each assignment. Evaluation and follow-up of the assignment are the last, and by no means necessarily the most important, steps in the teaching of composition.

This observation about the importance of planning individual theme assignments carefully is really not new; several recent writers have already made the point in general terms. Albert Kitzhaber remarks that "All teachers of composition should recognize that planning an assignment in writing is one of the most important aspects of teaching composition, and it should accordingly receive their closest attention. An offhand assignment or one poorly thought through places every student under a needless handicap and guarantees that a sizable proportion of the papers will be defective."[1] Arthur Carr of the University of Michigan, telling in one of the kinescopes of the Commission on English about a theme assignment dealing with "Fire-Walking in Ceylon," observes "I am persuaded that . . . one important way to do better [as teachers of composition] is to set the writing assignments less blindly . . . and that if we do this we shall be less frustrated as teachers and that our students will make greater headway, headway they themselves can perceive."[2] And the chapter on Composition in *Freedom and Discipline in English*, besides reminding readers that "No part of a teacher's job is more important or more a test of his mettle than the making of sound, well-framed assignments" describes quite specifically the characteristics that the Commission on English thinks a good assignment ought to exhibit.[3] (These suggestions—on pages 92–98 of *Freedom and Discipline*—ought to be required reading for all teachers of composition—in high school or college.) Haphazard assignments, all of these writers imply, are inefficient and often confusing. Only the planned assignment—the assignment that takes final form after the teacher has considered what he wants his students to learn and what problems they must solve in order to learn it—has much promise of success as an instrument of teaching.

Even some of these writers, however, do not deal very much with the specific steps a teacher ought regularly to take in thinking out the problems posed by a possible assignment, the tasks his students must perform in order to handle it, and the best ways of presenting the assignment to the class. (*Freedom and Discipline*, page 97, does offer some valuable suggestions on these points.) Moreover, these writers may encourage teachers to another doubtful assumption: that a theme can be assigned in isolation from those that surround it in the composition course. Yet many teachers now hold that even careful planning of the single assignment is not enough to insure that it will accomplish the maximum of teaching. These teachers argue persuasively that each assignment must fit into, and advance, the entire course, and that, ideally, the composition course in

1. Albert Kitzhaber, *Themes, Theories, and Therapy: The Teaching of Writing in College* (New York: McGraw-Hill, 1965), p. 33.
2. Arthur Carr, "A Student Writing Assignment Based on 'Fire-Walking in Ceylon'" (a *Kinescript* of the Commission on English, New York, 1965), pp. 6–7.
3. Commission on English, *Freedom and Discipline in English* (New York: College Entrance Examination Board, 1965), p. 92.

each secondary grade ought to be part of a plan for the curriculum in composition in all six secondary grades.

Much recent work on composition, in response to the arguments of these teachers, has been devoted to the planning of programs covering a full year or several years. Ever since Clarence Hach called in 1960 for a "sequential program in composition."[4] English departments and school districts have been responding with varied programs, some elaborate, some sketchy, but all designed to let the teacher know (or at any rate to force him to decide) what his course is to cover and how it fits into the school's total program in composition. The making of sequential programs of composition assignments has become a common pastime for departments under the leadership of progressive chairmen—and with good results. Leaders of the National Study of High School English programs conclude that in general those schools using or planning sequential programs in composition teach the subject more effectively than those without such a program. Many schools and districts, in fact, are so confident of the value of their programs that they are publishing or distributing them. Many a curriculum guide from one school district inspires imitation from other districts. Published texts on the teaching of English are beginning to contain detailed suggestions for composition curricula. Mary Elizabeth Fowler's *Teaching Language, Literature, and Composition,* for instance, contains an elaborate sequence based on the "spiral" principle—that the same general types of assignments can be given to students in successive grades, if the particular subject matter of work in the higher grades is more complex and demanding than that in the lower grades.[5]

Those who draft sequential programs, however, often neglect to advise teachers how to plan and present the individual assignments in their programs. Their plans, as a result, often are incomplete guides to the teaching of writing. Moreover, in many composition sequences, the principle of "sequence" is often no more than casually observed. In some curriculum guides a sequence of assignments consists simply of a list of subjects or types of writing, arranged in approximate chronological order of suggested use. (Some guides do not even suggest an order in which the types of writing might be assigned.) In many guides, the arrangement of subjects is not explained; often it appears haphazard. To be sure, such programs have the value of letting the teacher know at all times where his course is going (and reminding him of where it has been); they do not, however, encourage him always to think of each specific assignment in

4. Clarence Hach, "Needed: A Sequential Program in Composition," *English Journal,* XLIX (November, 1960), 536–47.
5. Mary Elizabeth Fowler, *Teaching Language, Literature, and Composition* (New York: McGraw-Hill, 1965), pp. 157–61.

relation to those that precede and follow, or to capitalize on what students have learned from one assignment as he moves on to the next. Each assignment, it appears, is treated in isolation, although the assignments, when viewed as a group, may assure that the course meets the responsibilities assigned it in the overall curriculum guide for grades 7–12.

But if an assignment is not likely to be an effective instrument of teaching unless carefully presented to students, neither is it likely to do its work fully unless the teacher can connect it to what the student has practiced in previous assignments and will be expected to attempt in later ones. Therefore, while agreeing that the teacher is wise to follow a "sequential" program, I suggest that he should carry out the principle to its conclusion. He should think of a sequential program not merely as a chronological arrangement of assignments but as a structure in which assignments are closely related to each other in service of the goals of the program. Instead of simply deciding what assignments are to be given and then arranging them in any convenient order (as some curriculum guides appear to encourage) he can consider in detail how and why one assignment should follow another and precede a third. He can view the course, to put the matter figuratively, not as a succession of steps to be taken singly, one after another, the later steps scarcely affected by the earlier ones, but as a staircase to be climbed so that at the end the student stands higher, and has a broader prospect beneath him, than when he began. The goal of each assignment in a true sequence should be to enlarge the student's powers of thinking, organizing, and expressing ideas so that he can cope with a more complex, more challenging problem in the next assignment.

A true "sequence" of assignments, then, is an arrangement in which each assignment builds on the one that preceded, and anticipates the assignment that is to follow. For each assignment in a well planned sequence, the teacher can ask students to draw upon and extend habits of thought and writing that they have just practiced or begun to acquire; in each assignment, the teacher may make sure that the student is gaining the preparation necessary for the next assignments in the series.

The planning of assignments requires that the teacher know at what point his students are starting the year, and in what ways each assignment is more demanding or complicated than the last. He must know what new "increments of complexity," if any—what techniques of thinking or organizing or expressing that students have not previously practiced—are demanded in each assignment. And, obviously, he must see that these new techniques of thought or writing are thoroughly understood by his students before they write. If he does not take care to teach new procedures as they are demanded by his assignments, the students will flounder and their papers will fail.

In order to see how each assignment differs from the last, the teacher must examine what mental processes, what operations of mind, the student must go through in order to carry out each assignment successfully. (Observe here my assumption that a teacher ought to know what characteristics the successful papers on any assignment will have, however they may vary in substance and in approach to the assigned topic.) To write an analysis of Lady Macbeth requires different techniques of thinking and composing, for example, than to compare one's school newspaper with that of a neighboring school, and the differences are not fully described by the two verbs "analyze" and "compare." The analysis of a character in a play requires, for example, the ability to draw inferences about the character from his actions, statements, and figures of speech, as well as from the comments of other characters and their reactions to him. It also requires some idea of the goal of "analysis"—to account for the behavior of a character by suggesting a theory? to reveal the importance of the character in the actions of the play? to discover the author's implied evaluation of her, if he implies one? A comparison of two school newspapers also requires a goal (the student must ask: to what discovery will the comparison lead me?), but it also requires powers of direct observation different from those required in the analysis of a play, demands the identification of some bases on which the papers can be compared, and may force the student to develop for himself standards useful in the evaluation of journalism. Again, to compare the newspapers requires different ways of thinking and writing from an assignment asking the student to analyze the significance of the Stamp Act in the years before the American Revolution. The latter assignment requires the student to sift varying kinds of historical evidence and display a lively sense of the potentials and limitations of analyses of cause and effect. The teacher should know the different tasks required by each assignment he gives, make some judgment of which tasks can come before others, and plan his lessons so that the class discusses and practices the necessary techniques before the theme requiring competence in these techniques is to be handed in.

Thus far I have been proposing three separate but closely related theses about the teaching of composition: that the teacher should plan every theme assignment with great care before presenting it to his students; that he should, as a part of this planning, identify the activities and operations of mind in which the student must engage if he is to cope with the assignment; and that he should see each assignment, if possible, as part of a truly sequential course in composition. Let me now try to translate these general suggestions into a series of steps that teachers might try to follow in designing their composition assignments. The proposal is, perhaps, idealistic in its rigor, but it need not be inflexible, and it does, I hope, point to the places where a teacher must make careful decisions about the focus of each assignment and about how he will present the assignment to his students.

First, plan the course at least in broad outline for a term and possibly a year in advance. Decide what you want your students to be able to do when they complete your course. (To be sure, the responsibilities of each course should be decided in general by teachers of several successive grades working together; they must determine what progress a student should make in each grade, and they may want to view the work of each grade as part of a complete sequential program in writing from grades 7–12 or 10–12. But the individual teacher is usually the one to plan a program that will meet the responsibilities assigned to his course.) Decide how many themes you want your students to write, and what tasks in thinking and writing each theme will require of them. You can slow the pace, give more time for some assignments than others, and repeat assignments as necessary, but knowing in advance the purposes of each assignment will give you an invaluable sense of direction as you start the term's work. No assignment need be decided upon in detail while you are planning the course in broad outline, but the major goals to be served and mental activities to be taught by each assignment ought to be at least tentatively determined.

Second, analyze each prospective assignment carefully before you give it. Among the questions to consider before you decide finally on a subject for the assignment are: what can these students reasonably be expected to accomplish at this point in their development? (You may wish on occasion to give an assignment that you know is beyond your students, but you should be aware that the assignment is probably beyond their reach and you should have clearly in mind your purpose in giving it.) What is the student expected to learn from this assignment? What is he to practice when doing it? What, in short, is the purpose of the assignment?

With the purpose of the assignment clearly in mind, you can decide the specific subject (or the kind of subject) you wish the students to discuss. The subject should be of value for itself, and should help students to learn about the act or process of composition. Test the subject to determine whether it will encourage the students to make some discovery, to develop, while planning and writing the theme, a new idea or perception about themselves, their environment, a work of literature, or some other significant object of inquiry. Whether the subject be presented to students in the form of a proposition (as recommended in *Freedom and Discipline in English,* p. 93), or a question, or a problem, or a broad topic which the student must restrict for himself, the assignment ought to help the student to new knowledge or new understanding of his subject.

Moreover, if this new understanding of his subject is to be sound, the student must have adequate data with which to work. The subject must be accessible to him; he must be able to locate the facts and other data needed in the development of his observations. And if he is asked to make a choice between alternatives, between conflicting interpretations of a character or novel, for example, he must have a genuine option; it must be possible for him to defend reasonably, with good evidence, whichever alternative he chooses. Few subjects present a useful problem for discussion if there is only one way to treat them.

Finally, after you have determined that the specific subject to be assigned is likely to be interesting and instructive to the students, check to be sure that, as you have framed it, the subject will serve the purpose of the assignment. If the purpose of the assignment, for example, is to force students to discriminate between facts and opinions on a subject, the assignment must be so presented that the student cannot evade making the discrimination (he might evade it, for instance, by writing a strictly factual narrative).

Third, consider what the student will need to know in order to do well on the assignment. These questions are pertinent: What operations of mind must the student go through in preparing to write the assignment? What powers of observation must he exercise? What acts of induction or deduction must he perform? What problems of rhetoric—selection of materials, organization of materials, and expression of simple or complex ideas—must he solve? Try to determine what a successful piece of writing on the assignment might look like—i.e., what features (of content and structure) it might have. One—admittedly time-consuming—way to determine these characteristics is to write the proposed assignment yourself in a form that you would consider satisfactory, and then determine what mental acts you had to perform in order to write it.

Fourth, decide what you must "teach" now in order to assure students a fair chance to do well on the assignment. This decision will be based on a comparison of what the students now know and can reasonably be expected to do with what the students will need to be able to do in order to carry out the assignment. You will need to consider how well previous assignments have prepared your students to do what you will now ask of them, and what new techniques and procedures—in both thinking and writing—they must master. Decide how you will help them to understand what is expected on this theme. Plan to discuss the special problems of observation, analysis, and organization that they will face. Try to anticipate difficulties the students will face with the assignment, and be prepared before you make the assignment to help the students surmount these difficulties.

Fifth, when the first four steps have been carefully taken, and you are sure that you know what activities and skills you are calling for, draft the written bulletin describing the assignment (or make the notes you will use in giving the assignment orally). Make sure that the instructions are complete and unambiguous. Be sure that the kind of performance—the action—required of the student is stipulated as precisely as possible. (Is he to compare two characters, trace a process, argue in support of a thesis, analyze a scene, and so on? You should even consider carefully what you mean by such verbs as "analyze," which direct the student's performance.) Often it is desirable for students to write as if they are filling a role in which precise communication with another person is required. In such assignments you should stipulate an imagined audience—a reader or a group of readers—to be addressed, an occasion for the writing, and a purpose or purposes to be accomplished. For example, instead of asking for a routine comparison of your school paper with that published in the other high school in town, try instructing the student to propose to his principal (or to the school's newspaper advisor) ways of improving the paper—ways of making it more like the good one in the other school. Instead of asking your aspiring aeronautical engineer to write a "process" paper, ask him to describe how a jet engine works in language that a grandmother taking her first jet flight could understand. Instead of asking routinely for an "analysis" of Lady Macbeth, urge the student to reply to someone who thinks the Lady was a foolish, misguided but loyal wife who was only trying to encourage her husband to better himself. Then check back through your reflections at step 4 to be sure that he has the tools and training (in selecting data, in recognizing and resolving interpretive problems raised by the data) that he will need to meet the problem you have set him.

Sixth, determine what your standards of evaluation on the assignment will be. The standards should, of course, reflect the purposes of the assignment and what you are trying to teach by means of it. Among the bases for evaluation should be the student's success in responding to the audience, occasion, and purpose you specified in making the assignment. The principal question that can be applied to almost any student's paper is: did he keep faith with his reader? did he do the job he set out to do for the audience that he was expected to address? But you will probably regard two or three of the tasks in reasoning, organization and expression presented by the assignment as especially important, and will plan to base your evaluation heavily on the students' success in performing these two or three tasks.

Seventh, explain the assignment to the students fully. Follow the explanation—or, perhaps better still, precede it—by some discussion of exercises or problems that will prepare the student to handle the task. Be sure that he sees the techniques of observation, discovery of ideas, organization, and expression that he needs to use as he writes. Not that writing is reducible always or even often to the application of techniques, but there are ways of drawing good generalizations, forming good hypotheses, drawing good inferences, introducing different kinds of papers effectively, concluding different discussions forcefully, and so on, that the students might know and use consciously as they work. If sources for materials to be used on the assignment are likely to be hard to find, suggest a few such sources. Here, in preliminary explanations of your assignments and perhaps in exercises that let students practice techniques you are teaching, is your chance to make the composition course seem not a guessing game but a program of instruction in a disciplined activity that a student can master.

Also, let the students know on what standards they will be judged. You may even wish to discuss with your students samples of successful work on analogous assignments, if you have such samples. Examples of professional writing that illustrate good solutions of the difficulties in an assignment have long been standard teaching materials for colleges; they can serve well in secondary schools, too. Although professional writing need not always be studied as a model for emulation, there is no harm, especially on difficult assignments, in giving your students a target of excellence at which to shoot.

Eighth, as part of your explanation of the assignment, allow time for students' questions, and be ready to point out pitfalls and difficulties they will encounter as they work on the assignment. You may even want to suggest ways of avoiding these pitfalls, if the assignment is especially demanding. You will not reduce the value of the assignment by alerting students to possible sources of trouble; the students will have difficulty enough in trying to avoid pitfalls they know about, and you may save yourself many unhappy experiences in reading and much red ink if you point out difficulties that students would almost surely not recognize unless forewarned. Some of these suggestions may be given after students have begun to work on first drafts, and possibly after you have looked at a few first drafts to see how the class is doing.

Ninth, in evaluating and commenting on papers, make special note of where the student has and has not succeeded in reaching the objectives of the assignment. Give praise where you can, and remember that the comment ought principally to be a tool for teaching. As such, it ought to point out precisely where a paper fell short of completing the assigned task, and to indicate what difficulties the writer ought specifically to guard against in the next paper, if a similar task is to confront him then. General comments on clarity of organization, accuracy of word choice, and economy of expression are almost always appropriate if warranted, but the teacher should not forget that the student is looking for some estimate of how well he met the specific assignment he faced. Whatever the focus of the comments, they should be full enough to let each student see exactly where he succeeded, where he failed, and why. And they should be constructive enough so that the student can profit from them in writing the next assignment. (Sometimes comments are more carefully heeded if no grade appears on the paper. Grades sometimes deflect students' attention completely from what the comments hope to teach.)

Tenth, discuss the assignments with students when you return them. Distribute, or read aloud, or show on the overhead projector, examples of comparatively successful performances on the assignment, demonstrating where they succeed and, if necessary, where they fall short. Resist the temptation to discuss only papers that show many difficulties; discuss examples of papers that handle the assignment well so that the student can learn by seeing what he should have done. Usually it is wise to involve students in discussion of strong and weak points of an essay; the teacher can intervene to comment if the discussion goes hopelessly astray from important strengths or weaknesses of the paper. But review the pitfalls that seized large numbers of students, and indicate once more (if you have already mentioned them) how these troubles might have been avoided.

Eleventh, ask students to revise or rewrite. For most students, revision ought not to consist simply of correcting errors in mechanics; it ought to be a thorough rewriting of the entire assignment. Some papers may be so good that revision is unnecessary. And on some assignments many students will do so badly that revision is unlikely to be rewarding. In such cases you may want to repeat approximately the same assignment (at the expense of slowing the pace of instruction) on an analogous subject. Whatever the procedure used, however, you should provide some way by which the student can follow up quickly and correct the difficulties he exhibited in handling the assignment.

Of the eleven steps in handling a theme assignment discussed here, eight are completed before the students even approach their final drafts. If the manuals for evaluating themes err in focusing too heavily on how the theme tests what the student has learned, this discussion may seem to focus unduly on what happens before the student has begun seriously to write. Moreover, the suggestions may appear to rigidify the curriculum and make giving even a short assignment into a forbiddingly complex task.

My emphasis on what the teacher must do before the student is allowed to go far with his assignment, though perhaps excessive, is intentional, and I hope the early pages of this essay will justify the emphasis. But this essay does not argue that the curriculum must be rigid. Each assignment should serve the purposes of the course and have a place in its total structure, but specific assignments need not always be decided before the course begins. Assignments often must be made up as the course progresses, to meet the needs of students as these needs appear. I argue only that whatever assignment is made, and whenever it is presented, it should be carefully considered in advance of presentation to the students. Of course, as the year progresses and the assignments become instruments for reviewing and reinforcing what has been taught rather than for the presentation of new techniques and concepts, the amount of explanation given to students before they write may diminish. But the thought given by the teacher to his assignment, I think, ought not to decrease even at the end of the year.

Some readers may object that if the teacher follows these suggestions, the student has less responsibility for learning than the teacher has for spelling out the lesson. Perhaps the charge has some merit. But students learn little from simply trying to outguess the teacher, from striving to write a theme in response to an assignment that seems pointless or confused. And they can hardly be expected to write a good theme if the assignment requires activities of mind that they have not practiced and do not know how to perform. They may, to be sure, learn from failures, but how frustrating it is to be told one has failed when one had no idea of how to seek success. For most students, composition is an uncomfortable subject; few enter with enthusiasm a course devoted primarily to exposition, and the morale even of the eager students is easily shattered by inept instruction. But if students have a goal in writing and are convinced that the teacher is helping them toward that goal, there is at least a better chance that their morale may remain strong.

We can not hope for much success in the teaching of composition unless our students want to learn, and continue wanting to learn throughout our courses. If we try to teach before we test and judge them, perhaps our students will discover that our assignments are helping them learn to write. They may even find that our assignments help them to use their minds more effectively and to organize more successfully their experiences in the world.

TIMOTHY R. DONOVAN

Seeing Students as Writers

Every teacher would welcome a classroom full of writers—people whose prose is thoughtful, vigorous and interesting (above all, interesting). But, of course, that is the teacher's pipe dream. The reality is that we have students, and students usually produce a "theme," a genre with the look and feel of writing that de-composes under honest scrutiny. But because they are students, we instruct them in formulas and reward conformity. I wonder, however, if too often we don't create the self-fulfilling prophecy, if by treating students as students instead of writers we aren't all settling for less than we need to.

Let me begin at the beginning, with writing assignments. Most are ill-conceived when the emphasis falls on "assignment" rather than writing. The word implies something that someone wants someone else to do, so the students' first task is to find out "what the teacher wants." The more non-directive the assignment, the more impatient they get because the more obscure is this thing the teacher wants. To be in a state of "negative capability," as Keats would have it, is worst of all because there are no easy answers, no keys to unlock the mystery. So let them be students.

This is a betrayal, wittingly or not, for those of us who like to think we teach writing because it is a process of growth and discovery or because the utility we presume for effective writing is best achieved when writing is presented in such a light. Assignments such as the following convey the not-so-subtle message that writing is at best merely communication and at worst a trivial, make-work exercise justified by something other than the worth of writing itself:

From *Composition and Teaching*, 1 (November, 1978), 13–16. Reprinted by permission of Goucher College, San Jose State University, and Timothy R. Donovan.

1. Tell about an interesting experience you have had while travelling;
2. Describe some object such as an orange, an egg slicer, a rock. Note its texture, its shape, smell, etc.;
3. Characterize one of the central figures in *A Farewell to Arms.*

What is depressing about such assignments is not just their pedagogical shortcomings (too clichéd, too trivial, too vague), but the way their very *artlessness* bespeaks of the teacher's limited expectations for the people who must do them. As writing teachers we must put ourselves in the position of seeing students as writers and, more importantly, of having students see themselves as writers.

I would like to outline some conventional problems—and some possible solutions—involved in creating assignments that demand students act like writers. A student asked to write his impressions of school responds thus:

> I thoroughly enjoy coming to class each day because I realize people are here to help me. If I have a problem with some subject, the teachers are more than willing to give me extra attention. They seem so energetic and are actively attacking the problems students have in learning the material. I know there are other schools where this doesn't happen, so I feel very fortunate in going to school here.

And so on. The exasperated teacher knows that there is nothing "wrong" with this paragraph except that it doesn't say anything. So he pleads with his little Pollyana for *honesty!* The next time he receives this paragraph:

> I honestly don't know what I'm doing in school. It's certainly not what I had in mind for my education. Teachers with their irrelevant projects and infantile rules. Snotty students with all their immature little plans. Not to mention my parents who are always looking over my shoulder and threatening this or that if I don't produce. I can't believe this is all there is to going to school. There must be something in it for *me!*

At last, the teacher says, I'm getting somewhere. Perhaps. But the basic problem with both pieces of writing lies not in the language, and no amount of fixing up the words will make for real writing or make the author a real writer. The act of composing is neither a skimming of experience nor a neurotic activity.

What prevents many students from being writers is not their failure to touch things around them or to get in touch with themselves. It is their failure to create a *literary* self on paper. The literary self grows out of a rhetorical context: the adoption of an appropriate voice, or persona, with which to speak about a topic. We should not expect that an inexperienced writer has a ready-made self within any more than we should feel the

need to give him one from without. But in the netherland of uncertainty
these things are worked out. Here he looks for relationships, categories,
conflicts, and inferences until he finds a way of controlling the flux of
his ideas.

For this reason we should encourage not the telling of what a writer
knows so much as the pursuit of what he really doesn't know. And by
having to become conscious of the writing process, of the need to develop
a persona, he may become more conscious, too, of the language by which
that persona is developed, refined or altered. Like a child reaching toward
individuation, a writer must make a conceptual leap in seeing himself as
a manipulator of language which is both part of and distinguishable from
him. His writing should be neither masked nor maskless but an artful way
of making others see what he sees.

Although the content of a writing course properly belongs to the
writer, assignments *can* be justified if they invite him to consider some
things for himself and to put them together in a way that has meaning for
him. We ask him to do, really, what a writer must do. So, perhaps assignments ought not to be assignments per se but problems for which there is
no one answer or solution. They should challenge the writer to imagine
and form a rhetorical context with which he may account for and illuminate the issue as he sees it. He needs tasks that demand the power to
look around the edges, to probe and withdraw until a suitable way of
talking emerges. In the course of doing so, he may also learn that writing
is not a trick or that it just doesn't happen to (other) people.

Following Walker Gibson's emphasis on writing as a self-creating activity, Edmund J. Farrell has suggested that we design composition assignments that offer "built-in selves."[1] These would involve the student in
a fictional situation, with an assumed persona and a specified audience for
the discourse. These can be fruitful exercises, but I think we must distinguish between an exercise and a writing assignment or between the
writer's adoption of a specified role and the capacious allowance for the
development of his own roles. Moreover, we must go beyond the concept
of "what works" in designing writing assignments to some rudimentary
questions that address the matter of the student's growth as a writer:

1. Does the assignment present issues that the writer can apply to
   his own experience?

2. Is the assignment open and flexible enough to encourage different and perhaps even experimental stances toward it?

1. "The Beginning Begets: Making Composition Assignments," *English Journal,* 58
(March 1969), 428–431.

3. Is it related to the assignment which preceded it and to the one that is to follow?

4. Does it take the writer inside, outside and, above all, just a bit beyond himself?

5. Does it suggest by its content and tone that writing carries intrinsic rewards beyond the fulfillment of academic requirements?

When questions such as these are asked, it becomes evident that assignment-making can be an art, like writing itself, that good assignments are created, not unearthed. Every teacher must evolve his own. However, I am game enough here to reconstruct an assignment as it might progress in my own mind.

I might start with and draw upon that predominant training ground of composition teachers—literature. (I would also suggest that not only is this fertile territory for assignments but also that a literary background is just as helpful to writing teachers as any other when it bestows imaginative and critical sensibility.) I might, for example, look into Melville and draw out a useful theme, say, the heart versus the mind, which does not mean I would have students read *Billy Budd*. I would begin by asking, or perhaps using a quotation that talks about, the importance or even the inevitability of following one's feelings and instincts. We would not stop here, however, for students are apt to think it a rhetorical question, agree enthusiastically and "support" it with a few reasons for examples. Such a question should be countered by acknowledgement of circumstances which seem to demand intellect, logic, judgement. This juxtaposition provides ample opportunity for prewriting in which students should indulge the free play of the mind over the issue it raises. But the success of an assignment (or lack of it) usually depends on a third question, one which, in some form, requests that the writer establish his own perspective, or synthesis, based upon his own experience and attitude. In essence, it is a problem he must work out as a writer and with the language that allows him to do so. The content is his, the writing is his, the theme is universal.

Undoubtedly we are making real demands on the writer when we encourage tentative and searching discourse. Moreover, the writing we are looking for is not going to appear magically in any one essay or even linearly through a series of essays, but as a spiral progression of recovery and discovery. But to give it a chance, we must begin to have students at least act like writers, that is, to have them always establishing perspectives toward objects, people, experience, ideas that, as they take shape on a page, stand for the best a writer can do. We must begin, in other words, by seeing students as writers.

ADDITIONAL READINGS

JAMES M. McCRIMMON, "A Cumulative Sequence in Composition," *English Journal,* 55 (April, 1966), 425–434.

JOHN E. JORDAN, "Theme Assignments: Servants or Masters?" *College Composition and Communication,* 14 (February, 1963), 51–53.

STEPHEN JUDY, "On Clock Watching and Composing," *English Journal,* 57 (March, 1968), 360–366.

ELEANOR M. HOFFMAN and JOHN P. SCHIFSKY, "Designing Writing Assignments," *English Journal,* 66 (December, 1977), 41–45.

The Uses—and Limits—of Grammar

INTRODUCTION

One of the more dispiriting discoveries of the Basic Writing teacher is that the study of grammar has been shown to have rather negligible effects upon student writing. The results with traditional grammar are uniformly discouraging, and the somewhat better results with structural and transformational grammars seem to depend less on any superiority in the grammatical analysis than on the fact that these grammars encourage students to manipulate the language as well as analyze it. Wherever it has been seriously researched, the analytical study of grammar has failed to produce significant results in student writing across the board—whether the result sought was improvement in the control of errors, increased sentence length, or increased variety of sentence structure; whether the students were in junior high school, high school, or college; whether they came from privileged or underprivileged backgrounds; whether the grammar studied was traditional, structural, or transformational generative. If there is one conclusion to be drawn which cuts across all the studies, it is this: the more time spent analyzing grammar as grammar, the less time spent writing; the less time spent writing, the less the improvement in the written product.

These hard facts cause many Basic Writing instructors to abandon the attempt to teach any grammar systematically. They hope, by emphasizing for the student the development of his unique voice and a number of

From *Journal of Basic Writing*, 1 (Spring/Summer, 1977), 1–20. Reprinted by permission of the *Journal of Basic Writing* and Sarah D'Eloia.

strategies for finding and organizing better content, to foster simultaneously an improved self-image, a confidence and pride in the act of writing, a desire to make it perfect on every level. They hope to avoid a psychologically debilitating, boring, and futile preoccupation with grammar and error, in the belief that the student can get it right readily enough when he genuinely has the motivation to do so and in the belief that repeated exposure to the written standard will enable the student to acquire standard forms by osmosis, much as his instructor acquired them.

These same hard facts leave other instructors with lingering doubts and suspicions. They are persuaded they became more astute observers of the language and better writers partly as a result of rigorous grammatical study, sometimes of English, sometimes of a foreign language. Resisting, in disbelief, the clear enough results of dozens of studies, they suspect that something was radically wrong with the research design or the instruction in grammar itself. They suspect, for example, that it takes longer than a single quarter, semester or even year for the study of grammar to manifest itself in improved fluency or correctness. They suspect that the study of grammar was boring: too deductive, facts-oriented, and passive, rather than inductive, actively analytical, stimulating, and discovery-laden. They suspect that the study of grammar was divorced from rather than thoroughly integrated into the process of writing, and perhaps intentionally, as a test of automatic rather than carefully mediated transference. They cannot bring themselves to believe that units combining the analysis of a grammatical principle with well-structured proofreading, imitation, paraphrase, and sentence consolidation exercises, and with directed writing assignments could fail to produce more significant results in both fluency and error control.

They suspect, in addition, that the research design did not take into account, nor teach across, first, the difference between the mental operations activated by reading for meaning, where one blocks out the interference of errors and miscues, and proofreading, in which one blocks out all but that meaning necessary to parse for errors and miscues, nor secondly, the difference between the parsing skills necessary for handbook exercises and the additional skill of psychological distancing necessary for proofing one's own work. Worst of all, they distrust the efficacy of linguistic osmosis, seeing the student's non-standard forms as a semi-permeable membrane across which new concepts and meanings—but not new linguistic patterns—will move with ease; they suspect that there are some errors, perhaps many, over which the student will have neither proofreading nor productive control until he has an analytical and conceptual control of the grammar of the standard dialect.

CATEGORIES OF GRAMMAR BASED ERRORS

The grammatical errors of beginning adult writers that one might hope to address through grammar are legion. They fall into several broad groups.

There are the inflectional omissions, redundancies, and leveling errors of the nouns, verbs, pronouns, adjectives and adverbs, involving plurality, possession, agreement, tense, case and degree which arise from different phonological and grammatical rules in the student's home dialect. (Omission: *two boy, John coat;* redundancy: *more better;* extension: *hisself, theirself(ves)*—like *myself, yourself, herself, ourselves;* I *seen* him do it—shared preterite and perfective form, as in *taught, bought, caught, slept, kept.*)

There are other less common forms derived from the more familiar spoken language which involve not so much the inflections of words but the choice, form, order, even the omission of words. These errors include the omitted ("zero") present tense copula; the omission of any contractible first auxiliary as in *he go* for *he will/would go;* the use of *-en* for *-ing* on participles where pronunciations are similar, as in *He is eaten his dinner;* durative *be; ain't* as a negative auxiliary before the unmarked (*go*), progressive (*going*), and perfect verb forms (variously *went* or *gone*); *done* or *been* as the perfective auxiliary; the reduced purposive future (*I'm gonna/gon/on/a/* put the cat out); the reduced conditional perfect (*I(woul)d of/a* done it myself); multiple negatives (John could*n't* do *nothing* for her. Could*n't nobody* do *nothing* for her. *Ain't nobody* can('*t*) do *nothing* for her.); and the indirect question (I asked him whose turn *was it.* I asked him *is it* his turn.)

There are the hypercorrect forms like *can walks, could walked, to finished, to be abled, he walk's,* forms which do not belong in either dialect, but which result from the student's attempt to produce standard inflections. In the absence of a pronunciation clue in his own dialect and in the absence of an abstract grasp of standard inflections, he must simply guess where *-s-'s,-s'* and *-ed* go.

On the one hand, there are the words lacking derivational affixes, like *courage* for *courageous* or *astonish* for *astonishment,* which bespeak the student's lack of familiarity with the system of derivational affixes that turn nouns to adjectives, verbs to nouns, and so on. In contrast, there are the coined words, many of them marvelously inventive, such as *enbodyness* for *embodiment,* which bespeak the student's attempt to manipulate a system he partially understands and the linguistic fact that the forms of many words are arbitrary. Here the student senses that he has heard the word he needs or that such a word ought to exist: he lacks familiarity with the specific word he needs.

There are the syntactically tangled sentences which result from the student's attempt to extend his syntactic control over longer stretches of related ideas, in order to show within a single sentence the complex patterns of logical and grammatical subordination, differential relation, and equivalence. Tangles increase with abstract topics because the student must perceive, consolidate, and clarify the complex relations between the observable facts and his conclusions. Thus the more perceptive and far-reaching a student's insights, the more difficulty he will have parcelling them out into sentences that properly order and relate them; the more inexperienced the student is as a writer, the less he will know how to start and, if off on the wrong foot, how to start over again. These syntactically tangled sentences may be classified according to the structures involved in the production of the tangle.[1]

In some cases, the student's problem seems to be a lack of familiarity with a particular structure, for example, the inverted subject verb and divided *but . . . also* of the co-ordinated clauses beginning "*Not only . . .*". In other cases, it seems clear enough that the student can produce well-formed subordinate clauses of cause, condition, concession, and so on most of the time, but that he may mismanage them when he is trying to handle a number of subordinations simultaneously, with the result that his sentence contains peculiar redundancies and lapses. In some cases, it appears that the student has access to a multiplicity of options for expressing his idea, but that having settled on an option as he begins, he is unable to keep other options from impinging as he continues. In other cases, one suspects that the student is limited to specific options for handling various parts of his sentence, and that these options do not mesh with each other and cannot be made to, without resort to a total recasting which exploits an option to which he has no productive, though perhaps passive, access.

Last of all there are the fragments, run-ons, and comma splices. These are of course errors of punctuation rather than grammar, yet they arise because the student cannot co-ordinate conventional punctuation with

1. See Mina Shaughnessy's *Errors and Expectations*, Chapter 3, "Syntax," for an illuminating discrimination between Accidental Errors (inadvertent word omissions or misspellings which miscue the reader), Blurred Patterns (a syntactically dissonant mixture of two or more patterns, as in "By going to college a young person could *get an increase his knowledge* about the world he lived in."), Consolidation Errors involving subordination, coordination, and juxtaposition, and Inversions (errors resulting from imperfect control of all departures from the most normal word order whether in simple sentences, relative clause structures, extraposed noun clauses, or unusual sentence patterns such as *the more, the merrier*).

anything more specific than length in number of words or pauses in speech or his sense that some parts of what he has written "are related" or "refer to each other" or "belong together" in some way. Thus a student may punctuate a long introductory prepositional phrase with a period because he pauses there and because "it's so long it has to be a sentence," or he may punctuate sentences like "The movie star Bruce Lee was a remarkable person, he didn't let his success go to his head" with a comma, and explain that the comma is used because *he* "refers back to" Bruce Lee. (Compare *who*.) These errors arise because the student is unable to establish sentence boundaries by distinguishing independent clauses from all the other structures which can attach to them and which often closely resemble them.

The question is, which of these problems will yield to the study of grammar? And how much grammar should a student be taught? How much does he need to know? Traditional, structural, transformational generative? What, in short, are the uses—and limits—of grammar?

USES OF GRAMMAR FOR TEACHERS

There are a number of benefits that can accrue to the instructor who has immersed himself in such works as Otto Jespersen's *Philosophy of Grammar* and *Essentials of English Grammar* or Labov's *Language in the Inner City* or a bone-crunching graduate course in transformational generative grammar or, better yet, comparative approaches to English grammar. These activities, apart from the hard information they impart, suggest alternative ways of viewing the world of language, and have the salutary effect of making one aware that very different kinds of rules are possible and valid, that there are constraints on the operation of "rules" which appear to defy explanation—aware of something he may have forgotten: what it feels like to be a student awash in a subject he does not comprehend. So important is it for the instructor to keep before himself a feeling for what it is not to know, a model of how it is he himself learns, and how the process of coming into knowledge works, that my gutsy high school geometry teacher spent some of her summers taking advanced graduate courses out of her field, without the proper prerequisites. Otherwise, she forgot, she said, why it was her students could not understand what was obvious to her; otherwise she could not teach. Otherwise she could only be impatient with our perverse stupidity. If, however, she had been recently confused herself, she could spot the likely sources of our confusion, though in subject matter intimately familiar to her, and move us past our confusions in a sensible order.

No capacity will better serve the Basic Writing teacher than this capacity to probe for the student's perspective on a particular problem. This capacity to imagine and project oneself into solutions, alternatives, world views other than one's own is, after all, just what we are asking of the student, in our classes and in the liberal arts curriculum. We can strengthen our pedagogy by consciously exercising it ourselves. By doing so, we discover more exactly the kinds of knowledge that separate us from the student. It is not enough to know that he is wrong, but that he is wrong for a reason.

There are a number of ways the Basic Writing instructor can serve the student better by having grammatical expertise. If he reads the available literature on non-standard dialects and second-language interference patterns, he will more readily see the sources of many of his student's errors, and what before seemed chaotic or careless mistakes will have explanations and often prove to have rules of their own.

If the instructor is familiar with several schools of grammar, he will be better able to practice an informed eclecticism, picking and choosing from a variety of explanations, possible presentations, and "discovery procedures" those that are most likely to shed light for the student on his error, to tell him exactly what to do exactly where in order to be correct, to give him a "mechanical" way both to produce correct forms and to proofread for correctness. Grammatical expertise will give him a sense for the times when he can simply explain a principle and for the other times when the principle to be explained is sufficiently complicated that it is better, though much more time-consuming, to lead the student inductively to a grasp of the principle, with the student drawing the increasingly complex generalizations from increasingly complex facts of standard grammar. It will give him a better perception of what it is the student has to "discover" and how this "discovery" can be "arranged."

Grammatical expertise will help him improve his exercises in a variety of other ways. He will improve his intuitions about the natural sequences in his instruction and have a means of thinking about areas of uncertainty. It will help him decide how to pull together all the forms which the student finds distractingly similar or distressingly contradictory, such as the base word ending with -s, the noun plural -s, the verb singular -s, the contraction 's, and the possessives (-'s, -s')[2] and how to begin with unrealistically simplified material, in order to establish the principle, and then add increasingly complicating distractors, as in teaching the recognition of sentence boundaries. It will help him reason in advance about which

2. See Patricia Lawrence, "Error's Endless Train," *Journal of Basic Writing*, I (Spring 1975), pp. 35–37, for a set of graduated perceptual exercises in recognizing the inflection -s.

distractors are likely to be most distracting for his students, or if he simply stumbles across an extremely discriminating test item, he will be able to understand and generalize the principle he has hit upon. In either case, he can better focus practice and measures of mastery in the areas where confusions or perceptual blocks are greatest. It will help him know why certain errors prove most recalcitrant, long after the student masters the principle, and it will suggest ways to use language forms and competencies the student already has in order to elicit and foster those he does not.

Grammatical expertise will replace the teacher's tendency to mark errors and supply the correct forms with a tendency to think in terms of interrelated systems which comprehend and address the sources of student error. It will give him the tools to address all of the kinds of error enumerated above. Indeed, the more standard and non-standard grammar the teacher knows, the more he may economize in his instruction to the student, out of knowing what is relevant and for what purposes.

None of the benefits I have mentioned accrue inevitably to the person who studies grammars. Pedants can become more pedantic. But the person who is familiar with some of the methods and results of linguistic analysis is likely to improve his grasp of various productive techniques of grammatical study, and to see that different grammars can be put to productive use in a variety of ways.

USES OF GRAMMAR FOR STUDENTS

Orientation toward error. Given our course objectives, that a student learn to write and to write more fluently and more cogently, as well as more correctly, it follows that all grammatical study should be subordinated to the elimination of error, so that grammatical study will take away as little time as possible from actual practice of writing. I would argue that the rigorous study of the grammatical subtleties of the language will, like the rigorous study of algebra, calculus, chemistry, Shakespeare, and symbolic logic, sharpen the critical faculties and "improve" the mind. The most significant question is, however, not whether students would profit in some general abstract way from rigorous grammatical study or whether this sort of study would not, in time, lead to a more sensitive and more correct use of the standard language, but whether, given the two or three semesters the student has in which to prove he can pass muster, it is the most gainful use he can make of his time, given his urgent need to write better and in the standard dialect. While it is necessary to address ourselves directly to the grammatical difficulties that make our student population different from "traditional" students, it would be folly to ignore the avalanche of studies that point to minimal connection between the ability to parse, label, diagram, and correct exercises and a more generalized correctness, fluency and elegance in writing.

From this general principle, two more follow. First, grammatical instruction should proceed with a minimum of terminology and the simplest terminology possible. In practice, this seems to mean using the traditional terms which many of our students have heard and to which they are attached, but supplementing them with the visible forms which we want our students to produce. Where our students have not learned a label—"gerund" is a case in point for most—"the -ing form in a noun position" will do. Whole sets of constructions can be handled in this manner. Exercises practicing transformational paraphrases can describe the paraphrases to be produced as the -'s-ing paraphrase, the -'s-xxx (special ending) paraphrase, the *for . . . to . . .* paraphrase, and the *it . . . that* paraphrase, for example, in an exercise of this sort:

Convert the italicized *the fact that* clause to the following paraphrases as in the example below:

> *The fact that his best student failed the exam* surprised Prof. Helton.
> *'s-ing*
> > *His best student's failing the exam surprised Prof. Helton.*
> *-'s -xxx*
> > *His best student's failure of the exam surprised Prof. Helton.*
> *for . . . to . . .*
> > *For his best student to fail the exam surprised Prof. Helton.*
> *It . . . that . . .*
> > *It surprised Prof. Helton that his best student failed the exam.*

One need not refer to "gerund phrases," "infinitive phrases," "extra-position" and the like, for these terms simply divert attention from the operations to be accomplished and from the visible forms by which they are accomplished. Nothing is to be gained, when the objective is error reduction, by covering the grammatical ground, in order to round out the grammar, unless the constructions being discussed are not readily accessible to the student or are a source of error, and in a way clear to the instructor.

Second, at the sime time that the instructor is attempting to minimize the time devoted to grammar, he must be careful to teach whatever makes standard English predictable for the student—not only what is necessary, but also, *all* that is necessary. Otherwise his instruction in grammar falls short of its objective, the elimination of error. The standard dialect remains intractable and unruly for our students until they can impose the right rules. The student who is told that all verb phrases are marked for present or past tense is likely to produce forms like *can walks* and *could walked,* unless he is also led to see that a first auxiliary, if present, bears the only tense marking, and that other endings have other sources.

Integration of grammar study and writing. The instructor should integrate the study of a grammatical concept into the process of writing as thoroughly as he can contrive the mix, so that the student transfers an abstract grasp of grammatical principles to correct production, and so that he addresses matters of fluency, maturity, cogency, and correctness simultaneously. Integrating grammatical study and actual writing is not so difficult a task as may first appear, once one has this in mind as an important objective and once one has a repertoire of techniques at his disposal. The two may be integrated in a variety of ways, but the objective is always to integrate the actual production of forms with an understanding of the forms to be produced and with actual proofreading for those forms. Four strategies are discussed below.

1. Dictation. One highly productive way to integrate production and proofreading is old-fashioned dictation. The instructor can write and dictate short passages heavily laden with troublesome forms, let us say present and past perfectives of regular verbs ending in consonant clusters, where the student is least likely to pronounce or hear the terminal *-ed.* The practice is most beneficial if it follows by one class hour the study of the construction of the tenses at hand but if the structural point of the dictation is at first unremarked. The student, having taken down the passage, is then told the "real" content, and told to go back and supply and circle every *-ed* he missed. This dictation can be followed by another immediately, of like kind. The point is to make the student aware of his aural perceptual block and aware of the fact that he has the analytical skill to overcome it, by matching up *have's* with perfective endings, and to give him chances to practice overcoming his perceptual resistance to the correct form, at the point where that resistance is highest, by applying his analytical knowledge of the construction of these phrases.

2. Grammatical follow-ups to writing assignments. The sort of practice in simultaneous production and proofreading that occurs in dictation can be supplemented by another in which production and proofreading are more discrete. The student may be instructed to write an essay using one of several topic sentences establishing a present perfect frame ("My parents have (not) had a lot of influence on my beliefs and values," "The person who has had the most influence on my present beliefs and values is . . ." "I have had to reject (come to accept) a lot of the things I was taught by my family."). He is also instructed, as a part of his proofreading, to sunburst 🌟 every use of *have, has,* or *had* as a simple, one-word verb, and to box every *have* which appears as an auxiliary, and to box the past participle form of the verb that occurs with it, making sure he has used the past participle form. This sort of grammatical follow-up to the writing assignment forces the student to reread his paper, and to proofread it for one kind of error. It encourages him to transfer the skills he uses to correct workbook exercises to his own writing and to develop the psychological distance toward his own work that proofreading, and more importantly, rewriting, require.

Other grammatically oriented follow-ups appropriate to other grammatical lessons would include such exercises as using a slash to divide every complete subject from every complete verb in every sentence; circling every dependent clause marker, to be sure every dependent clause is punctuated to tie it to its main clause; underlining every tense marked verb and verb phrase in the paper; and underlining every present tense verb and its subject, having first had the student write an essay using a topic sentence which established a third person singular topic (and potential subject for the sentences) and a clearly present time frame ("My father always encourages me to. . . ." "Aunt Emma is always telling me. . . .").

3. Paraphrases and conversions. Yet another way to integrate writing and grammatical practice is to construct grammatical exercises so that they require considerable rewriting and recasting rather than simply picking the correct option or marking the error and supplying the correct form. While the latter kinds of exercises are useful for determining quickly whether the student has mastered the principle involved, they do not reveal the extent to which the student has moved from a conceptual grasp of the principle to an internalized operational knowledge of the principle, that is, to the ability to produce the correct forms under the stresses and distractions of writing. Nor do they give the student the opportunity to internalize the operation of the principle by practicing the production of the correct forms in the context of a modified form of actual composition.

Exercises of this sort may require the student to convert sentences or entire passages from *of-plus-noun* prepositional phrases to possessives thereof, and vice versa; from the third person singular to the plural, and vice versa, picking up pronoun and subject verb agreement; from the present to the past, and vice versa; from the active voice to the passive and vice versa; from sets of simple sentences to "combined" sentences, and vice versa; from full noun clauses to phrasal equivalents and vice versa; from direct discourse, especially questions, to indirect discourse and vice versa; and so on. There is a natural sequence to many of these exercises, later exercises assuming previous exposure to some grammatical fact. The student who had trouble with simple noun and pronoun possessives will have an opportunity for review in sentence-combining or imitation exercises requiring nominalized structures, including the *-'s -ing*, *-'s -xxx* (special ending) paraphrases mentioned above, as for example, in sentence-combining exercises of this sort:

Combine the two sentences below, using *is -ing* and *-'s -xxx* to convert the second sentence to a phrase replacing SOMETHING, as in the example:

I was worried about SOMETHING.
My parents had disappeared mysteriously.
-s -ing
   I was worried about my parents' disappearing mysteriously.
-s -xxx
   I was worried about my parents' mysterious disappearance.

4. Imitation. Still another way to integrate writing and grammatical practice is through imitation exercises of various sorts. In one kind of close imitation, emphasizing function words and word endings, the student matches one sentence with another of his own, by filling in the blanks appropriately. It is sometimes helpful to suggest the topic of the new sentence, especially in the early exercises (see B below), lest students inadvertently pick a topic, like the abstract word *aspect*, that makes parallelism difficult. Thus:

Match these sentences with three of your own:

A.   I *was* worried *about* my parents' disappear*ing* mysterious*ly*.

1.   _____ was _____ ed about _____ _____ s'
      _____ ing _____ ly.
2.   _____ was _____ ed about _____ _____ s'
      _____ ing _____ ly.
3.   _____ was _____ ed about _____ _____ s'
      _____ ing _____ ly.

Now write a sentence of your own, making it structurally identical to the three you have already produced.
1.   _____

B.   *The* gent*ly* fall*ing* snow sift*ed* *through* *the* denud*ed* branch*es* *of* *the* tree.

1.   The _____ ly _____ ing man _____ ed
      through the _____ ed _____ (e)s of the _____ .
2.   The _____ ly _____ ing snob _____ ed
      through the _____ ed _____ (e)s of the _____ .
3.   The _____ ly _____ ing face _____ ed

through the _____ ed _____ (e)s of the _____ .
Now write two sentences of your own, making them structurally identical to
the three you have already produced.

1. _____
    _____

2. _____
    _____

Sentences with multiple "levels" or "layers" of co-ordination and modification impose their own semantic constraints, and with this sort of
sentence it is best to use a much looser kind of imitation which emphasizes these larger structural relations, and to preface "pure" imitation with
practice combining short sentences where these larger relations have been
worked out. Sentence combining has already been shown to increase the
maturity of student sentences as measured in T-units (essentially all main
clauses with all their modifiers, even if mispunctuated as fragments).[3]
Combining "canned" sentences appears to be less effective than combining student-generated sentences, at least with some remedial students.[4]
Preliminary investigation suggests that imitation exercises have a greater
effect than sentence combining.[5]

It seems likely that a combination of sentence combining and sentence
imitation will prove as or more effective than either strategy alone. Neither
sentence combining nor sentence imitation is exactly comparable to the
process of composing, where the writer simultaneously generates ideas
and wrestles with the various structural options for setting them forth.
But sentence combining allows a student to practice using an option he
underexploits in a context that is right, by supplying ready-made content,
and sentence imitation encourages him to generate both the structure he
underexploits as well as a semantically appropriate context for it. Of the
two, imitation is the more difficult and the more similar to actual composition, unlike it in imposing sharp restrictions on both content and form
that are absent in ordinary spontaneous composition. But these restric-

3. See John C. Mellon's *Transformational Sentence Combining*, Research Report No. 6
(Champaign, Ill.: NCTE, 1966) and Frank O'Hare's *Sentence Combining*, Research
Report No. 15 (Champaign, Ill.: NCTE, 1971).
4. Studies of sentence combining with remedial students include James Wesley
Howell's "A Comparison of Achievement of Students in Remedial English Using a
Linguistic and a Traditional Approach" (Diss. New York Univ., 1973), Andrea Luns-
ford's "An Historical, Descriptive, and Evaluative Study of Remedial English in
American Colleges and Universities" (Diss. Ohio State Univ., 1977), and Leslie
Freede's, "The Impact of Sentence Combining on the Syntactic Maturity of College
Students at the Remedial Level (Master's Thesis, City College, 1976).
5. Rosemary Hake (Chicago State) and Joseph Williams (University of Chicago)
have noted these results in carefully matched sentence-combining and imitation
exercises.

tions may channel thought productively, actually suggesting lines of development as well as limiting them.

An exercise combining the techniques of sentence generation, sentence combining and imitation generally needs four components of incremental difficulty: (1) an example showing shorter separate sentences and how they might be combined according to a specific structural pattern, (2) a structurally parallel group of sentences which the student is to combine using the specified pattern, (3) an incomplete group of sentences with the most difficult parts of the content and the structurally crucial elements given, which the student is to complete and then combine according to the same pattern, (4) space for the student to work out his own sentences and his own combination of them, with the structurally crucial elements given. If the student is likely to become stalled because he cannot find appropriate content, the instructor may want to give the sentence(s) or suggest topics suitable to parallel development. These four stages are isolated at steps A though D in two exercises. The first exercise results in single descriptive sentences of some complexity, the second in expository paragraphs of four sentences. As a finale for the second exercise, the student is given strategies for doubling the length—and substance—of these paragraphs, and an opportunity to practice these strategies.

These sorts of exercises are turned to best use when they move from narrative and descriptive passages to the exposition we want our students to learn to produce. Then they can be used to teach the student to develop and order kinds of content such as different examples, different reasons for coming to the same conclusion, different results and their place in the cause-effect chain. We can also use them to teach the student to recognize and exploit the semantic equivalence and syntactic differences of the words and phrases that specify the relationships between clauses such as *but, however,* and *although,* and *as a result, with the result that* and *so that* in the second sample exercise.

A final word about imitation exercises. They can and should be turned to rhetorical questions. The necessity of imitating may lead a student to omit ideas or to raise his points in an infelicitous order. Students may discuss, for example, whether the three reasons given for opposing gun control in Exercise 2 in the Appendix are raised in the most effective order, moving as they do from large matters of political wisdom in governance to matters of private inconvenience or private sacrifice. Are there different effective orders? One for arguing the case, another for rebutting it? Imitation exercises may well conclude with the suggestion that the student start over with the same topic from scratch, free of the restrictions that imitation imposed on the development of his ideas.

The discovery approach. I have argued that it is most productive for Basic Writing students if their instructors teach only that grammar necessary for the student to address error, and even *that* grammar as economically and as thoroughly integrated into the process of writing as possible.

I would argue further that what turns out to be economical in the long run is often time-consuming over the short haul. The paradoxical economy of the longer explanation arises for two reasons. First, some phenomena, such as the construction of verb phrases, are so complex that nothing other than a long drawn out analysis makes the total system comprehensible. Second, almost any grammatical point is more interesting to the student when he himself discovers the "rule" or "convention" from examples of its operation, instead of the more customary handbook method of stating the rule and giving examples. For any point of instruction, the instructor must weigh the complexity of the point and gains in student interest against the inevitable expenditure of extra time lost to other purposes.

The inductive or discovery approach has three further advantages. The student tends to remember the conclusion he has drawn himself better than one he has been given, and if his memory begins to slip, he has access to a method for recovering the rule. In addition, the approach fosters an exploratory, open classroom tone which encourages the student to interact with, challenge, and one-up his classmates in a spirit of friendly competitiveness and mutual inquiry. Finally, it respects the student's intelligence, treating the student as the teacher's equal, not in acquired knowledge, certainly, but in insight and perceptiveness.

1. Sharp focus on significant differences. The success of the discovery method depends upon the instructor's skill with two strategies. The first of these is the strategy of pulling together, into one place, all the structures the student finds confusing. Sometimes these structures are closely related in meaning but significantly different in form, as with the phrase and dependent clause variants of an independent clause; sometimes the structures are essentially unrelated, but superficially similar, as in the case of the *-s*'s ending words. In either case, the student experiences the structures as an imperfectly discriminated, only partially articulated whole. Thus, the instructor should operate out of a strictly conceived contrastive approach, which excludes, at first, all of the distracting variables which are the actuality of real language use but off the structural point at hand. By the term "strictly conceived contrastive approach," I do not mean the method of foreign language teaching based upon "contrastive analysis" of the structures of the native language and the foreign language, though I do not recommend against this approach for students with many deeply seated native language or dialect differences for whom relatively few standard inflections come easily, even in conferences, and for whom the overt translation may be productive. What I have in mind is the simultaneous presentation of the structural variants for essentially identical kinds of logical relation or semantic content in the target dialect. This strategy not only emphasizes the resourcefulness and variety of the language; it forces the student to focus on those function words and inflectional endings by which structural differences are signalled—precisely those words and endings which escape or bedevil him in the proofreading.

For example, in introducing the sentence, it has proven illuminating and economical to give the student lists of semantically related structures like these, asking him to identify the *one* complete sentence in each group by giving it a capital and period:

for the child to sing sweetly
the child's sweet song
the sweetly singing child
the child singing sweetly
the child is singing sweetly
that the child is singing sweetly
if the child is singing sweetly
whenever the child is singing sweetly

for the woman to smile knowingly
the woman's knowing smile
the knowingly smiling woman
the woman smiling knowingly
the woman was smiling knowingly
that the woman was smiling knowingly
because the woman was smiling knowingly
so that the woman was smiling knowingly

for the bomb to explode suddenly
the bomb's sudden explosion
the suddenly exploding bomb
the bomb exploding suddenly
the bomb exploded suddenly
that the bomb exploded suddenly
when the bomb exploded suddenly
unless the bomb exploded suddenly

for the student to be genuinely astonished
the student's genuine astonishment
the genuinely astonished student
the student being genuinely astonished

the student was genuinely astonished
that the student was genuinely astonished
since the student was genuinely astonished
although the student was genuinely astonished

The students are then asked to try to define a sentence—not as a complete idea—but in terms of its structural parts: what it must have and what it must lack. The instructor leads the class at the board in identifying all the things that change from line to line with circles, underlining the things that do not change; for example, in the first group, *the, child, sing, sweet* would be underlined, and *for, to, -ly, -ing, is, that, if, whenever* circled. When the instructor reaches the addition of the word *is,* he makes the point that this word marks the noun-verb relationship for time, as one can tell by substituting another time-marked word, *was.* None of the earlier word groups were marked for time. The time of the action expressed by these verbs will vary according to the time expressed in the verbs that must be added to turn these word groups into sentences: "The child's sweet song *is bringing/ brought/ will bring* tears to my eyes." As the instructor moves through the dependent clauses, he leads students to note that they are identical to the complete sentence, except that they contain an extra word which marks the clause as a part of some other sentence. The students are led to the conclusion that a sentence must have a subject and a tense-marked verb and must lack a dependent clause marker. The teacher should work through one or two sets of sentences on the board, then have the students do the circles and underlinings for another one or two independently at their desks.

At the next stage, the instructor has the class give the non-sentence equivalents of *Flight 110 is arriving promptly; The infant whimpered weakly, Gus laughs easily* and *My mother was truly pleased;* the first one or two as board work, the last independently. Students then use the same system of circling the variables and underlining the constants, to be sure they got their versions right.

Last of all the students look at three structures which are ambiguous grammatically: they can be sentences or not, depending on context: *which woman was smiling knowingly* (as direct question or noun clause), *the student genuinely astonished* (as nominative absolute, as noun with non-restrictive participle, as direct object noun with direct object participial complement, as sentence with an omitted, context-clear object) and *the child's singing sweetly* (as gerund phrase paraphrasable as *the child's sweet singing* and as a sentence with a contracted *is*). Obviously the students do not struggle with labels; they simply produce sentence and non-sentence examples, by adding words, paraphrasing, changing intonation, and supplying the situational context to illustrate their insights. From this point the class can move in one of several directions—for example, to a discussion of the different kinds of -*s*, all of which they have had to use in these paraphrases, or to sentence expansion and contraction exercises.

2. Incrementation. The second strategy necessary for a successful discovery process, especially for the weaker students, is a very careful and purposeful incrementation, moving from the state of extremely simplified contrasts of bare-bones structures through the stages by which increasingly complex variables and distracting items are added, in the order which will prove most helpful to the students. For instance, familiar words are easier than unfamiliar words, short words are easier than long ones, verbs which require no derivational ending when converted to noun function (*smile*) are easier than those that do (*astonishment*), active-voice verbs are easier than passives, common derivational patterns (*astonish/astonishment*) are easier than less common ones (*demean, demeanor*), unambiguous structures are easier than ambiguous ones. The purpose of incrementation is to avoid overwhelming the less confident or weaker student with more information than he can process simultaneously. Like the llama bearing only one stick too many, the student may be unable to rise. In the exercise just above, for example, it may be a good idea to eliminate the adjective-to-adverb conversion (*sweet, sweetly*) for some or all of the groups of sentences, depending upon the entry level of the students and the rate at which they are mastering the phrase and dependent clause variants of the simple sentence. Similarly, the common adjective-to-adverb conversion should be practiced before flat adverbs like *early* and *fast*, or irregular conversions like *good/well*, or converted prepositional phrases (*arriving at noon/noon arrival*); and intransitive complete verbs before intransitive linking verbs and transitive verbs taking direct objects. In sentences with both indirect and direct objects, or direct objects and direct object complements, some of the phrase variants are so clumsy that a few examples serve as an admonishment to avoid them, and students should be encouraged to develop ugliness scales for such structures as *my giving Mary a little help* and *my gift to Mary of a little help*, and *the gift to Mary from me of a little help*.

Finally, at the same time the instructor laboriously learns how, like a slow-motion instant-replay camera, to delay and replay the flow of language events, he must also be able to fast-forward through them as rapidly as progress admits, even to drop all his painstakingly developed exercises as soon as it becomes apparent the exercises address problems the students do not or no longer have.

THE LIMITS OF GRAMMARS

Every grammatical approach is limited. Each has a bias growing out of some central assumption, some central problem to be solved, some central question to be answered. Each has, as a result, strengths of a certain kind and weaknesses of other kinds. Traditional grammar, with its emphasis on words and meanings and its assumption that Latin was the model, tends to be prescriptive, even inaccurate, and often about matters of little moment, has little to say useful on word order, and gives a static rather than dynamic view of language. But much is of value: the labels for parts of speech and their functions, and much of the semantic subcategorization of the parts of speech, such as the subclassification of nouns as concrete or abstract, count or mass, common or proper, has been incorporated into subsequent grammars. Structural grammar, with its emphasis on the linearity of language and on discovery procedures that would reveal the internal structures of that linear sequence, has much more to say that is useful about the discovery process, about defining the parts of speech by function word signals, inflections and derivational affixes rather than meaning, and about the order of syntactic elements. But it has relatively little to say about the kinds of relations that undergird, cut across, or transcend word order. Transformational generative grammar, with its emphasis on these transformational relations between structures and its disputes about what should be regarded as transforms, has much to say of use about these relations and suggests many useful strategies such as sentence combining and transformational paraphrasing, but in a language of symbols and diagrams so foreign and technical that it remains inaccessible to most.

There appear to be, regrettably, limits upon every attempt to deal with the full range of possibilities in the language in a simple way. The extremely elegant transformation rule for verb-phrase structure which I take up below does not tidily account for the way *ought to* lacks a present equivalent (*owe* is obsolete), or the way *must go* is the present equivalent of *had to go,* nor the behavior of other modal-like structures. Fortunately, these structures are not the source of written errors for many students. Similarly, the x-word grammar strategy of having students turn declarative sentences to questions is extremely useful in teaching subject-verb agreement, tense-marking, subject location and in overcoming the sentence fragment. Instructors will be delighted to discover that the question technique will locate the subject of "There's the book you wanted me to read" by normalizing the order: 'Is the book you wanted me to read there?" Many will be dismayed to find the word *there* identified as the subject in sentences like "There are things I can do to help" when the sentence is converted: "Are there things I can do to help?" This same strategy will help students who write frequent fragments find most of them: long introductory phrases, subjects divided from verbs, verbs separated from subjects, and adverb clauses simply will not convert. Neither will a few other structures which are, nonetheless, complete sentences. Sentences with subject infinitives such as "For Nixon to deny involvement angered the public" do not convert as "Did for Nixon to deny involvement anger the public?" but as "Did it anger the public for Nixon to deny involvement?" and sentences with comparisons on the pattern of *the more, the merrier,* such as "The less the student writes, the less he improves" do not convert gracefully to "Is the less the student writes, the less he improves?" Something like "Is it true that the less the student writes, the less he improves?" is the grammatical paraphrase. Furthermore, some fragments can be converted to questions: The author's intent can escape the strategic net if the author intends a single sentence in such constructions as "I didn't know. Which waitress would come to my table" and "I hadn't realized. That was the book. She wanted me to read." Every system has the painful exceptions that require elaboration of the "simple" rule.

Beyond the conceptual limitations of any given grammar, and the limitations imposed by the complexity of language itself, there is the fact that no grammar that is taught to Basic Writing students as it would be taught to upperclassmen or graduate students, that is, largely divorced from practice in perception, intensive writing, and enforced proofreading, will have a significant effect on the writing of these students. As suggested earlier, the better results obtained with structural and generative grammars as theoretical bases seem to depend upon the fact that they suggested exercises which involved actually operating the language rather than merely dissecting it. A further limit upon the effectiveness of grammatical instruction is the human limitation of the instructor: limited time, limited information, and limited imagination in addressing the problems of perception, production, and proofreading. We can do a great deal to overcome the weaknesses of individual grammars, to expand our knowledge, and to stimulate our imaginations by reading widely and by consciously mediating between grammatical analysis and the synthesis of writing. For the chief limit of grammar is that grammatical analysis has no necessary connection to the synthetic process of writing. Perception is not production. Production is not proofreading. By whatever system the instruction is done, diagraming and parsing are about as similar to writing as admiring the dance and executing it, watching pro ball and playing it. We minimize our effectiveness anytime we lose sight of this first principle.

Putting Error in Its Place

I began teaching Basic Writing six years ago by, first of all, doing my homework: aside from reading the popular classics on ghetto life, I found articles about dialect and went to lectures. On the first day of my first class, I presented my students with a list of all the errors they would most likely be making during the semester. In the left margin of this sheet, I had handwritten all the symbols I would be using to indicate their errors in red, and for each one, I supplied sentences with examples of subject-verb agreement mistakes, verb tense inconsistencies, plural *s*'s left off, *etc.*—sentences I had either gleaned from the texts I had been reading or had made up, using Relevant contexts. (In those days, relevant was spelled with a capital R.) By the end of the semester, I was quite satisfied that many of the students had learned, for example, that subjects should agree with verbs, that "John book" circled in red was a problem to do with possession. Students who showed they knew what these errors were got good grades—they passed the tests—and if they continued to slip up in their own writing, I figured it mainly would just take time.

It was only when the special program I was working in established a work-study system where older students could tutor others that I began to learn something about teaching students how to write. I eavesdropped while Tony, whom I had hired to tutor some of my "weaker" students, worked with Deborah on one of her papers in my office. I cannot remember now exactly what they were saying as they looked at the sheet; what I do remember is how they were both attacking it with pleasure—drawing

From *Journal of Basic Writing*, 1 (Spring, 1975), 72–86. Reprinted by permission of the *Journal of Basic Writing* and Isabella Halsted.

marks across it, writing in, starting anew upside down on the side—because it really didn't say what she meant at all. His saying: "Look, man, this doesn't make sense, to me anyway. I just don't get the scene. And by the way, that was *yesterday*." "Oh, yeah," (she sighs, scratching it in) "-*ed*, right?" "Right . . . sure . . . So, go on tell me what you *really* felt when he looked at you that way on the bus." "Well . . . ," she begins, "I . . ." "So why didn't you say so in the first place? Put it *down*." (She starts in.) "*Good!*" I could say that of course Deborah felt more comfortable with another student, and in this case, another Black, and leave it at that. But to do so would be skirting the issue: Tony was teaching writing, not Error.

The novice teacher of remedial writing may never be as misguided as I was, but I believe that most of us even after years of experience in this field still tend to fall back on Error, sometimes as an old friend. This is most likely because here we are on solid ground—for if we are rightfully questioning everything else we are doing, we can never doubt our growing expertise in the recognition of Error. We need only look at the kind of feedback we tend to give our students on their papers—especially when in a hurry. The words circled in vivid color ("blood," as one student puts it), the cop-out comment "awkward" (or "AWK!"), or "This paper is better than the last one, *but* . . ."—all show the penchant we have for teaching the *good* in terms of what it is *not*. And whether we mean it to be so, our students recognize what they already have learned so well: this is what the teacher looks for, this is what writing is all about: The Avoidance of Error. Our students tell us so, in many ways.

Witness Lois, a student whose anxiety runs high, though her writing is superior to most in my class this semester:

> I'm sorry my typing is so bad and its' rather messy, I was going to type it agin. But I just couldn't make it (This is why I didn't go to class today) I hope you will take into account my effort and disregard the untidyness.

"What do you do when you sit down to write?" I ask Diane, who is biting the end of her ballpoint, unable to start. "Well, first I figure out what you want me to say, then I try to say it." Merline writes in pencil so light that you can hardly read it. Stan writes pages and pages with never a single indentation, the -*ed* and -*s* endings sometimes there, sometimes not, and all of it joined by commas. He leaves as soon as his hand gets tired or the bell rings, flinging it all at me. David, in an hour's time, writes, rewrites, rewrites and hands in six sentences, in very neat, impeccably neat script. Sam, during a free-writing exercise ("just write, forget grammar, write anything that's in your mind, write until I say stop"), lets it all out:

I am behind in my writing for my English class. I have dealt with my writing in the past but. I think this time it's got the best of me. When it comes to writing I have the right idea in my mind but I am can not put it down on paper. I know how important it is to stay in college and to be able to express your self in writing. I know I have troubles in my writing and in my mind I said I want to overcome these probelms but these is allway something on my mind that stops me from writing.

(What is that "something" on Sam's mind?)

These students have in common their alienation from writing—writing is a foreign activity. Little in their experience has shown them the significance of written language in their lives—its daily necessity, its possibilities for discovery, its pleasures—or the many purposes to which they can put this kind of language. True, their school experience has drilled them to comply with, if not necessarily to respect, certain pragmatic uses for writing, but the focus has often been the avoidance of Error. The student whose egregious grammatical, syntactical, and proofreading habits place him in English 1 and the student in English 2 or 3 who writes what she figures I want her to say are alike in their distance from the process of writing and their preoccupation with the possibility of wrongdoing. Sam, of course, has an enormous obstacle: he lacks the basic skills required for communication in written standard English, and knows this so well that it "stops me from writing." But Diane is also deprived—she writes brief, vapid, generalized essays, organized simplistically, never reflecting her complicated person, her intelligence, or her desire in spoken dialogue to express her often opinionated views. Sam has an important edge on her: he knows he wants to "put it down on paper."

In a departmental exam, one student was outspoken in his view of the problem:

> Is writing easier than talking? I believe it is not because writing has a lot of regulations where talking doesn't have so many. . . . Grammer happens to be something that requires rules and regulations. Grammer includes things such as, noun and verb agreement, when is the proper time to use adjectives and adverbs, and then what punctuation mark is needed at the end of the sentence. English happens to be the worst language to write in because this is the only language which has exception. . . . Spelling is another hardship for many people. English being a rotten language anyway encounters many difficulties because English is derived from many languages and also many words have different spellings in different situations dued to these so-called exceptions to the exceptions. . . . After one has conquered these mistakes in writing, there is the main problem left which is trying to project one's ideas in writing to another person. . . . In talking the main thing is communi-

cation. . . . In talking you can forget a few things and make it up but in writing it is disastorous.

This student is freer than most from the curse he describes—he has taken a clear stance of resigned disgust and calls it all "disastorous"—, but I feel that he is speaking for the rest of them: Writing is a burden; English "grammer" is full of rules, regulations and hardships ("being a rotten language anyway"); the goal is first to *conquer the mistakes*. All would agree: talking is easier, yes, because thank god—and by contrast—in talking, at least, "the main thing is communication." (In writing, it's not.)

Like this one, our students come to us with a thorough misconception of what writing is all about. Only a rare few say they enjoy it. Some will admit outright that they fear it. When I asked a class to describe how their attitude had changed, if at all, since the beginning of the semester, one wrote: "I guess it's changed. I don't think I'm as afraid as I was before. Maybe that made all the difference." Another: "I can write more words and ideas than I normally did in the past. I am not scared to write about anything I feel." Others, as I have suggested, reveal their fear and dislike through the way they do it, rather than what they directly say— *e.g.*, in the refusal to proofread, the anxiety to "find out what you want me to say," the manic concern with neatness, or conversely, the wish to be unreadable, or to get it all out of the way as fast as possible. At the ages of eighteen or nineteen, they are so engaged to the fear of Error (read that also: "What is Right?" "What do you want me to say?" "What is the Rule?" "Forgive my typing errors.") that they are incapable of spontaneity or trust in themselves. And lacking these, how can they begin to break through to writing? How can they hope to succeed—or be willing to fail here and there along the way? And where do we come in?

I believe that the students' fixation on Error is equally matched by our own, however well-meaning we be. We must look again at our own attitudes and the images of language and of writing we project in the classrooms and in our offices as we read and mark our students' papers. Yet so often here it is Error, not communication, that is being taught. A case in point: the other day a former student came to my office extremely upset with the first long paper she had written for her present English teacher. I turned each page, looking at red marks: circled commas (misplaced); carets (word missing); every misspelled word underlined with an occasional remonstratory remark like "What, Miss X, you've done it *again!*"; and one or two "good points" in the margin. I got to the end of the paper and found an oversized *F* with the brief comment: "Although this paper shows considerable thought and is well-organized, your run-ons and spelling mistakes are *inexcusable*." This teacher had doubtless thought that by emphasizing errors, he might jolt the student into doing something about them. Needless to say, the effect was the opposite. Rather than emphasizing and so encouraging her performance where it mattered—her thought and her ability to communicate it logically to her reader—he reinforced her pessimism and sense of despair. He was teaching Error, not writing.

Are we unwittingly perpetuating attitudes which are a major cause of our students' problems with writing? As we become masters of Error, more and more skillful in this pursuit, it seems that we are very hard put to agree on what good writing is—and this is part of where the trouble lies.

It is doubtful that in the last analysis writing effectiveness can be measured wholly objectively—and those who claim this, I feel, ignore the subtleties involved in what constitutes communication—but it is surely possible to find a middle ground between that extreme and the other, which refuses objectivity altogether. That teachers do apply standards they consider absolute to their students' writing is a fact, yet the vast discrepancy in teachers' standards is legion. At a Basic Writing meeting recently, teachers were asked to be "blind readers" of several papers, to simply place these students on various levels and to justify their choice. Of a group of merely twenty-five or thirty teachers, all with considerable experience in the field, there were those who placed a student's paper in English 3 where others would have put it in English 1. Some teachers focussed on grammar mistakes; others ignored these in favor of logic; others loved style. Yet very few, I think, had they read any of these papers at leisure, would have said: "This is a student who can write, who doesn't need my help."

And if that is so—if teachers generally acknowledge a student's need for help—there must be a means of defining what constitutes writing that is *not* in need of help. What *do* we mean by good writing? Why do we sometimes sense that student X, with the occasional dropped *-ed*'s and peculiar word order configurations, might actually make it on his own? What is it about Y's writing, grammatically competent, neatly organized, that makes us feel she needs at least a semester more? Why do we place a student in English 2 rather than English 1? Why do we decide the English 2 student can skip English 3? We are given decisions like this to make, but can we define our standards for judgment? If we acknowledge that a major problem our students (and we ourselves) have is a fixation on Error, an anxiety about "conquering the mistakes," what can we do to put Error in its place?

We should begin by a reconsideration of what Error is, for writing, and reaffirm in the process what we mean by *good* writing so that we may instead teach *that*. As I have suggested so far, Error fixation includes the whole range: from what we might call the "details" of the language to the broadest areas—the logic and substance of the whole. So often, that attitude of mind in the student which worries to the point of paralysis about whether or not the grammar is "right" is the same attitude which automatically responds to a teacher's suggestion with "What do you want me to say? How do you want me to say it?"—attitudes which, of course, mirror the way the student has been taught to view writing.

How do we put Error in its place and so get on to the business of writing? Of course, we must become fully acquainted with the sources of errors of whatever nature in our students' papers and, if we don't have it already, build respect in ourselves for the validity of the languages our students are masters of and the cultures they reflect. This knowledge will help us to see Error in a different light and alter the ways in which we deal with it together, our students and we. We should give due respect to the importance of Error for what it is—no more *and* no less. Error is certainly *not* Sin; it is not Crime punishable by *F*. As Orwell once wrote, "Good prose is like a window pane." Like soot on the pane, Error is something that gets in the way of the clear vision. We know this: we are irritated by misused words and clumsy sentences just as we are by faulty logic or misused facts—and in our reading, by a printer's mistake. Error on all levels is distracting, annoying, obstructive. Error is inexcusable ultimately, yes, not because it is Wrong *per se*, but because, as Jimmy Breslin once remarked to one writing class to make a wider point: "Look, I wouldn't be caught dead with a misspelled word! *Who wants to read* a misspelled word? If I couldn't spell, I'd cut my fingers off!" In plain pragmatic terms, the absence of Error is useful; but when our students take pains to avoid it—by writing short sentences, by sticking to one tense, by writing as little as possible—I doubt very much that they do so in order to better communicate with a reader, but rather to play safe, to avoid the red marks.

The *CCCC* position paper of last year ("Students' Right to Their Own Language") states:

> Perhaps the most serious difficulty facing non-standard dialect speakers in developing writing ability derives from their exaggerated concern for the *least* serious aspects of writing. If we can convince our students that spelling, punctuation, and usage are less important than content, we have removed a major obstacle in their developing the ability to write.[1]

The statement correctly identifies the students' "exaggerated concern" and implicitly, our *own* exaggerated concern, but in suggesting that such mat-

1. "Students' Right to Their Own Language," *College Composition and Communication*, Special Issue, 25 (Fall 1974), 8.

ters as spelling, punctuation and usage are not serious and that teachers should focus instead on content, it distorts the problem. The problem is not an "either/or," "correctness" v. "content" issue. The problem is, rather, that in our teaching of spelling, punctuation, usage, we are going about it the wrong way; that in our teaching of other important aspects—sentence complexity, paragraph logic, or essay organization—we tend to teach negatively; and sometimes, too, when we focus on content, we are as authoritarian in our expectations as we are in our handing out of prescripts for the way to learn the so-called "least serious aspects." Typically, teachers who reject the teaching of "the least serious aspects" rush off to teach "content," feeling that such challenging topics as "abortion," "capital punishment" or "Watergate" will really turn the student on to communicating—or if these topics don't, by the way, they *should*. Yet, were we to pick up pencil and paper and sit down to write on these topics, we might find them as interesting as the proverbial "What did you do on your summer vacation?" Any of them may or may not be interesting to a student; what is so often deadly dull about all of them, for a writing course in search of subject matter, is that, out of context, they are false topics and too often taught with as much singleminded expectation of "right thinking" as are the "less serious matters" like subordination or -*s* on the verb.

When we are not teaching the language in terms of its pitfalls, we are often reinforcing in other ways the student's sense that writing has little to do with the communication of his or her thought to someone else. Setting ourselves up as the source of Right, by implication, we confirm the student's sense that whatever his or her offering, it must be short of the mark, if not Wrong. Positive remarks on a paper, or in the classroom, are so often to be found in subordinate clauses or overshadowed by "buts" ("*Although* such and such is good, . . .") ("That was an interesting remark, *but* . . ."). "Try harder" means "Not good enough." And we become, of course, the model for what *is*. I needn't spend much time here pointing out that there still do exist teachers who carry on dialogues with themselves in a classroom ("What is the topic sentence of this paragraph?"—with rising inflection, a pause, some furrowed brows, silence—"As usual, the topic sentence of this paragraph is at the beginning, and it is . . ."—falling inflection, pause, some relieved looks, more silence. "And how is it developed?" *Etc.*). This is an extreme, but it can be argued that what passes for "Socratic" teaching is often a much more subtle variation of the same thing. We are agile, clever and bright—artful dodgers—, but as we manipulate our class discussions, we are usually teaching the avoidance of Error: in this case, "What do I have in mind that I want you to say?"

This holds true as much for a lesson in syntax as for a discussion of the latest scandal in the *News,* Ralph Ellison's *Prologue,* or a student's description of someone she saw on the bus. Scene: I write a student sentence on the board. "Well, now," I say with a smile, "and what do we have here? Let's read it together." There is probably not a student in the class who doesn't instantly translate my words as, "What does she think of this? And if she's written it on the board, that means it's Wrong, and I wonder what it is she has in mind that's Right." We all bandy about alternatives for a while, Stan and Lois and Tony all coming up with very good ones and good explanations for them (usually safely phrased as a question: "Wouldn't it be better if the student had added a such-and-such?") No one else in the class says anything, but (I say to myself) they are all at least listening to, witnessing, the process of discovery. And in the friendly, open atmosphere of "let's hear from anyone," when Diane provides an unacceptable solution, fraught with new problems, what can Ms. Halstead say (if she wants to get to where she's going by the end of the hour) but: "Hmmmmm, yes, well, that's an interesting possibility, but . . . ," and Diane also smiles and decides wisely to keep her mouth shut from now on.

("What do you do when you sit down to write a paper?" I figure out what you want me to say, and then I try to say it.")

The so-called non-traditional teacher who wants to make sure that this classroom is a democracy where "It is not I who am right; your answer is just as good as mine as long as you can back it up" is so often lying. It *is* I who am right. My evidence is always stronger and in the end, I always win. Few students are unaware that there is a hidden agenda, and in this scene, classes become guessing games; "dialogue" is a matter of carrying on the game in an atmosphere of tease. It is a good class, for teacher and students alike, if finally someone provides an answer to the riddles and if, for the teacher, anyway, there's been quite a lot of tension, excitement, along the way (with at least fifty percent participation).

But we all know that this is not what writing is all about: writing does not mean the prating of someone else's views any more than it means the avoidance of errors. In encouraging students to focus on what the teacher has in mind, we reinforce the student's basic assumption: if he/she is not careful, he/she will do or say something wrong. The risk of Error will remain the fixed point, the main preoccupation. We must instead put Error in its place by shifting our own and our students' perspective away from where the students' work or thought falls *short* to where it genuinely succeeds.

When *does* it succeed? What is good writing? I suspect that no matter what we do in conference and in the classroom, we probably judge our students' papers no more by the objective interest or import of the subject matter than we do by the absence of errors—these are weighty factors, but factors only. I suspect we judge their writing by whether or not, as we read the first paragraph or two, we find ourselves interested in *whatever* it is the student is trying to say. Too many errors get very much in the way of course; and an opener like "Humbleness is a virtue, everyone has heard this saying at one time or another there lifetime" frankly gets in *my* way, but not chiefly because of the run-on, the spelling, or the missing word. *Is this really Philip talking? Who is he talking to? I really can't believe he cares.* We read on, and our interest is sustained, or it is not. This writer is saying something to me, or, somehow, he is not.

The focus of a writing course should be communication. A student we judge to be well on the way to good writing shows basic awareness of what it is all about: there is a sensed audience and a point of view to be expressed, involving thought and demonstration. It is this basic awareness that we should develop in the class, in conference, in reading their papers. At all times, we should provide our students with an experience where no matter what the material, they are encouraged to discover their individual points of view and are given the chance to see that these are worthy of attention, that others are listening, and that there are effective ways to communicate them in writing. And by focussing on this, we will help our students to understand, and even enjoy, the process of writing.

In conferences, or in our "silent" comments on our students' papers, we should create a dialogue which makes clear that the word, the sentence, or the organization of the essay are all simply ways of getting across what the student has in mind to say to *someone else.* If we are dealing with the "least serious aspects," let us in our emphasis show our students that errors are important for only one reason: they interrupt the flow between writer and reader. Thus, when the student-tutor Tony saw a dropped *-ed,* he pointed it out to Deborah almost as an aside, in the context of "didn't this all happen yesterday?" His emphasis was on meaning, rather than the rules. A dangler misleads, muddles, sometimes amuses; that it doesn't stand next to the word it modifies is not the main issue at all. That group of sentences has me going in three directions at once! What is your main point? (Not: "There is no topic sentence; you need conjunctions.")

In this dialogue, we function not as "Teacher" and therefore Right, as our students tend to think, but as interested, skeptical and close readers who want to know what our students have to say. Because we have more resources and experience, we can help to figure out how something can be said more effectively. To project this novel view, for our students, is very important. If they could eventually internalize this "intelligent reader" voice we speak with, they would not so often be saying to us,

"When *you* read it and ask me those questions, I see what you mean. . . ."

But to talk here about the refinements of writing is starting, perhaps, at the end, rather than the beginning. We meet in conference with our students, usually, *after* the fact—when it is the time to proofread what's on paper, to refine, to rewrite, to think of the final product. Before this, our students must have gone through all the various aspects that make up the writing process—a process, which, as we have already said, they have little or no love for and scarce practice in doing.

We must do all we can to make that process meaningful, workable. Generally, we tend to stress writing as a finished product, forgetting what William Stafford, the poet, has expressed well: "A writer is not so much someone who has something to say as he is someone who has found a process that will bring about new things he would not have thought of if he had not started to say them."[2] If this is so for all writers, we must rethink much of what many of us do to set off the writing process. Is it really valid, for example, to urge that students take notes, organize these into an outline, into a topic outline, into a sentence outline, *before* starting to write? "How can I know what I think 'til I see what I say?" our students so justly complain, echoing Forster's neat phrase. We seldom give as much importance to the draft copies our students write—if we allow them—as we do to the final product, and in dismissing the draft as a mechanical step, we force the student to picture only some abstract "perfect paper," by which standard any of his or her productions must fall into Error's grasp. A near impossible task, for anyone, usually provides a good incentive to lose interest, if not give up, in anticipation of failure.

"I must be willing to fail," Stafford goes on. "If I am to keep on writing, I cannot bother to insist on high standards. I must get into action and not let anything stop me, or even slow me much."[3] Stafford might well be talking for the free-writing advocates (e.g. Macrorie, Elbow) who contend persuasively that most of us in the classroom go about teaching/ learning how to write backwards. Peter Elbow traces the progression of his paralysis as a writer, until in graduate school, which involved "deciding to try *very hard* and plan my writing *very carefully* . . . I finally

---

2. William Stafford, "A Way of Writing," *Field*, Spring, 1970, p. 10.
3. *Ibid.* By standards, here, Stafford specifies that he does not mean spelling, punctuation, etc. (details of "correctness" which he feels will "become mechanical for anyone who writes for a while"); he means "what many people would consider 'important' standards, such matters as social significance, positive values, consistency, etc." For the purposes of my argument here, I would include *both* "correctness" and "significance" or "consistency" as standards which must be set aside for the moment in this stage of writing.

reached the point where I could not write at all."[4]) He discovered what should be obvious to us all—that the obsession with the final product, the "high standards" we have had imposed on us and have internalized for ourselves, is what leads ultimately to serious writing block. More importantly, it is a sure way to close off avenues to discovering what it is you have to say. "Writing is a way to end up thinking something you couldn't have started out thinking."[5] Elbow suggests a reverse: start writing, write and write without stopping, do not think, do not pause, do not criticize for a while. . . . *Later* for the critical eye, later for the editing, the organizing, the skills—the "standards."

Students go giddy at the happy notion that they can write about anything without looking back, that when they can't think of anything to write, they have to write something anyway. Free writing, at its freest, helps to restore the spontaneity and confidence that have been so successfully killed by Error-consciousness—to |be |replaced\ by |the |archenemies of writing: fear, caution, resentment, boredom. Returning to Sam, from whose free-written paper I quoted at the beginning of this article: for the first time in the semester he wrote steadily, two full pages. "I am can not put it down on paper," he wrote. "Sam," I said afterwards, "you just did."

I have found that teaching students to write freely, helping them to temporarily exorcise the censor in them, is in itself a project that takes time, but it is valid and fruitful. Not only does it help to put Error where it belongs (in this case, later), and so free the student to discover private thought; it becomes a way of teaching students that writing is also a "public" endeavour. As students and teacher share each other's writings (perhaps we have all taken off from the same general topic), we discover *not* that "Sam writes better/worse than I do" but we all think differently on this same subject. Free-writing is non-competitive: it produces many different, but equally valid and interesting points of view and ways of expressing them. We all begin to listen to each other and to discuss ways these first outspillings might be later developed into something more focussed, perhaps, more easily accessible to another, a reader.

In the classroom, there must be opportunity for the airing of many points of view. Students must want to express themselves and will do so only if they feel that each of them has a point of view valid to be expressed. If the class centers around what the teacher wants the students to know about something "out there," then the student feels, of course, that his or her writing should be at the very best a reflection of what the

---

4. Peter Elbow, *Writing Without Teachers* (New York: Oxford, 1973), p. 17.
5. *Ibid.*, p. 15.

teacher has in mind about "that." If instead, the focus is on discovering what "I" have to say, on listening to what someone else says, how another reacts, what is said to reinforce the idea and how, how the other responds, etc., then the kinds of questions, the voices, the dialogue that goes on privately in our heads as we write with an audience in mind, are being experienced directly and out loud for the benefit of all.

Free writing is only one of the many ways that have been described elsewhere for restructuring what happens in the classroom so as to shift the emphasis from the teacher to the student, from emulating a model to tangling directly with the problems inherent to communication. I will only briefly mention some options: as much as possible, *let students teach each other,* by running class discussions, by being listeners and commentators, readers and evaluators of each other's work. By so doing, they all become aware of audience and discover first hand what standards for effective communication are. (We may be vague when asked to spell out standards, but our students seldom are. Usually kind and generous, they are still very frank when it comes to asking key questions such as "Look, man, why didn't you say so?" "You didn't finish that sentence and made me go on reading, so I had to go back and read it all over again.")

Groups: A student who is part of a group working together to present something to the rest of the class can suddenly discover that without him or her some input is lacking, and that the putting over, to the others, is a project important in itself. Groups for teaching grammar, groups for presenting concepts, for analyzing a reading, groups for acting out argument (put Antigone on trial?)— students are involved without being told what they are supposed to be doing in defining a point of view, presenting it, communicating clearly to a willing and critical audience.

Media: Slides and films heighten individual perception, a key to good writing, and they do more than that: they provide a direct shortcut to the teaching of the equality of point of view, the subjectivity of inference, the necessity for substantiation and the need to persuade. Too, when students produce their own, they become involved in thinking processes fundamental to written composition: a student who made a collage as a pre-writing project for a definition of Justice discovered, as she explained to the class, that she had found many aspects she hadn't realized she could talk about, and that in making it, one of her most difficult tasks was which pictures to select and how to arrange them to achieve the focus she wanted so that they could see what she had to say.

These various possibilities imply a departure from what either our students or we have known as the traditional English class. For our students, if all goes well, they mean an opportunity which many have never experienced before to discover that genuine communication does not end at the door of the classroom and that writing is a significant and absorbing part of it.

If all goes well. For ourselves as teachers, the departure is problematical, by no means easy. It means breaking long-entrenched habits of thought about what we are there for and how to proceed. What seems to be a "turning over" of authority, the opening up of the classroom (to let the students in?) is threatening. Genuine dialogue means listening and respecting the unexpected. Groups mean not only careful planning but a lot of noise, seeming chaos. Letting students run discussions means having to bite your tongue to keep quiet. Media means machines and *their* quirks. Freewriting means permitting the sentence fragment, doubting the perfected paragraph, for the moment. All of this takes such a lot of time that seems time wasted, if not violated, by our old standards. It is small consolation that in shifting the center, we free ourselves of the burden of feeling we must control every word in a lesson hour from beginning to end. Opening the class up to allow for dialogue means seeing our role as teachers differently and taking on a different kind of responsibility. It is much more difficult to be a guide than a director, a catalyst than a determiner, to suggest than to dictate. In this new situation, we must find ways to provide structure in such a way that, rather than giving students only an illusion of freedom and exploration, we create a framework which in fact allows our students to freely explore and produce. Only in this context will writing become meaningful to them.

We are teaching courses designated as skills courses. We are told to make up in four months or eight or twelve for twelve years of schooling which have failed to meet our students' various needs, else they wouldn't be with us. If we see our task as primarily something that must be done quickly, we are in danger of not doing it at all. There is no short-cut to teaching writing, and in my view, "skills" cannot be considered separate from all the factors that make up the process. This is particularly true for our students whose negative attitudes about writing are nearly insuperable obstacles. A student who does not want to learn something will not, and so our main concern must be to convince our students that writing—with all its components, including acceptable forms—is more than worth the effort. This can only be done where we make clear what it is for, by giving them opportunity to sense that what they have to say is worth listening to, that others are there, and the work involved in putting it in writing opens up new possibilities for communication. If we can do this, we may also find ourselves learning much more than we ever could about our students, their language, and, incidentally, ourselves.

ANDREA A. LUNSFORD

Cognitive Development and the Basic Writer

In her article, "Writing as a Mode of Learning," Janet Emig argues that

> Writing . . . connects the three major tenses of our experience to make meaning. And the two major modes by which these three aspects are united are the processes of analysis and synthesis: analysis, the breaking of entities into their constituent parts; and synthesis, combining or fusing these, often into fresh arrangements or amalgams.[1]

I agree with Professor Emig, and her work as well as that of Mina Shaughnessy has led me to ponder the relationship of writing and the processes of analysis and synthesis to the teaching of basic writers. In general, my study of basic writers—their strategies, processes, and products[2]—leads me to believe that they have not attained that level of cognitive development which would allow them to form abstractions or conceptions. That is, they are most often unable to practice analysis and synthesis and to apply successfully the principles thus derived to college tasks. In short, our students might well perform a given task in a specific situation, but they have great difficulty abstracting from it or replicating it in another context.

Let me offer one concrete example to illustrate this point. Asked to read ten consecutive issues of a comic strip, choose one of the major char-

From *College English*, 41 (September, 1979), 39–46. Reprinted by permission of the National Council of Teachers of English and Andrea A. Lunsford.

1. "Writing as a Mode of Learning," *CCC*, 28 (1977), 127.
2. "The Ohio State University Remedial English Pilot Project: Final Report and Follow-Up Study," Ohio State University, 1977, and "An Historical, Descriptive, and Evaluative Study of Remedial English in American Colleges and Universities," Diss. Ohio State University, 1977.

acters, and infer the basic values of that character from the information provided in the ten issues, typical basic writing students find it almost impossible to articulate anything about the values of characters unlike themselves. In short, they have problems drawing inferences or forming concepts based on what they have read. Instead, they tend either to describe the characters or, more typically, to drop the comic strip character after a few sentences and shift to what they see as their own values. When I first began teaching basic writers, their response to this type of assignment gave me the first hint of how their difficulties were related to cognitive development.

In *Thought and Language*, the Russian psychologist Lev Vygotsky identifies three basic phases in the ascent to concept formation: the initial syncretic stage, in which "word meaning denotes nothing more to the child than a vague syncretic conglomeration of individual objects that have . . . coalesced into an image"; the "thinking in complexes" stage during which "thought . . . is already coherent and objective . . . , although it does not reflect objective relationships in the same way as conceptual thinking"; and, finally, the true-concept formation stage.[3] Vygotsky cautions, however, that

> even after the adolescent has learned to produce concepts, . . . he does not abandon elementary forms; they continue for a long time to operate, indeed to predominate, in many areas of his thinking. . . . The transitional character of adolescent thinking becomes especially evident when we observe the actual functioning of the newly acquired concepts. Experiments specially devised to study the adolescent's operations bring out . . . a striking discrepancy between his ability to form concepts and his ability to define them. (p. 79)

Vygotsky goes on to distinguish between "spontaneous" concepts, those which are formed as a result of ordinary, day-to-day experiences, and "scientific" concepts, which are formed largely in conjunction with instruction. The student described above by Vygotsky is like my basic writing students confronted with the comic strips in that they all are able to formulate spontaneous concepts, but not able to remove themselves from such concepts, to abstract from them, or to define them into the scientific concepts necessary for successful college work. In my experience, basic writing students most often work at what Vygotsky calls the "thinking in complexes" stage and the spontaneous-concept stage rather than at the true-concept formation stage. While these writers may have little difficulty in dealing with familiar everyday problems requiring abstract thought

3. Lev Semenovich Vygotsky, *Thought and Language*, trans. Eugenia Hanfmann and Gertrude Vakar (Cambridge, Mass.: MIT Press, 1962), pp. 59–61.

based on concepts, they are *not aware of the processes they are using.* Thus they often lack the ability to infer principles from their own experience. They are not forming the "scientific concepts" which are basic to mastery of almost all college material.

Jean Piaget categorizes mental development basically into four stages: the sensori-motor stage; the pre-operational stage; the concrete-operations stage; and the formal-operations stage characterized by the ability to abstract, synthesize, and form coherent logical relationships.[4] At the stage of concrete operations, the child's thought is still closely linked to concrete data; completely representational, hypothetical, or verbal thought still eludes him. As the child moves through the stages of cognitive development, he goes through what Piaget calls the process of "de-centering," a process further defined by Lee Odell as "getting outside one's own frame of reference, understanding the thoughts, values, feelings of another person; . . . projecting oneself into unfamiliar circumstances, whether factual or hypothetical; . . . learning to understand why one reacts as he does to experience."[5] Although children first begin to "de-center" as early as the pre-operational stage, egocentricity is still strong in the concrete stage, and, indeed, we apparently continue the process of "de-centering" throughout our lives.

The relationship of Piaget's concrete stage to Vygotsky's "thinking in complexes" stage and "spontaneous-concept formation" stage is, I believe, clear. Furthermore, the work of both Piaget and Vygotsky strongly indicates that cognitive development moves first from doing, to doing consciously, and only then to formal conceptualization. As Eleanor Duckworth says in an essay in *Piaget in the Classroom*, "thoughts are our way of connecting things up for ourselves. If somebody else tells us about the connections he has made, we can only understand him to the extent that we do the work of making those connections ourselves."[6] This notion is directly related to the highly influential work of Gilbert Ryle. In *The Concept of Mind* (New York: Barnes and Noble, 1949), Ryle makes his crucial distinction between knowing *how* and knowing *that.*

> Learning *how* or improving in ability is not like learning *that* or acquiring information. Truths can be imparted, procedures can only be inculcated, and while inculcation is a gradual process, imparting is relatively sudden. It makes sense to ask at what moment someone became apprised of a truth, but not to ask at what moment someone acquired a skill. "Part-trained" is a significant phrase, "part-informed" is not. Train-

4. *Six Psychological Studies* (New York: Random House, 1967).

5. "Teaching Reading: An Alternative Approach," *English Journal*, 22 (1973), 455.

6. "Language and Thought," in *Piaget in the Classroom*, ed. Milton Schwebel and Jane Raph (New York: Basic Books, 1973), p. 148.

ing is the art of setting tasks which the pupils have not yet accomplished but are not any longer quite incapable of accomplishing. . . . Misunderstanding is a by-product of knowing how. Only a person who is at least a partial master of the Russian tongue can make the wrong sense of a Russian expression. Mistakes are exercises of competences. (pp. 59–60)

Chomsky's distinction between "competence" and "performance" has similar implications. Chomsky's views as expressed in *Aspects of the Theory of Syntax* (Cambridge, Mass.: MIT Press, 1965) can be used to argue against the notion that "language is essentially an adventitious construct, taught by 'conditioning' . . . or by a drill and explicit explanation" (p. 51). In other words, students learn by doing and *then* by extrapolating principles from their activities. This theory informs an educational model proposed by James Britton in a recent lecture at Ohio State University (and based on his 1970 *Language and Learning*). Essentially, this paradigm incorporates learning by doing as opposed to learning solely by the study of abstract principles or precepts.

Britton's model is closely related to that articulated in Michael Polanyi's discussion of skills in *Personal Knowledge* (New York: Harper and Row, 1964). Polanyi begins his discussion by citing "the well-known fact that the *aim of a skillful performance is achieved by the observance of a set of rules which are not known as such to the person following them*" (p. 49). Polanyi uses examples of the person who rides a bicycle, keeps afloat in the water, or plays a musical instrument without at all comprehending the underlying rules. "Rules of art can be useful," Polanyi says, "but they do not determine the practice of an art; they are maxims, which can serve as a guide to an art only if they can be integrated into the practical knowledge" (p. 50). Polanyi goes on to discuss the importance of apprenticeship in acquiring a skill or an art, by which he means that we learn by doing *with* a recognized "master" or "connoisseur" better than by studying or reading about abstract principles. Vygotsky puts it quite succinctly: "What a child can do in cooperation today he can do alone tomorrow. Therefore the only good kind of instruction is that which marches ahead of development and leads it; it must be aimed not so much at the ripe as at the ripening functions" (*Thought and Language*, p. 104).

I have attempted this very cursory theoretical review partially in support of the premise asserted at the beginning of my essay: that most of our basic writing students are operating well below the formal-operations or true-concept formation stage of cognitive development, and hence they have great difficulty in "de-centering" and performing tasks which require analysis and synthesis. But once we are convinced that our basic writing students are most often characterized by the inability to analyze and synthesize, what then? How can we, as classroom teachers, use what we know about theory and about our students' levels of cognitive development to guide the ways in which we organize our basic writing classes and create effective assignments?

The theory reviewed above offers, I believe, a number of implications which will help us answer these questions. First, basic writing classes should never be teacher-centered; set lectures should always be avoided. Instead, the classes should comprise small workshop groups in which all members are active participants, apprentice-writers who are "exercising their competence" as they learn *how* to write well. Class time should be spent writing, reading what has been written aloud to the group/audience, and talking about that writing. Such sessions require an atmosphere of trust, and they demand careful diagnosis and preparation by the teacher. But these suggestions offer only a very general guide. Exactly *what* preparation should the basic writing teacher do?

The best way to move students into conceptualization and analytic and synthetic modes of thought is to create assignments and activities which allow students to practice or exercise themselves in these modes continuously. While an entire course plan would take more space than is available here, I can offer a series of examples, from activities focusing on grammatical categories and sentence-building to essay assignments, each of which is designed to foster conceptualization and analytic thinking.

One reason drill exercises have so often failed to transfer a skill into a student's own writing is that the student is operating below the cognitive level at which he or she could abstract and generalize a principle from the drill and then apply that principle to enormously varied writing situations. Memorizing precepts has been equally ineffective. Instead of either one, why not present students with a set of data, from their own writing or from that of someone else, and help them approach it inductively? Following is an exercise on verb recognition which attempts to engage students in inferential reasoning.

RECOGNIZING VERBS

Read the following sentences, filling in the missing word(s) in each one:

a. The cow _____ over the moon.
b. The farmer _____ a wife.
c. Jack Sprat _____ _____ no fat; his wife _____ _____ no lean.
d. Jack Horner _____ in a corner.
e. Jack _____ over the candlestick.
f. Don't _____ on my blue suede shoes.
g. The cat _____ away with the spoon.

h. Sunshine on my shoulder _____ me happy.
i. Little Miss Muffett _____ on a tuffet.
j. He _____ for his pipe, and he _____ for his fiddlers three.
k. The three little kittens _____ their mittens.
l. Little Boy Blue, come _____ your horn.
m. They all _____ in a yellow submarine.
n. The three little pigs _____ to market.
o. Jack and Jill _____ up the hill.
p. One _____ over the cuckoo's nest.
q. Everywhere that Mary _____, the lamb was sure to _____.

Whether or not you recognize the songs and rhymes these sentences come from, you will have filled in the blanks with VERBS. Look back over the verbs you have used, and then list five other lines from songs or rhymes and underline the verbs in them.

1.
2.
3.
4.
5.

Now try your hand at formulating the rest of the following definition: Verbs are words which _____

_____

You may have noted in your definition that verbs *do something;* or you may have remembered learning a traditional definition of verbs. No matter what definition we come up with, though, verbs are essential to our communication: they complete or comment on the subjects of our sentences. Now revise your definition so that it includes the major *function* which verbs have in sentences:

_____

_____

CHARACTERISTICS OF VERBS

In this assignment, your job is to discover some major characteristics of verbs. To find the first one, begin studying the following lists of verbs. Then try to determine what characterizes each group. How do the groups differ?

Group One	Group Two	Group Three
break	prayed	will go
sweep	climbed	will run
strikes	altered	will fall
say	passed	will listen
heeds	dug	will look
catch	failed	will move
engages	wrote	will organize
operates	chose	will win
arrests	swore	will answer
play	questioned	will ride
reads	promised	will act
study	gave	will sing

Can you state what characterizes each group? _____

If you are having difficulty answering this question, try answering the next three questions first.

The action named by the verbs in Group One takes place at what time?

_____

The action named by the verbs in Group Two takes place at what time?

_____

The action named by the verbs in Group Three takes place at what time?

_____

Now go back and fill in an answer to the first question about what characterizes each group.

By now, you will have been able to identify the TENSE of the verbs in the three groups. Tense, or relation to time, is one of the major characteristics of verbs; it distinguishes them from other kinds of words such as nouns. Do you know the names of the three tenses represented in Group One, Group Two, and Group Three?

This same inductive or analytic approach can be applied to any grammatical concept or convention we wish our students to become familiar with. Rather than asking students to memorize the functions of the semi-colon, for instance, workshop groups can be presented with a passage or short essay which uses semi-colons frequently. The students' task is to isolate those sentences which use semi-colons and then draw some conclusions based on their data: they might be asked to group sentences which use semi-colons in the same way, to define the semi-colon, etc. Whatever the task, the group will be engaged in inferential problem-solving rather than in isolated drill or memorization. In Vygotsky's terms, analytic thinking is the "ripening function" we are attempting to foster.

In spite of their general effectiveness, sentence-combining drills will often fail to transfer new patterns into the basic writer's own writing—unless the sentence-combining work helps build inferential bridges. The sequential sentence-combining exercise below is designed to give students practice in inferring and analyzing. It is based primarily on the ancient practice of *imitatio,* which we would do well to introduce in all of our basic writing classes.

Pattern Sentence: The General Motors assembly line grinds out cars swiftly, smoothly, and almost effortlessly.

A. After studying the sentence pattern, combine each of the following sets of sentences into a sentence which imitates the pattern.

1. The cat eyed its prey.
2. The cat was scruffy.
3. The cat was yellow.
4. The prey was imaginary.

5. The cat eyed it craftily.
6. It eyed it tauntingly.
7. It even eyed it murderously.

---

1. Oil massages you.
2. The oil is bath oil.
3. It is Beauty's oil.
4. The massaging is gentle.
5. The massaging is soothing.
6. The massaging is almost loving.

---

1. We tend to use technologies.
2. The technologies are new.
3. Our use of them is profuse.
4. Our use is unwise.
5. Our use is even harmful.

---

1. H. L. Mencken critized foibles.
2. The foibles belonged to society.
3. The society was American.
4. The criticism was witty.
5. It was sarcastic.
6. It was often unmerciful.

---

1. The lecturer droned.
2. The lecturer was nondescript.
3. The lecturer was balding.
4. The droning went on and on.
5. The droning was mechanical.
6. It was monotonous.
7. It was interminable.

B. Now fill in appropriate words to complete the following sentence, again being careful to imitate the pattern sentence.

The _____ _____ wins _____

_____ly, _____ly, and almost _____ ly.

C. Now write a series of seven sentences and then combine them into one sentence which imitates the pattern sentence. Then write at least one more sentence which imitates the pattern.

Such exercises are not difficult to create; they can easily be adapted to specialized interests of any particular group or class. And they can lead to the kind of paragraph- and theme-length sentence-combining exercises recommended recently by Donald Daiker, Andrew Kerek, and Max Morenberg of Miami of Ohio.[7] Furthermore, such exercises can be sup-

---

7. *The Writer's Options: College Sentence Combining* (New York: Harper and Row, 1979).

plemented by visual stimuli, pictures or video tapes, which can be used as raw material from which to generate new sentences in imitation of the pattern. But to be maximally effective, sentence-combining exercises must be designed to lead basic writing students to bridge the cognitive gap between imitating and generating.

I have yet to offer any sample essay assignments, but I do not thereby mean to imply that writing whole essays should only occur at or toward the end of a basic writing course. On the contrary, basic writers should begin composing whole paragraphs and essays, practicing the entire process of writing, from the very onset of the course. A pitcher does not practice by articulating one mini-movement at a time but by engaging in an entire, continuous process, from warm-up and mental preparation, to the wind-up, the release, and the follow-through: an analogy, to be sure, but one which I hope is not overly strained. In addition to having students write paragraphs and essays early in the course, I would like especially to emphasize the importance of working with analytic modes in basic writing classes. Basic writers often fall back on narrative and descriptive modes because these modes are more adaptable to their own experience, or to what Linda Flower has described as "writer-based prose."[8] Yet the work of Ed White in California and of James Britton and his colleagues in England has shown us that little correlation exists in student performance between the spatial and temporal modes of narration and description and the logical and analytic modes of exposition and argumentation. Therefore, the basic writing course that works exclusively on narration and description will probably fail to build the cognitive skills its students will need to perform well in other college courses.

The comic-strip assignment I described earlier in this essay helped me learn that my students needed practice in using and assimilating analytic modes; it also helped me see that I had made several crucial mistakes in giving that assignment. First, I assigned it when the students had had little or no formal practice in inferential reasoning; second, I asked students to do the assignment at home rather than in workshop groups. In short, I ignored one of the lessons both Polanyi and Vygotsky have taught us: that often we learn best by working at a task in cooperation with a "master" or "connoisseur." I have since profited from these mistakes, and that same assignment, properly prepared for by workshop discussion and practice, has proven considerably more effective. Following are two other assignments, one calling for a brief response, the other for a longer essay, which are designed to help students gain control of analytic modes.

8. Linda Flower and John R. Hayes, "Problem Solving Strategies and the Writing Process," *College English*, 39 (1977), 449–461.

WRITING ASSIGNMENT A

Study the following set of data:

1. New York City lost 600,000 jobs between 1969–76.
2. In 1975, twenty buildings in prime Manhattan areas were empty.
3. Between 1970–75, ten major corporations moved their headquarters from New York City to the Sunbelt.
4. In 1976, New York City was on the brink of bankruptcy.
5. Between February, 1977 and February, 1978, New York City gained 9,000 jobs.
6. Since January, 1978, one million square feet of Manhattan floor space has been newly rented.
7. AT&T has just built a $110 million headquarters in New York.
8. IBM has just built an $80 million building at 55th and Madison in New York.
9. Co-op prices and rents have increased since 1977.
10. Even $1 million luxury penthouses are sold out.
11. There is currently an apartment shortage in Manhattan.
12. The President recently signed a bill authorizing $1.65 billion in federal loan guarantees for New York City.

After reading and thinking about the information listed above, how would you describe the current economic trend in New York City? Using your answer to that question as an opening sentence, write a paragraph in which you explain and offer support for your conclusion by using the information provided in the original set of data.

An assignment like the one above, which gives students practice in analyzing, generalizing, and abstracting, can be readily adapted to workshop groups in which discussion, criticism, and revision can take place.

WRITING ASSIGNMENT B

Preparing: Choose a person (but NOT someone you know well) whom you can observe on at least 5–7 occasions. You might choose someone who rides the same bus as you do, or one of your instructors, or someone who is in one of your classes. Be sure that you are on no closer than "how are you today?" terms with the person you choose.

Gathering Data: Arrange the times you can observe your person so that you can make notes during or immediately after the observation. Note down anything that seems important to you. For a start, answer these questions after each observation.

1. What is X wearing? (Be detailed; include colors, types of fabric, etc.)
2. How is X's hair fixed? (What kind of hair-cut, length of hair, style, etc.)
3. What, if anything, does X have with him or her? (Bag, knapsack, purse, books, etc.)
4. What is X doing? (Be as detailed as possible.)
5. What does X say? (Get exact wording whenever you can.)
6. Who does X associate with?
7. What seems to be X's mood?

Grouping Data: Study all your notes. Then group them under the following headings: APPEARANCE, ACTIONS, WORDS.

Analyzing Data: Now study all the information you have categorized. Based on that information, what would you say is X's lifestyle? What does your observation suggest about X's top priorities? What is most important to X?

Writing About your Data: Write a short essay which begins by answering the questions asked under "Analyzing Data." Use the data you have grouped in your notes to explain and support your analysis of the lifestyle and priorities of X.

This assignment begins with workshop discussion; the results of each stage are discussed by the group. Revision, sorting, and excluding are thus continuous, with the teacher helping students move more and more surely from *describing* their subjects to *analyzing* them. To save space, I have omitted the revising stages, which involve group response to and criticism of the essays and which vary, of course, with the particular difficulties encountered by each group.

Writing projects based on inference-drawing and conceptualization are easily adapted to almost any topic. I have used excerpts from the *Foxfire* books as the basis for essays in which students draw conclusions and generalize about the people interviewed. David Bartholomae, of the University of Pittsburgh, recommends Studs Terkel's *Working* as the basis for similar assignments building conceptual skills. Role-playing exercises and persona paraphrases offer other effective means of helping students "decenter" and hence gain the distance necessary to effective analysis and synthesis. In fact, it is possible and, I would urge, highly profitable, to build an entire basic writing course on exercises like the ones described above, assignments which "march ahead of development and lead it." If we can do so successfully, and if we can find valid ways to substantiate our success, certainly we will have put all our theory to the best practical use. And as a bonus, we will help to establish what Janet Emig argues is the unique value of writing to the entire learning process.

Writer-Based Prose:
A Cognitive Basis for Problems in Writing

If writing is simply the act of "expressing what you think" or "saying what you mean," why is writing often such a difficult thing to do? And why do papers that do express what the writer meant (to his or her own satisfaction) often fail to communicate the same meaning to a reader? Although we often equate writing with the straightforward act of "saying what we mean," the mental struggles writers go through and the misinterpretation readers still make suggest that we need a better model of this process. Modern communication theory and practical experience agree; writing prose that actually communicates what we mean to another person demands more than a simple act of self-expression. What communication theory does not tell us is how writers do it.

An alternative to the "think it/say it" model is to say that effective writers do not simply *express* thought but *transform* it in certain complex but describable ways for the needs of a reader. Conversely, we may find that ineffective writers are indeed merely "expressing" themselves by offering up an unretouched and underprocessed version of their own thought. Writer-Based prose, the subject of this paper, is a description of this undertransformed mode of verbal expression.

As both a style of writing and a style of thought, Writer-Based prose is natural and adequate for a writer writing to himself or herself. However, it is the source of some of the most common and pervasive problems in academic and professional writing. The symptoms can range from a mere missing referent or an underdeveloped idea to an unfocused and

From *College English,* 41 (September, 1979), 19–37. Reprinted by permission of the National Council of Teachers of English and Linda Flower.

apparently pointless discussion. The symptoms are diverse but the source can often be traced to the writer's underlying strategy for composing and to his or her failure to transform private thought into a public, reader-based expression.

In *function*, Writer-Based prose is a verbal expression written by a writer to himself and for himself. It is the record and the working of his own verbal thought. In its *structure*, Writer-Based prose reflects the associative, narrative path of the writer's own confrontation with her subject. In its *language*, it reveals her use of privately loaded terms and shifting but unexpressed contexts for her statements.

In contrast, Reader-Based prose is a deliberate attempt to communicate something to a reader. To do that, it creates a shared language and shared context between writer and reader. It also offers the reader an issue-centered rhetorical structure rather than a replay of the writer's discovery process. In its language and structure, Reader-Based prose reflects the *purpose* of the writer's thought; Writer-Based prose tends to reflect its *process*. Good writing, therefore, is often the cognitively demanding transformation of the natural but private expressions of Writer-Based thought into a structure and style adapted to a reader.

This analysis of Writer-Based prose style and the transformations that create Reader-Based prose will explore two hypotheses:

1. Writer-Based prose represents a major and familiar mode of expression which we all use from time to time. While no piece of writing is a pure example, Writer-Based prose can be identified by features of structure, function, and style. Furthermore, it shares many of these features with the modes of inner and egocentric speech described by Vygotsky and Piaget. This paper will explore that relationship and look at newer research in an effort to describe Writer-Based prose as a verbal style which in turn reflects an underlying cognitive process.

2. Writer-Based prose is a workable concept which can help us teach writing. As a way to intervene in the thinking process, it taps intuitive communication strategies writers already have, but are not adequately using. As a teaching technique, the notion of transforming one's own Writer-Based style has proved to be a powerful idea with a built-in method. It helps writers attack this demanding cognitive task with some of the thoroughness and confidence that comes from an increased and self-conscious control of the process.

My plan for this paper is to explore Writer-Based prose from a number of perspectives. Therefore, the next section, which considers the psychological theory of egocentrism and inner speech, is followed by a case study of Writer-Based prose. I will then pull these practical and theoretical issues together to define the critical features of Writer-Based prose.

The final section will look ahead to the implications of this description of Writer-Based prose for writers and teachers.

INNER SPEECH AND EGOCENTRISM

In studying the developing thought of the child, Jean Piaget and Lev Vygotsky both observed a mode of speech which seemed to have little social or communicative function. Absorbed in play, children would carry on spirited elliptical monologues which they seemed to assume others understood, but which in fact made no concessions to the needs of the listener. According to Piaget, in Vygotsky's synopsis, "In egocentric speech, the child talks only about himself, takes no interest in his interlocutor, does not try to communicate, expects no answers, and often does not even care whether anyone listens to him. It is similar to a monologue in a play: The child is thinking aloud, keeping up a running accompaniment, as it were, to whatever he may be doing."[1] In the seven-year-olds Piaget studied, nearly fifty percent of their recorded talk was egocentric in nature.[2] According to Piaget, the child's "non-communicative" or egocentric speech is a reflection, not of selfishness, but of the child's limited ability to "assume the point of view of the listener: [the child] talks of himself, to himself, and by himself."[3] In a sense, the child's cognitive capacity has locked her in her own monologue.

When Vygotsky observed a similar phenomenon in children he called it "inner speech" because he saw it as a forerunner of the private verbal thought adults carry on. Furthermore, Vygotsky argued, this speech is not simply a by-product of play; it is the tool children use to plan, organize, and control their activities. He put the case quite strongly: "We have seen that egocentric speech is not suspended in a void but is directly related to the child's practical dealings with the real world . . . it enters as a constituent part into the process of rational activity" (*Thought and Language*, p. 22).

The egocentric talk of the child and the mental, inner speech of the adult share three important features in common. First, they are highly elliptical. In talking to oneself, the psychological subject of discourse (the old information to which we are adding new predicates) is always known.

---

1. Lev Vygotsky, *Thought and Language,* ed. and trans. Eugenia Hanfmann and Gertrude Vakar (Cambridge, Mass.: M.I.T. Press, 1962), p. 15.
2. Jean Piaget, *The Language and Thought of the Child,* trans. Majorie Gabin (New York: Harcourt, Brace, 1932), p. 49.
3. Herbert Ginsberg and Sylvia Opper, *Piaget's Theory of Intellectual Development* (Englewood Cliffs, N.J.: Prentice-Hall, 1969), p. 89.

Therefore, explicit subjects and referents disappear. Five people straining to glimpse the bus need only say, "Coming!" Secondly, inner speech frequently deals in the sense of words, not their more specific or limited public meanings. Words become "saturated with sense" in much the way a key word in a poem can come to represent its entire, complex web of meaning. But unlike the word in the poem, the accrued sense of the word in inner speech may be quite personal, even idiosyncratic; it is, as Vygotsky writes, "the sum of all the psychological events aroused in our consciousness by the word" (*Thought and Language,* p. 146).

Finally, a third feature of egocentric/inner speech is the absence of logical and causal relations. In experiments with children's use of logical-causal connectives such as *because, therefore,* and *although,* Piaget found that children have difficulty managing such relationships and in spontaneous speech will substitute a non-logical, non-causal connective such as *then.* Piaget described this strategy for relating things as *juxtaposition:* "the cognitive tendency simply to link (juxtapose) one thought element to another, rather than to tie them together by some causal or logical relationship."[4]

One way to diagnose this problem with sophisticated relationships is to say, as Vygotsky did, that young children often think in *complexes* instead of concepts.[5] When people think in complexes they unite objects into families that really do share common bonds, but the bonds are concrete and factual rather than abstract or logical. For example, the notion of "college student" would be a complex if it were based, for the thinker, on facts such as college students live in dorms, go to classes, and do homework.

Complexes are very functional formations, and it may be that many people do most of their day-to-day thinking without feeling the need to form more demanding complex concepts. *Complexes* collect related objects; *concepts,* however, must express abstract, logical relations. And it is just this sort of abstract, synthetic thinking that writing typically demands. In a child's early years, the ability to form complex concepts may depend mostly on developing cognitive capacity. In adults this ability appears also to be a skill developed by training and a tendency fostered

4. John Flavell, *The Developmental Psychology of Jean Piaget* (New York: D. Van Nostrand, 1963), p. 275. For these studies see the last chapter of Piaget's *Language and Thought of the Child* and *Judgment and Reasoning in the Child,* trans. M. Warden (New York: Harcourt, Brace, 1926).

5. *Thought and Language,* p. 75. See also the paper by Gary Woditsch which places this question in the context of curriculum design, "Developing Generic Skills: A Model for a Competency-Based General Education," available from CUE Center, Bowling Green State University.

by one's background and intellectual experience. But whatever its source, the ability to move from the complexes of egocentric speech to the more formal relations of conceptual thought is critical to most expository writing.

Piaget and Vygotsky disagreed on the source, exact function, and teleology of egocentric speech, but they did agree on the features of this distinctive phenomenon, which they felt revealed the underlying logic of the child's thought. For our case, that may be enough. The hypothesis on which this paper rests is not a developmental one. Egocentric speech, or rather its adult written analogue, Writer-Based prose, is not necessarily a stage through which a writer must develop or one at which some writers are arrested. But for adults it does represent an available mode of expression on which to fall back. If Vygotsky is right, it may even be closely related to normal verbal thought. It is clearly a natural, less cognitively demanding mode of thought and one which explains why people, who can express themselves in complex and highly intelligible modes, are often obscure. Egocentric expression happens to the best of us; it comes naturally.

The work of Piaget and Vygotsky, then, suggests a source for the cognitive patterns that underlie Writer-Based prose, and it points to some of the major features such a prose style would possess. Let us now turn to a more detailed analysis of such writing as a verbal style inadequately suited for the needs of the reader.

WRITER-BASED PROSE:
A CASE STUDY OF A TRANSFORMATION

As an introduction to the main features of Writer-Based prose and its transformations, let us look at two drafts of a progress report written by students in an organizational psychology class. Working as consulting analysts to a local organization, the writers needed to show progress to their instructor and to present an analysis with causes and conclusions to the client. Both readers—academic and professional—were less concerned with what the students did or saw than with *why* they did it and *what* they made of their observations.

To gauge the Reader-Based effectiveness of this report, skim quickly over Draft 1 and imagine the response of the instructor of the course, who needed to answer these questions: As analysts, what assumptions and decisions did my students make? Why did they make them? At what stage in the project are they now? Or, play the role of the client-reader who wants to know: How did they define my problem, and what did they conclude? As either reader, can you quickly extract the information the report should be giving you? Next, try the same test on Draft 2.

DRAFT 1: GROUP REPORT

(1) Work began on our project with the initial group decision to evaluate the Oskaloosa Brewing Company. Oskaloosa Brewing Company is a regionally located brewery manufacturing several different types of beer, notably River City and Brough Cream Ale. This beer is marketed under various names in Pennsylvania and other neighboring states. As a group, we decided to analyze this organization because two of our group members had had frequent customer contact with the sales department. Also, we were aware that Oskaloosa Brewing had been losing money for the past five years and we felt we might be able to find some obvious problems in their organizational structure.

(2) Our first meeting, held February 17th, was with the head of the sales department, Jim Tucker. Generally, he gave us an outline of the organization from president to worker, and discussed the various departments that we might ultimately decide to analyze. The two that seemed the most promising and most applicable to the project were the sales and production departments. After a few group meetings and discussions with the personnel manager, Susan Harris, and our advisor Professor Charns, we felt it best suited our needs and the Oskaloosa Brewing's to evaluate their bottling department.

(3) During the next week we had a discussion with the superintendent of production, Henry Holt, and made plans for interviewing the supervisors and line workers. Also, we had a tour of the bottling department which gave us a first hand look into the production process. Before beginning our interviewing, our group met several times to formulate appropriate questions to use in interviewing, for both the supervisors and workers. We also had a meeting with Professor Charns to discuss this matter.

(3a) The next step was the actual interviewing process. During the weeks of March 14-18 and March 21-25, our group met several times at Oskaloosa Brewing and interviewed ten supervisors and twelve workers. Finally during this past week, we have had several group meetings to discuss our findings and the potential problem areas within the bottling department. Also, we have spent time organizing the writing of our progress report.

(4) The bottling and packaging division is located in a separate building, adjacent to the brewery, where the beer is actually manufactured. From the brewery the beer is piped into one of five lines (four bottling lines and one canning line), in the bottling house where the bottles are filled, crowned, pasteurized, labeled, packaged in cases, and either others, is production manager, Phil Smith. Next in line under him in di-shipped out or stored in the warehouse. The head of this operation, and

rect control of the bottling house is the superintendent of bottling and packaging, Henry Holt. In addition, there are a total of ten supervisors who report directly to Henry Holt and who oversee the daily operations and coordinate and direct the twenty to thirty union workers who operate the lines.

(5) During production, each supervisor fills out a data sheet to explain what was actually produced during each hour. This form also includes the exact time when a breakdown occurred, what it was caused by, and when production was resumed. Some supervisors' positions are production staff oriented. One takes care of supplying the raw material (bottles, caps, labels, and boxes) for production. Another is responsible for the union workers' assignment each day.

These workers are not all permanently assigned to a production line position. Men called "floaters" are used filling in for a sick worker, or helping out after a breakdown.

(6) The union employees are generally older than 35, some in their late fifties. Most have been with the company many years and are accustomed to having more workers per a slower moving line. They are resentful to what they declare "unnecessary" production changes. Oska-Brewery also employs mechanics who normally work on the production line, and assume a mechanics job only when a breakdown occurs. Most of these men are not skilled.

Draft 2: Memorandum

TO: Professor Martin Charns

FROM: Nancy Lowenberg, Tod Scott, Rosemary Nisson, Larry Vollen

DATE: March 31, 1977

RE: *Progress Report: The Oskaloosa Brewing Company*

Why Oskaloosa Brewing?

(1) Oskaloosa Brewing Company is a regionally located brewery manufacturing several different types of beer, notably River City and Brough Cream Ale. As a group, we decided to analyze this organization because two of our group members have frequent contact with the sales department. Also, we were aware that Oskaloosa Brewing had been losing money for the past five years and we felt we might be able to find some obvious problems in their organizational structure.

Initial Steps: Where to Concentrate?

(2) Through several interviews with top management and group discussion, we felt it best suited our needs, and Oskaloosa Brewing's, to

evaluate the production department.   Our first meeting, held February 17, was with the head of the sales department, Jim Tucker. He gave us an outline of the organization and described the two major departments, sales and production. He indicated that there were more obvious problems in the production department, a belief also implied by Susan Harris, personnel manager.

NEXT STEP

(3) The next step involved a familiarization of the plant and its employees. First, we toured the plant to gain an understanding of the brewing and bottling process. Next, during the weeks of March 14–18 and March 21–25, we interviewed ten supervisors and twelve workers. Finally, during the past week we had group meetings to exchange information and discuss potential problems.

THE PRODUCTION PROCESS

(4)   Knowledge of the actual production process is imperative in understanding the effects of various problems on efficient production; therefore, we have included a brief summary of this process.

The bottling and packaging division is located in a separate building, adjacent to the brewery, where the beer is actually manufactured. From the brewery the beer is piped into one of five lines (four bottling lines and one canning line) in the bottling house where the bottles are filled, crowned, pasteurized, labeled, packaged in cases, and either shipped out or stored in the warehouse.

PEOPLE BEHIND THE PROCESS

(5) The head of this operation is production manager, Phil Smith. Next in line under him in direct control of the bottling house is the superintendent of bottling and packaging, Henry Holt. He has authority over ten supervisors who each have two major responsibilities: (1) to fill out production data sheets that show the amount produced/hour, and information about any breakdowns—time, cause, etc., and (2) to oversee the daily operations and coordinate and direct the twenty to thirty union workers who operate the lines. These workers are not all permanently assigned to a production line position. Men called "floaters" are used to fill in for a sick worker or to help out after a breakdown.

(6) The union employees are a highly diversified group in both age and experience. They are generally older than 35, some in their late fifties. Most have been with the company many years and are accustomed to having more workers per a slower moving line. They are resentful to what they feel are unnecessary production changes. Oskaloosa Brewing also employs mechanics who normally work on the production line, and assume a mechanic job only when a breakdown occurs. Most of these men are not skilled.

PROBLEMS

Through extensive interviews with supervisors and union employees, we have recognized four apparent problems within the bottle house operations. First, the employees' goals do not match those of the company. This is especially apparent in the union employees whose loyalty lies with the union instead of the company. This attitude is well-founded as the union ensures them of job security and benefits. . . .

In its tedious misdirection, Draft 1 is typical of Writer-Based prose in student papers and professional reports. The reader is forced to do most of the thinking, sorting the wheat from the chaff and drawing ideas out of details. And yet, although this presentation fails to fulfill our needs, it does have an inner logic of its own. The logic which organizes Writer-Based prose often rests on three principles: its underlying focus is egocentric, and it uses either a narrative framework or a survey form to order ideas.

The *narrative framework* of this discussion is established by the opening announcement: "Work began. . . ." In paragraphs 1–3 facts and ideas are presented in terms of when they were discovered, rather than in terms of their implications or logical connections. The writers recount what happened when; the reader, on the other hand, asks, "Why?" and "So what?" Whether he or she likes it or not, the reader is in for a blow-by-blow account of the writer's discovery process.

Although a rudimentary chronology is reasonable for a progress report, a narrative framework is often a substitute for analytic thinking. By burying ideas within the events that precipitated them, a narrative obscures the more important logical and hierarchical relations between ideas. Of course, such a narrative could read like an intellectual detective story, because, like other forms of drama, it creates interest by withholding closure. Unfortunately, most academic and professional readers seem unwilling to sit through these home movies of the writer's mind at work. Narratives can also operate as a cognitive "frame" which itself generates ideas.[6] The temporal pattern, once invoked, opens up a series of empty slots waiting to be filled with the details of what happened next, even though those details may be irrelevant. As the revision of Draft 2 shows, our writers' initial narrative framework led them to generate a shaggy project story, instead of a streamlined logical analysis.

6. The seminal paper on frames is M. Minsky's "A Framework for Representing Knowledge" in P. Winston, ed., *The Psychology of Computer Vision* (New York: McGraw Hill, 1973). For a more recent discussion of how they work see B. Kuipers, "A Frame for Frames" in D. Bowbow and A. Collins, eds., *Representation and Understanding: Studies in Cognitive Science* (New York: Academic Press, 1975), pp. 151–184.

The second salient feature of this prose is its focus on the discovery process of the writers: the "I did/I thought/I felt" focus. Of the fourteen sentences in the first three paragraphs, ten are grammatically focused on the writers' thoughts and actions rather than on issues: "Work began," "We decided," "Also we were aware . . . and we felt. . . ."

In the fourth paragraph the writers shift attention from their discovery process to the facts discovered. In doing so they illustrate a third feature of Writer-Based prose: its idea structure simply copies the structure of the perceived information. A problem arises when the internal structure of the data is not already adapted to the needs of the reader or the intentions of the writer. Paragraph five, for example, appears to be a free-floating description of "What happens during production." Yet the client-reader already knows this and the instructor probably does not care. Lured by the fascination of facts, these writer-based writers recite a litany of perceived information under the illusion they have produced a rhetorical structure. The resulting structure could as well be a neat hierarchy as a list. The point is that the writers' organizing principle is dictated by their information, not by their intention.

The second version of this report is not so much a "rewrite" (i.e., a new report) as it is a transformation of the old one. The writers had to step back from their experience and information in order to turn facts into concepts. Pinpointing the telling details was not enough: they had to articulate the meaning they saw in the data. Secondly, the writers had to build a rhetorical structure which acknowledged the function these ideas had for their reader. In the second version, the headings, topic sentences, and even some of the subjects and verbs reflect a new functional structure focused on Process, People, and Problems. The report offers a hierarchical organization of the facts in which the hierarchy itself is based on issues both writer and reader agree are important. I think it likely that such transformations frequently go on in the early stages of the composing process for skilled writers. But for some writers the under-transformed Writer-Based prose of Draft 1 is also the final product and the starting point for our work as teachers.

In the remainder of this paper I will look at the features of Writer-Based prose and the ways it functions for the writer. Clearly, we need to know about Reader-Based prose in order to teach it. But it is also clear that writers already possess a great deal of intuitive knowledge about writing for audiences when they are stimulated to use it. As the case study shows, the concept of trying to transform Writer-Based prose for a reader is by itself a powerful tool. It helps writers identify the lineaments of a problem many can start to solve once they recognize it as a definable problem.

WRITER-BASED PROSE:
FUNCTION, STRUCTURE, AND STYLE

While Writer-Based prose may be inadequately structured for a reader, it does possess a logic and structure of its own. Furthermore, that structure serves some important functions for the writer in his or her effort to think about a subject. It represents a practical strategy for dealing with information. If we could see Writer-Based prose as a *functional system*—not a set of random errors known only to English teachers—we would be better able to teach writing as a part of any discipline that asks people to express complex ideas.

According to Vygotsky, "the inner speech of the adult represents his 'thinking for himself' rather than social adaptation [communication to others]: i.e., it has the same function that egocentric speech has in the child" (*Language and Thought*, p. 18). It helps him solve problems. Vygotsky found that when a child who is trying to draw encounters an obstacle (no pencils) or a problem (what shall I call it?), the incidence of egocentric speech can double.

If we look at an analogous situation—an adult caught up in the complex mental process of composing—we can see that much of the adult's output is not well adapted for public consumption either. In studies of cognitive processes of writers as they composed, J. R. Hayes and I observed much of the writer's verbal output to be an attempt to manipulate stored information into some acceptable pattern of meaning.[7] To do that, the writer generates a variety of alternative relationships and trial formulations of the information she has in mind. Many of these trial networks will be discarded; most will be significantly altered through recombination and elaboration during the composing process. In those cases in which the writer's first pass at articulating knowledge was also the final draft—when she wrote it just as she thought it—the result was often a series of semi-independent, juxtaposed networks, each with its own focus.

Whether such expression occurs in an experimental protocol or a written draft, it reflects the working of the writer's mind upon his material. Because dealing with one's material is a formidable enough task in itself, a writer may allow himself to ignore the additional problem of accommodating a reader. Writer-Based prose, then, functions as a medium for thinking. It offers the writer the luxury of one less constraint. As we shall

7. L. Flower and J. Hayes, "Plans That Guide the Composing Process," in *Writing: The Nature, Development and Teaching of Written Communication*, C. Frederikson, M. Whiteman, and J. Dominic, eds. (Hillsdale, N.J.: Lawrence Erlbaum, in press).

see, its typical structure and style are simply paths left by the movement of the writer's mind.

The *structure* of Writer-Based prose reflects an economical strategy we have for coping with information. Readers generally expect writers to produce complex concepts—to collect data and details under larger guiding ideas and place those ideas in an integrated network. But as both Vygotsky and Piaget observed, forming such complex concepts is a demanding cognitive task; if no one minds, it is a lot easier to just list the parts. Nor is it surprising that in children two of the hallmarks of egocentric speech are the absence of expressed causal relations and the tendency to express ideas without proof or development. Adults too avoid the task of building complex concepts buttressed by development and proof, by structuring their information in two distinctive ways: as a narrative of their own discovery process or as a survey of the data before them.

As we saw in the Oskaloosa Brewing Case Study, a *narrative* structured around one's own discovery process may seem the most natural way to write. For this reason it can sometimes be the best way as well, if a writer is trying to express a complex network of information but is not yet sure how all the parts are related. For example, my notes show that early fragments of this paper started out with a narrative, list-like structure focused on my own experience: "Writer-Based prose is a working hypothesis because it works in the classroom. In fact, when I first started teaching the concept. . . . In fact, it was my students' intuitive recognition of the difference between Writer-Based and Reader-Based style in their own thought and writing. . . . It was their ability to use even a sketchy version of the distinction to transform their own writing that led me to pursue the idea more thoroughly."

The final version of this sketch (the paragraph numbered 2 on pp. 274–75) keeps the reference to teaching experience, but subordinates it to the more central issue of why the concept works. This transformation illustrates how a writer's major propositions can, on first appearance, emerge embedded in a narrative of the events or thoughts which spawned the proposition. In this example, the Writer-Based early version recorded the raw material of observations; the final draft formed them into concepts and conclusions.

This transformation process may take place regularly when a writer is trying to express complicated information which is not yet fully conceptualized. Although much of this mental work normally precedes actual writing, a first draft may simply reflect the writer's current place in the process. When this happens, rewriting and editing are vital operations. Far from being a simple matter of correcting errors, editing a first draft is often the act of transforming a narrative network of information into a more fully hierarchical set of propositions.

A second source of pre-fabricated structure for writers is the internal structure of the information itself. Writers use a *survey* strategy to compose because it is a powerful procedure for retrieving and organizing information. Unfortunately, the original organization of the data itself (e.g., the production process at Oskaloosa Brewing) rarely fits the most effective plan for any given piece of focused analytical writing.

The prose that results from such a survey can, of course, take as many forms as the data. It can range from a highly structured piece of discourse (the writer repeats a textbook exposition) to an unfocused printout of the writer's memories and thoughts on the subject. The form is merely a symptom, because the governing force is the writer's mental strategy: namely, to compose by surveying the available contents of memory without adapting them to a current purpose. The internal structure of the data dictates the rhetorical structure of the discourse, much as the proceedings of Congress organize the *Congressional Record*. As an information processor, the writer is performing what computer scientists would call a "memory dump": dutifully printing out memory in exactly the form in which it is stored.

A survey strategy offers the writer a useful way into the composing process in two ways. First, it eliminates many of the constraints normally imposed by a speech act, particularly the contract between reader and writer for mutually useful discourse. Secondly, a survey of one's own stored knowledge, marching along like a textbook or flowing with the tide of association, is far easier to write than a fresh or refocused conceptualization would be.

But clearly most of the advantages here accrue to the writer. One of the tacit assumptions of the Writer-Based writer is that, once the relevant information is presented, the reader will then do the work of abstracting the essential features, building a conceptual hierarchy, and transforming the whole discussion into a functional network of ideas.

Although Writer-Based prose often fails for readers and tends to preclude further concept formation, it may be a useful road into the creative process for some writers. The structures which fail to work for readers may be powerful strategies for retrieving information from memory and for exploring one's own knowledge network. This is illustrated in Linde and Labov's well-known New York apartment tour experiment.[8] Inter-

8. C. Linde and W. Labov, "Spatial Networks as a Site for the Study of Language and Thought," *Language,* 51 (1975), 924–939.

ested in the strategies people use for retrieving information from memory and planning a discourse, Linde and Labov asked one hundred New Yorkers to "tell me the layout of your apartment" as a part of a "sociological survey." Only 3% of the subjects responded with a map which gave an overview and then filled in the details; for example, "I'd say it's laid out in a huge square pattern, broken down into 4 units." The overwhelming majority (97%) all solved the problem by describing a tour: "You walk in the front door. There was a narrow hallway. To the left, etc." Furthermore, they had a common set of rules for how to conduct the tour (e.g., you don't "walk into" a small room with no outlet, such as a pantry; you just say, "on the left is . . ."). Clearly the tour structure is so widely used because it is a remarkably efficient strategy for recovering all of the relevant information about one's apartment, yet without repeating any of it. For example, one rule for "touring" is that when you dead-end after walking through two rooms, you don't "walk" back but suddenly appear back in the hall.

For us, the revealing sidenote to this experiment is that although the tour strategy was intuitively selected by the overwhelming majority of the speakers, the resulting description was generally very difficult for the listener to follow and almost impossible to reproduce. The tour strategy— like the narrative and textbook structure in prose—is a masterful method for searching memory but a dud for communicating that information to anyone else.

Finally, the *style* of Writer-Based prose also has its own logic. Its two main stylistic features grow out of the private nature of interior monologue, that is, of writing which is primarily a record or expression of the writer's flow of thought. The first feature is that in such monologues the organization of sentences and paragraphs reflects the shifting focus of the writer's attention. However, the psychological subject on which the writer is focused may not be reflected in the grammatical subject of the sentence or made explicit in the discussion at all. Secondly, the writer may depend on code words to carry his or her meaning. That is, the language may be "saturated with sense" and able to evoke—for the writer—a complex but unexpressed context.

Writers of formal written discourse have two goals for style which we can usefully distinguish from one another. One goal might be described as stylistic control, that is, the ability to choose a more embedded or more elegant transformation from variations which are roughly equivalent in meaning. The second goal is to create a completely autonomous text, that is, a text that does not need context, gestures, or audible effects to convey its meaning.

It is easy to see how the limits of short-term memory can affect a writer's stylistic control. For an inexperienced writer, the complex transformation of a periodic sentence—which would require remembering and relating a variety of elements and optional structures such as this sentence contains—can be a difficult juggling act. After all, the ability to form parallel constructions is not innate. Yet with practice many of these skills can become more automatic and require less conscious attention.

The second goal of formal written discourse—the complete autonomy of the text—leads to even more complex problems. According to David Olson, the history of written language has been the progressive creation of an instrument which could convey complete and explicit meanings in a text. The history of writing is the transformation of language from utterance to text—from oral meaning created within a shared context of a speaker and listener to a written meaning fully represented in an autonomous text.[9]

In contrast to this goal of autonomy, Writer-Based prose is writing whose meaning is still to an important degree in the writer's head. The culprit here is often the unstated psychological subject. The work of the "remedial" student is a good place to examine the phenomenon because it often reveals first thoughts more clearly than the reworked prose of a more experienced writer who edits as he or she writes. In the most imaginative, comprehensive and practical book to be written on the basic writer, Mina Shaughnessy has studied the linguistic strategies which lie behind the "errors" of many otherwise able young adults who have failed to master the written code. As we might predict, the ambiguous referent is ubiquitous in basic writing: *he's, she's* and *it's* are sprinkled through the prose without visible means of support. *It* frequently works as a code word for the subject the writer has in mind but not on the page. As Professor Shaughnessy says, *it* "frequently becomes a free-floating substitute for thoughts that the writer neglects to articulate and that the reader must usually strain to reach if he can."[10]

> With all the jobs available, he will have to know more of *it* because thire is a great demand for *it*.

For the writer of the above sentence, the pronoun was probably not ambiguous at all; *it* no doubt referred to the psychological subject of his sentence. Psychologically, the subject of an utterance is the old information, the object you are looking at, the idea on which your attention has been focused. The predicate is the new information you are adding. This

9. David R. Olson, "From Utterance to Text: The Bias of Language in Speech and Writing," *Harvard Educational Review*, 47 (1977), 257–281.
10. Mina Shaughnessy, *Errors and Expectations* (New York: Oxford University Press, 1977), p. 69.

means that the psychological subject and grammatical subject of a sentence may not be the same at all. In our example, "college knowledge" was the writer's psychological subject—the topic he had been thinking about. The sentence itself is simply a psychological predicate. The pronoun *it* refers quite reasonably to the unstated but obvious subject in the writer's mind.

The subject is even more likely to be missing when a sentence refers to the writer herself or to "one" in her position. In the following examples, again from *Errors and Expectations,* the "unnecessary" subject is a person (like the writer) who has a chance to go to college.

> Even if a person graduated from high school who is going on to college to obtain a specific position in his career [ ] should first know how much in demand his possible future job really is.
>
> [he]

> If he doesn't because the U.S. Labor Department say's their wouldn't be enough jobs opened, [ ] is a waste to society and a "cop-out" to humanity.
>
> [he]

Unstated subjects can produce a variety of minor problems from ambiguous referents to amusing dangling modifiers (e.g., "driving around the mountain, a bear came into view"). Although prescriptive stylists are quite hard on such "errors," they are often cleared up by context or common sense. However, the controlling but unstated presence of a psychological subject can lead to some stylistic "errors" that do seriously disrupt communication. Sentence fragments are a good example.

One feature of an explicit, fully autonomous text is that the grammatical subject is usually a precise entity, often a word. By contrast, the psychological subject to which a writer wished to refer may be a complex event or entire network of information. Here written language is often rather intransigent; it is hard to refer to an entire clause or discussion unless one can produce a summary noun. Grammar, for example, normally forces us to select a specific referent for a pronoun or modifier: it wants referents and relations spelled out.[11] This specificity is, of course, its strength as a vehicle for precise reasoning and abstract thought. Errors arise when a writer uses one clause to announce his topic or psychological subject and a second clause to record a psychological predicate, a response to that old information. For example:

11. "Pronouns like *this, that, which* and *it* should not vaguely refer to an entire sentence or clause," and "Make a pronoun refer clearly to one antecedent, not uncertainly to two." Floyd Watkins, et al., *Practical English Handbook* (Boston: Houghton Mifflin, 1974), p. 30.

The jobs that are listed in the paper, I feel you need a college degree.

The job that my mother has, I know I could never be satisfied with it.

The preceding sentences are in error because they have failed to specify the grammatical relationship between their two elements. However, for anyone from the Bronx, each statement would be perfectly effective because it fits a familiar formula. It is an example of topicalization or Y-movement and fits a conventionalized, Yiddish-influenced, intonation pattern much like the one in "Spinach—you can have it!" The sentences depend heavily on certain conventions of oral speech, and insofar as they invoke those patterns for the reader, they communicate effectively.[12]

However, most fragments do not succeed for the reader. And they fail, ironically enough, for the same reason—they too invoke intonation patterns in the reader which turn out to be misleading. The lack of punctuation gives off incorrect cues about how to segment the sentence. Set off on an incorrect intonation pattern, the thwarted reader must stop, reread and reinterpret the sentence. The following examples are from Maxine Hairston's *A Contemporary Rhetoric* (Boston: Houghton Mifflin, 1974):

> The authorities did not approve of their acts. These acts being considered detrimental to society. (society, they . . .)
>
> Young people need to be on their own. To show their parents that they are reliable. (reliable, young people . . .)
>
> (p. 322)

Fragments are easy to avoid; they require only minimal tinkering to correct. Then why is the error so persistent? One possible reason is that for the writer the fragment is a fresh predicate intended to modify the entire preceding psychological subject. The writer wants to carry out a verbal trick easily managed in speech. For the reader, however, this minor grammatical oversight is significant. It sets up and violates both intonation patterns and strong structural expectations, such as those in the last example where we expect a pause and a noun phrase to follow "reliable." The fragment, which actually refers backward, is posing as an introductory clause.

The problem with fragments is that they are perfectly adequate for the writer. In speech they may even be an effective way to express a new idea which is predicated on the entire preceding unit thought. But in a written text, fragments are errors because they do not take the needs of the reader into consideration. Looked at this way, the "goodness" of a

12. I am greatly indebted here to Thomas Huckin for his insightful comments on style and to his work in linguistics on how intonation patterns affect writers and readers.

stylistic technique or grammatical rule such as parallelism, clear antecedents, or agreement is that it is geared to the habits, expectations, and needs of the reader as well as to the demands of textual autonomy.

Vygotsky noticed how the language of children and inner speech was often "saturated with sense." Similarly, the words a writer chooses can also operate as code words, condensing a wealth of meaning in an apparently innocuous word. The following examples come from an exercise which asks writers to identify and transform some of their own pieces of mental shorthand.

The students were asked to circle any code words or loaded expressions they found in their first drafts of a summer internship application. That is, they tried to identify those expressions that might convey only a general or vague meaning to a reader, but which represented a large body of facts, experiences, or ideas for them. They then treated this code word as one would any intuition—pushing it for its buried connections and turning those into a communicable idea. The results are not unlike those brilliant explications one often hears from students who tell you what their paper really meant. This example also shows how much detailed and perceptive thought can be lying behind a vague and conventional word:

> First Draft: "By having these two jobs, I was able to see the business in an entirely different perspective." (Circle indicates a loaded expression marked by the writer.)

> Second Draft with explanation of what she actually had in mind in using the circled phrase: "By having these two jobs, I was able to see the true relationship and relative importance of the various departments in the company. I could see their mutual dependence and how an event in one part of the firm can have an important effect on another."

The tendency to think in code words is a fact of life for the writer. Yet the following example shows how much work can go into exploring our own saturated language. Like any intuition, such language is only a source of potential meanings, much as Aristotle's topics are places for finding potential arguments. In this extended example, the writer first explores her expression itself, laying out all the thoughts which were loosely connected under its name. This process of pushing our own language to give up its buried meanings forces us to make these loose connections explicit and, in the process, allows us to examine them critically. For the writer in our example, pushing her own key words leads to an important set of new ideas in the paper.

First Draft: "I want a career that will help other people while at the same time be challenging scientifically. I had the opportunity to do a biochemical assay for a neuropsychopharmacologist at X— Clinic in Chicago. Besides learning the scientific procedures and techniques that are used, I realized some of the (organizational, financial and people problems) which are encountered in research. This internship program would let me pursue further my interest in research, while concurrently exposing me to (relevant and diverse) areas of bioengineering."

EXCERPT FROM WRITER'S NOTES WORKING ON THE CIRCLED PHRASES

How did research of Sleep Center tie into overall program of X— Clinic? Not everyone within dept. knew what the others were doing, could not see overall picture of efforts.

Brainstorm

Dr. O.—dept. head—trained for lab yet did 38–40 hrs. paperwork. Couldn't set up test assay in Sleep Center because needed equip. from biochem.

Difficulties in getting equipment

1. Politics between administrators
   Photometer at U. of — even though Clinic had bought it.
2. Ordering time, not sufficient inventory, had to hunt through boxes for chemicals.
3. Had to schedule use by personal contact on borrowing equipment—done at time of use and no previous planning.

No definite guidelines had been given to biochem. people as to what was "going on" with assay. Partner who was supposed to learn assay was on vacation. Two people were learning, one was on vac.

No money from state for equipment or research grants.
Departments stealing from each other.
Lobbying, politics, included.

My supervisor from India, felt prejudices on job. Couldn't advance, told me life story and difficulties in obtaining jobs at Univ. Not interested in research at Clinic per se, looking for better opportunities, studying for Vet boards.

REVISION (ADDITIONS IN ITALICS)

"*As a biomedical researcher, I would fulfill my goal of a career* that will help other people while at the same time be challenging scientifically. I had exposure to research while doing a biochemical assay for a neuropsychopharmacologist at X— Clinic in Chicago. Besides learning the scientific procedures and techniques that are used, I realized some of the organizational, financial and people problems which are encountered in research. *These problems included a lack of funds and equipment, disagreements among research staff, and the extensive amounts of time, paperwork and steps required for testing a hypothesis which was only one very small but necessary part of the overall project. But besides knowing some of the frustrations, I also know that many medical advancements, such as the cardiac pacemaker, artificial limbs and cures for diseases, exist and benefit many people because of the efforts of researchers.* Therefore I would like to pursue my interest in research by participating in the NIH Internship Program. The exposure to many *diverse projects, designed to better understand and improve the body's functioning, would help me to decide which areas of biomedical engineering to pursue."*

We could sum up this analysis of style by noting two points. At times a Writer-Based prose style is simply an interior monologue in which some necessary information (such as intonation pattern or a psychological subject) is not expressed in the text. The solution to the reader's problem is relatively trivial in that it involves adding information that the writer already possesses. At other times, a style may be Writer-Based because the writer is thinking in code words at the level of intuited but unarticulated connections. Turning such saturated language into communicable ideas can require the writer to bring the entire composing process into play.

IMPLICATIONS FOR WRITERS AND TEACHERS

From an educational perspective, Writer-Based prose is one of the "problems" composition courses are designed to correct. It is a major cause of that notorious "breakdown" of communication between writer and reader. However, if we step back and look at it in the broader context of cognitive operations involved, we see that it represents a major, functional stage in the composing process and a powerful strategy well-fitted to a part of the job of writing.

In the best of all possible worlds, good writers strive for Reader-Based prose from the very beginning: they retrieve and organize information within the framework of a reader/writer contract. Their top goal or initial question is not, "What do I know about physics, and in particular the physics of wind resistance?" but, "What does a model plane builder need to know?" Many times a writer can do this. For a physics teacher this particular writing problem would be a trivial one. However, for a person ten years out of Physics 101, simply retrieving any relevant information would be a full-time processing job. The reader would simply have to wait. For the inexperienced writer, trying to put complex thought into written language may also be task enough. In that case, the reader is an extra constraint that must wait its turn. A Reader-Based strategy which includes the reader in the entire thinking process is clearly the best way to write, but it is not always possible. When it is very difficult or impossible to write for a reader from the beginning, writing and then transforming Writer-Based prose is a practical alternative which breaks this complex process down into manageable parts. When transforming is a practiced skill, it enters naturally into the pulse of the composing process as a writer's constant, steady effort to test and adapt his or her thought to a reader's needs. Transforming Writer-Based prose is, then, not only a necessary procedure for all writers at times, but a useful place to start teaching intellectually significant writing skills.

In this final section, I will try to account for the peculiar virtues of Writer-Based prose and suggest ways that teachers of writing—in any field—can take advantage of them. Seen in the context of memory retrieval, Writer-Based thinking appears to be a tapline to the rich sources of episodic memory. In the context of the composing process, Writer-Based prose is a way to deal with the overload that writing often imposes on short-term memory. By teaching writers to use this transformation process, we can foster the peculiar strengths of writer-based thought and still alert writers to the next transformation that many may simply fail to attempt.

One way to account for why Writer-Based prose seems to "come naturally" to most of us from time to time is to recognize its ties to our episodic as opposed to semantic memory. As Tulving describes it, "episodic memory is a more or less faithful record of a person's experiences." A statement drawn from episodic memory "refers to a personal experience that is remembered in its temporal-spatial relation to other such experiences. The remembered episodes are . . . autobiographical events, describable in terms of their perceptible dimensions or attributes."[13]

Semantic memory, by contrast, "is the memory necessary for the use of language. It is a mental thesaurus, organized knowledge a person possesses about words and other verbal symbols, their meaning and referents, about relations among them, and about rules, formulas, and algorithms for the manipulation of these symbols, concepts, and relations." Although we know that table salt is NaCl and that motivation is a mental

13. Edel Tulving, "Episodic and Semantic Memory," in Edel Tulving and Wayne Donaldson, eds., *Organization of Memory* (New York: Academic Press, 1972), p. 387.

state, we probably do not remember learning the fact or the first time we thought of that concept. In semantic memory, facts and concepts stand as the nexus for other words and symbols, but shorn of their temporal and autobiographical roots. If we explored the notion of "writing" in the semantic memory of someone we might produce a network such as this:

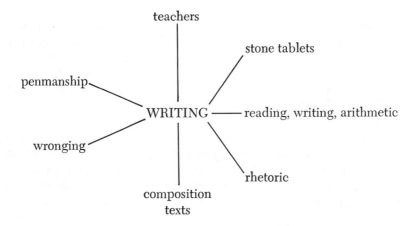

In an effort to retrieve what she or he knew about stone tablets, for example, this same person might turn to episodic memory: "I once heard a lecture on the Rosetta stone, over in Maynard Hall. The woman, as I recall, said that . . . and I remember wondering if. . . ."

Writers obviously use both kinds of memory. The problem only arises when they confuse a fertile source of ideas in episodic memory with a final product. In fact, a study by Russo and Wisher argues that we sometimes store our ideas or images (the symbols of thought) with the mental operations we performed to produce these symbols.[14] Furthermore, it is easier to recall the symbols (that fleeting idea, perhaps) when we bring back the original operation. In other words, our own thinking acts can serve as memory cues, and the easiest way to recover some item from memory may be to *reprocess* it, to reconstruct the original thought process in which it appeared. Much Writer-Based prose appears to be doing just this—reprocessing an earlier thinking experience as a way to recover what one knows.

Writing is one of those activities that places an enormous burden on short-term or working memory. As George Miller put it, "The most glar-

14. J. Russo and R. Wisher, "Reprocessing as a Recognition Cue," *Memory and Cognition*, 4 (1976), 683–689.

ing result [of numerous experiments] has been to highlight man's inadequacy as a communication channel. As the amount of input information is increased, the amount of information that the man transmits increases at first but then runs into a ceiling. . . . That ceiling is always very low. Indeed, it is an act of charity to call man a channel at all. Compared to telephone or television channels, man is better characterized as a bottleneck."[15]

The short-term memory is the active central processor of the mind, that is, it is the sum of all the information we can hold in conscious attention at one time. We notice its capacity most acutely when we try to learn a new task, such as driving a car or playing bridge. Its limited capacity means that when faced with a complex problem—such as writing a college paper—we can hold and compare only a few alternative relationships in mind at once.

Trying to evaluate, elaborate, and relate all that we know on a given topic can easily overload the capacity of our working memory. Trying to compose even a single sentence can have the same effect, as we try to juggle grammatical and syntactic alternatives plus all the possibilities of tone, nuance, and rhythm even a simple sentence offers. Composing, then, is a cognitive activity that constantly threatens to overload short-term memory. For two reasons, Writer-Based prose is a highly effective strategy for dealing with this problem.

1. Because the characteristic structure of Writer-Based prose is often a list (either of mental events or the features of the topic) it temporarily suspends the additional problem of forming complex concepts. If that task is suspended indefinitely, the result will fail to be good analytical writing or serious thought, but as a first stage in the process the list-structure has real value. It allows the writer freedom to generate a breadth of information and a variety of alternative relationships before locking himself or herself into a premature formulation. Furthermore, by allowing the writer to temporarily separate the two complex but somewhat different tasks of generating information and forming networks, each task may be performed more consciously and effectively.

2. Taking the perspective of another mind is also a demanding cognitive operation. It means holding not only your own knowledge network but someone else's in conscious attention and comparing them. Young children simply can't do it.[16] Adults choose not to do it when their cen-

15. George Miller, *The Psychology of Communication* (New York: Basic Books, 1967), p. 48.
16. Marlene Scardamalia, "How Children Cope with the Cognitive Demands of Writing," in *Writing: The Nature, Development and Teaching of Written Communication,* C. Frederikson, M. Whiteman, and J. Dominic, eds.

tral processing is already overloaded with the effort to generate and structure their own ideas. Writer-Based prose simply eliminates this constraint by temporarily dropping the reader out of the writer's deliberations.[17]

My own research suggests that good writers take advantage of these strategies in their composing process. They use scenarios, generate lists, and ignore the reader, but only for a while. Their composing process, unlike that of less effective writers, is marked by constant re-examination of their growing product and an attempt to refine, elaborate, or test its relationships, plus an attempt to anticipate the response of a reader. Everyone uses the strategies of Writer-Based prose; good writers go a step further to transform the writing these strategies produce.

But what about the writers who fail to make this transformation or (like all of us) fail to do it adequately in places? This is the problem faced by all teachers who assign papers. I think this study has two main and quite happy implications for us as teachers and writers.

The first is that Writer-Based prose is not a composite of errors or a mistake that should be scrapped. Instead, it is a half-way place for many writers and often represents the results of an extensive search and selection process. As a stage in the composing process, it may be a rich compilation of significant thoughts which cohere *for the writer* into a network she or he has not yet fully articulated. Writer-Based prose is the writer's homework, and so long as the writer is also the audience, it may even be a well-thought-out communication.

The second happy implication is that writing Reader-Based prose is often simply the task of transforming the groundwork laid in the first stage of the process.[18] Good analytical writing is not different in kind from the writer-based thought that seems to come naturally. It is an extension of our communication with ourselves transformed in certain predictable ways to meet the needs of the reader. The most general transformation is simply to try to take into account the reader's purpose in reading. Most people have well-developed strategies for doing this when they talk. For a variety of reasons—from cognitive effort to the illusion of the omniscient teacher/reader—many people simply do not consider the reader when they write.

17. Linda Flower and John R. Hayes, "The Dynamics of Composing: Making Plans and Juggling Constraints," in *Cognitive Processes in Writing: An Interdisciplinary Approach,* Lee Gregg and Irwin Steinberg, eds. (Hillsdale, N.J.: Lawrence Erlbaum, 1979).

18. For a study of heuristics and teaching techniques for this transformation process see L. Flower and J. Hayes, "Problem-Solving Strategies and the Writing Process," *College English,* 39 (1977), 449–461.

More specifically, the transformations that produce Reader-Based writing include these:

Selecting a focus of mutual interest to both reader and writer (e.g., moving from the writer-based focus of "How did I go about my research or reading of the assignment and what did I see?" to a focus on "What significant conclusions can be drawn and why?").

Moving from facts, scenarios, and details to concepts.

Transforming a narrative or textbook structure into a rhetorical structure built on the logical and hierarchical relationships between ideas and organized around the purpose for writing, rather than the writer's process.

Teaching writers to recognize their own Writer-Based writing and transform it has a number of advantages. It places a strong positive value on writing that represents an effort and achievement for the writer even though it fails to communicate to the reader. This legitimate recognition of the uncommunicated content of Writer-Based prose can give anyone, but especially inexperienced writers, the confidence and motivation to go on. By defining writing as a multi-stage process (instead of a holistic act of "expression"), we provide a rationale for editing and alert many writers to a problem they could handle once it is set apart from other problems and they deliberately set out to tackle it. By recognizing transformation as a special skill and task, we give writers a greater degree of self-conscious control over the abilities they already have and a more precise introduction to some skills they may yet develop.

ADDITIONAL READINGS

Mina P. Shaughnessy, "Basic Writing," *Teaching Composition: 10 Bibliographical Essays,* ed. Gary Tate (Fort Worth: Texas Christian University Press, 1976), pp. 137–167.

Harvey S. Wiener, "Questions on Basic Skills for the Writing Teacher," *College Composition and Communication,* 28 (December, 1977), 321–324.

Robert de Beaugrande, "Linguistic Theory and Composition," *College Composition and Communication,* 29 (May, 1978), 134–140.

Elaine Chaika, "Grammars and Teaching," *College English,* 39 (March, 1978), 777–783.

Barry M. Kroll and John C. Schafer, "Error-Analysis and the Teaching of Composition," *College Composition and Communication,* 29 (October, 1978), 242–248.

Paul Roberts, "Linguistics and the Teaching of Composition," *English Journal,* 52 (May, 1963), 331–335.

Muriel Harris, "Individualized Diagnosis: Teaching for Causes, Not Symptoms, of Writing Deficiencies," *College English,* 40 (November, 1978), 318–323.

When Is a Paragraph?

For the past few years, for reasons that will soon become apparent, I have asked students in one of my courses to take part in a small, informal experiment. Each student receives a duplicated copy of the same 500-word expository passage. The passage, I explain, has been transcribed verbatim from Cleanth Brooks and Robert Penn Warren's *Fundamentals of Good Writing* (New York: Harcourt, Brace & Co., 1950), pp. 290–291, departing from the original in only one respect: the original passage was divided into two or more paragraphs; the copy contains no paragraph indentations. Their task is simply to decide into how many paragraphs they think it should be divided and to note the precise point (or points) at which they would make their divisions.

The exercise usually takes fifteen minutes or so, and we spend another ten or fifteen analyzing the results, which are invariably intriguing. We discover that some students have divided the passage into two paragraphs, others into three, still others into four or five. What is more, nearly all of these possible divisions seem justifiable—they "feel right." Most surprising of all is the fact that only five students out of the more than 100 who have tried the experiment have paragraphed the passage precisely, as Brooks and Warren originally did.

These results are hardly earthshaking, I realize. They prove, if they prove anything, only that different students have different intuitions about paragraphing and that many of these intuitions turn out to be equally acceptable, equally "correct." But perhaps a few facts I have so

From *College Composition and Communication*, 27 (October, 1976), 253–257. Reprinted by permission of the National Council of Teachers of English and Arthur A. Stern.

far neglected to mention will make this discovery less trivial than it may at first appear.

First of all, the students who took part in the exercise were not college freshmen; they were teachers of English. Secondly, most of them were committed to the theory, promulgated by many handbooks, that the paragraph is a purely "logical" unit of discourse. They believed, that is to say, that a paragraph is a group of sentences developing one central idea. They believed that good paragraphs always (or usually) contain identifiable topic sentences which always (or usually) occur toward the beginning of the paragraphs. They believed that a well-developed paragraph is "a composition in miniature." They believed, accordingly, that good English teachers should concentrate on teaching their students to write good paragraphs, because good paragraphs are really good essays writ small.

My purpose in having them try my little experiment was to induce them to question the adequacy of the theory they had accepted. If, as the handbooks declare, a paragraph represents a "distinct unit of thought," why is it that we can't recognize a unit of thought when we see one? If every paragraph contains an identifiable topic sentence, then why don't all of us identify the same topic sentence? If good paragraphs are really compositions in miniature, why do some of us, given a passage not marked off into paragraphs, find in it two mini-compositions, while others find three or four or five? Aren't compositions—even miniature ones—supposed to have clear beginnings, middles, and conclusions?

Too many of us, I suspect, have based our teaching of the paragraph on a theory whose origins we do not know and whose validity we have not tested. Like the poet's neighbor in Frost's "Mending Wall," we go on repeating our fathers' sayings without ever going behind them.

Behind the logical (or "organic") theory of the paragraph lies a history replete with facts that cast doubt upon its authenticity. That history, as Paul C. Rodgers, Jr. has told us, begins a little more than a hundred years ago with Alexander Bain, a Scottish logician.[1] The fact that Bain was a logician, not a teacher of rhetoric, is itself of first importance; for he conceived the paragraph as a deductive system, a collection of sentences animated by unity of purpose, a purpose announced in an opening topic statement and developed through a logically ordered sequence of statements that "iterate or illustrate the same idea."[2] What is more, Bain appears to have constructed his deductive model

1. Paul C. Rodgers, Jr., "Alexander Bain and the Rise of the Organic Paragraph," *Quarterly Journal of Speech*, 51 (December, 1965), 399–408.
2. Alexander Bain, *English Composition and Rhetoric* (London: Longmans, Green, 1866), cited by Rodgers, p. 404.

by a purely deductive procedure. Making no empirical analysis of actual paragraphs, he simply transferred to his collection of sentences the classical rules governing the individual sentence—rules, now discredited, which defined the sentence as a group of words containing a subject and predicate and expressing a "complete and independent thought." Bain's paragraph, notes Rodgers, "is simply a sentence writ large,"[3] that is, an extension by analogy of logic-based grammar.

Others—John Genung, Barrett Wendell, and George R. Carpenter among them—subsequently refined Bain's theory without questioning its assumptions, reducing Bain's original six principles of paragraph construction to the now familiar triad of Unity, Coherence, and Emphasis, and tacking on the added notion that the paragraph is the discourse in miniature. Bain's influence is thus responsible, Rodgers observes, "for placing twentieth-century paragraph rhetoric in a deductive cage, from which it has yet to extricate itself."[4]

The work of extrication has been quietly going forward, however. The most recent empirical testing of Bain's theory, and the most damaging to it, was undertaken by Richard Braddock in 1974.[5] Braddock's study, completed shortly before his untimely death, took specific aim at two of Bain's assertions: that all expository paragraphs have topic sentences and that topic sentences usually occur at the beginnings of paragraphs. Braddock's method of research and his findings call into question not only Bain's century-old paragraph theory but also, as I shall try to show, the procedures and generalizations of such "new" rhetoricians as Francis Christensen and Alton L. Becker.

Braddock began by making a random selection of essays published in *The Atlantic, Harper's, The Reporter, The New Yorker,* and *The Saturday Review.* Almost immediately, he ran into trouble, finding it extremely difficult to define the very item he was looking for—the topic sentence. "After several frustrating attempts to underline the appropriate T-unit where it occurred," Braddock reported, "I realized that the notion of what a topic sentence is, is not at all clear."[6] In an effort to define this central term, he developed an entire catalogue of "types" of topic sentence: the *simple* topic (the kind the handbooks say all paragraphs should contain); the *delayed-completion* (a topic stated in two T-units, not necessarily adjacent); the *assembled* (not actually a sentence at all, but a composite, gummed together from fragments of several sentences running through

3. Rodgers, Alexander Bain," p. 406.
4. Ibid., p. 408.
5. Richard Braddock, "The Frequency and Placement of Topic Sentences in Expository Prose," *Research in the Teaching of English,* 8 (Winter, 1974), 287–302.
6. Ibid., p. 291.

the paragraph); and the *inferred* (a "topic sentence" nowhere explicitly stated by the writer, but construed by the reader).

But even after thus extending—one might say stretching—the definition of "topic sentence," Braddock found that a considerable proportion of the paragraphs in his sample contained no topic sentence of any type. In some instances, a single topic sentence governed a sequence running to several paragraphs; in others, the indentations seemed "quite arbitrary." All told, fewer than half the paragraphs contained a simple topic sentence; even when topic sentences of the delayed-completion type were included, the total came to little more than half (55%). How many paragraphs *began* with topic sentences? Fewer than one out of seven (13%) in all the paragraphs Braddock analyzed.

These findings, Braddock noted with quiet understatement, "did not support the claims of textbook writers about the frequency and location of topic sentences in professional writing."[7] Although scientific and technical writing might present a different case, with respect to contemporary professional exposition the textbooks' claims were "just not true."[8]

Braddock's study thus effectively disposes of the hand-me-down Bainalities of the textbooks. But it does more than that: as I have already suggested, Braddock's empirical method and his findings cast some doubt upon certain conclusions reached by Francis Christensen and A. L. Becker, and upon the evidence those conclusions are based on.

In his "Generative Rhetoric of the Paragraph," Professor Christensen proposes, as did Alexander Bain, "that the paragraph has, or may have, a structure as definable and traceable as that of the sentence and that it can be analyzed in the same way."[9] From this premise he moves rather swiftly to conclusions hardly distinguishable from Bain's:

1. The paragraph may be defined as a sequence of structurally related sentences.

2. The top sentence of the sequence is the topic sentence.

3. The topic sentence is nearly always the first sentence of the sequence.[10]

Although he subsequently allows for exceptions (some paragraphs have no topic sentence; some paragraphing is "illogical"), there is no mistaking that Christensen's second and third "rules" are essentially those which Braddock found to be false. Unlike Braddock, Christensen seems to be-

---

7. Ibid., p. 301.
8. Ibid., p. 298.
9. *Notes Toward a New Rhetoric* (New York: Harper & Row, 1967), p. 54.
10. Ibid., pp. 57–58.

lieve that the term *topic sentence* is self-explanatory, requiring no precise definition. In support of his claims, Christensen cites the "many scores of paragraphs I have analyzed for this study."[11] He does not tell us how these paragraphs were selected or from what sources; he tells us only that in the paragraphs he analyzed "the topic sentence occurs almost invariably at the beginning."[12] Had he detailed his procedures as he did in his study of sentence openers,[13] we would have reason to be more confident of his conclusions. But he doesn't. The evidence underlying his statements about the paragraph is soft and rather vague.

A. L. Becker's "Tagmemic Approach to Paragraph Analysis," viewed in the light of Braddock's study, seems similarly flawed. Like Christensen, Becker applies to the paragraph the instruments of sentence-analysis, with the purpose of "extending grammatical theories now used in analyzing and describing sentence structure . . . to the description of paragraphs."[14] He cautions at the outset that he intends to examine the paragraph from only one of three possible perspectives—the "particle" perspective—and that his description will necessarily be somewhat distorted because it suppresses the "wave" and "field" aspects of paragraph structure. But this disclaimer hardly prepares us for his subsequent assertion that there are "two major patterns of paragraphing in expository writing,"[15] and only two: the TRI (Topic-Restriction-Illustration) pattern and the PS (Problem-Solution) pattern. Becker continues:

> Although there are more kinds of expository paragraphs than these two, I would say that the majority of them fall into one of these two major types. Many expository paragraphs which at first appear to be neither TRI or [*sic*] PS can be interpreted as variations of these patterns. . . . There are also minor paragraph forms (usually transitional paragraphs or simple lists)—and, finally, there are "bad" paragraphs, like poorly constructed, confusing sentences.[16]

Again, one is left in doubt as to the evidence on which these generalizations rest. Surely, in preparing his study, Professor Becker cannot have read *all* expository paragraphs; how, then, can he justify a claim concerning a "majority" of them? What were his sampling procedures? Were "bad" paragraphs included in his total count, or were they summarily re-

11. Ibid., p. 58.
12. Ibid.
13. Ibid., pp. 39–51.
14. A. L. Becker, "A Tagmemic Approach to Paragraph Analysis," in Francis Christensen *et al.*, *The Sentence and the Paragraph* (Champaign, Ill.: National Council of Teachers of English, 1966), p. 33.
15. Ibid., p. 34.
16. Ibid., p. 36.

jected as unworthy of consideration? To these and other questions he provides no answers. We know only that his findings conflict sharply with Braddock's, and that, in Becker's case as in Christensen's, we find, somewhat disguised by modern terminology, the century-old claim that a "good" paragraph begins with a topic sentence and develops the idea stated by the topic sentence.

If we are ever to rid ourselves of Bain's lingering legacy we must, it seems clear, abandon his exclusively sentence-based, "particle" approach to paragraph description, an approach that treats the paragraph as if it were an isolated, self-contained unit, and imposes upon it a rigid set of logical and quasi-grammatical rules. We must adopt an approach that describes not only the internal structure of a paragraph but also its external connections with adjoining paragraphs and its function in the discourse as a whole. What we need, Paul Rodgers proposes, is "a flexible, open-ended *discourse-centered* rhetoric of the paragraph":

> All we can usefully say of *all* paragraphs at present [Rodgers explains] is that their authors have marked them off for special consideration as *stadia of discourse,* in preference to other stadia, other patterns, in the same material. Paragraph structure is part and parcel of the discourse as a whole; a given stadium becomes a paragraph not by virtue of its structure but because the writer elects to indent, his indentation functioning, as does all punctuation, as a gloss upon the overall literary process under way at that point.[17]

Paragraphing, Rodgers here suggests, is governed by rhetorical choice rather than by logical or grammatical rule. Like the structure of a sentence or that of a fully developed essay, the structure of a paragraph arises out of an *ethos* and a *pathos* as well as out of a *logos*—out of the writer's personality and his perception of his reader as well as out of his perception of the structure of his subject-matter. The logic and "grammar" of a given paragraph are conditioned—sometimes powerfully—by what may be termed the psychologic and socio-logic of a particular rhetorical occasion.

As every experienced writer knows, paragraphing helps establish a tone or "voice." (Editors know this, too. That is why they frequently reparagraph a writer's prose to bring it into conformity with their publication's image.) Short paragraphs appear to move more swiftly than long ones; short paragraphs lighten up the appearance of a page, whereas long ones, containing the identical information, give the page a heavier, more

17. Paul C. Rodgers, Jr., "A Discourse-Centered Rhetoric of the Paragraph," in Francis Christensen *et al., The Sentence and the Paragraph* (Champaign, Ill.: National Council of Teachers of English, 1966), p. 12.

scholarly look. Just as he adjusts his sentences and his diction, the writer may adjust his paragraphs, deliberately or intuitively, to achieve a variety of rhetorical effects—formality or informality, abruptness or suavity, emphasis or subjunction.

Paragraphing practices are also governed by changes in fashion and social convention. Today's paragraphs are considerably shorter than those of fifty or a hundred years ago. "In books of the last century," Paul Roberts reminds us, "a paragraph often ran through several pages, but the modern reader wants to come up for air oftener. He is alarmed by a solid mass of writing and comforted when it is broken up into chunks."[18] In consequence of this change in literary fashion, nineteenth-century rules of "logical" paragraphing, dubious in their own day, are outmoded now. What might once have appeared as a single paragraph is today routinely broken up into smaller units which, taken together, comprise what William Irmscher has labeled a "paragraph bloc."[19] Indeed, when Richard Braddock observed that one topic sentence frequently governed an entire sequence of paragraphs, he was suggesting that contemporary professional writers use blocs rather than single paragraphs as logical units much of the time.

In sum, today's paragraph is not a logical unit and we should stop telling our students it is. It does not necessarily begin with a topic sentence; it does not necessarily "handle and exhaust a distinct topic," as the textbooks say it must do. It is not a composition-in-miniature, either—it is not an independent, self-contained whole but a functioning part of discourse; its boundaries are not sealed but open to the surrounding text; it links as often as it divides. Shaped by the writer's individual style and by the reader's expectations as well as by the logic of the subject-matter, the paragraph is a flexible, expressive rhetorical instrument.

Perhaps some day it will be possible to teach paragraphing by rule and formula, though I frankly doubt it. In any case, the rules and formulas that govern the paragraphing practices of professional writers have yet to be discovered. Let us, therefore, focus our students' attention on what they have to say—on the arguments they want to present, the points they want to make—and not on the number of indentations they should use in saying it. Let us make them think about the topics they plan to discuss rather than about the "correct" location of their topic sentences. Let us, in other words, make our teaching discourse-centered. If the whole does indeed determine the parts, their paragraphs should improve as their essays mold them into form.

18. Paul Roberts, *Understanding English* (New York: Harper & Row, 1958), p. 423.
19. William F. Irmscher. *The Holt Guide to English* (New York: Holt, Rinehart and Winston, Inc., 1972), p. 86.

W. ROSS WINTEROWD

The Grammar of Coherence

Just at the point where it could best serve rhetoric, transformational generative grammar fails: it does not jump the double-cross mark (#) that signifies "sentence boundary" or, more accurately, "transformational unit boundary." The significance of this limitation is underscored by the inability of grammarians to write a rule for the simplest of all transformations: clause coordination.

> Since the number of sentences that can be conjoined in this way is, theoretically at least, unlimited, it is not immediately obvious how to write a constituent-structure rule to permit the generation of compound sentences. . . . It is clearly unsatisfactory to have to postulate an infinity of rules. . . .[1]

As a result, transformational generative grammar has been tremendously useful in the study of style, but it has had little application (except metaphorically) to invention and organization. That is, it has cast only dim light on concepts of form and coherence.

The following discussion will argue that there is a grammar of *coherence* (or *form,* for in the following, the two terms are virtually synonymous). If one perceives form in discourse, he also perceives coherence, for form is the internal set of consistent relationships in any stretch of discourse, whether poem, play, essay, oration, or whatever. This set of relationships—like the relationships that rules of grammar describe—must be finite in number; otherwise: formlessness, for the very concepts of form and coherence imply a finite number of relationships that can be

From *College English,* 31 (May, 1970), 828–835. Reprinted by permission of the National Council of Teachers of English and W. Ross Winterowd.

1. D. Terence Langendoen, *The Study of Syntax* (New York, 1969), p. 31.

perceived. (A generative grammar implies a finite number of rules, some of which may be applied recursively.) Following the model of grammar, one might look for some sort of "constituent structure rules" that underlie coherent utterances beyond the sentence, and then for the equivalent of "lexical rules," and finally for something approximating "transformational rules." In a very rough, loosely analogous way, the following discussion concentrates only on the "phrase structure rules" of coherence and, as a result, excludes "lexical" data which is undoubtedly significant. For instance, one reason that a paragraph "hangs together" or is a convention is that chains of equivalent words run through it. A switch in equivalence chains signals: new paragraph.[2] The present discussion will ignore everything but the abstract configurations or sets of relationships that constitute coherence. (This, of course, is not to say that any one component of the whole body of discourse is unimportant.)

Modern grammar nicely describes the first two stadia in the hierarchy of discourse relationship sets that make up coherence. The first set of relationships is one that can develop from the application of rules to S and then to all constituents that develop from S. The result (after lexical rules have been applied) will be a sentence, divided into two parts: Modality and Proposition. As Charles J. Fillmore explains:

> In the basic structure of sentences . . . we find what might be called the "proposition," a tenseless set of relationships involving verbs and nouns (and embedded sentences, if there are any), separated from what might be called the "modality" constituent. This latter will include such modalities on the sentence-as-a-whole as negation, tense, mood, and aspect.[3]

Each noun in the proposition stands in a *case* relationship with the verb, thus:

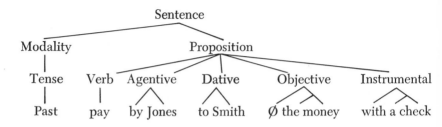

2. A. L. Becker, "A Tagmemic Approach to Paragraph Analysis," *The Sentence and the Paragraph* (Champaign, Ill., 1966), pp. 33–38.

3. "The Case for Case," *Universals in Linguistic Theory,* ed. Emmon Bach and Robert T. Harms (New York, 1968), p. 23.

This *deep structure* can have the following surface manifestations, all of them synonymous:

1. Jones paid Smith the money with a check.
2. Jones paid the money to Smith with a check.
3. The money was paid Smith by Jones with a check.
4. The money was paid to Smith by Jones with a check.
5. The money was paid by Jones to Smith with a check.
6. Smith was paid the money by Jones with a check.

And with the cleft sentence transformation: *A check is what Jones paid Smith the money with.* It is worth pointing out that syntactic relationships in these sentences change, but case relationships ("who did what and with which and to whom") are invariable. Thus, in 1 and 2, "Jones" is the grammatical subject of the verb; in 3, 4, and 5, "the money" is the grammatical subject; in 6, "Smith" is the subject. But "Jones" is always in the agentive case, "the money" is always in the objective case, and "Smith" is always in the dative. That is, we never lose sight of the relationships among the noun phrases or of their relationships with the verb. It is also worth noting—in fact, crucial to this discussion—that certain "particles" which are represented in the deep structure diagram may or may not appear in the surface structure. Thus, the agentive "by" does not appear until after the passive transformation has been applied, and dative "to" disappears with application of the indirect object inversion transformation. These signals of case relationships may or may not be in the surface structure.

The first "layer" of relationships that make up coherence, then, is *cases*.

The second "layer" might well be called *syntax* (in a somewhat specialized and restricted use of the word). The relationships of syntax are described by those transformations that have to do with inserting sentences within other sentences by any means but coordination. Thus, the relationships characteristic of syntax (as I use the word) are, for instance,

complements:
  It is strange. He is here.
  It is strange that he is here.
  It is strange for him to be here.
  His being here is strange.

relatives:
  The banker owned the town. The banker was rich.

The banker who was rich owned the town.
The rich banker owned the town.

subordinates:
He chews tobacco. He likes it.
He chews tobacco because he likes it.

absolutes:
The airport being fogged in, the plane circled for an hour.
The airport was fogged in. The plane circled for an hour.
and so on.

This is the cat. The cat chased the rat. The rat ate the malt. The malt lay in the house. Jack built the house.

This is the cat that chased the rat that ate the malt that lay in the house that Jack built.

And this, of course, is just the point at which grammar ends—that very point at which *inventio* and *dispositio* really begin.

I argue that there is a set of relationships beyond case and syntax and that this set constitutes the relationships that make for coherence—among the transformational units in a paragraph, among the paragraphs in a chapter, among the chapters in a book. I call these relationships *transitions,* and I claim that beyond the sentence marker, the double-cross, we perceive coherence only as the consistent relationships among transitions. All of this, of course, is more easily illustrated than explained, and illustration is forthcoming. For the moment, however, I should like to underscore my claim that the relationships I am about to describe constitute the grammar of coherence for *all* units of discourse beyond the level of what I have called "syntax."[4]

In another place, I will detail the method whereby I arrived at the following conclusions. But for the time being, I will concentrate on results and their applications.

Analysis of thousands of transformational units in sequences reveals that there are seven relationships that prevail among T-units and, I would argue, in any stretch of discourse that is perceived as coherent. I have

4. The reader who is familiar with modern logic will immediately perceive the similarity between what I am about to outline and the relationships among propositions listed in logic. They are *initial, additive* (and), *adversative* (but), *alternative* (or), *explanatory* (that is), *illustrative* (for example), *illative* (therefore), *causal* (for). I would urge the reader, however, to be more conscious of the differences between the two systems than of the similarities. What I call transitions are not merely an adaptation, but, it seems to me, are manifestations of some of the most basic properties of language.

called these relationships (1) coordinate, (2) obversative, (3) causative, (4) conclusive, (5) alternative, (6) inclusive, and (7) sequential. These relationships can be either *expressed* or *implied*. They are expressed in a variety of ways: through coordinating conjunctions, transitional adverbs, and a variety of other moveable modifiers. Just how they are implied remains a mystery.[5] However, the relationships are easily demonstrated.

Coordination can always be expressed by *and*. (Synonyms: *furthermore, in addition, too, also, again, etc.*)

Boswell was a Rousseau-ite, one of the first of the Romantics, an inveterate sentimentalist, AND nothing could be more complete than the contrast between his career and Gibbon's.

Lytton Strachey

They almost hid from us the front, but through the dust and the spaces between running legs we could see the soldiers in the trench leap their barricade like a breaking wave. AND then the impenetrable dust shut down AND the fierce stabbing needle of the machine guns sewed the mighty jumble of sounds together.

John Reed

. . . Marat is, in most of his speeches, tinsel, stage scenery, or an element in a great painting. AGAIN, the Brechtian songs are touching, but ironically and allusively touching; Charlotte Corday, the mad, beautiful country girl mouthing her lines, is AGAIN an element in a picture, an aesthetic contrivance.

Stuart Hampshire

Obversativity can always be expressed by *but*. (Synonyms: *yet, however, on the other hand, etc.*)

It has been ambitious and plucky of me to attempt to describe what is indescribable, and I have failed, as I knew I would. BUT I have discharged my duty to society. . . .

E. B. White

5. When I first began working on these ideas, I communicated my findings to Charles Fillmore of Ohio State. His comment on my tentative conclusions is revealing. I was talking strictly about the relationships in the paragraph, and he said, "Your ideas about paragraph structure are appealing, but it's hard to see, as you admit, how they can lead to any clarification of the problems of coherence on the paragraph level. The 'coherence' of clauses in a sentence is just as unsolved an issue as ever, but to the extent that your proposals are right you can at least claim to have demonstrated that what might have appeared to be two separate mysteries are reducible to one and the same mystery." The fact that coherence among clauses in a T-unit and coherence among T-units are reducible to the same mystery is, of course, the point here, not that coherence is mysterious. In general, I am indebted to Professor Fillmore for a great variety of insights.

And Johnson, as Kennedy has often acknowledged, was a man of force and decision to whom, in case anything happened, the government could responsibly be assigned.

ON THE OTHER HAND, the designation of Johnson would outrage the liberal wing of the party.

Arthur Schlesinger, Jr.

Causativity can always be expressed by *for.* It is interesting to note that among the transitional adverbs commonly used (nevertheless, however, moreover, hence, consequently, nonetheless, accordingly, then, besides, likewise, indeed, therefore), none expresses the causative relationship.

Now, on that morning, I stopped still in the middle of the block, *FOR* I'd caught out of the corner of my eye a tunnel-passage, an overgrown courtyard.

Truman Capote

Conclusivity can always be expressed by *so.* (Synonyms: *therefore, thus, for this reason, etc.*)

She has a rattling Corsican accent, likes Edith Piaf records, and gives me extra shrimp bits in my shrimp bit salad. *SO* some things change. Last time I heard no Edith Piaf and earned no extra forkful of shrimp.

Herbert Gold

Alternativity can always be expressed by *or.*

Now such an entity, even if it could be proved beyond dispute, would not be God: it would merely be a further piece of existence, that might conceivably not have been there—*OR* a demonstration would not have been required.

John A. T. Robinson

Inclusivity is often expressed with a *colon.*

In the first century B.C., Lucretius wrote this description of the pageant of Cybele: Adorned with emblem and crown . . . she is carried in awe-inspiring state. . . .

Harvey Cox

The inclusive relationship is that of the example to the generality or the narration of the case to the statement of the case. Often, inclusivity is expressed by the transformational possibility of complementization:

He realized that their discovery [Aristotle's discovery of the statues of Daedalus] would shatter his own "natural" law: Managers would no longer need subordinates, masters could dispense with slaves.

Michael Harrington

With the last two clauses complementized, the sentence reads like this:

> He realized that their discovery would shatter his own "natural" law, that managers would no longer need subordinates, and that masters could dispense with slaves.

The *sequential relationship* is expressed by such transitions as "first . . . second . . . third," "earlier . . . later," "on the bottom . . . in the middle . . . on top," and so on.

Three types of relationships, then, constitute coherence: cases, syntax, and transitions (with the transitions either expressed or implied). And it is, indeed, obvious that transitions can be implied, for it is common to find series of transformational units with no expressed transitions.

> It is possible to love the theater and to revel in theatricality, to find the pretense and unreality of the stage wholly absorbing in its own right. It must be supposed that most actors and directors, if left to their own tastes and impulses, would strive after theatrical effects above all else. The satisfaction of any broader human interest might be quite secondary.
> *Stuart Hampshire*

I read this as an "and . . . and" series, but another interpretation is possible: "and . . . for." That is, there can be ambiguity in transitions as well as in lexicon and syntax.

The interesting possibility, however, is that the seven relationships that prevail among T-units also prevail among larger elements of discourse. For instance, applied at the level of the T-unit, the seven constitute a series of topics that will automatically generate discourse, for the second T-unit must stand in one of the seven relationships to the first, and the third must stand in one of the seven relationships to the second, and so on. Therefore, transitions are topics for a generative rhetoric. But a rhetoric that will generate only paragraphs has limited usefulness. If, however, the seven topics isolate the relationships among any segments of discourse (except those related to one another by the grammar of the T-unit), then they might well be the basis for a true generative rhetoric.

Shakespeare's sonnets have proved to be useful models for my purposes, and they will serve here to demonstrate that the seven relationships prevail in "whole works," though, of course, one might argue that a sonnet is, after all, just another kind of paragraph. Expressed transitions in the following will be in capitals; implied transitions (according to my reading) will be in bracketed capitals.

Sonnet XVII

Who will believe my verse in time to come,
If it were fill'd with your most high deserts?

THOUGH YET, heaven knows, it is but as a tomb
Which hides your life and shows not half your parts.
[BUT] If I could write the beauty of your eyes
And in fresh numbers number all your graces,
The age to come would say 'This poet lies;
[FOR] Such heavenly touches ne'er touch'd earthly faces.'
SO should my papers, yellowed with their age,
Be scorn'd, like old men of less truth than tongue,
And your true rights be term'd a poet's rage
And stretched metre of an antique song:
    BUT were some child of yours alive that time,
    You should live twice, in it and in my rhyme.

In his cycle, Shakespeare upon occasion needs two sonnets rather than one to express his complete idea. In such cases, he supplies the proper transition. The relationship between V and VI is conclusive, expressed as *then.* (*So* is the minimal transition to express conclusivity.)

Sonnet V

Those hours that with gentle work did frame
The lovely gaze where every eye doth dwell,
Will play the tyrants to the very same
And that unfair which fairly doth excel:
FOR never-resting time leads summer on
To hideous winter and confounds him there;
Sap check'd with frost and lusty leaves quite gone,
Beauty o'ersnow'd and bareness every where:
THEN, were not summer's distillation left,
A liquid prisoner pent in walls of glass,
Beauty's effect with beauty were bereft,
Nor it, nor no remembrance what it was:
    BUT flowers distill'd, though they with winter meet,
    Leese but their show; [FOR] their substance still lives sweet.

Sonnet VI

THEN let not winter's ragged hand deface
In thee thy summer, ere thou be distill'd:
[BUT] Make sweet some vial; [AND] treasure thou some place
With beauty's treasure, ere it be self-kill'd.
[FOR] That use is not forbidden usury,
Which happies those that pay the willing loan;
[FOR] That's for thyself to breed another thee,
OR ten times happier, be it ten for one;
[FOR] Ten times thyself were happier than thou art,

If ten of thine ten times refigured thee:
THEN what could death do, if thou shouldst depart,
Leaving thee living in posterity?
[SO] Be not self-will'd, FOR thou art much too fair
To be death's conquest and make worms thine heir.

To apply this test to a series of paragraphs that make up an essay, for instance, is too cumbersome a job for the present discussion and is, in any case, unnecessary. The reader can make his own test. "What relationships prevail among the sections—paragraphs or other—of an extended piece of discourse?" is the question. If the seven outlined here are the answer, then the system has stood the test. (By the way, the question transformation might be viewed as a transition in itself. That is, it predicts some kind of answer.)

Finally, it is necessary to clarify the exact sense in which I take these seven relationships (they might be called "topics") to constitute a generative rhetoric. The term "generative" is of itself productive, for it exactly designates the process whereby discourse—at the sentence level and beyond—comes into being. An oversimplified explanation of the language process is to say that at any level of generality, one unit has the potential for generating other units and of combining these units in some meaningful way. Any set of topics is merely a way of triggering the process. Thus the student, say, who has difficulty with the invention of arguments, can use the seven-item list to tell him what might come next—not what content, to be sure, but what relation his next unit must take to the previous one. There are only seven possibilities.

Inability to write sentences stems not from the writer's lack of subject matter (everyone is the repository of an infinitude of subject matter), but from his not knowing how to get the subject matter into structures. The problem at levels beyond the sentence is, I think, exactly the same. The seven relation-oriented "topics" that I have outlined name the structures that can hold the writer's ideas.

A generative rhetoric, a heuristic model, even a grammar of form— whatever it might be called, the schema of these seven relationships ought to be easily applicable in the classroom. But equally important, they should have wide ranging theoretical possibilities, for instance, in explaining the disjunction of schizoid language, in identifying "the eighth ambiguity" (that which takes place between units larger than the sentence and results from the inability to perceive transitions) and in dealing with form in literature.

RICHARD BRADDOCK

The Frequency and Placement
of Topic Sentences in Expository Prose

Most textbooks on English composition have presented some concerted treatment of topic sentences, long hailed as means of organizing a writer's ideas and clarifying them for the reader. In the most popular composition textbook of the nineteenth century, for example, Alexander Bain recognized that topic sentences may come at the end of a descriptive or introductory paragraph, but he emphasized that expository paragraphs have topic sentences and that they usually come at the beginnings of paragraphs:

> 19. The opening sentence, unless obviously preparatory, is expected to indicate the scope of the paragraph. . . . This rule is most directly applicable to expository style, where, indeed, it is almost essential (Bain, 1890, p. 108).

In one of the more popular composition textbooks of the present, Gorrell and Laird present a similar statement about topic sentences—a statement which is paralleled in many other textbooks these days:

> Topic sentences may appear anywhere, or even be omitted. . . . but most modern, carefully constructed prose rests on standard paragraphs, most of which have topic sentences to open them.

And of 15 items on "Paragraph Patterns" in a commercial test of "writing," three involve the identification of topic sentences in brief paragraphs. In each of the three, the correct answer is the first sentence in the paragraph (*Basic Skills*, 1970).

How much basis is there for us to make such statements to students

From *Research in the Teaching of English*, 8 (Winter, 1974), 287–302. Reprinted by permission of the National Council of Teachers of English.

or to base testing on the truth of them? To clarify the matter, I studied the paragraphs in representative contemporary professional writing, seeking the answers to these two questions:

1. What proportion of the paragraphs contain topic sentences?
2. Where in the paragraphs do the topic sentences occur?

PROCEDURE

As a body of expository material representing contemporary professional writing, I used the corpus of 25 complete essays in American English selected by Margaret Ashida, using random procedures, from 420 articles published from January, 1964, through March, 1965, in *The Atlantic, Harper's, The New Yorker, The Reporter,* and *The Saturday Review.* Ashida indicated possible uses of the corpus:

> . . . this corpus could be used for a wealth of investigations by students, teachers, and research scholars—for anything from a relatively superficial examination of controversial matters of usage, to the exploration of the deep (and equally controversial) questions being raised by theoreticians of the new rhetorics. Because the sample has its own built-in validity, it represents a *common* corpus for use by many different scholars—something we desperately need in rhetorical research . . . (Ashida, 1968, pp. 14–23).

Paragraphs. Working one-by-one with xerographic copies of the 25 articles,[1] I numbered each paragraph from the first paragraph of the essay to the last. For this study, a paragraph was what we normally take to be one in printed material—a portion of discourse consisting of one or more sentences; the first line of type of which is preceded by more interlinear space than is otherwise found between lines in the text and the first sentence of which begins either with an indentation or with an unindented large initial capital.

Headnotes and footnotes were not counted as parts of the text for this study and hence were not numbered and analyzed. A problem appeared when one article included an insert, consisting of a diagram and some ten sentences of explanation, which was crucial to an understanding of the text proper.[2] This insert arbitrarily was not counted as a paragraph in

1. The copies were supplied through the generosity of the Department of English, University of Iowa.
2. Here and hereafter, reference to specific articles in the corpus will be made simply by using the author's last name—or, in the cases of the two articles by individuals of the same last name, by using the first initial and last name (see Table 1)—The paragraph referred to here is in Lear, p. 89.

the article. In those few essays in which dialog was quoted, each separately indented paragraph was counted as a paragraph, even though it consisted in one case merely of one four-word sentence (Taper, p. 138).

T-units. After numbering the paragraphs in an essay, I proceeded to insert a pencilled slash mark after each T-unit in each paragraph and to write the total number of T-units at the end of each paragraph.

The T-unit, or "minimal terminable unit," is a term devised by Kellogg Hunt to describe the "shortest grammatically allowable sentences into which . . . [writing can] be segmented" (Hunt, 1965, pp. 20–21). In other words, consideration of the T-units of writing permits the researcher to use a rather standard conception of a sentence, setting aside the differences occurring between writers when they use different styles of punctuation. A T-unit, then, "includes one main clause plus all the subordinate clauses attached to or embedded within it. . . . (Hunt, p. 141). Hunt wrote that an independent clause beginning with "and" or "but" is a T-unit, but I also included "or," "for," and "so" to complete what I take to be the coordinating conjunctions in modern usage.

Although in the vast majority of cases, there was no difficulty knowing where to indicate the end of a T-unit, several problems did arise. Take, for instance, the following sentence:

> The Depression destroyed the coalfield's prosperity, but the Second World War revised it, and for a few years the boom returned and the miner was again a useful and honored citizen (Caudill, p. 49).

Obviously, one T-unit ends with "prosperity" and another with "revived it," but is what follows "revived it" one T-unit or two? I made the judgment that "for a few years" was an integral part of both clauses following it and that "and for a few years the boom returned and the miner was again a useful and honored citizen" was one T-unit. Similarly, I counted the following sentence as one T-unit, not two, judging the intent of the first clause in the speech of the Protocol man to be subordinate, as if he had said "If you put an ambassador in prison":

> For another, as a Protocol man said recently, "You put an ambassador in prison and you can't negotiate with him, which is what he's supposed to be here for" (Kahn, p. 75).

In marking off T-units, a person must be prepared for occasional embedding. Sometimes a writer uses parentheses to help accomplish the embedding:

Gibbs & Cox (Daniel H. Cox was a famous yacht designer who joined the firm in 1929, retired in 1943, and subsequently died) is the largest private ship-designing firm in the world (Sargeant, p. 49).

That sentence, of course, has one T-unit embedded within one other. In the following example, dashes enclose two T-units embedded within another, and the entire sentence consists of four T-units:

> "They're condescending, supercilious bastards, but when the 'United States' broke all the transatlantic records—it still holds them, and it went into service in 1952—they had to come down a peg" (Sargeant, p. 50).

But embedding does not prove to be a problem in determining what is and what is not a T-unit. With the exception of perhaps a dozen other problems in the thousands of sentences considered in the 25 essays, marking off and counting the T-units was a fairly mechanical operation.

Topic sentences. The next problem was to decide which T-unit, if any, constituted a topic sentence in each paragraph. After several frustrating attempts merely to underline the appropriate T-unit where it occurred, I realized that the notion of what a topic sentence is, is not at all clear.

Consultation of composition textbooks provided no simple solution of the problem. Gorrell and Laird, for example, offered this definition of a topic sentence:

> Most paragraphs focus on a central idea or unifying device expressed in topical material. Occasionally this topical material is complex, involving more than one sentence and some subtopics; sometimes it carries over from a previous paragraph and is assumed to be understood or is referred to briefly; but usually it simply takes the form of a sentence, sometimes amplified or made more specific in a sentence or two following it. This topic sentence may appear at the end of the paragraph as a kind of summary or somewhere within the paragraph, but most frequently it opens the paragraph or follows an opening introduction or transition (Gorrell and Laird, p. 25).

The authors further clarify their definition (pp. 25–26) by stating that a topic sentence has three main functions: (1) to provide transition, (2) to suggest the organization of the paragraph, (3) to present a topic, either by naming or introducing a subject or by presenting a proposition or thesis for discussion. In the next several pages, the authors consider various types of "topic sentences as propositions" (or theses) and the problems in writing them with precision.

From my preliminary attempts to identify topic sentences in paragraphs, I could see the truth of a complex definition like Gorrell and Laird's. But such a comprehensive definition presents problems. Sometimes a paragraph opens with a sentence which we could all agree is transitional but which does not reveal much about the content of the paragraph. The second sentence may name the topic of the paragraph but not make a statement about it. The actual thesis of the paragraph may be stated explicitly in a succeeding sentence or in several sentences, or it may merely be inferred from what follows, even though it is never stated explicitly. In such a paragraph, which is the topic sentence—the first, second, a succeeding sentence, perhaps even all of them? Many of the sentences seem to fit the definition. An all-embracing definition does not seem helpful to me in deciding which sentence can be named the topic sentence.

Furthermore, as Paul Rodgers demonstrated (1966), paragraphing does not always correspond to a reader's perceived organization of ideas. Sometimes a paragraph presents an illustration of the thesis of the preceding paragraph. The second paragraph thus extends the previous paragraph, and the paragraph indentation seems quite arbitrary. Or sometimes a thesis is stated in a one-sentence paragraph and the following paragraph explains that thesis without restating it. In such situations, one cannot simply identify a topic sentence in each paragraph.

It seemed to me that the best test of topic sentences is the test a careful reader might make—the test offered when one constructs a sentence outline of the major points of an essay, drawing the sentences insofar as possible from the sentences the author has written. In constructing a sentence outline, one usually omits transitional and illustrative statements and concentrates on the theses themselves. Consequently, I decided to prepare a sentence outline of each of the 25 essays and *then* determine which paragraphs had topic sentences and where in the paragraphs they occurred.

Outlines. From the beginning of the first one, I was aware of the serious problems in constructing a sentence outline to study the organization of another person's writing. To what degree would I tend to impose on an essay my own interpretation of what was written? Does it do violence to discursive writing to cast it into the form of a sentence outline, trying to make the outline understandable by itself when the essay includes details of thought and qualities of style omitted in the process? Would the paragraphing and other typographical features of the edited essay distract me from the ideas and structure of the written essay? Of course I would try to preserve the author's intent in all of these matters, but what I actually did would be so much a matter of judgment that I should expose my outlines for the criticism of others, permitting comparison to the original articles. Moreover, the outlines might be helpful to other investigators who would like to use them without going to the extensive effort of preparing their own. Although it is impractical to include the outlines here, I will make them available to others for the cost of the copying.

In outlining an article, I read it through in sections of a number of paragraphs which seemed to be related, underlining topic sentences where I could find them and constructing topic sentences where they were not explicit in the article. In constructing a topic sentence, I tried to include phrases from the original text as much as possible. Whatever sentences, phrases, or key words I did use from the original I was careful to enclose in quotation marks, indicating by ellipsis marks all omissions and by brackets all of my own insertions. Opposite each entry in the outline I indicated the number of the paragraph and T-unit of each quotation used. Thus the notation 20:2,3 and 4 indicates that quoted portions of the outline entry were taken from the second, third, and fourth T-units of the twentieth paragraph in the essay. On a few occasions where I took an idea from a paragraph but it did not seem possible to cast it in the author's original words at all, I put the paragraph number in parentheses to indicate that. But I tried to use the author's words as much as I could, even, in some cases, where it yielded a somewhat unwieldy entry in the outline.

To illustrate the approach, let me offer in Figure 1 the opening paragraphs from the first article in the corpus, indicating the corresponding entries in the outline.

Notice the different types of outline entries necessitated by the various kinds of paragraphs the author writes. Topic Sentence B is an example of what I would call a *simple topic sentence,* one which is quoted entirely or almost entirely from one T-unit in the passage, wherever that T-unit occurs. (Incidentally, the last sentence in Paragraph 2 is not reflected in Topic Sentence B because that last sentence is an early foreshadowing of the main idea of the entire article.)

Topic Sentence C is a fairly common type, one in which the topic sentence seems to begin in one T-unit but is completed in a later T-unit. In Paragraph 3, the first sentence does not make a specific enough statement about the two existing statutes to serve as a complete topic sentence, even though it reveals the subject of the paragraph. One must go to the third sentence to find the predicate for the topic sentence. Let us term this type a *delayed-completion topic sentence.* Not all delayed completion topic sentences stem from separated subjects and predicates, though. Sometimes the two sentences present a question and then an answer (Fischer, 18:1,2), a negative followed by a positive (Fischer, 38:

FIGURE 1. Sample Paragraphs and Outline Entries

Opening Paragraphs from Drew, p. 33	Excerpt from Outline	
(1) Among the news items given out to a shocked nation following the assassination of President Kennedy was the fact that Lee Harvey Oswald had purchased his weapon, a 65-mm Italian carbine, from a Chicago mail-order house under an assumed name. The rifle was sent, no questions asked, to one "A. Hidell," in care of a post office box in Dallas. The transaction was routine in the mail-order trade: about one million guns are sold the same way each year.	1. "By the ordinary rules of the game, the events in Dallas should have ensured prompt enactment . . ." of gun control legislation by Congress. A. "President Kennedy" had recently been shot with one of the "one million guns . . . sold . . . each year" through "the mail-order business in guns."	2:2 1:1,3,4
(2) At the same time, a bill was pending in Congress to tighten regulation of the rapidly expanding mail-order business in guns. By the ordinary rules of the game, the events in Dallas should have ensured prompt enactment, just as the news of Thalidomide-deformed babies has provided the long-needed impetus for passage of stricter drug regulations in 1962. But Congress did not act—a testimonial to the deadly aim of the shooting lobby.	B. "At the same time, a bill was pending in Congress to tighten regulation of the rapidly expanding mail-order business in guns."	2:1
(3) Two existing statutes presumably deal with the gun traffic. Both were passed in reaction to the gangsterism of the prohibition era. But because of limited coverage, problems of proof, and various other quirks, they have had a negligible impact on the increasing gun traffic.	C. "Two existing statutes . . . [had] a negligible impact on the increasing gun traffic."	**3:1,3**
(4) The investigation of the mail-order traffic in guns began in 1961 under the auspices of the Juvenile Delinquency subcommittee. . . .		

1,2), or metaphoric language subsequently explained by straight language (Drucker, 8:1,2). The T-units from which a delayed-completion topic sentence is drawn are not always adjoining. In one instance, I discovered them separated by three T-units (Collado, 29:1,2,6); in another, in adjoining paragraphs (Caudill, 17:2 and 18:1); in still another, nine paragraphs apart (Lear, 1:1,2 and 10:1).

Notice that Topic Sentence A is an example of a statement assembled by quotations from throughout the paragraph. The first sentence in Paragraph 1 cannot properly be considered the topic sentence: it includes such phrases as "the news item" and "a shocked nation" and such details as the name of the assassin, the size and make of the carbine, and the location of the mail order house—such matters as are not essential to the topic sentence; and it omits such a detail as the scope of the problem—"one million guns . . . sold . . . each year"—which helps convey the idea in Statement I. To ease later reference to this type of topic sentence, let us call it an *assembled topic sentence.*

Finally, there is what we might call an *inferred topic sentence,* one which the reader thinks the writer has implied even though the reader cannot construct it by quoting phrases from the original passage. Though the paragraph in Figure 2 comes out of context—from an article on cutting the costs of medical care—it may still be clear why the corresponding topic sentence had to be inferred.

As I was determining what were the topic sentences of an article, I was also keeping an eye out for what we might call the *major topic sentences* of the larger stadia of discourses. That is, a series of topic sentences all added up to a major topic sentence; a group of paragraphs all added up to what William Irmscher (1972) calls a "paragraph bloc" within the entire article. A major topic sentence (designated with a

FIGURE 2. Sample of Paragraph Yielding Inferred Topic Sentence

Paragraph from Sanders, p. 24	Excerpt from Outline
Fortunately most ailments do not require such elaborate treatment. Pills cost a good deal less but even they are no small item in the medical bill. From 1929 to 1956 prescription sales climbed from $140 million to $1,466 million a year, and the average price per prescription rose from 85 cents to $2.62. Citing the findings of the Kefauver Committee, Professor Harris makes a strong case for more—and more stringent—regulation of the pharmaceutical industry by the government.	Prescription drug costs have risen.

Roman numeral) might head as few as two topic sentences (designated with capital letters) in the outline or as many as 12 topic sentences (in the Kahn outline) or 15 (the most, in the Mumford outline). On the other hand, it was frequently apparent that the main idea of a paragraph was really a subpoint of the main idea of another paragraph. Let us call these *subtopic sentences.* As few as two and as many as seven subtopic sentences (in the Taper outline) were headed by a topic sentence. Sometimes a major topic sentence or a subtopic sentence was simply stated in a single T-unit, but sometimes it had to be assembled, sometimes inferred. Some occurred as delayed-completion topic sentences.

After completing the rest of the outline, I arrived at the main idea (the thesis) or, in the case of the Kahn and Sargeant articles (both *New Yorker* "Profiles"), the purpose. And as with the various types of topic sentences, I drew quoted phrases from the article to construct the statement of the main idea whenever possible, but with one exception—if a term or phrase occurred frequently in the article, I would not enclose it in quotations and note its location unless it seemed to me to have been put by the author in a particular place or signalled in a particular way to suggest that he was at that time intentionally indicating to readers the nature of his main idea.

After all of the outlines were completed, I went back through each one, classifying each topic sentence as one of the four types and checking the outline against the text of the original essay.

FINDINGS

A tabulation of the frequency of each type of topic sentence for each of the 25 essays is presented in Table 1. It should not escape the reader that the number of topic sentences in an outline does not correspond directly to the number of paragraphs in its essay. Sometimes a major topic sentence and a topic sentence occurred in the same paragraph, and sometimes several paragraphs seemed devoted to the presentation of one topic sentence. (The total number of topic sentences—including the main idea or purpose, major topic sentences, topic sentences, and subtopic sentences, if any—and the total number of paragraphs are given in the two columns at the right of the table.)

One conclusion from Table 1 is that the use made of the different types of topic sentences varies greatly from one writer to the next. Another is that the four articles taken from the *New Yorker* (each one a "Profile") tend to have yielded a higher proportion of assembled topic sentences than most of the other essays.

TABLE 1. Frequency of Types of Topic Sentences in Each of the 25 Essays

Essay No.	Author	Magazine	Main Idea	Simple			Del-comp.			Assembled			Inferred			Total TS's	Total Pars.
				MTS	TS	STS	MTS	TS	STS	MTS	TS	STS	MTS	TS	STS		
1	Drew	Reporter	Inf.	3	8	2	0	2	0	2	2	2	0	0	0	22	20
2	Tebbel	Sat. Rev.	D-C	1	5	2	1	2	0	0	5	2	1	2	1	23	25
3	Collado	Sat. Rev.	Sim.	3	8	3	1	1	2	0	4	9	0	1	0	33	50
4	Sargeant	New York.	Inf.	1	3	0	0	0	0	1	13	6	3	3	1	32	26
5	Chamberlain	Atlantic	Inf.	3	5	2	0	2	0	1	7	3	0	0	0	24	24
6	Daniels	Sat. Rev.	Sim.	3	8	0	0	0	0	0	6	0	0	0	0	18	27
7	E. Taylor	Reporter	Ass.	3	8	0	0	2	0	1	2	2	0	0	0	17	19
8	Kaufman	Atlantic	Ass.	2	13	5	1	2	7	1	0	0	0	1	0	35	41
9	Kahn	New York.	Inf.	0	7	0	0	1	0	1	25	2	4	5	0	44	45
10	Handlin	Atlantic	Sim.	4	11	0	0	7	0	1	4	0	0	0	0	28	35
11	Francois	Reporter	Ass.	2	5	0	0	1	0	1	3	0	0	1	0	13	13
12	Sanders	Harper's	Sim.	3	12	0	0	4	0	1	6	0	2	3	0	32	35
13	Lear	Sat. Rev.	Sim.	0	7	0	2	2	0	2	15	0	2	1	0	32	67
14	Lyons	Atlantic	Sim.	4	8	0	1	1	0	1	13	0	0	2	0	31	53
15	Ribman	Harper's	Inf.	5	20	1	0	4	0	1	12	0	1	0	0	44	56
16	Taper	New York.	Inf.	4	14	0	0	3	0	3	16	11	0	0	0	53	53
17	Fischer	Harper's	Inf.	4	11	9	0	0	1	1	9	3	0	1	0	41	42
18	Mumford	New York.	Inf.	2	17	0	0	2	0	3	27	0	2	0	0	54	49
19	Drucker	Harper's	Sim.	5	15	1	0	5	1	0	16	1	0	0	0	45	53
20	Caudill	Atlantic	Sim.	2	10	3	0	7	0	2	6	0	0	1	0	31	39
21	C. Taylor	Atlantic	Sim.	1	11	0	0	1	1	2	7	3	1	1	0	29	29
22	Cousins	Sat. Rev.	Sim.	1	2	0	1	2	1	1	3	0	0	0	0	11	13
23	Clark	Harper's	Sim.	4	8	0	1	0	1	0	4	1	0	0	0	21	26
24	Durrell	Atlantic	Sim.	1	5	0	1	0	0	1	6	0	0	0	0	15	13
25	Rule	Atlantic	Ass.	3	15	0	1	3	0	1	9	0	0	0	0	33	36
Totals			25	64	236	28	10	56	13	27	220	43	16	21	2	761	889

MTS = major topic sentence   TS = topic sentence   STS = subtopic sentence

Frequency of types of topic sentences. Table 2 combines the data for the 25 essays, indicating the distribution of topic sentences of each type. It is clear that less than half of all the topic sentences (45%) are simple topic sentences and almost as many (39%) are assembled. It is also apparent that—except for the statements of the main idea or purpose—the more of the text that the topic sentence covers, the more likely it is to be a simple topic sentence. That is, of the 117 major sentences, 55% were simple; of the 533 topic sentences, 44% were simple; of the 80 subtopic sentences, 33% were simple.

One might well maintain that simple and delayed-completion topic sentences are relatively explicit, that assembled and inferred topic sentences are relatively implicit. Pairing the types of topic sentences in that fashion, Table 2 reveals no great changes in the tendencies of the percentages. Slightly more than half of all the topic sentences (55%) are explicit, slightly less than half (45%) implicit. Again, with the exception of statements of main idea and purpose, the more of the text which the topic sentence covers, the more likely it is to be explicit.

If what the composition textbooks refer to as "the topic sentence" is the same thing as this study terms the simple topic sentence, it is apparent that claims about its frequency should be more cautious. It just is not true that most expository paragraphs have topic sentences in that sense. Even when simple and delayed-completion topic sentences are combined into the category "explicit topic sentences"—a broader conception than many textbook writers seem to have in mind—the frequency reaches only 55% of all the entries in a sentence outline. And when one remembers that only 761 outline topic sentences represent the 889 paragraphs in all 25 essays, he realizes that considerably fewer than half of all the paragraphs in the essays have even explicit topic sentences, to say nothing of simple topic sentences.

TABLE 2. Percentages of Topic Sentences of Various Types

Types of Topic Sentences	No.	Percentages					
		Sim.	D.C.	Ex-plicit	Ass.	Inf.	Im-plicit
Main idea or purpose	25	48	4	52	16	32	48
Major topic sentences	117	55	9	63	23	14	37
Topic sentences	533	44	11	55	41	4	45
Subtopic sentences	86	33	15	48	50	2	52
All types together	761	45	11	55	39	6	45

Placement of simple topic sentences. How true is the claim that most expository paragraphs open with topic sentences? To find out, I studied the paragraph location of the 264 topic sentences and subtopic sentences in the outline. Gorrell and Laird, like others, had written that the "topic sentence may appear at the end of the paragraph as a kind of summary or somewhere within the paragraph, but most frequently it opens the paragraph or follows an opening introduction or transition (p. 25). Thus I decided to tabulate the occurrence of each simple topic sentence as it appeared in each of four positions: the first T-unit in the paragraph, the second T-unit, the last, or a T-unit between the second and last. To do that, of course, I could consider only paragraphs of four or more T-units. Consequently, I excluded from consideration paragraphs with three or fewer T-units. The results are presented in Table 3.

More than a fourth (28%) of all those paragraphs presenting simple topic sentences or simple subtopic sentences contained fewer than four T-units. Of the rest, 47% presented a simple topic sentence or simple subtopic sentence in the first T-unit, 15% in the second T-unit, 12% in the last T-unit, and 26% elsewhere. But these figures are based on the 190 paragraphs of four or more T-units which contain simple topic sentences or simple subtopic sentences. There were 355 paragraphs from which other topic sentences or subtopic sentences were drawn—delayed-completion, assembled, and inferred. One cannot say that they "have topic sentences to open them." Consequently, it is obvious that much smaller percentages than the above pertain to expository paragraphs in general. Furthermore, there were at least 128 paragraphs from which no topic sentences at all were drawn. If one adds the 190, 355, and 128, he has a total of 673 from which percentages may be computed, if he wishes to estimate what percentage of *all* of the paragraphs in the 25 essays open with a topic sentence. Using those figures, I estimate that only 13% of the expository paragraphs of contemporary professional writers begin with a topic sentence, that only 3% end with a topic sentence.

IMPLICATIONS FOR TEACHING

Teachers and textbook writers should exercise caution in making statements about the frequency with which contemporary professional writers use simple or even explicit topic sentences in expository paragraphs. It is abundantly clear that students should not be told that professional writers usually begin their paragraphs with topic sentences. Certainly teachers of reading, devisers of reading tests, and authors of reading textbooks

TABLE 3. Location of Simple Topic Sentences and Simple Subtopic Sentences

										Essay Number																	
Location	1	2	3	4	5	6	7	8	9	10	11	12	13	14	15	16	17	18	19	20	21	22	23	24	25	Tot.	%
(Paragraph shorter than 4 T-units)	1	1	4	0	3	2	6	5	0	4	1	7	4	0	9	0	6	1	4	2	0	1	6	1	6	74	(28)
First T-unit	6	2	2	3	3	2	0	2	6	4	2	2	1	2	7	5	7	3	6	5	8	1	0	3	7	89	47
Second T-unit	1	4	2	0	0	1	1	2	0	1	0	1	0	1	1	0	4	5	0	2	2	0	1	0	0	29	15
Last T-unit	0	0	1	0	0	1	1	4	0	0	0	0	2	0	1	1	1	4	3	2	1	0	0	1	0	22	12
Elsewhere	2	0	2	0	1	2	1	5	1	2	2	2	0	5	3	9	2	4	3	2	0	0	0	1	1	50	26
Total no. of TS's and STS's in essay	10	7	11	3	7	8	8	18	7	11	5	12	7	8	20	15	20	17	16	13	11	2	8	5	15	264	
Total no. of paragraphs in essay	20	25	50	26	24	27	19	41	45	35	13	35	67	53	56	53	42	49	53	39	29	13	26	13	36	889	

should assist students in identifying the kinds of delayed-completion and implicit topic statements which outnumber simple topic sentences in expository paragraphs.

This sample of contemporary professional writing did not support the claims of textbook writers about the frequency and location of topic sentences in professional writing. That does not, of course, necessarily mean the same findings would hold for scientific and technical writing or other types of exposition. Moreover, it does not all mean that composition teachers should stop showing their students how to develop paragraphs from clear topic sentences. Far from it. In my opinion, often the writing in the 25 essays would have been clearer and more comfortable to read if the paragraphs had presented more explicit topic sentences. But what this study does suggest is this: While helping students use clear topic sentences in their writing and identify variously presented topical ideas in their reading, the teacher should not pretend that professional writers largely follow the practices he is advocating.

REFERENCES

Ashida, M. E.   Something for everyone: a standard corpus of contemporary American expository essays. *Research in the Teaching of English*, 1968, 2, 14–23.

Bain, A.   *English Composition and Rhetoric*, enl. ed. London: Longmans, Green, 1890.

Basic skills system: writing test, Form A. New York: McGraw Hill, 1970.

Gorrell, R. M. and Laird, C.   *Modern English handbook*, 4th ed. Englewood Cliffs, New Jersey: Prentice-Hall, 1967.

Hunt, K. W.   *Grammatical structures written at three grade levels*. Reserach Report No. 3. Urbana, Illinois: NCTE, 1965.

Irmscher, W. F.   *The Holt guide to English*. New York: Holt, Rinehart, and Winston, 1972.

Rodgers, P. Jr.   A discourse-centered rhetoric of the paragraph. *College Composition and Communication*, 1966, 17, 2–11.

ADDITIONAL READINGS

James R. Bennett et al., "The Paragraph: An Annotated Bibliography," *Style*, 11 (Spring, 1977), 107–118.

The Sentence and the Paragraph (Urbana, Ill.: National Council of Teachers of English, 1966). This collection from *College Composition and Communication*, 17 (May, 1966) contains articles by Francis Christensen (pp. 60–66), A. L. Becker (pp. 67–72), Paul C. Rodgers, Jr. (pp. 72–80), Josephine Miles (pp. 80–82), David H. Karrfalt (pp. 82–87).

Richard A. Meade and W. Geiger Ellis, "Paragraph Development in the Modern Age of Rhetoric," *English Journal*, 59 (February, 1970), 219–226.

William Stalter, "A Sense of Structure," *College Composition and Communication*, 29 (December, 1978), 341–345.

Leo Rockas, "Further Comments on the Paragraph," *College Composition and Communication*, 17 (October, 1966), 148–151.

Richard Warner, "Teaching the Paragraph as a Structural Unit," *College Composition and Communication*, 29 (December, 1978), 341–345.

Teaching Style: A Possible Anatomy

A general approach to the teaching of style can embrace any number of pedagogical tasks and obligations. There are three tasks, however, that seem obligatory: (1) making the teaching of style significant and relevant for our students, (2) revealing style as a measurable and viable subject matter, and (3) making style believable and real as a result of our own stylistic practices. These are all *sine qua non,* and to neglect them, one or all, is to do our discipline a disservice. They are not the only tasks involved in teaching style, of course, but they are the underlying concerns in all our particular classroom procedures. A discussion of these three tasks—the questing for relevance, viability, and credibility—may possibly serve as a kind of mapping of our pedagogical territory.

First, making style significant for our students. To teach style well, to reach the final goals we have in mind for the written page, we must confront our students not only with the discipline of style itself but with its justification. F. L. Lucas, the Cambridge professor, said that after forty years of trying, he had come to the conclusion that it was impossible to teach students to write well. "To write well," Professor Lucas said, "is a gift inborn; those who have it teach themselves; one can only try to help and hasten the process." But surely one of the best ways to "hasten the process" is to make it seem important. It is difficult to imagine any successful technical approach being made in teaching style if students are not aware of the great values involved. Surely many a student needs, at least in the context of freshman English, relevance pointed out to him, for otherwise he may think of style as a kind of aesthetic luxury, if not beyond his grasp at least beyond his interests.

From *College Composition and Communication,* 21 (May, 1970), 144–149. Reprinted by permission of the National Council of Teachers of English and Winston Weathers.

I fear, though, that we often neglect to explain the significance of the discipline. In teaching *literature* we seem much more inclined to indicate relevance; in teaching *language,* once we have made the pitch about better communication we have a tendency, don't we, to drop the task of relevance altogether.

I think we should confirm for our students that style has something to do with better communication, adding as it does a certain technicolor to otherwise black-and-white language. But going beyond this "better communication" approach, we should also say that style is the proof of a human being's individuality; that style is a writer's revelation of himself; that through style, attitudes and values are communicated; that indeed our manner is a part of our message. We can remind students of Aristotle's observation, "character is the making of choices," and point out that since style, by its very nature, is the art of selection, how we choose says something about who we are.

In addition, we can tell students that style is a gesture of personal freedom against inflexible states of mind; that in a very real way—because it is the art of choice and option—style has something to do with freedom; that as systems—rhetorical or political—become rigid and dictatorial, style is reduced, unable as it is to exist in totalitarian environments. We can reveal to students the connection between democracy and style, saying that the study of style is a part of our democratic and free experience. And finally we can point out that with the acquisition of a plurality of styles (and we are after pluralities, aren't we? not *just* the plain style?) the student is equipping himself for a more adaptive way of life within a society increasingly complex and multifaceted.

To some, this "publicizing" task may seem beside the point in our discussion of approaches to style. Yet if we perform this task well, no student of ours will ever assume that we are teaching some dainty humanistic pastime; our students will know that we are playing the game for real. And I am convinced that it's this preparatory task that makes any other approach meaningful. Many students write poorly and with deplorable styles simply because they do not care; their failures are less the result of incapacity than the lack of will.

Now if this first approach, a la propaganda, can be successfully made, we can move on to the task of revealing style as a viable subject matter. Certainly we must keep rescuing style from what Professor Louis Milic has called the metaphysical approach—elevated descriptions that finally prove terribly nebulous—for if we find style unteachable because students see no relevance, we can also find style unteachable because students never get their fingers on it, never see it in measurable, quantitative terms.

To make style viable, we must teach students some rather specific skills—(1) how to recognize stylistic material, (2) how to master this stylistic material and make it a part of a compositional technique, (3) how to combine stylistic materials into particular stylistic modes, and (4) how to adapt particular stylistic modes to particular rhetorical situations. In teaching these four "how to's" we are providing students with a *modus operandi* for learning style and an overall strategy for using it. It is in these ways that style becomes a reality, a true discipline and a true art.

To begin, we do well to emphasize the concept of stylistic material; to explain to students that in the art of choosing, one *can* and must choose *from something*. We need to explain that certain real materials exist in style—measurable, identifiable, describable: Demetrius's "phrases, members, and periods," or Professor Josephine Miles' "linear units" (the terms do not really matter): but real material that serves as the substantive foundation of style, this material being of three general kinds: individual words; collections of words into phrases, sentences, and paragraphs; and larger architectural units of composition.

A certain amount of stylistic material is already a part of the student's repertoire when he comes to college, of course; the simple sentence, after all, is an ingredient of stylistic material, and any given word in a vocabulary is an element of style. But now, in college, the student must enlarge his collection of usable stylistic materials. The student learned a compound sentence in high school; he will now learn a periodic sentence. He learned a simile in high school; he will now learn reification. And it becomes our task to lead students to the storehouses of material from which they can make acquisition, to help students encounter the sources of stylistic materials and to draw from them.

There is certainly the traditional source—the established schemes and tropes, the established arrangements and procedures of writing. A metaphor, an oxymoron, an inductive paragraph. The student can draw upon the wealth of materials in classical and subsequent rhetorics. In addition, the student can draw upon materials that are not a part of tradition, but are the results of current achievements in the study of style. In the past decade or so, the great interest in rhetoric and style has effected new identifications of materials—such elements as serial sentences, patterned paragraphs, and the like are being analyzed and described in our professional literature. And finally—through the creative analysis of literary texts—the student can himself discover new materials. If, for instance, a student observes a writer habitually using a construction of "opening prepositional phrase, a subject, a compound predicate, a closing prepositional phrase" the student may note that sequence as a usable stylistic element. Admittedly, the student may be discovering material already discovered by Longinus—but that's fine; the student has the pleasure of confirming established knowledge. And if the student makes a discovery of material not heretofore identified, so much the better. Let the student name it: the D. H. Lawrence construction, the Hemingway verb, the Faulkner paragraph. The ingredients of style are that much more a reality. Indeed, this seems to me—this inductive approach—one of the great values in the stylistic analysis of a text; it is a chance to make discoveries about style that have not, amazingly enough, already been made.

Teaching the recognition of stylistic material, old or new, brings us to an interesting juncture, however, for it is easy to assume that with recognition and identification of an adequate supply of material, the student somehow has mastered style itself. But recognition of stylistic material is not the same as the practice of it; the knowledge must be converted into performance.

One widespread approach to the task of moving stylistic material from the depot of the student's mind to the front line of his writing fingers is, alas, the contemplative approach. If we use the contemplative approach, we tell students that by looking at style long enough they will finally find themselves practicing style—by a kind of osmosis. We say "read a lot of good literature, make a lot of good stylistic analyses, and someday you'll wake up a writer." But can one learn to drive a car simply by taking a lot of car rides as a passenger? Surely one needs, in addition to contemplation, a great deal of involvement. One learns metaphor, not just by analysis, but by writing metaphors.

Some of us would advocate, therefore, a definite exercise system. We would advocate setting up recognized stylistic material as models; the models to be copied until the student can create similar but original versions of his own. It is a process of creative imitation that works like this: If we are going to teach a tricolon, an established bit of stylistic material, we first locate a tricolon in a text and point it out to our student; let us say the tricolon "of the people, by the people, for the people." The student learns to identify and recognize the tricolon. But our second step is to isolate the tricolon sentence from the text, set it up as a model, and ask the student to make an exact copy of it in his own hand—word for word, comma for comma. After the student has made his perfect copy and we have checked it for accuracy, we then ask the student to discuss with us—or at least learn *from* us—the nature of the model tricolon, its use in the text in which it occurred, and the use of such tricola in general. Finally, we ask the student to compose a sentence of his own containing a tricolon—on some subject far removed from that which Lincoln was discussing. We ask the student to write a sentence or a topic of his own choosing, but following the "model" he has just studied.

In this process, the student is asked to *recognize, copy, understand,* then *imitate creatively*. And this process can be used to master all possible stylistic materials: from the use of particular words to the more complex combinations of materials found in long passages. Creative imitation or generative copying is not new, of course; we all know the famous essay by Rollo Walter Brown on "How the French Boy Learns to Write" and certainly Professor Edward P. J. Corbett has given great support to this method in his *Classical Rhetoric for the Modern Student*.

Teaching viability of style does not end here, however. The student must not be left in the lurch at this point either; he must not be left with the ability to recognize and imitate stylistic materials without having a rationale for using them. A student has the legitimate right to ask, "Now what do I do? I know how to recognize and compose a tricolon, but what do I do with one?"

What students are actually asking for at this point is a strategy of style—and we can establish such a strategy by doing two primary things: (1) identifying the categories of style, and (2) describing the constituency of those categories in terms of stylistic material.

First, a word about categories. The categories of style we choose to identify will depend upon our own individual way of seeing things: some of us may still use the four levels of style acknowledged by Demetrius; some of us may use the fairly conventional levels of usage—formal, informal, colloquial; some of us may prefer more elaborate categories combining both levels and intensities of language into a complex of rhetorical profiles; some of us may prefer such new categories as the styles of certitude, judiciousness, emotion, and absurdity, or "tough, sweet, and stuffy"; or some of us may even be so reductive as to prefer a simple two-category system of plain and literary style. But whatever our preferences, we must identify some *set* of *categories*, some *system* of categories, to serve as a framework in which various styles can be achieved.

Second, the constituency of these categories. Having established a system of diverse styles, we must establish recipes for achieving individual styles within the system. We must teach our students that certain stylistic material goes here; certain material goes there; that a certain combination and sequence of stylistic material creates one style; a certain combination and sequence creates another. Though given enough time a student might, by induction, discover the constituency of given categories himself, the burden of the description falls upon the teacher who is obligated to list the observable characteristics of the various styles. Indeed, I suspect that a good deal of our homework as teachers is, or should be, spent in discovering, in as great a detail as possible, these characteristics and pointing them out to our classes.

If we are able to effect for our classes these primary conditions of strategy—identification and description of categories—then we can exercise our students in the following ways:

Exercise One—We call for a student to write down all the possible verbalizations he can think of for any given message. How many ways can he say, "It's a beautiful day"? How many ways can he say, "Space exploration is too expensive"? Having made a list of all the possible ways, the student is then asked to allocate the various verbalizations on his list, placing them in the categories of style we have taught him. That is, given the recipes for a number of different styles—which verbalizations go where. Practicing this exercise over a period of time, the student—under our guidance—comes to realize that nearly any verbalization he can think of per given message can play its part in a total system of style; he stops seeking one eternally correct verbalization, but seeks rather to place all verbalizations in their appropriate communities.

Exercise Two—We ask a student to write a paragraph—on any topic—and to identify the particular style he has used in that paragraph. Having done so, the student next transforms the paragraph into another style. If he has written about campus revolution in a militant style, we ask him to transform his composition—with the same facts, observations, data, and opinions—into the judicious style. If he has written about his flower garden in an elegant style, we ask him now to write about it in a plain style. If in a colloquial style, now in a formal style. The point of the exercise is to teach the student how to add or subtract or substitute particular stylistic materials so as to change one style to another. Ultimately by means of this transformational exercise, the student will be able to decline—as it were—any sentence, paragraph, or essay through all possible styles.

Finally, of course, after the exercises, we ask students to write complete compositions. Though in teaching viability perhaps we err too often by beginning with whole compositions, by plunging the student into the middle of stylistic performance without making it truly viable for him, step by step, we do not err by asking the student to make the final effort of demonstrating all that we have been talking about—to demonstrate a knowledge of stylistic material, piece by piece, and a capacity for its strategic incorporation into stylistic wholeness.

The third task in our general approach to style—after the tasks of relevance and viability—is that of making the practice of style tremendously believable as the result of our performances in front of students. Robert Zoellner recently wrote in *College English* that he had "never, repeat never, seen a composition instructor, whether full professor or graduate student, walk into a composition classroom cold-turkey, with no preparation, ask the class for a specific theme-topic . . . and then—off the top of his head—actually compose a paragraph which illustrates the rhetorical principles that are the current concern of the class."

Professor Zoellner was surely exaggerating with the "never, repeat never" but I suspect that in general his charge is valid. We are an amazing lot of piano players refusing to play the piano. Yet should not the student's most significant model, so far as style is concerned, be the teacher himself? Isocrates, that ancient member of the profession, did not, as Werner Jaeger points out in *Paideia*, "merely discuss the technique of language and composition—the final inspiration was derived from the art of the master himself." And surely this is so: what the teacher writes on the blackboard in front of the student, or even what the teacher writes outside of class and brings to read to his students, is the teacher's commitment to the style he is urging his students to learn. Perhaps some of the difficulties in teaching style arise because of teacher failure: not failure in sincerity or industry or knowledge, but failure in demonstrating an art and a skill. Teacher failure ever to write and perform as a master stylist creates an amazing credibility gap.

I would propose a definite incorporation of teacher performance into our approach to style. Such a program would entail original composition by the teacher, at the blackboard, at least three to five minutes each class—or at least a five-to-ten minute performance once a week. We are limited by the physical circumstances of the classroom and by the pressures of time, but every blackboard is large enough for five or six sentences or a short paragraph, and every class period is long enough for a few minutes of teacher composition. Even if our demonstration of style is faulty and less than excellent, the fact that the teacher "did something" *for all to see* is noteworthy. And I have found that students actually learn a great deal from watching a teacher put in a word, take out a word, rewrite a sentence, even misspell, and then correct a spelling, ponder over the use of a comma or a semicolon. Believe me: the teacher's struggle amidst the chalk dust can become the student's education.

And to prove to our class that we are not conning them, we can have one student call out a noun, another call out a verb—then using the noun and verb, we can write without prearrangement what needs to be written that day: a balanced sentence, a serial sentence, a circular paragraph. We may be reluctant to do this sort of impromptu writing—yet we are obligated. We are supposed to be professionals, and we should know enough about style to do a passing job, if not a brilliant job, and do the job "on call."

Teacher performance can go beyond the blackboard even. I think a certain amount of talk—modest and judicious, but enthusiastic—about the writing we do outside the class is important in the teaching of style. And I wonder if we shouldn't write some of the essays we ask our students to write—or write something comparable at least—and on occasion read to our classes what we have written. We could risk offending students with our vanity in an attempt to convince them that composition, rhetoric, and style are things we really do, that they are a part of our lives, that *we* are involved.

Such are the three obligations that must be met, three important tasks that must be performed in a general approach to teaching style. Our decisions how best to make style relevant, viable, and credible in the classroom may indeed vary; you and I may not agree about the details; we may use different syllabi and different textbooks. But I hope we will agree concerning the obligations themselves. At least I offer this anatomy for teaching as a possibility.

EDWARD P. J. CORBETT

A Method of Analyzing Prose Style
with a Demonstration Analysis
of Swift's "A Modest Proposal"

Most of us teachers have felt rather frustrated in our efforts to analyze prose style, either for ourselves or for our students in the classroom. This frustration has been brought on not only by a certain vagueness about what style is but also by the lack of a technique for analyzing prose style. As a result, we content ourselves in the classroom with enunciating such general, subjective labels for a particular author's style as "vigorous," "urbane," "ponderous," "curt," "mannered," "jaunty," "explosive," and that favorite all-purpose epithet "smooth-flowing." Some of us may have arrived at the point where we feel confident enough to designate more specific features of a prose style, such as the preponderance of Latinate diction, the mannerism of balanced sentence structure, or the high proportion of concrete images. But usually by the time we have gone that far, we have exhausted our resources for describing prose style, and we spend the rest of the class period discussing the ideas of the essay under consideration.

The New Criticism, especially as it was presented in Brooks and Warren's influential textbook *Understanding Poetry*, gave us teachers a technique for analyzing the verbal strategies of a poem. Consequently, we feel very secure when we come to analyze poetry for or with our students. What we need now is comparable training in a method of analyzing prose style.

What would lay the groundwork for the development of such a method would be a number of descriptions of prose style comparable to the descriptions of English grammar that we have had from modern linguists. It is surprising how few of these studies have been produced. At the end

From *Reflections on High School English*, edited by Gary Tate (Tulsa, Oklahoma: The University of Tulsa, 1966), pp. 106–124. Reprinted by permission.

of the last century, Edwin H. Lewis's *The History of the English Paragraph* (University of Chicago Studies, 1894), L. A. Sherman's *Some Observations upon Sentence-Length in English Prose* (University of Nebraska Studies, 1892), and G. W. Gerwig's *On the Decrease of Predication and of Sentence Weight in English* (University of Nebraska Studies, 1894) presented statistical studies of several prose stylists. In this century, we have had a few stylistic studies of specific authors, such as Warner Taylor's *The Prose Style of Johnson* (Madison, 1918), Zilpha E. Chandler's *An Analysis of the Stylistic Techniques of Addison, Johnson, Hazlitt and Pater* (Iowa City, 1928), and W. K. Wimsatt's *The Prose Style of Samuel Johnson* (New Haven, 1941).[1] Very shortly, I understand, Mouton of the Hague will publish Louis Milic's study of Jonathan Swift's style.

As more of these stylistic descriptions appear, we will gain a basis for more valid generalizations about English prose style, and we may find that we have to relinquish some of our illusions about how certain writers create their stylistic effects. Such studies will also help us to develop techniques for analyzing style and to prepare textbooks for the classroom. Those of us who are interested in doing something with style in the classroom are looking forward to the publication of textbooks on style now being prepared by such teachers as Richard Ohmann, Francis Christensen, Winston Weathers and Otis Winchester, Harriet Sheridan, and Josephine Miles.

I will outline here a procedure for analyzing prose style. There will be very little in this proposed method that is original. I have merely brought together what I have learned about style from the ancient rhetoricians and from modern expositors of verbal strategies. After I have outlined the various features of style that one might look for in studying any prose piece, I will illustrate the method with a fairly detailed analysis of one of the most anthologized prose essays in English literature, Jonathan Swift's *A Modest Proposal.*

Any stylistic analysis must start out, I think, with some close observation of what actually appears on the printed page. One might, for instance, sense that a particular author uses a great many short sentences. Now, sentence-length is one of the features that can tell us something about an author's style. But it should be obvious that we cannot make a tenable generalization about an author's characteristic sentence-length until we have determined, by some rather tedious counting and tabulating, just how long or short his sentences are. Such a procedure would make counters and measurers of us all—"a slide-rule method," to use

---

1. We must not forget, of course, the pioneering work that Morris W. Croll did in the 1920's on sixteenth and seventeenth-century English prose style. These studies will soon be published in a single volume.

Leslie Whipp's term,[2] that we humanistically trained teachers may find repellent—but this is a necessary step if we are to learn something about style in general and about style in particular.

If teachers and students survive the tedium of such counting and tabulating, they will then have a chance to bring to bear their aesthetic sensibilities. The next step in the procedure—and a more significant step—is to relate what the statistics reveal to the rhetoric of the piece being analyzed. Determining the length of a prose sentence is much like scanning a line of verse. Just as it is fairly easy to determine that a particular line of verse is written in iambic pentameter, so it is easy to determine that a particular sentence in prose is, say, twenty-one words long. But so what? The more important consideration is the function of that meter or that sentence-length. What contribution does this meter or this sentence-length make to the effect that the writer was seeking to produce? Here is where our judgment or our aesthetic sensibility or our rhetorical sense will have an opportunity to exercise itself. And it is here, in our relating of fact to function, that we will experience a perceptible growth in our powers of analysis and criticism.

A note of caution should be raised at this point. Inductive logic has taught us that the strength of a generalization rests partly on the number of observed facts. Just as one swallow does not make a summer, so a prevalent stylistic feature observed in a single piece of prose does not necessarily constitute a characteristic of the author's style. An author's style may change as his subject-matter or his purpose or his audience changes. Moreover, his style may have evolved over a period of time, and the stylistic feature that we have observed in this particular prose piece may be a mannerism that he eventually outgrew. True, certain characteristics of an author's style will be fairly constant, but we would be wise to withhold any generalizations about those constants until after we have studied a reasonably large body of a man's prose. All that we may be able to conclude from our inductive study of a single essay is that this particular stylistic device is a feature of this particular prose piece. But of course even that limited generalization represents some gain in our knowledge of an author's style.

Another caution is that we must be careful in our effort to relate fact to function. Dr. Johnson, you recall, said about Pope's celebrated doctrine of suiting sound to the sense, "This notion of representative metre, and the desire of discovering frequent adaptations of the sound to the sense, have produced, in my opinion, many wild conceits and imaginary

2. See Leslie T. Whipp and Margaret E. Ashida, "A Slide-Rule Composition Course," *College English*, XXV (October, 1963), 18–22.

beauties." We can indeed become excessively ingenious in our efforts to make a stylistic feature fit a rhetorical function. The pitfalls of such speculation, however, should not discourage us from at least making the attempt. Even a strained speculation about the aptness of a particular stylistic feature is better than leaving an observed fact hanging in mid-air. We can later revise or reject our forced speculation when our knowledge or skill grows. If I may indulge in a platitude, nothing ventured, nothing gained.

With these general observations and cautions about the method in mind, we can now look at a listing of some of the objectively observable features of style. These features will be considered under the three main heads of words, sentences, and paragraphs.

What is there that we can observe about words or, to use the more common rhetorical term, diction? Well, we can seek to determine whether an author's diction is predominantly general or specific; abstract or concrete; formal or informal; polysyllabic or monosyllabic; common or special; referential or emotive. Judgments about the either-or will be more subjective in some cases than in others. We can, for instance, determine precisely the proportion between monosyllabic and polysyllabic diction; but since the difference between, say, formal and informal diction is relative, our judgments about some words on this score will necessarily be subjective. Making allowances for those subjective judgments, however, we still can determine, in cases of relative difference, the general tenor of a man's diction. After studying the diction of an A. J. Liebling piece on boxing, for instance, we would find it fairly easy to conclude that although Mr. Liebling adroitly mixes formal and informal words, his diction is predominantly informal.

The frequency of proper nouns in a piece will also tell us something about a man's style. In the readability formula that Rudolf Flesch devised several years ago, the incidence of proper nouns was one of the factors that enhanced the readability of prose. Then too there will always be some few words in an essay that will tell us a great deal about an author's period, milieu, range of interest, education, and bias. We would do well to look for such indicative words.

Studying the diction of a prose piece from these various angles will help us to determine the "weight" of a man's style and to account for the effect that a man's style creates. Sometimes, for instance, when we get the general impression that a man's style is heavy and opaque, we are surprised to learn, after a close study of the diction, that the peculiar texture of his style has *not* been produced by his choice of words. And that kind of revelation is a real gain for us, because then we know that we will have to look elsewhere for the cause of the ponderous effect.

In moving on from a study of word-choice to a study of words in col-location, we find that the most fruitful syntactical unit to study is the sentence. What can we look for when we study the sentences in a prose piece? For one thing, we can study the length of sentences (measured in number of words). Once the total number of sentences and the total number of words are known, we can, by a simple exercise in long division, figure out the average sentence-length. We can then get an idea of variations of sentence-length by tabulating the percentage of sentences which *exceed*, and the percentage which *fall short of*, the average by a specified number of words.

One can also make a study of the *kinds* of sentences in a prose piece. One can tabulate the grammatical types of sentences (simple, compound, complex, compound-complex); or the rhetorical types (loose, periodic, balanced, antithetical); or the functional types (statement, question, command, exclamation). In studying varieties of sentence patterns, one can look at such things as inversions of normal word-order, the frequency and kinds of sentence-openers (infinitive, gerund, or participial phrases; adverb clauses; absolute constructions; expletive patterns; conjunctive words and phrases); and the methods and location of expansion in the sentences.

Although tropes (words with transferred meanings) could be observed when we are studying diction, and schemes (unusual sentence patterns) could be observed when we are studying sentences, it is probably better to make a separate step of recording figures of speech. Under tropes we would be noting such things as metaphor, simile, synecdoche, metonymy, irony, litotes, oxymoron, antonomasia. Under schemes we would be noting such things as anaphora, apposition, parallelism, antithesis, chiasmus, climax, anastrophe. The study of schemes and tropes can reveal a great deal about the degree of vividness, vivacity, and ornateness in an author's style.

The rhetoric of the next largest unit, the paragraph, has been one of the most neglected aspects of stylistic study. Modern rhetoric books have paid a great deal of attention to the topic sentence, to the various methods of developing paragraphs, and to the qualities of unity, coherence, and emphasis, but a study of these aspects does not reveal very much about a man's style. Perhaps the reason why classical rhetorics did not deal at all with the paragraph is that classical rhetoric was concerned primarily with spoken discourse. Paragraphing of course is a typographical device to punctuate units of thought in written discourse only, and this kind of punctuation often reveals no more about a man's style than the punctuation used within sentences. But there must be an approach to the study of the paragraph that would reveal something about style, and perhaps Professor Francis Christensen's projected book on the rhetoric of the sentence and paragraph will provide the approach that will yield significant information about the style of the paragraph.

As a beginning, meanwhile, we can look at such things as the length of paragraphs (measured in number of words and/or number of sentences), the various levels of movement or development in the paragraph, the means of articulating sentences within the paragraph, and the transitional devices used between paragraphs. By observing the length of paragraphs and the modes of development and articulation, we will get a sense of the density, pace, and readability of an author's style.

The tabulation of objectively observable items, such as I have been outlining, might be called the stage of "gathering the data." It is a wearisome, time-consuming inductive exercise, but it is a necessary stage if our generalizations about a man's style are to be at all tenable. Needless to say, one does not have to look at *all* of the features in every stylistic analysis, and one does not have to follow the order outlined above. Sometimes concentration on a few salient features will bring us closer to the essence of a man's style than will an exhaustive analysis. Style is a complex of many linguistic devices cooperating to produce a peculiar effect, but it may not always be necessary to expose all of the linguistic devices in order to account for the effect.

Let me recommend one fruitful practice for this gathering of the data. You might try copying out by hand long passages of the essay or even the entire essay. You will be amazed at the number of additional things you will detect about a man's style when you write out his text. From my experience with transcribing a text, I would estimate that by copying you will detect at least three times as many features as you will by merely reading and rereading the text. In gathering the data for my analysis of Swift's *A Modest Proposal,* I detected some of the most significant features of his style only after I had laboriously copied out the entire text of the essay.

Gathering the data is a prelude for the more important, the more difficult stage—relating this data to the author's rhetorical strategies. It does not take much intelligence to gather the data; it takes only patience and accuracy. But it does take intelligence and perhaps a good measure of imagination to be able to see the rhetorical function of a particular stylistic feature.

The "why" of any stylistic feature can be answered only in relation to something else—the subject-matter or the occasion or the genre or the author's purpose or the nature of the audience or the ethos of the writer. To be able to relate stylistic features to their rhetorical function then, we must have a secure knowledge of the essay we are analyzing. As a minimum, we must know its purpose, its thesis, and its organization. In addition, we may need to know something about the author, something about the situation that prompted the essay, something about the audience to whom the essay was directed. We should be able to gain a good deal of this kind of knowledge from internal evidence alone. But we may find it helpful to resort to external sources in order to supplement what internal evidence tells us. So we may have to turn to biographical reference works, to literary histories, to critical articles. The point is that the more profound our understanding of the essay is, the easier it will be to relate a stylistic feature to its rhetorical function.

Before launching into my analysis of *A Modest Proposal,* let me suggest some follow-up exercises. Once your students have done an analysis of one or more stylistic features of an essay, they can be asked to study another essay by the same author. They may discover thereby that an author's style changes noticeably as his subject-matter or his purpose or his audience changes. The value to your students of such an observation will be the realization that an author must be in command, not of one style, but of many styles. Next, you may want to direct your students to study another author, either from the same period or from a later period, preferably an author writing on a similar subject or with a similar purpose. Such comparisons can make meaningful to the students Buffon's famous statement, "Style is the man." And such comparisons can also make the students aware that styles change not only as the subject or genre or audience or purpose changes but as the period changes. Twentieth-century style in general is distinctively different from seventeenth-century style, and it will represent a real gain in the students' education if they come to realize that the radical changes in modern man's way of life have had a marked influence on the dominant style of the age.

Eventually, students should be turned loose on an analysis of their own prose style. This exercise may well be the most fruitful one for the students. They will be fascinated not only by what they learn about their own style but also by what they learn from comparing their style with that of professional writers. Let us hope that the students will be intelligent enough to recognize that the differences between their style and other authors' styles do not mean that their style is necessarily inferior to the styles of the other authors.

The best themes I have received from students during my teaching career have been those written by freshmen who were asked to comment on what they had learned from a series of stylistic studies. One of the reasons why these themes were fascinating enough to keep me up until 2:00 in the morning reading them was, I think, that the students were writing from a body of specific knowledge that they themselves had derived inductively. In other words, the problem of invention having been solved for them, the students had something to say—and somehow, for the first time, they were finding apt words to say what they had to say. Try this with your students. You may for the first time in your teaching career become excited about a batch of themes.

I have gone on long enough now about a general procedure for analyzing prose style. The method should become more meaningful for you as I apply it to a specific piece of prose—in this case, Jonathan Swift's famous satirical essay *A Modest Proposal*.

I might begin this stylistic analysis by defining what kind of discourse *A Modest Proposal* is, since genre makes its own demands on the kind of style that an author will employ. With reference to the literary genres, *A Modest Proposal* can be classified as a satire, and with reference to the four forms of discourse, satire must be classified as argumentation. If we were using the classical rhetorician's three kinds of persuasive discourse to further specify what type of argumentation we have here, we would classify *A Modest Proposal* as an instance of "deliberative" discourse, since Jonathan Swift is bent on changing the attitude of the propertied class toward the Irish poor and ultimately on moving this class to take some action that would remedy the lot of the poor.

In 1728, a year before *A Modest Proposal* was published, there had been a devastating famine in Ireland caused by three successive failures of the harvest. This famine had aggravated the misery of a people that had already been reduced to abject poverty by years of heavy taxation, repressive laws, and absentee landlordism. As Louis A. Landa has pointed out,[3] Swift hoped to expose the contradiction between a favorite maxim of the mercantilist economic writers—namely, that people are the riches of a nation—and the practice of reducing the majority of subjects to a condition of grinding poverty. The prevalence of the poverty was plain to see, and there had been no lack of proposals, from the political economists, of ways to remedy the condition of the poor. But the ruling class and the absentee landlords were not listening; battening on the revenues from the land, they were not much concerned about the condition of the peasants who were producing their wealth. Swift was determined to get their ear. He would shock them into attention. And he would shock them into attention with a monstrous proposal presented by means of two of his favorite satiric techniques—using a mask and using irony.

To make his use of the mask or *persona* effective, Swift must create a character who is consistent, credible, and authoritative. This must be a

3. See Louis A. Landa, "*A Modest Proposal* and Populousness," *Modern Philology*, XL (1942), 161–70, and "Swift's Economic Views and Mercantilism," *Journal of English Literary History*, X (1942), 310–35.

character who, in a sense, "sneaks up" on the reader, a character who lulls the reader into expecting a sensible, practicable solution of the Irish problem and who, even after he has dropped his bombshell, maintains his pose and his poise. This character will exert a curious kind of ethical appeal—a man who at the beginning of the essay gives the impression of being serious, expert, and well-meaning but who gradually reveals himself to be shockingly inhuman and naive. The character that eventually emerges is that of a fool whose insanity becomes, as Martin Price puts it, "a metaphor for the guilt of responsible men."[4]

One of the consequences of this use of a *persona* is that the style of the essay will not be Swift's style; rather it will be a style appropriate to the character that Swift has created. True, some of the characteristics of Swift's style will be present; no author can entirely submerge his own style, except perhaps when he is engaged in writing a parody of another author's style. But if Swift does his job properly, the message of the essay will be conveyed to us in a style that differs, at least in some respect, from the style that Swift displays when he is speaking in his own voice.

One of the respects in which the style of *A Modest Proposal* differs noticeably from Swift's usual style is the sentence-length. The average sentence-length in this essay is 56.9 words per sentence. And we note some remarkable variations above and below that average. Although 46 per cent of his sentences are composed of less than 47 words, almost 30 per cent of his sentences are longer than 67 words (see Appendix for additional statistics on sentence-length). It is interesting to compare this sentence-length with that in two other works where Swift used a *persona*. In studying 200 paragraphs of *Gulliver's Travels* and 100 paragraphs of *A Tale of a Tub,* Edwin Herbert Lewis discovered the average sentence-length to be 40.7 words—almost 50 per cent shorter than the average sentence in *A Modest Proposal.*[5] What has happened to the "conciseness" that Herbert Davis says is the most distinctive quality of Swift's style?[6] What has happened of course is that in *A Modest Proposal* we are listening to a man who is so filled with his subject, so careful about qualifying his statements and computations, so infatuated with the sound of his own words, that he rambles on at inordinate length.

We note this same tendency to qualify and ramify his thoughts in other characteristics of the proposer's sentence structure. We note this,

---

4. Martin Price, *Swift's Rhetorical Art* (New Haven: Yale University Press, 1953), p. 88.
5. Edwin H. Lewis, *History of the English Paragraph* (Chicago: University of Chicago Press, 1894), pp. 35–6.
6. Herbert Davis, "The Conciseness of Swift," *Essays on the Eighteenth Century Presented to David Nichol Smith* (Oxford: At the Clarendon Press, 1945), pp. 15–32.

for one thing, in his frequent use of parentheses. Sometimes the parenthetical matter throws in a gratuitous aside—"(as I must confess the times require)"; or editorializes—"(although indeed very unjustly)"; or qualifies a statement—"(I mean in the country)"; or insinuates an abrupt note of ethical appeal—"(it would, I think with humble submission, be a loss to the public)." Interpolated gestures like these, especially when they are as frequent as they are in this essay, betray a man who is unusually concerned for the accuracy of his statements and for the image he is projecting to his audience.

Something of the same tendency is evident in the many absolute constructions in the essay. Most of these occur at the end of fairly long sentences—e.g. "the charge of nutriment and rags having been at least four times that value" (para. 7); "their corn and cattle being seized and money a thing unknown" (para. 33). These trailing-off phrases create the effect of a thought suddenly remembered and desperately thrown in. What is clever, though, about Swift's use of these trailing-off phrases, placed as they are in an emphatic position, is that in many cases they carry the real sting of the sentence. Here is that topsy-turviness of values that constitutes one of the main strategies of the essay—important things couched in ironical terms or hidden away in weak structures.

This tendency to ramify, qualify, or refine statements is evident too in the proposer's habit of compounding elements. I am referring not so much to the common eighteenth-century practice of using doublets and triplets, of which there are a conspicuous number in *A Modest Proposal,* as to the proposer's habit of stringing out words and phrases beyond the common triad, so that we get the effect almost of an exhaustive cataloguing of details or qualifiers. I am referring to instances like these:

> stewed, roasted, baked, or boiled (para. 9)
>
> of curing the expensiveness of pride, vanity, idleness, and gaming in our women (para. 29)
>
> equally innocent, cheap, easy, and effectual (para. 32)
>
> by advancing our trade, providing for infants, relieving the poor, and giving pleasure to the rich (para. 33)[7]

What is observable about the proposer's amplifications is that his epithets are rarely just synonymous variations, such as the displays of *copia* that

7. There is nothing in *A Modest Proposal* that approaches the crushing catalogue of words in Book IV of *Gulliver's Travels:* "Hence it follows of necessity that the vast numbers of our people are compelled to seek their livelihood by begging, robbing, stealing, cheating, pimping, forswearing, flattering, suborning, forging, gaming, lying, fawning, hectoring, voting, scribbling, star-gazing, poisoning, whoring, canting, libelling, free-thinking, and the like occupations."

were common in Anglo-Saxon poetry and Euphuistic prose. In a phrase like "innocent, cheap, easy, and effectual," each adjective adds a distinct idea to the predication.

Along with this heavy compounding, Swift occasionally uses the scheme of polysyndeton—e.g. "in the arms or on the back or at the heels" (para. 2); "dying and rotting by cold and famine and filth and vermin" (para. 19). Multiplying conjunctions like this has the effect of further stringing out the list. Swift sometimes adds to the compounded elements the scheme of alliteration, as in the just-quoted "famine and filth and vermin" or in the triplet "parsimony, prudence, and temperance" (para. 29). In these examples, we get the impression of a man who is beginning to play with words. In the only other conspicuous use of alliteration, "in joints from the gibbet" (para. 18), our impulse to laugh at this sporting with words is suddenly restrained by our realization of the horror of the image. At other times, Swift will reinforce the compounding with the scheme of climax, as in the two or three examples in the first paragraph of the essay, or with the scheme of anticlimax, as in the example quoted above from paragraph 33.

Although all of this compounding is done within the framework of parallelism, parallelism is not a characteristic of the proposer's style or of Swift's style in general. But Swift demonstrates that he knows how and when to use parallel structure. In paragraph 29, the key paragraph of the essay, he lays out his long enumeration of "other expedients" on a frame of parallel structure. The list is long, the list is important, and Swift wants to make sure that his readers do not get lost in this maze of coordinate proposals.

Another thing that the long rambling sentences and the frequent compounding might suggest is a "spoken" style. If one compares spoken style with written style, one notes that spoken style tends to be paratactic—a stitching together of coordinate units. We have just observed this kind of rhapsodic structure in the word and phrase units of *A Modest Proposal*, but when we look at the kinds of grammatical sentences (see Appendix), we observe a marked predominance of the subordinate structures that typify a sophisticated written style. Over half of the sentences are complex, and almost a third of the sentences are compound-complex. Although there are five simple sentences in the essay, there is not a single compound sentence, which is the commonest structure in extemporaneous spoken discourse. So although the essay may give the impression of a certain colloquial ease, this impression is not being produced by the syntax of the sentences.

Further evidence of a calculated literary style is found in the proposer's inclination to periodic structure. As Walter J. Ong said in a recent article on prose style, "Oral composition or grammatical structure is typically nonperiodic, proceeding in the 'adding' style; literary composition tends more to the periodic."[8] We see this periodic structure exemplified in a sentence like the first one of paragraph 4: "As to my own part, having turned my thoughts, for many years, upon this important subject, and maturely weighed the several schemes of other projectors, I have always found them grossly mistaken in their computations." No one *speaks* a sentence like that; sentences like that are produced by someone who has time to plot his sentences.

This tendency to delay the main predication of the sentence is most pronounced within another structural pattern that is so common in the essay as to be a mannerism. I refer to the proposer's habit of putting the main idea of the sentence into a noun clause following the verb of the main clause. These noun clauses follow either personal structures like "I am assured by our merchants that . . . ," "I have reckoned that . . . ," "he confessed that . . ." or impersonal structures like "it is not improbable that . . ." and "it is very well known that. . . ." There are at least nineteen instances like these, where the main idea of the sentence is contained in the noun clause. And frequently the proposer further delays the main idea by making us read almost to the end of the noun clause before he gives us the main predication. A prime example of this is the final sentence of paragraph 18:

> Neither indeed can I deny, that if the same use were made of several plump young girls in this town, who, without one single groat to their fortunes, cannot stir abroad without a chair, and appear at the playhouse and assemblies in foreign fineries, which they will never pay for, the kingdom would not be the worse.

Reading a sentence like this, we wonder whether the man will ever get to the point, and in this case, when the point is finally reached, we find that it is deflatingly anti-climactic.

This tendency toward periodic structure is evidence not only of a deliberate written style but of a habit of the *persona* that suits Swift's rhetorical purpose. I suggested earlier that part of Swift's rhetorical strategy is to create a character who will, as it were, "sneak up" on the reader. The frequent use of periodic structure is one of the ways in which the proposer "sneaks up" on the reader.

And we see this same tactic in the early paragraphs of the essay. In the first two paragraphs we see the long, leisurely, meandering sentences in which the proposer, in a matter-of-fact tone, describes the present con-

8. Walter J. Ong, "Oral Residue in Tudor Prose Style," *PMLA*, LXXX (June, 1965), 149.

dition of the poor. There is further dawdling in paragraph 4, where in two rambling sentences he seeks to establish his credentials with his audience. Then in paragraph 6, the second longest paragraph of the essay, we are subjected to a litany of cold, hard figures or "computations." In the short paragraph 9, we hear the disturbing sputter of a lighted fuse as the proposer retails the testimony of his American acquaintance about what a delicacy a year-old child is. Then in paragraph 10, after the expenditure of almost a thousand words on preliminaries (almost a third of the essay), the proposer drops his bombshell. Nor does his pace become any more frenetic from this point on. He continues to "leak out" information, testimony, and arguments.

The noticeable periodic structure of many of the sentences, then, is part of Swift's strategy of sneaking up on the audience, of disarming the reader in order to render him more sensitive to the blow that will be delivered to the solar plexus. The proposer tells us in paragraph 27 that he is "studious of brevity." But he is not brief at all; he takes his own good time about dealing out what he has to say to his audience. This is not the curt Senecan amble; this is the rambling Ciceronian cadence. The Ciceronian cadence does not fit Jonathan Swift, of course, but it does fit the character he has created and does contribute to the rhetorical effectiveness of the essay.

We could pursue this discussion of sentences and schemes, but let us move on to a consideration of the diction of the essay. Let us see what a study of the diction tells us about Swift's strategies and about the proposer's style.

To begin with, we might advert briefly to the words and idioms that mark the essay as a product of the eighteenth century. One of the things that has often been remarked of Swift's style is that it is strikingly modern. As one of my students said to me, "When I'm reading Swift, I have the feeling that I'm reading George Orwell all over again." One of the reasons certainly for this impression of modernity is the diction and idiom. Swift uses very few words and idioms that are outdated. But he does use just enough dated words and expressions to prevent our getting the impression that we are reading the morning newspaper. I counted about a dozen idioms which were peculiar to the eighteenth century or were still current in the eighteenth century but are no longer current—expressions like "of towardly parts" (para. 6), "no gentleman would *repine* to give ten shillings" (para. 14), "I cannot be altogether *in* his sentiments" (para. 17) (see Appendix for additional examples). If one were attempting to date this piece from internal evidence, probably the two words that would be the best index of the period in which this essay was written would be *shambles* (para. 16) and the *chair* (para. 18) in which the plump young girls ride about town. The *OED* would tell us that in the eighteenth century *shambles* meant "a place where meat is sold," "a slaughter house" and that *chair* designated a means of transportation. Expressions like these give the essay its Augustan flavor, but aside from these, the diction and idiom are remarkably modern.

The Appendix carries a note about the monosyllabism of the essay. Only about one-third of the nouns in the first ten paragraphs are monosyllabic, and I suspect that there is a much higher percentage of polysyllabic, Latinate diction in *A Modest Proposal* than we will find in most of Swift's other prose works, especially in that prose where he is speaking in his own voice. This polysyllabic diction is appropriate of course for the kind of pedantic character that Swift has created in *A Modest Proposal*. The proposer wants to pass himself off on his audience as a man who has indulged in a great deal of scientific, scholarly study of the problem, so as to enhance his authority—"having turned my thoughts, for many years, upon this important subject, and maturely weighed the several schemes of other projectors" (para. 4).

The mathematical and mercantile terminology is also contributing to the image of the dedicated investigator and the political arithmetician. Besides the many figures cited, there are repeated uses of words like "compute," "reckon," "calculate," "shillings," "pounds," "sterling," "accounts," "stock," "commodity," "*per annum*." By putting jargon like this in the mouth of his proposer, Swift is making him talk the language of the other political economists who had turned their attention to the problem. We might say of the cold-bloodedness with which the proposer delivers himself of these terms that it represents his disinterested endeavor to propagate the worst that is known and thought about the problem in the Anglo-Irish world.

The most notable of the lexical means that Swift uses to achieve his purpose is the series of animal metaphors (see the Appendix). Charles Beaumont has pointed out that Swift is here employing the ancient rhetorical device of diminution, the opposite effect of amplification.[9] Swift first reduces his human beings to the status of animals and then to the status of food furnished to the table when these animals are slaughtered. So we pass from animal images like "dropped from its dam" and "reserved for breed" to such slaughtered-animal images as "the carcass," "the fore or hind quarters," and "the skin of which, artificially dressed." We feel the impact of these metaphors when we realize that Swift is suggest-

9. See Charles Allen Beaumont, "A Modest Proposal," *Swift's Classical Rhetoric* (Athens, Ga.: University of Georgia Press, 1961), pp. 15–43. After my own gathering of data, it was reassuring to me to discover that I had noted many of the same stylistic features that Beaumont had found.

ing that the Anglo-Irish landlords were treating human beings no better than they treated their domestic animals. The proposer points up this inhuman treatment when he says, in paragraph 26, that if his proposal were adopted, "men would become as fond of their wives, during the time of pregnancy, as they are now of their mares in foal, their cows in calf, or sows when they are ready to farrow."

Another trope that Swift uses to achieve diminution is litotes—the opposite trope to hyperbole. Here are four prominent examples of litotes or understatement. In paragraph 2, the proposer refers to the burden of the prodigious number of beggar children as "a very great additional grievance." In paragraph 17, he speaks of the practice of substituting the bodies of young lads and maidens for venison as "a little bordering on cruelty." At the end of the periodic sentence in paragraph 18, he says that "the kingdom would not be the worse" if the bodies of plump young girls were sold as a delicacy for the table. The most notable example of litotes in the essay—and the one that serves as the chief tip-off to the irony of the essay—is found in the first sentence of the key paragraph 29: "I can think of no one objection that will possibly be raised against this proposal, unless it should be urged that the number of people will be thereby much lessened in this kingdom." The frequent use of litotes fits in well with the proposer's tendency to underplay everything.

The proposer not only underplays his proposal (note "a modest proposal") and his arguments to justify the proposal but also underplays his emotions. One has a hard time of it finding emotionally freighted words in the essay. Only in paragraphs 1 and 5 do I find conspicuous clusters of what I. A. Richards calls "emotive words":

> paragraph 1: Melancholy, all in rags, helpless infants, dear native country, crowded
>
> paragraph 5: abortions, horrid practice, murdering their bastard children, alas, tears and pity, poor innocent babes, savage and inhuman breast

The only other place in the essay where I sense the proposer losing a tight rein on his emotions is in his outburst in paragraph 18 against the plump young girls of the town, and in this instance, the anger simmering under these words is, I suspect, the emotional reaction of the clergyman Swift rather than of the worldly proposer. And this is the one place in the essay where I feel that Swift momentarily drops the mask and speaks in his own voice.

Swift considerably enhances the emotional impact of his message by this underplaying. And the other trope that is responsible for the emotional power of the essay is irony. As I remarked before, irony is an overarching device for the entire essay: the proposer means what he says, but Swift does not. Irony, however, is a prevalent device within the essay too. I counted at least fifteen instances of words being used ironically. Rather than weary you with the entire catalogue, let me quote a few representative examples (the ironical words are italicized):

will make two dishes at an *entertainment* for friends (para. 10)

the fore and hind quarters will make a *reasonable* dish (para. 10)

will make admirable gloves for *ladies* and summer boots for *fine gentlemen* (para. 14)

some *scrupulous* people might be apt to censure (para. 17)

The horror of this irony hits us all the harder when we realize that the proposer, in his naivety, intends his words to be taken literally. These are the places where I can almost see Swift grinning through the lines of print.

Swift does something with words in this essay that I had not noticed him doing in any of his other prose works. He repeats key words so that they almost become motifs in the essay. The Appendix lists some of these repeated words and records the frequency of repetition. Note particularly the repetitions and variations of the words *child* and *parent*. Swift realizes that the proposal violates one of the most fundamental of human relations—the child-parent relation. When this violation of the normal child-parent relation is joined with a suggestion of cannibalism, a practice that almost universally offends the sensibilities of mankind, we get a proposal of the utmost monstrosity. And if Swift can get his audience to react violently enough to the revolting proposal, there is hope that they will resort to some of the "other expedients" for a solution to the problem of poverty. Basically that is his main rhetorical strategy in the essay.

I cannot wholly account for the rhetorical function of the repetition of the kingdom-country-nation diction. Swift may be seeking to emphasize that the poverty of the people is a problem of national scope, one in which the welfare of the entire nation is crucially involved. Hasn't this been the theme that President Johnson has been urging in his efforts to promote his Poverty Program? Another explanation may be that Swift is suggesting that just as, on the domestic level, the normal child-parent relationships have broken down, the kingdom-citizen relationships have broken down on the national level.

This kind of repetition of key words and phrases is a device that we have come to associate with Matthew Arnold's style. Anyone who has read Arnold's prose extensively knows how effective this tactic can be for purposes of exposition. Although repetition is not a mannerism of Swift's style in general, we can appreciate the emotional effect that Swift achieves in this argumentative piece with these drumbeat repetitions. These insistent repetitions keep bringing us back to the full implications of the modest proposal.

Before this exhaustive analysis becomes prostratingly exhausting, I had better bring it to a quick conclusion. Maybe a good way to conclude this study is for me to quote two estimates of Swift's style and then to ask you which of these two estimates seems to be, in the light of the foregoing analysis, the more just.

The first quotation is from Dr. Johnson's *Life of Swift:*

> For purposes merely didactic, when something is to be told that was not known before [his style] is in the highest degree proper, but against that inattention by which known truths are suffered to lie neglected, it makes no provision; it instructs but does not persuade.

There is no denying that Swift's style does achieve an "easy and safe conveyance of meaning," but do you find Dr. Johnson's denial of persuasive value in Swift's style too harsh? Perhaps you are more disposed to accept Coleridge's judgment on Swift's style: "The manner is a complete expression of the matter, the terms appropriate, and the artifice concealed."

But maybe it is unfair to ask you to choose between these two estimates, for one of my points has been that in this essay we are observing not so much Swift's style as a style that Swift has created for his modest proposer. And who, after all, remembers this essay for its style? This analysis has revealed, I hope, that there is considerable stylistic artifice in *A Modest Proposal*, but hasn't this essay become memorable mainly because of the monstrousness of the proposal and the cleverness of the ironical form? As a matter of historical fact, Swift did *not* succeed in persuading his audience to do something about a lamentable situation. But he did succeed in producing a great piece of literature.

APPENDIX

SOME STATISTICS ON SWIFT'S *A MODEST PROPOSAL*

3474 words
  33 paragraphs
  61 sentences (For this study, a sentence is defined as a group of words beginning with a capital letter and ending with some mark of terminal punctuation.)

Average number of words per paragraph 105.2
Average number of sentences per paragraph 1.84
    18 one-sentence paragraphs
     7 two-sentence paragraphs
     4 three-sentence paragraphs
     3 four-sentence paragraphs
     1 five-sentence paragraph (#29)

Shortest paragraph #8 (20 words)—a transitional paragraph (other transitional paragraph, #20, is 34 words long)
Longest paragraph #29 (289 words)—"other expedients" (a key paragraph)

Average number of words per sentence 56.9
Number of sentences 10 words or more *above* average 18
Percentage of sentences above average 29.5%
Number of sentences 10 words or more *below* average 28
Percentage of sentences below average 45.9%
Longest sentence .... 179 words (para. 32)
Other long sentences: 164 words (para. 6); 141 words (para. 29); 119 words (para. 18); 109 words (para. 4); 102 words (para. 13)
Shortest sentence .... 11 words (last sentence of para. 27)
    (other short sentence: first sentence of transitional paragraph #20)
34 Complex sentences
18 Compound-complex sentences
 5 Simple sentences (paragraph 4, 19, 20, 27)
 4 Elliptical or incomplete sentences (paragraph 10, 29 (two), 31)

REPEATED WORDS

child (children) .....25 ⎫		kingdom ....13 ⎫
infants ....6 ⎬ 33		country ....9 ⎬ 27
babes ....2 ⎭		nation ....5 ⎭

		the year ....6 ⎫
mother ....6 ⎫		one year old ....1 ⎪
parents ....7 ⎬ 20		annually ....3 ⎬ 16
breed (breeders) ......7 ⎭		solar year ....2 ⎪
		per annum ....4 ⎭

number ....7 ⎫		food ....7 ⎫
compute ....5 ⎪		flesh ....4 ⎪
reckon ....2 ⎬ 15		carcass ....5 ⎬ 19
calculate ....1 ⎭		plump ....3 ⎭

propose ....5 ⎫ 9		gentlemen ....5 ⎫
proposal ....4 ⎭		persons of quality .....2 ⎬ 12
		beggars ....5 ⎭

DICTION OR IDIOM PECULIARLY EIGHTEENTH-CENTURY

(The number in parentheses refers to the paragraph in which the expression occurs.)

(6) of *towardly* parts
(10) increas*eth* to twenty-eight pounds
(13) fish being a *prolific* diet
(14) no gentleman would *repine* to give ten shillings
(16) *shambles* may be appointed
(16) dressing them hot from the knife
(17) the *want* of venison . . . for *want* of work and service
(17) I cannot be altogether *in* his sentiments
(18) who came from *thence, above* twenty years ago
(18) without a *chair*
(19) and I have been desired to employ my thoughts what course may be taken
(19) But I am not *in the least pain upon* that matter
(19) and thus the country and themselves are *in a fair way* of being delivered from the evils to come
(25) bring great *custom* to taverns where the *vintners* will certainly be so prudent
(26) emulation among the married women, *which* of them could bring
(32) to reject any offer, proposed by wise men, *who* [which?] shall be found equally innocent, cheap, easy, and effectual

ANIMAL IMAGERY

(3) at the *heels* of their mother
(4) a child just *dropped* from its *dam*
(10) reserved for breed
(10) more than we allow to sheep, black-cattle, or swine
(10) therefore one *male* will be sufficient *to serve* four *females*
(10) to let them *suck* plentifully . . . to render them plump and fat for a good table
(10) the fore or hind quarter
(14) for the *carcass* of a good fat child
(15) flay the *carcass* . . . the skin of which, artificially *dressed*
(16) as we do roasting pigs
(26) men would become as fond of their wives, during the time of their pregnancy, as they are now of their mares in foal, their cows in calf, or sows when they are ready to farrow
(27) propagation of swine's flesh
(27) the great destruction of pigs
(27) fat *yearling* child

MONOSYLLABISM

In the first ten paragraphs of the essay, there are 1127 words; of these, 685 (60%) are monosyllabic. But since a good many of these monosyllabic words are pronouns, prepositions, conjunctions, or auxiliary verbs, we get an unreliable estimate of Swift's diction. If we look at the nouns only, we get a different picture. In these same ten paragraphs, there are 204 nouns. Of these, 73 are monosyllabic (36%), 131 are polysyllabic. If we regard only the substantive words in these paragraphs, we get, for Swift, an unusually high number of polysyllabic words.

A Generative Rhetoric
of the Sentence

We do not have time in our classes to teach everything about the rhetoric of the sentence. I believe in "island hopping," concentrating on topics where we can produce results and leaving the rest, including the "comma splice" and the "run-on sentence," to die on the vine. The balanced sentence deserves some attention in discursive writing, and the enormous range of coordinate structures deserves a bit more. The rhythm of good modern prose comes about equally from the multiple-tracking of coordinate constructions and the downshifting and backtracking of free modifiers. But the first comes naturally; the other needs coaxing along.

This coaxing is the clue to the meaning of *generative* in my title. (It is not derived from generative grammar; I used it before I ever heard of Chomsky.) The teacher can use the idea of levels of structure to urge the student to add further levels to what he has already produced, so that the structure itself becomes an aid to discovery.

This system of analysis by levels is essentially an application of immediate constituent analysis. IC analysis reveals what goes with what. In such analysis the free modifiers are cut off first. The order in which initial, medial, and final elements are cut off is immaterial, but one might as well start at the beginning. Thus, in sentence 2 below, the first cut would take off the whole set of initial modifiers. Then the members of a coordinate set are separated and, if the dissection is to be carried out to the ultimate constituents, analyzed one by one in order. In sentence 1, the first cut would come at the end of the base clause, taking off levels 2, 3,

From *Notes Toward a New Rhetoric,* Second Edition, edited by Bonniejean Christensen. New York: Harper & Row, 1978, pp. 23–44. Reprinted by permission of Bonniejean Christensen.

and 4 together since they are dependent on one another. Another cut would come at the end of level 2, taking off levels 3 and 4 together since 4 is a modifier of 3. Medial modifiers have to be cut *out* rather than *off*.

If the new grammar is to be brought to bear on composition, it must be brought to bear on the rhetoric of the sentence. We have a workable and teachable, if not a definitive, modern grammar; but we do not have, despite several titles, a modern rhetoric.

In composition courses we do not really teach our captive charges to write better—we merely *expect* them to. And we do not teach them how to write better because we do not know how to teach them to write better. And so we merely go through the motions. Our courses with their tear-out workbooks and four-pound anthologies are elaborate evasions of the real problem. They permit us to put in our time and do almost anything else we'd rather be doing instead of buckling down to the hard work of making a difference in the student's understanding and manipulation of language.

With hundreds of handbooks and rhetorics to draw from, I have never been able to work out a program for teaching the sentence as I find it in the work of contemporary writers. The chapters on the sentence all adduce the traditional rhetorical classification of sentences as loose, balanced, and periodic. But the term *loose* seems to be taken as a pejorative (it sounds immoral); our students, no Bacons or Johnsons, have little occasion for balanced sentences; and some of our worst perversions of style come from the attempt to teach them to write periodic sentences. The traditional grammatical classification of sentences is equally barren. Its use in teaching composition rests on a semantic confusion, equating complexity of structure with complexity of thought and vice versa. But very simple thoughts may call for very complex grammatical constructions. Any moron can say "I don't know who done it." And some of us might be puzzled to work out the grammar of "All I want is all there is," although any chit can think it and say it and act on it.

The chapters on the sentence all appear to assume that we think naturally in primer sentences, progress naturally to compound sentences, and must be taught to combine the primer sentences into complex sentences—and that complex sentences are the mark of maturity. We need a rhetoric of the sentence that will do more than combine the ideas of primer sentences. We need one that will *generate* ideas.

For the foundation of such a generative or productive rhetoric I take the statement from John Erskine, the originator of the Great Books courses, himself a novelist. In the essay "The Craft of Writing" (*Twentieth Century English*, Philosophical Library, 1946) he discusses a principle of the writer's craft which, though known he says to all practitioners, he has never seen discussed in print. The principle is this: "When you write, you make a point, not by subtracting as though you sharpened a pencil, but by adding." We have all been told that the formula for good writing is the concrete noun and the active verb. Yet Erskine says, "What you say is found not in the noun but in what you add to qualify the noun. . . . The noun, the verb, and the main clause serve merely as the base on which meaning will rise. . . . The modifier is the essential part of any sentence." The foundation, then, for a generative or productive rhetoric of the sentence is that composition is essentially a process of *addition*.

But speech is linear, moving in time, and writing moves in linear space, which is analogous to time. When you add a modifier, whether to the noun, the verb, or the main clause, you must add it either before the head or after it. If you add it before the head, the direction of modification can be indicated by an arrow pointing forward; if you add it after, by an arrow pointing backward. Thus we have the second principle of a generative rhetoric—the principle of *direction of modification* or *direction of movement*.

Within the clause there is not much scope for operating with this principle. The positions of the various sorts of close, or restrictive, modifiers are generally fixed and the modifiers are often obligatory—"The man who came to dinner remained till midnight." Often the only choice is whether to add modifiers. What I have seen of attempts to bring structural grammar to bear on composition usually boils down to the injunction to "load the patterns." Thus "pattern practice" sets students to accreting sentences like this: "The small boy on the red bicycle who lives with his happy parents on our shady street often coasts down the steep street until he comes to the city park." This will never do. It has no rhythm and hence no life; it is tone-deaf. It is the need that will burgeon into gobbledegook. One of the hardest things in writing is to keep the noun clusters and verb clusters short.

It is with modifiers added to the clause—that is, with sentence modifiers—that the principle comes into full play. The typical sentence of modern English, the kind we can best spend our efforts trying to teach, is what we may call the *cumulative sentence*. The main clause, which may or may not have a sentence modifier before it, advances the discussion; but the additions move backward, as in this clause, to modify the statement of the main clause or more often to explicate or exemplify it, so that the sentence has a flowing and ebbing movement, advancing to a new position and then pausing to consolidate it, leaping and lingering as the popular ballad does. The first part of the preceding compound sentence has one addition, placed within it; the second part has 4 words in the main clause and 49 in the five additions placed after it.

The cumulative sentence is the opposite of the periodic sentence. It does not represent the idea as conceived, pondered over, reshaped, packaged, and delivered cold. It is dynamic rather than static, representing the mind thinking. The main clause ("the additions move backward" above) exhausts the mere fact of the idea; logically, there is nothing more to say. The additions stay with the same idea, probing its bearings and implications, exemplifying it or seeking an analogy or metaphor for it, or reducing it to details. Thus the mere form of the sentence generates ideas. It serves the needs of both the writer and the reader, the writer by compelling him to examine his thought, the reader by letting him into the writer's thought.

Addition and direction of movement are structural principles. They involve the grammatical character of the sentence. Before going on to other principles, I must say a word about the best grammar as the foundation for rhetoric. I cannot conceive any useful transactions between teacher and students unless they have in common a language for talking about sentences. The best grammar for the present purpose is the grammar that best displays the layers of structure of the English sentence. The best I have found in a textbook is the combination of immediate constituent and transformation grammar in Paul Roberts's *English Sentences*. Traditional grammar, whether oversimple as in the school tradition or overcomplex as in the scholarly tradition, does not reveal the language as it operates; it leaves everything, to borrow a phrase from Wordsworth, "in disconnection dead and spiritless." *English Sentences* is oversimplified and it has gaps, but it displays admirably the structures that rhetoric must work with—primarily sentence modifiers, including nonrestrictive relative and subordinate clauses, but, far more important, the array of noun, verb, and adjective clusters. It is paradoxical that Professor Roberts, who has done so much to make the teaching of composition possible, should himself be one of those who think that it cannot be taught. Unlike Ulysses, he does not see any work for Telemachus to work.

Layers of structure, as I have said, is a grammatical concept. To bring in the dimension of meaning, we need a third principle—that of *levels of generality* or *levels of abstraction*. The main or base clause is likely to be stated in general or abstract or plural terms. With the main clause stated, the forward movement of the sentence stops, the writer shifts down to a lower level of generality or abstraction or to singular terms, and goes back over the same ground at this lower level.[1] There is no theoretical limit to the number of structural layers or levels, each[2] at a lower level of generality, any or all of them compounded, that a speaker or writer may use. For a speaker, listen to Lowell Thomas; for a writer, study William Faulkner. To a single independent clause, he may append a page of additions, but usually all clear, all grammatical, once we have learned how to read him. Or, if you prefer, study Hemingway, the master of the simple sentence: "George was coming down in the telemark position, kneeling, one leg forward and bent, the other trailing, his sticks hanging like some insect's thin legs, kicking up puffs of snow, and finally the whole kneeling, trailing figure coming around in a beautiful right curve, crouching, the legs shot forward and back, the body leaning out against the swing, the sticks accenting the curve like points of light, all in a wild cloud of snow." Only from the standpoint of school grammar is this a a simple sentence.

This brings me to the fourth, and last, principle, that of texture. *Texture* provides a descriptive or evaluative term. If a writer adds to few of his nouns or verbs or main clauses and adds little, the texture may be said to be thin. The style will be plain or bare. The writing of most of our students is thin—even threadbare. But if he adds frequently or much or both, then the texture may be said to be dense or rich. One of the marks of an effective style, especially in narrative, is variety in the texture, the texture varying with the change in pace, the variation in texture producing the change in pace. It is not true, as I have seen it asserted, that fast action calls for short sentences; the action is fast in the sentence by Hemingway above. In our classes, we have to work for greater density and variety in texture and greater concreteness and particularity in what is added.

I have been operating at a fairly high level of generality. Now I must downshift and go over the same points with examples. The most graphic way to exhibit the layers of structure is to indent the word groups of a sentence and to number the levels. The first three sentences illustrate the

1. Cf. Leo Rockas "Abstract and Concrete Sentences," *CCC*, May 1963. Rockas describes sentences as abstract or concrete, the abstract implying the concrete and vice versa. Readers and writers, he says, must have the knack of apprehending the concrete in the abstract and the abstract in the concrete. This is true and valuable. I am saying that within a single sentence the writer may present more than one level of generality, translating the abstract into the more concrete in added levels.

2. This statement is not quite tenable. Each helps to make the idea of the base clause more concrete or specific, but each is not more concrete or specific than the one immediately above it. See pp. 56, 80.

various positions of the added sentence modifiers—initial, medial, and final. The symbols mark the grammatical character of the additions: SC, subordinate clause; RC, relative clause; NC, noun cluster; VC, verb cluster; AC, adjective cluster; A + A, adjective series; Abs, absolute (i.e., a VC with a subject of its own); PP, prepositional phrase. The elements set off as on a lower level are marked as sentence modifiers by junctures or punctuation. The examples have been chosen to illustrate the range of constructions used in the lower levels; after the first few they are arranged by the number of levels. The examples could have been drawn from poetry as well as from prose. Those not attributed are by students.

1

1 He dipped his hands in the bichloride solution and shook them,
    2 a quick shake, (NC)
        3 fingers down, (Abs)
            4 like the fingers of a pianist above the keys. (PP)

Sinclair Lewis

2

    2 Calico-coated, (AC)
    2 small-bodied, (AC)
        3 with delicate legs and pink faces in which their mismatched eyes
            rolled wild and subdued, (PP)
1 they huddled,
    2 gaudy motionless and alert, (A + A)
    2 wild as deer, (AC)
    2 deadly as rattlesnakes, (AC)
    2 quiet as doves. (AC)

William Faulkner

3

1 The bird's eye, / , remained fixed upon him;
    2 / bright and silly as a sequin (AC)
1 its little bones, / , seemed swooning in his hand.
    2 / wrapped . . . in a warm padding of feathers (VC)

Stella Benson

4

1 The jockeys sat bowed and relaxed,
    2 moving a little at the waist with the movement of their horses.
    (VC)

Katherine Anne Porter

5

1 The flame sidled up the match,
   2 driving a film of moisture and a thin strip of darker grey before
      it. (VC)

6

1 She came among them behind the man,
   2 gaunt in the gray shapeless garment and the sunbonnet, (AC)
   2 wearing stained canvas gymnasium shoes. (VC)

Faulkner

7

1 The Texan turned to the nearest gatepost and climbed to the top of it,
   2 his alternate thighs thick and bulging in the tight trousers, (Abs)
   2 the butt of the pistol catching and losing the sun in pearly gleams.
      (Abs)

Faulkner

8

1 He could sail for hours,
   2 searching the blanched grasses below him with his telescopic eyes,
      (VC)
   2 gaining height against the wind, (VC)
   2 descending in mile-long, gently declining swoops when he curved
      and rode back, (VC)
   2 never beating a wing. (VC)

Walter Van Tilburg Clark

9

1 They regarded me silently,
   2 Brother Jack with a smile that went no deeper than his lips, (Abs)
      3 his head cocked to one side, (Abs)
      3 studying me with his penetrating eyes; (VC)
   2 the other blank-faced, (Abs)
      3 looking out of eyes that were meant to reveal nothing and to stir
         profound uncertainty. (VC)

Ralph Ellison

10

1 He stood at the top of the stairs and watched me,
   2 I waiting for him to call me up, (Abs)
   2 he hesitating to come down, (Abs)
      3 his lips nervous with the suggestion of a smile, (Abs)
      3 mine asking whether the smile meant come, or go away. (Abs)

11

1 Joad's lips stretched tight over his long teeth for a moment, and
1 he licked his lips,
   2 like a dog, (PP)
      3 two licks, (NC)
         4 one in each direction from the middle. (NC)

                                             Steinbeck

12

1 We all live in two realities:
   2 one of seeming fixity, (NC)
      3 with institutions, dogmas, rules of punctuation, and routines,
        (PP)
         4 the calendared and clockwise world of all but futile round on
           round; (NC) and
   2 one of whirling and flying electrons, dreams, and possibilities, (NC)
   3 behind the clock. (PP)

                                               Sidney Cox

13

1 It was as though someone, somewhere, had touched a lever and
  shifted gears, and
1 the hospital was set for night running,
   2 smooth and silent, (A + A)
   2 its normal clatter and hum muffled, (Abs)
   2 the only sounds heard in the whitewalled room distant and unreal:
     (Abs)
      3 a low hum of voices from the nurses' desk, (NC)
         4 quickly stifled, (VC)
      3 the soft squish or rubber-soled shoes on the tiled corridor, (NC)
      3 starched white cloth rustling against itself, (NC) and, outside,
      3 the lonesome whine of wind in the country night (NC) and
      3 the Kansas dust beating against the windows. (NC)

14

1 The beach sounds are jazzy,
   2 percussion fixing the mode—(Abs)
      3 the surf cracking and booming in the distance, (Abs)
      3 a little nearer dropped bar-bells clanking, (Abs)
      3 steel gym rings, / , ringing, (Abs)
         4 / flung together, (VC)
      3 palm fronds rustling above me, (Abs)
         4 like steel brushes washing over a snare drum, (PP)
      3 troupes of sandals splatting and shuffling on the sandy cement,
     (Abs)

4 their beat varying, (Abs)
   5 syncopation emerging and disappearing with changing paces. (Abs)

15

1 A small Negro girl develops from the sheet of glare-frosted walk,
2 walking barefooted, (VC)
   3 her bare legs striking and coiling from the hot cement, (Abs)
     4 her feet curling in, (Abs)
       5 only the outer edges touching. (Abs)

16

1 The swells moved rhythmically toward us,
2 irregularly faceted, (VC)
2 sparkling, (VC)
2 growing taller and more powerful until the shining crest bursts, (VC)
   3 a transparent sheet of pale green water spilling over the top, (Abs)
     4 breaking into blue-white foam as it cascades down the front of the wave, (VC)
     4 piling up in a frothy mound that the diminishing wave pushes up against the pilings, (VC)
       5 with a swishmash, (PP)
     4 the foam drifting back, (Abs)
       5 like a lace fan opened over the shimmering water as the spent wave returns whispering to the sea. (PP)

The best starting point for a composition unit based on these four principles is with two-level narrative sentences, first with one second-level addition (sentences 4, 5), then with two or more parallel ones (6, 7, 8). Anyone sitting in his room with his eyes closed could write the main clause of most of the examples; the discipline comes with the additions, provided they are based at first on immediate observation, requiring the student to phrase an exact observation in exact language. This can hardly fail to be exciting to a class: it is life, with the variety and complexity of life; the workbook exercise is death. The situation is ideal also for teaching diction—abstract-concrete, general-specific, literal-metaphorical, denotative-connotative. When the sentences begin to come out right, it is time to examine the additions for their grammatical character. From then on, the grammar comes to the aid of the writing, and the writing reinforces the grammar. One can soon go on to multilevel narrative sentences (1, 9–11, 15, 16) and then to brief narratives of three to six or seven sen-

tences on actions with a beginning, a middle, and an end that can be observed over and over again—beating eggs, making a cut with a power
saw, or following a record changer's cycle or a wave's flow and ebb.
(Bring the record changer to class.) Description, by contrast, is static,
picturing appearance rather than behavior. The constructions to master
are the noun and adjective clusters and the absolute (13, 14). Then the
descriptive noun cluster must be taught to ride piggyback on the narrative sentence, so that description and narration are interleaved: "In the
morning we went out into a new world, a glistening crystal and white
world, each skeleton tree, each leafless bush, even the heavy, drooping
power lines sheathed in icy crystal." The next step is to develop the sense
for variety in texture and change in pace that all good narrative demands.

In the next unit, the same four principles can be applied to the expository paragraph. But this is a subject for another paper.

I want to anticipate two possible objections. One is that the sentences are
long. By freshman English standards they are long, but I could have produced far longer ones from works freshmen are expected to read. Of the
sentences by students, most were written as finger exercises in the first
few weeks of the course. I try in narrative sentences to push to level after
level, not just two or three, but four, five, or six, even more, as far as the
students' powers of observation will take them. I want them to become
sentence acrobats, to dazzle by their syntactic dexterity. I'd rather have to
deal with hyperemia than anemia. I want to add my voice to that of
James Coleman (*CCC,* December 1962) deploring our concentration on
the plain style.

The other objection is that my examples are mainly descriptive and
narrative—and today in freshman English we teach only exposition. I deplore this limitation as much as I deplore our limitation to the plain style.
Both are a sign that we have sold our proper heritage for a pot of message. In permitting them, the English department undercuts its own discipline. Even if our goal is only utilitarian prose, we can teach diction
and sentence structure far more effectively through a few controlled exercises in description and narration than we can by starting right off with
exposition (Theme One, 500 words, precipitates *all* the problems of writing). There is no problem of invention; the student has something to
communicate—his immediate sense impressions, which can stand a bit of
exercising. The material is not already verbalized—he has to match language to sense impressions. His acuteness in observation and in choice of
words can be judged by fairly objective standards—is the sound of a bottle of milk being set down on a concrete step suggested better by *clink* or
clank or *clunk?* In the examples, study the diction for its accuracy, rising

at times to the truly imaginative. Study the use of metaphor, of comparison. This verbal virtuosity and syntactical ingenuity can be made to carry over into expository writing.

But this is still utilitarian. What I am proposing carries over of itself into the study of literature. It makes the student a better reader of literature. It helps him thread the syntactical mazes of much mature writing, and it gives him insight into that elusive thing we call style. Last year a student told of rereading a book by her favorite author, Willa Cather, and of realizing for the first time *why* she liked reading her: she could understand and appreciate the style. For some students, moreover, such writing makes life more interesting as well as giving them a way to share their interest with others. When they learn how to put concrete details into a sentence, they begin to look at life with more alertness. If it is liberal education we are concerned with, it is just possible that these things are more important than anything we can achieve when we set our sights on the plain style in expository prose.

I want to conclude with a historical note. My thesis in this paragraph is that modern prose like modern poetry has more in common with the seventeenth than with the eighteenth century and that we fail largely because we are operating from an eighteenth-century base. The shift from the complex to the cumulative sentence is more profound than it seems. It goes deep in grammar, requiring a shift from the subordinate clause (the staple of our trade) to the cluster and the absolute (so little understood as to go almost unnoticed in our textbooks). And I have only lately come to see that this shift has historical implications. The cumulative sentence is the modern form of the loose sentence that characterized the anti-Ciceronian movement in the seventeenth century. This movement, according to Morris W. Croll,[3] began with Montaigne and Bacon and continued with such men as Donne, Browne, Taylor, Pascal. To Montaigne, its art was the art of being natural; to Pascal, its eloquence was the eloquence that mocks formal eloquence; to Bacon, it presented knowledge so that it could be examined, not so that it must be accepted.

But the Senecan amble was banished from England when "the direct sensuous apprehension of thought" (T. S. Eliot's words) gave way to Cartesian reason or intellect. The consequences of this shift in sensibility are well summarized by Croll:

3. "The Baroque Style in Prose," *Studies in English Philology: A Miscellany in Honor of Frederick Klaeber* (1929), reprinted in *Style, Rhetoric, and Rhythm: Essays by Morris W. Croll* (1966) and A. M. Witherspoon and F. J. Warnke, *Seventeenth-Century Prose and Poetry*, 2nd ed. (1963). I have borrowed from Croll in my description of the cumulative sentence.

To this mode of thought we are to trace almost all the features of modern literary education and criticism, or at least of what we should have called modern a generation ago: the study of the precise meaning of words; the reference to dictionaries as literary authorities; the study of the sentence as a logical unit alone; the careful circumscription of its limits and the gradual reduction of its length; . . .[4] the attempt to reduce grammar to an exact science; the idea that forms of speech are always either correct or incorrect; the complete subjection of the laws of motion and expression in style to the laws of logic and standardization—in short, the triumph, during two centuries, of grammatical over rhetorical ideas. (*Style, Rhetoric and Rhythm,* p. 232.)

Here is a seven-point scale any teacher of composition can use to take stock. He can find whether he is based in the eighteenth century or in the twentieth and whether he is consistent—completely either an ancient or a modern—or is just a crazy mixed-up kid.

POSTSCRIPT

I have asserted that "syntactical ingenuity" can best be developed in narrative-descriptive writing and that it can be made to carry over into discursive writing. The count made for the article on sentence openers included all sentence modifiers—or free modifiers, as I prefer to call them. In the total number of free modifiers, the 2000 word samples were almost identical—1545 in the fiction and 1519 in the nonfiction, roughly one in three sentences out of four. But they differ in position:

| Nonfiction | initial 575 | medial 492 | final 452 |
| Fiction | initial 404 | medial 329 | final 812 |

And they differ in some of the grammatical kinds used in the final position:

| Nonfiction | NC 123 | VC 63 | Abs   9 |
| Fiction | NC 131 | VC 218 | Abs 108 |

Thus the differences are not in the structures used, only in the position and in the frequency of the various kinds of structures. It will be well to look at a few more sentences of discursive prose.

4. The omitted item concerns punctuation and is not relevant here. In using this scale, note the phrase "what we should have called modern a generation ago" and remember that Croll was writing in 1929.

17

1 His [Hemingway's] characters, / , wander through the ruins of
  Babel,
  2 / expatriates for the most part, (NC)
  2 smattering many tongues (VC) and
  2 speaking a demotic version of their own. (VC)

Harry Levin

18

1 From literal to figurative is one range that a word may take:
  2 from *foot* of a person to *foot* of a mountain, (PP)
    3 a substituted or metaphoric use. (NC)

1 From concrete to abstract is another range:
  2 from *foot to extremity,* (PP)
    3 stressing one of the abstract characteristics of foot, (VC)
      4 a contrast for which the terms *image* and *symbol* as distin-
      guished from *concept* are also used. (NC)

Josephine Miles

19

  2 Going back to his [Hemingway's] work in 1944, (VC)
1 you perceive his kinship with a wholly different group of novelists,
  2 let us say with Poe and Hawthorne and Melville: (PP)
    3 the haunted and nocturnal writers, (NC)
    3 the men who dealt in images that were symbols of an inner
    world. (NC)

Malcolm Cowley

20

1 Even her style in it is transitional and momentous,
  2 a matter of echoing and reminiscing effects, and of little clarion
  notes of surprise and prophecy here and there; (NC)
    3 befitting that time of life which has been called the old age of
    youth and the youth of old age, (AC or VC)
      4 a time fraught with heartache and youthful tension. (NC)

Glenway Wescott, of Colette's Break of Day

21

  2 Aglow with splendor and consequence, (AC)
1 he [Sterne] rejoined his wife and daughter,
  2 whom he presently transferred to his new parsonage at Coxwold,
  (RC)
    3 an old and rambling house, (NC)
      4 full of irregular, comfortable rooms, (AC)

4 situated on the edge of the moors, (VC)
    5 in a neighborhood much healthier than the marshy lands of
        Sutton. (PP)

Peter Quennell

22

1 It is with the coming of man that a vast hole seems to open in nature,
  2 a vast black whirlpool spinning faster and faster, (NC)
    3 consuming flesh, stones, soil, minerals, (VC)
    3 sucking down the lightning, (VC)
    3 wrenching power from the atom, (VC)
      4 until the ancient sounds of nature are drowned out in the ca-
          cophony of something which is no longer nature, (SC)
        5 something instead which is loose and knocking at the
            world's heart, (NC)
        5 something demonic and no longer planned—(NC)
          6 escaped, it may be—(VC)
          6 spewed out of nature, (VC)
          6 contending in a final giant's game against its master. (VC)

Loren Eiseley

The structures used in prose are necessarily the structures used in
poetry, necessarily because prose and poetry use the same language.
Poets may take more liberties with the grammar than prose writers are
likely to do; but their departures from the norm must all be understood
by reference to the norm. Since poets, like the writers of narrative, work
more by association than by logical connection, their sentences are likely
to have similar structures. They seem to know the values of the cumulative sentence.

The first example here consists of the first two stanzas of "The Meadow
Mouse"; the slashes mark the line ends. The other example constitutes the
last four of the five stanzas of "The Motive for Metaphor." It shows well
how structural analysis of the sentence reveals the tactics of a difficult
poem.

23

1 In a shoebox stuffed in an old nylon stocking / Sleeps the baby
    mouse I found in the meadow, /
  2 Where he trembled and shook beneath a stick / Till I caught him
      up by the tail and brought him in, / (RC)
    3 Cradled in my hand, / (VC)
    3 a little quaker, (NC)
      4 the whole body of him trembling, / (Abs)
    3 His absurd whiskers sticking out like a cartoon mouse, / (Abs)

3 His feet like small leaves, / (Abs)
  4 Little lizard-feet, / (NC)
  4 Whitish and spread wide when he tried to struggle away, / (AC)
    5 Wriggling like a minuscule puppy. (VC)

1 Now he's eaten his three kinds of cheese and drunk from his bottle-cap watering trough— /
  2 So much he just lies in one corner, / (AC)
    3 His tail curled under him, (Abs)
    3 his belly big / As his head, (Abs)
    3 His bat-like ears / Twitching, (Abs)
      4 tilting toward the least sound. (VC)

Theodore Roethke

24

2 In the same way, (PP)
1 you were happy in spring,
  2 with the half colors of quarter-things, (PP)
    3 The slightly brighter sky, (NC
    3 the melting clouds, (NC)
    3 the single bird, (NC)
    3 the obscure moon—(NC)
      4 The obscure moon lighting an obscure world of things that would never be quite expressed, (NC)
        5 where you yourself were never quite yourself and did not want nor have to be, (RC)
          6 desiring the exhilarations of changes: (VC)
            7 the motive for metaphor, (NC)
          6 shrinking from the weight of primary noon, (VC)
            7 the ABC of being, (NC)
            7 the ruddy temper, (NC)
            7 the hammer of red and blue, (NC)
            7 the hard sound—(NC)
              8 steel against intimation—(NC)
            7 the sharp flash, (NC)
            7 the vital, arrogant, fatal, dominant X. (NC)

Wallace Stevens

An Outline for Writing
Sentence-Combining Problems

Every teacher would welcome a systematic classroom activity that would enable his students to write sentences of greater structural variety and complexity. Every child does eventually come to write more complex sentences—and several recent studies have traced that development[1]—but every teacher watching this glacially slow development feels compelled to intervene. He cannot avoid asking what Piaget calls the American question: "How can I speed it up?" Now that formal grammar study has been discredited as an instructional tool for enhancing syntactic dexterity,[2] the well-informed upper elementary or secondary teacher has been relying on naturalistic methods for strengthening his students' sentence dexterity, methods such as wide silent reading, reading aloud, dramatic activities, discussion, sentence games, much writing and the informal examination of the students' own sentences. Probably all language activities foster syntactic dexterity, and there is no reason why the teacher must consider it a separate, isolated problem.

However, beginning in Grade 4, there may be a distinct developmental gain in control of written syntax for most children if they are asked to

From *English Journal*, 62 (January, 1973), 96–102, 108. Reprinted by permission of the National Council of Teachers of English and Charles R. Cooper.

1. Kellogg W. Hunt, *Grammatical Structures Written at Three Grade Levels*, 1965; Walter Loban, *The Language of Elementary School Children*, 1963; and Roy C. O'Donnell *et al.*, *Syntax of Kindergarten and Elementary School Children*, 1967. All published at Urbana, Illinois, as research reports of the National Council of Teachers of English.

2. See the very thorough and readable review of research on grammar and writing in John C. Mellon, *Transformational Sentence-Combining* (Urbana, Illinois: National Council of Teachers of English, 1969).

direct their attention to syntax. Grade 4 is about the time when complexity of written syntax catches and surpasses complexity of spoken syntax (O'Donnell, p. 95). As teachers know, students seem to make a breakthrough here in willingness to write and in sheer quantity of writing. It seems an appropriate time to provide them direct help with sentences. Boys particularly appear to need this help, since they temporarily fall behind the girls in written-sentence dexterity (though never in spoken-language dexterity) at about this point (O'Donnell, p. 96).

How can the teacher provide this direct assistance? A significant recent research report by John Mellon[3] provides evidence that sentence-combining problems of a special kind can enhance the syntactic dexterity of students' written sentences. The problems are presented apart from the writing program (which should be concerned with whole pieces of discourse); they confront the student with sentences more complex than ones he would be likely to write at that point in his development; they ask the student to write out fully-formed sentences, and they provide him the content of the sentences so that his attention can remain focused on the *structural* aspects of the problem. The appended Outline offers examples. The first problem asks the student to write out a new, well-formed sentence by embedding the sentence, "The canary is yellow," in the sentence, "The canary flew out the window." Simple indentation indicates which sentence is the insert. Sentence ID shows a multiple embedding problem. Clues for making the insertion are included for adjective clauses and for noun substitutes.

The studies in language development referred to above show that the structures covered in Parts I and II of the Outline are highly significant in distinguishing mature from "immature" syntax. In other words, the teacher can accelerate growth toward written syntactic maturity if he can help students increase the amount of modification around their nouns and help them use noun substitutes (phrases and clauses) in place of single-word nouns.

Loban's study of oral language development implies that there is no point in having the student write sentence patterns he already controls (in the manner of most grammar texts); what the student needs—and what separates high-verbal from low-verbal students—is to expand the

3. Mellon, *op. cit.* A replication of Mellon's study by Frank O'Hare of the University School of Florida State University supports Mellon's findings. Working with seventh-graders, Mellon got two years' growth in one in syntactic dexterity. Working with eighth-graders, O'Hare got four years' growth in one; his subjects were writing words per T-unit, words per clause, and a ratio of clauses to T-units equal to that of twelfth-graders.

patterns themselves. This is Loban's often-quoted conclusion: *"Not pattern but what is done to achieve flexibility within the pattern* proves to be a measure of effectiveness and control of language at this level of language development" (Loban, p. 84; italics are his).

Hunt's study of grammatical structures written at Grades 4, 8, and 12 leaves no doubt that critical factors in written language development are longer and more varied nominals (using noun phrases and clauses in place of simple-word nouns) and amount and depth of adjective modification of nouns. In discussing the implications of his study for instruction in the classroom, Hunt has this to say: "This study suggests a kind of sentence-building program that probably has never been produced, or at least not systematically and fully. The aim would be to widen the student's span of grammatical attention and concern. The method would be for him to reduce independent clauses to subordinate clauses and non-clauses, consolidating them with adjoining clauses and T-units. He could work up to structures of considerable depth and complexity comparable to those exhibited by twelfth-graders and superior adults" (Hunt, p. 157).

Mellon, the first researcher to examine the effects in the student's own writing of a sentence-building program like the one recommended by Hunt, concludes that sentence-combining problems "will increase the rate at which the sentence structure of the student's own writing becomes more highly elaborated (or differentiated) and thus more mature." Mellon thinks that ". . . this increase in growth rate is of sufficient magnitude to justify one's regarding the programs that produce it as valuable supplements to reading, writing, and discussing, which will obviously remain the staple activity content of elementary and junior high school English and language arts curriculums" (Mellon, p. 73).

In building a case for using sentence-combining problems in the classroom on a systematic basis, I do not want to ignore two important criticisms of this approach. One comes from James Moffett, who argues that any nonnaturalistic approach to language development should be avoided, that workbooks and exercises should be thrown out, the teacher working only with the student's own language production. And yet Moffett does recommend one sentence-writing activity that is very much like these sentence-combining problems. His activity has elementary children practice expanding and filling in the telegraphic speech of babies.[4] I am satisfied that these problems do not violate Moffett's curriculum if they are regarded as another language game in the teacher's repertory and if they are used in the spirit of a game, a set of puzzles to be solved.

4. *A Student-Centered Language Arts Curriculum, Grades K-13: A Handbook for Teachers* (New York: Houghton Mifflin, 1968) pp. 150–152.

The other criticism comes from Francis Christensen, who argues that the cumulative sentence, rather than the embedded sentence, is more characteristic of modern prose styles.[5] The cumulative sentence with its final free modifiers is very common in modern prose, but it has not replaced the embedded sentence, an impression one can get on reading Christensen. Embeddings and accumulations can occur in the same sentences, of course. The fact remains that mature syntax is characterized *in large part* by amount and depth of embedding, and this is a developmental task the child must master. To meet this criticism the teacher could also prepare some sentence-*additive* problems based on those in *The Student Workbook, The Christensen Rhetoric Program: The Sentence and the Paragraph* (Harper and Row, 1969). One exercise format very much like the format of Mellon's sentence-combining problems appears three times in Christensen's workbook (pp. 53, 65, 67), but in every other exercise format the student is writing to a pattern, making up the content of the sentence out of his own head.

My considered opinion is that teachers should be using these sentence-combining problems on a regular basis with their students. Used with an informal approach in correcting deviancy from standard English usage and punctuation (Mellon, pp. 5–7),[6] they permit the teacher to guiltlessly eliminate the teaching of a formal grammar, since both these activities—informal approach to deviancy and sentence-combining problems—fulfill the traditional goals of grammar study: standard usage and control of written syntax. Presented as another language game in a class where there is also an engaging writing program, they will increase the child's facility with the nominal and adjective structures of written English. Even so, the increased facility will still come very slowly. Learning to write sentences is like learning to read—a lifelong process. In "A Week on the Concord and Merrimack Rivers," Thoreau said it well: "A perfectly healthy sentence, it is true, is extremely rare."

Teachers can easily write all the sentence-combining problems they need. The Outline is a guide to constructing them systematically to cover all the kinds of embeddings and substitutions students need to practice. For children in the upper elementary grades the emphasis should be on the adjective problems (Part I). Beginning in Grade 7 the problems can be balanced between adjective embeddings and noun substitutions (Part II). Multiple embeddings and substitutions (ID and IIC) should be pre-

5. *Notes Toward a New Rhetoric* (New York: Harper and Row, 1967).
6. Mellon reviews the research on the utility of learning usage rules in correcting usage problems and concludes that the informal or incidental approach to correcting usage problems is more efficient and successful.

sented as soon as the students can handle them. Very capable high school students can move almost immediately to multiple embedding and substitution problems.

The sentence-combining problems can be presented a few at a time on a single worksheet. In doing further research on the value of these problems, I have been presenting them to large numbers of fourth- and seventh-graders of all abilities in schools in San Bernardino, California. Students do two worksheets in class each week (a total of ten or twelve problems) in connection with whatever other language activities the teacher has planned. Like Mellon, I have found that students seem to remain interested in "solving" the problems. Obviously, they can be given to the entire class at once, or they can be independent work for each student or for students who choose the activity. Pairs or small groups of students can work together on the problems. The teacher can put up a key somewhere in the room for students to check their new sentences against. The worksheets should never be presented as tests or as punishment or as time-fillers. Ideally the problems would be designed so that all the students write out perfect solutions, although some may puzzle over the problems longer than others.

An Outline for Writing Sentence-
Combining Problems:
Noun Modifiers and Noun Substitutes

I. Noun modifiers
  A. Adjective word embeddings
    1. Simple
      a. before subject
        The canary flew out the window.
          The canary is *yellow*.
        • The yellow canary flew out the window.
      b. before object
        I saw a canary.
          The canary is *yellow*.
        • I saw a yellow canary.
      c. before predicate nominative
        He was a student.
          The student was *serious*.
        • He was a serious student.
      d. before object of a preposition
        He was in the house when it caught fire.
          The house was *old*.
        • He was in the old house when it caught fire.
        He fell from the roof.

The roof was *steep*.
* He fell from the steep roof.

2. Participle
   a. *ing*
      He saw the dog.
         The dog *sleeps*.
      * He saw the sleeping dog.
      The plane crashed into the house.
         The plane *burns*.
      * The burning plane crashed into the house.
   b. *ed*
      The house had a pool.
         The owners *abandoned* the house.
      * The abandoned house had a pool.
      The police captured the convict.
         The convict *escaped* from prison.
      * The police captured the escaped convict.
      The students did their homework.
         The homework was *assigned*.
      * The students did their assigned homework.

3. Compound-adjectives
   He dated the girl.
      The girl *loves fun*.
   * He dated the fun-loving girl.
   He saw the dog.
      Fleas bite the dog.
   * He saw the flea-bitten dog.

4. From adverbs
   The man is a fireman.
      The man is *outside*.
   * The man outside is a fireman.
   The number is the answer.
      The number is *below*.
   * The number below is the answer.
   The sky was full of stars.
      The sky was *above*.
   * The sky above was full of stars.
   The people on the boat asked us to come aboard.
      The boat was *alongside*.
   * The people on the boat alongside asked us to come aboard.

B. Adjective phrase embeddings
   1. Prepositional phrases
      The man is my teacher.
         The man is *in the room*.
      * The man in the room is my teacher.

We sailed in the boat.

> The boat was the one *with the blue sail.*

- We sailed in the boat with the blue sail.

2. Appositive phrases

My old friend is a plumber.

> My old friend is *Bill Jones.*

- My old friend Bill Jones is a plumber.

My neighbor took me around the track.

> My neighbor is *the race car driver.*

- My neighbor the race car driver took me around the track.

3. Participle phrases

a. *ing*

I stepped on the ant.

> The ant was *carrying a crumb.*

- I stepped on the ant carrying a crumb.

The runner wins.

> The runner was *making the best effort.*

- The runner making the best effort wins.

b. *ed*

We ate the food.

> The food was *prepared by the chef.*

- We ate the food prepared by the chef.

The homework took too long.

> The homework was *assigned by the math teacher.*

- The homework assigned by the math teacher took too long.

4. Infinitive phrases

We were given food.

> The food was *to eat.*

- We were given food to eat.

The team was our next opponent.

> The team was the *one to beat for the championship.*

- The team to beat for the championship was our next opponent.

C. Adjective clause embeddings (using who, when, which, that, when, or where)

People shouldn't throw stones.

> People live in glass houses. (who)

- People who live in glass houses shouldn't throw stones.

The man is a congressman.

> The man is the one I admire most. (whom)

- The man whom I admire most is a congressman.

He read a story.

> The story had a surprise ending. (which)

- He read a story which had a surprise ending.

There are days.
> I am discouraged. (when)
* There are days when I am discouraged.

That was the town.
> We stopped for a hamburger. (where)
* That was the town where we stopped for a hamburger.

D. Multiple adjective embeddings (use of two or more embeddings from A-C)

The girl went to San Francisco.
>> The girl was *tall*.
>> The girl was *slender*.
>> The girl won the beauty contest. (who)
>>> The contest was *local*.
>> The girl competed in the finals. (where)
>>> The finals were *state-wide*.

* The tall, slender girl who won the local beauty contest went to San Francisco, where she competed in the state-wide finals.

II. Noun substitutes

A. Noun clauses

1. Fact clauses

SOMETHING pleased him.
> It snowed. (the fact that)
* The fact that it snowed pleased him.

SOMETHING alarmed his parents.
> He might not have grades high enough to get him into Mugwamp College. (the fact that)
* The fact that he might not have grades high enough to get him into Mugwamp College alarmed his parents.

SOMETHING made the teacher feel very good.
> Jimmy volunteered to give a report to the class. (that)
* That Jimmy volunteered to give a report to the class made the teacher feel very good.

The policeman was convinced (of) SOMETHING.
> He had caught the guilty person. (that)
* The policeman was convinced that he had caught the guilty person.

Each of the candidates said SOMETHING.
> He was the best man for the office of student body president. (that)
* Each of the candidates said that he was the best man for the office of student body president.

2. Question clauses

Johnny never did understand SOMETHING.
> The teacher made him stay after school for some reason. (why)

- Johnny never did understand why the teacher made him stay after school.

SOMETHING made her angry.

She read something in the note. (what)

- What she read in the note made her angry.

Suzy tried to figure out SOMETHING.

The gift was for SOMETHING. (what)

- Suzy tried to figure out what the gift was for.

The fans wondered SOMETHING.

The coach would send in the second string sometime. (when)

- The fans wondered when the coach would send in the second string.

We didn't know SOMETHING.

Those other guys came from somewhere. (where)

- We didn't know where those other guys came from.

The pilot tried to explain SOMETHING.

He had drifted so far off course somehow. (how)

- The pilot tried to explain how he had drifted so far off course.

His scoutmaster could best tell him SOMETHING.

His money will go so far on the trip. (how far)

- His scoutmaster could best tell him how far his money would go on the trip.

The engineer knew exactly SOMETHING.

The cables should be so long. (how long)

- The engineer knew exactly how long the cables should be.

The coach knew just SOMETHING.

A fullback had to be so tough. (how tough)

- The coach knew just how tough a fullback had to be.

Janet was afraid to find out SOMETHING.

She had so much make-up work to do in algebra. (how much)

- Janet was afraid to find out how much make-up work she had to do in algebra.

(others: how often, how little, how few, how many, etc.)

My guitar teacher did not say SOMETHING.

Someone practices the chords so often. (how often to)

- My guitar teacher did not say how often to practice the chords. My father is not sure of SOMETHING.

Someone calls someone if the car breaks down. (who + to)

- My father is not sure who to call if the car breaks down.

The fisherman didn't know SOMETHING.

Someone finds worms someplace (where + to)

- The fisherman didn't know where to find the worms.

Leinegen wondered about SOMETHING.

> Someone stops the ants somehow. (how + to)

• Leinegen wondered about how to stop the ants.

Suzy could not decide SOMETHING.

> Someone does SOMETHING next. (what + to)

• Suzy could not decide what to do next.

B. Noun phrases
  1. Gerund phrases

SOMETHING was his favorite way of exercising.

> He ran on the beach. (running)

• Running on the beach was his favorite way of exercising.

He enjoyed SOMETHING.

> He wrote his name on fences. (writing)

• He enjoyed writing his name on fences.

The teacher could not understand SOMETHING.

> Jim did not finish the homework. (Jim's + *ing*)

• The teacher could not understand Jim's not finishing the homework.

SOMETHING causes night and day.

> The earth rotates on its axis. (the earth's + *ing*)

• The earth's rotating on its axis causes night and day.

  2. Infinitive phrases

SOMETHING was his dream.

> He wanted to win an Olympic medal in swimming. (to win)

• To win an Olympic medal in swimming was his dream.

He tried SOMETHING.

> He avoided hitting the tree. (to avoid)

• He tried to avoid hitting the tree.

My recommendation would be SOMETHING.

> The councilmen build more parks. (for + to)

• My recommendation would be for the councilmen to build more parks.

SOMETHING is very hard.

> A smoker gives up the habit. (for + to)

• For a smoker to give up the habit is very hard.

C. Multiple embeddings (use of two or more embeddings from I A-C and II A, B above)

SOMETHING upset my father.

> The smog persisted for ninety days above the danger level. (the fact that)
>
> The smog was deadly.
>
> My father sat down and wrote a letter to the governor. (who)
>
> The letter was long.

The letter was angry.

• The fact that the deadly smog persisted for ninety days above the danger level upset my father, who sat down and wrote a long, angry letter to the governor.

My friends and I enjoy SOMETHING.

We race our bicycles around the paths in the park. (racing)

Our bicycles are lightweight.

Our bicycles are ten-speed.

The paths are narrow.

The paths are winding.

• My friends and I enjoy racing our lightweight, ten-speed bicycles around the narrow, winding paths in the park.

SOMETHING is highly frustrating to a(n) student.

Some teachers only exhort students to write sentences. (the fact that)

The teachers are naive.

The sentences are mature.

The sentences are deeply-embedded.

The student is eager.

The student recognizes his lack of fluency but cannot see SOMETHING. (who)

The fluency is syntactic.

He can correct this deficiency somehow. (how to)

• The fact that some naive teachers only exhort students to write mature, deeply-embedded sentences is highly frustrating to an eager student who recognizes his lack of syntactic fluency but cannot see how to correct this deficiency.

Use Definite, Specific,
Concrete Language

My title is Rule 12 from Strunk and White's *The Elements of Style*, and it probably comes as close as any precept to claiming the unanimous endorsement of writing teachers. After E. D. Hirsch, Jr., in *The Philosophy of Composition*, develops his principle of "relative readability,"grounding it in historical and psychological evidence, he turns for support to "the accumulated wisdom of the handbooks." (The ones he chooses are Strunk and White, Crews, McCrimmon, Lucas, Gowers.) He reduces their wisdom to ten or a dozen maxims each: there is much overlap from book to book, but only two maxims appear in nearly the same form in all five books, and my title is also one of those two.[1]

Does anyone besides me feel uneasy when Strunk and White begin exemplifying this reasonable advice? For "A period of unfavorable weather set in," they substitute "It rained every day for a week." The rewrite is indeed more definite, specific, and concrete, and less pompous to boot. But it doesn't say the same thing, and in that difference there is a loss as well as a gain, especially if the writer means to relate the weather to some undertaking rather than just describing it. The original conveys—however inadequately—a more complex idea. The same is true when "He showed satisfaction as he took possession of his well-earned reward" becomes for Strunk and White "He grinned as he pocketed the coin."

In this essay I want to look at the way some authors of textbooks show students how to be definite, specific, and concrete. The questions I

From *College English*, 41 (December, 1979), 390–397. Reprinted by permission of the National Council of Teachers of English and Richard Ohmann.

1. The other is, avoid padding. *The Philosophy of Composition* (Chicago: University of Chicago Press, 1977) pp. 148–49.

have in mind as I do so are whether in teaching a skill like this we may inadvertently suggest to students that they be less inquiring and less intelligent than they are capable of being, and whether the teaching of basic skills is an ideological activity. To bring suspense down to a tolerable level, let me reveal now that my answer to both questions is Yes.

I will examine just three textbooks, chosen not as bad examples—they seem to me lively, serious, and honest—but for these reasons: They are current (1978). They are second editions, an indication of acceptance in the market. Their authors teach in a large city university, a community college in a large northern city, and two community colleges in a southern town and a southern city; such institutions are close to the center of the freshmen composition industry. All three textbooks give unusually ample attention to style, and in particular to the matters I am concerned with here.

I will look first at the recently published second edition of David Skwire and Frances Chitwood, *Student's Book of College English* (Glencoe Press), and refer to a section in it on "Specific Details" (pp. 347–49). Skwire and Chitwood introduce the section by saying "The use of specific details is the most direct way to avoid abstract writing." (And students *should* avoid it, since "abstract writing is the main cause of bored readers" [p. 346].) Detail is a plus. In fact, "within reason, the more specific the details, the better the writing." "Within reason" means that the detail must be relevant and neither obvious nor trivial. To illustrate, they offer three passages, labeled "Abstract (weak)," "More Specific (better)," and "Still More Specific (much better)." Here are the first and third.

1. Abstract (weak)

   The telephone is a great scientific achievement, but it can also be a great inconvenience. Who could begin to count the number of times that phone calls have come from unwelcome people or on unwelcome occasions? Telephones make me nervous.

3. Still More Specific (much better)

   The telephone is a great scientific achievement, but it can also be a great big headache. More often than not, that cheery ringing in my ear brings messages from the Ace Bill Collecting Agency, my mother (who is feeling snubbed for the fourth time that week), salesmen of encyclopedias and magazines, solicitors for the Policemen's Ball and Disease of the Month Foundation, and neighbors complaining about my dog. That's not to mention frequent wrong numbers—usually for someone named "Arnie." The calls always seem to come at the worst times, too. They've interrupted steak dinners, hot tubs, Friday night parties, and Saturday morning sleep-ins. There's no escape. Sometimes I wonder if there are any telephones in padded cells. (pp. 348–9)

Consider now how revision has transformed the style of the first passage. Most obviously, one generalization—"unwelcome people"—disappears entirely, to be replaced by a list of eight people or types of people the writer doesn't want to hear from; and another generalization—"unwelcome occasions"—is changed to "worst times," then amplified in another list. Seriation has become the main principle of structure. When items are placed in a series, the writer implies that they are alike in some respect. But in what respect? Here the angry neighbors and possessive mother are placed on par with salesmen and others connected to the writer only through the cash nexus. Are the callers unwelcome because the writer does not get along with his or her family and neighbors, or for a less personal reason: that businesses and other organizations in pursuit of money use the phone as a means of access to it? The answer may be both, of course, but in expanding the idea of "unwelcome people," Skwire and Chitwood add no insight to it. The specific details close off analysis.

The same holds for their treatment of "unwelcome occasions." An occasion is a time that is socially defined and structured: a party or a steak dinner, yes, but sleep and a bath are more private activities, hardly occasions. Of course a phone call is usually as unwelcome in the middle of a bath as during a party. My point is that in changing "occasions" to "times" and letting detail do the work, the germ of an idea has been lost: the idea that we like to control our own social time, and that the telephone allows other people to intervene and impose *their* structure. What the details communicate instead is a loose feeling of harassment—easier to visualize, more specific, but certainly not more precise in thought.

Other changes have a similar effect. "Headache" is more sensory than "inconvenience," but less exact, and personal rather than social. The phrase, "cheery ringing in my ears," is a distraction, from the perspective of developing an idea: the point is not the sound, but the fact, of the intrusions and their content, the social relations they put the writer into or take him or her out of. And where the final sentence of the original implicitly raised a fruitful question (why "nervous"?), the new conclusion—"Sometimes I wonder if there are any telephones in padded cells"—closes off inquiry with a joke and points up the writer's idiosyncrasy rather than the social matter that is under discussion.

On the level of speech acts, too, the rewrite personalizes, moves away from social analysis. In the first passage, emphasis falls on the general claims made about phones and the people who use them and are used by them. The rewrite buries those claims in a heap of reports of "my" experience, reports for which only the writer need vouch. The speaker of an assertion must be in a position to make it, or it isn't "felicitous," in Austin's terms. (I cannot felicitously assert that there is life in the next galaxy.) The writer of the second passage *risks* less by moving quickly from generalizations that require support from history and social analysis, to those that stand on private terrain. This reduction in scope accords well with the impression given by the rewrite of a person incapable of coping with events, victimized by others, fragmented, distracted—a kind of likable schlemiel. He or she may be a less "boring" writer, but also a less venturesome and more isolated person, the sort who chatters on in a harmless gossipy way without much purpose or consequence: a *character*.

If a student showed me the first passage (as the outline of a composition or the beginning of a draft), I would want to say that it expresses an interesting idea, inadequately handled to be sure, but begging for a kind of development that amplification by detail, alone, can never supply. The contradiction with which it begins is familiar but perplexing: How is it that so many of our scientists' "achievements," with all their promise of efficiency and ease, turn out to be inconvenient or worse in the long run? Why does an invention designed to give people control over their lives make many of us feel so often in the control of others? Why does a device for bringing people together (as its proprietors are constantly telling us in commercials) in fact so often serve as the carrier of frictions and antagonisms?

To make any headway with such questions, it is necessary to stay with the abstractions a while, penetrate them, get at the center of the contradictions they express, not throw them out in favor of lists of details. "Achievement": By whom? Who calls "science" into being and engineers its discoveries into commodities? The telephone as we have it is a hundred-year-long achievement, of patent lawyers and corporate planners more than of Alexander Graham Bell. "Inconvenience": For whom? Not for the salesmen and bill collectors, presumably. And certainly not for executives barricaded behind secretaries making sure the boss talks only with people he wants to talk with, and at a time of his choosing. The telephone represents a network of social relations embedded in history. In order to gain any leverage on the badly expressed contradiction of the first passage, it is necessary to unpack some of those relations. Piling on the details, as in the rewrite, may create a kind of superficial interest, but no gain in insight. The strategy, as exemplified here, is a strategy for sacrificing thought to feckless merriment.

Skwire and Chitwood are concerned with adding detail. In the section I wish to consider from Winston Weathers and Otis Winchester's *The*

New Strategy of Style (McGraw-Hill), the authors show how to make detail more specific. They do this under the heading of "Texture" (pp. 135–44), explaining that different subjects call for different textures: the simpler the subject, the more elaborate the texture. The maxim begs the question to an extent, since whether or not a given subject is simple or complex depends partly upon the diction used in exploring it. But apparently the first passage below is about a simple subject, since as the authors take it through four revisions their instructions all advise elaboration of texture. (*"Make your nouns more specific." "Make your adjectives more specific."*) Passage 2 is the second of the rewrites.

1. The country store was an interesting place to visit. In the very heart of the city, it had the air of a small town grocery store combined with a feed and hardware supply house. There were flower seeds and milk churns, coal buckets and saddle blankets, all mixed together. Walking down the crowded aisles, you felt you had gone back to the past—to the time of pot-belly stoves and kerosene lamps and giant pickle jars. You could smell the grain, you could touch the harnesses, you could even sit down in the old wooden chair. When you finally left the store and were once more in the activity of the city, you felt as you sometimes do when you come out of an old movie into the bright light of reality.

2. Charlie's Country Store was a *spell-binding* emporium. In the very heart of Minneapolis, Charlie's had the *dubious* charm of a smalltown grocery combined with a feed and hardware supply house. There were *zinnia* seeds and milk churns, *shiny* coal buckets and *garish* saddle blankets, all mixed together. Walking down its *quaint* passageways—*narrow, poorly lighted, but nevertheless immaculate*—you felt you had gone back to nineteenth-century America—to the lost years, the *faintly remembered* days of *squat* pot-belly stoves and *sturdy* kerosene lamps and *rotund, ceramic* crocks—meant for pickles or pastries. You could smell the cornmeal, you could touch the *leather* harnesses, you could even sit in the *stern* wooden rocker. And when you finally left this anachronism—and were once more in the bustle of the city—you felt as you sometimes do when you come out of an old cinema into the *blinding* glare of a *rocket-age* reality. (pp. 135–38: emphasis in original)

Passage 2 is the result of making nouns and adjectives more specific and also (though Weathers and Winchester don't say so) of adding adjectives. Setting aside some words that might be criticized as elegant variations (e.g., "emporium," which suggests a grander establishment than is implied by the rest of the passage), consider the ways the description has become more specific.

1. The scene is particularized. The store is now Charlie's; the city,

Minneapolis; the past, nineteenth-century America. Note that this change blurs the two main contrasts in which the description is grounded, country versus city and present versus past. For the sharpening of these contrasts, it does not matter whose store it is or in what city, or whether the visitor travels back in imagination to America or England. Some of the other specifics are equally irrelevant: zinnia seeds, pastries, cornmeal. The point, I take it, is not the kind of flowers people used to grow, but that they had gardens; not what kind of grain they used, but that they did more of the work of preparing their own food, and that the arts of preserving, packaging, and marketing were in a primitive state of development compared to our present attainments as represented by freezers full of TV dinners and by the Golden Arches.

2. The writer's own impressions and values are foregrounded, most often adjectivally. The store is now *spell-binding*, its passageways *quaint*, and so on through "dubious charm," "faintly remembered," "stern," and "blinding." The writer has become much more of a presence, reacting, exercising taste, judging. These responses seem to issue from no particular perspective; for instance, what's "dubious" about the store's charm? They scarcely relate to the content of the original passage, certainly not to the ideas latent in it. They seem like the reflexes of a dilettantish tourist whose fugitive sensations and values clutter the picture and block analysis.

3. Similarly, the adjectives highlight the thinginess of things, their physical appearance, rather than what they are, what they meant, how life might have been organized around them. "Shiny," "garish," "poorly lighted," "squat," "sturdy," "rotund," "ceramic." The picture turns into a kind of still life, crowded with visual detail apparently valuable in itself. Such emphasis on visible surfaces, along with the esthetic perspective, draws attention to a detached present experience, dissipating the image of an earlier kind of civilization in which most people lived on farms, the family was the main productive unit, few of people's needs were commercialized, and technology was manageable and local.

Like the telephone, the objects in the country store embody social relations. And even more clearly than the initial passage about telephones, Weathers and Winchester's original version supports a sense of history, of a society that has been utterly transformed so that most of the things in the store have lost their usefulness. The society these artifacts imply—in which local people grew the grain, harvested it, ground it into flour, and baked it into bread—has given way to one in which almost all of our labor is sold in the market and controlled by employers rather than expended at our own pace and to our own plans; and almost all of our consumption takes place through markets organized not by a village merchant but by distant corporations.

Of course the first passage doesn't say what I have just said, even by implication. But in the way it sets up contrasts and in the details it presents, it provides the ground and even the need for such analysis. The student who takes Weathers and Winchester's guidance in making the passage "richer," more "vivid," and more "intense" will lose the thread of *any* analysis in a barrage of sensory impressions, irrelevant details, and personalized or random responses. Once again, the rhetorical strategy scatters thought.

With my final example, I turn to the injunction to use concrete language. The textbook is the second edition of *Composition: Skills and Models,* by Sidney T. Stovall, Virginia B. Mathis, Linda C. Elliot, G. Mitchell Hagler, Jr., and Mary A. Poole (Houghton Mifflin). Here are two of the passages they present for comparison in their chapter on forming a style, the first from Fielding's *Tom Jones,* and the second from Nevil Shute's *On the Beach:*

> 1. The charms of Sophia had not made the least impression on Blifil; not that his heart was pre-engaged, neither was he totally insensible of beauty, or had any aversion to women; but his appetites were by nature so moderate that he was easily able by philosophy, or by study, or by some other method to subdue them; and as to that passion which we have treated of in the first chapter of this book, he had not the least tincture of it in his whole composition.
>
> But though he was so entirely free from that mixed passion of which we there treated, and of which the virtues and beauty of Sophia formed so notable an object, yet was he altogether as well furnished with some other passions that promised themselves very full gratification in the young lady's fortune. Such were avarice and ambition, which divided the dominion of his mind between them. He had more than once considered the possession of this fortune as a very desirable thing, and had entertained some distant views concerning it, but his own youth and that of the young lady, and indeed, principally a reflection that Mr. Weston might marry again and have more children, had restrained him from too hasty or too eager a pursuit.
>
> 2. He went back to bed. Tomorrow would be an anxious, trying day; he must get his sleep. In the privacy of his little curtained cabin he unlocked the safe that held the confidential books and took out the bracelet; it glowed in the synthetic light. She would love it. He put it carefully in the breast pocket of his uniform suit. Then he went to bed again, his hand upon the fishing rod, and slept.
>
> They surfaced again at four in the morning, just before dawn, a little

to the north of Gray Harbor. No lights were visible on the shore, but as there were no towns and few roads in the district that evidence was inconclusive. They went down to periscope depth and carried on. When Dwight came to the control room at six o'clock the day was bright through the periscope and the crew off duty were taking turns to look at the desolate shore. He went to breakfast and then stood smoking at the chart table, studying the minefield chart that he already knew so well, and the well-remembered entrance to the Juan de Fuca Strait. (p. 390)

The authors have couched their discussion of style in historically relative terms. Styles change, and students will want to choose from among styles suited to contemporary life. Eighteenth-century readers could "idle" over "long sentences"; "leisure is at a premium" now. Stovall and his colleagues do not absolutely value Shute's style over Fielding's, but since they say that the earlier style would strike the modern reader as awkward, stilted, colorless, complex, plodding, tedious and wordy, their counsel to the student is reasonably plain.

They direct their judgment partly against Fielding's long and complex sentences, partly against the quality of his diction. The latter is my concern. Stovall et. al. object to phrases like "entertained some distant view" and "had not the least tincture," and especially to Fielding's dependence on the big abstractions, "passion," "virtues," "avarice," "ambition," words which "elicit no emotional response from the reader." They praise Shute for "concrete words" that give life to the passage, citing "curtained cabin," "glowed in the synthetic light," "surfaced," and "desolate shore." Later in the chapter they urge the student to "Strive for the concrete word" (pp. 390–91).

Abstract nouns refer to the world in a way quite different from concrete nouns. They do not point to a set of particulars—all curtained cabins—or to any one cabin. They are relational. For instance, in speaking of Blifil's "avarice," Fielding calls up at least the relation of a series of acts to one another (a single act of acquiring or hoarding is not enough); of Blifil's feelings to these actions and to the wealth that is their goal; of those acts and feelings to a scale of values that is socially established (avarice is a sin, and so related to salvation and damnation); and of Bilfil to other people who make such judgments, as well as to people whose wealth he might covet and who would become poorer were he to become richer. The term also evokes a temporal relationship: an avaricious person like Blifil seeks to become wealthy over time, and it is this future goal that informs his conduct. Abstract nouns that characterize people do so through bundles of relationships like these.

In short, one need not adopt an eighteenth-century faculty psychology, or expect Nevil Shute to adopt it, to see that Fielding's abstract nouns give a rich social setting to Blifil's sordid intentions. This setting is made more rich as, in context, Fielding humorously brings avarice into parity with love, under the higher-level abstraction of passion. (Herein another relationship, that of the narrator to his subject and his reader.) Abstractions are for Fielding a speculative and interpretive grid against which he can examine the events of the novel, and which themselves are constantly tested and modified by those events.

Shute's language in this passage, by contrast, sets his hero's actions against a background mainly of objects and of other people treated more or less as objects. The moral implications of the passage will have to be supplied by the reader. And there is no way for the narrator, given his style, to place that moral content in a dynamic relationship with social values, at least within the passage cited. This may be appropriate enough in a story from which society has literally disappeared; I do not mean to disparage Shute's diction, only to question the wisdom of commending it to students as plainly superior (for the twentieth-century reader) to Fielding's. Some important kinds of thinking can be done only with the help of abstractions.

In sum, as this textbook teaches the skill of using definite, specific, concrete language, it joins the other two in preferring realia to more abstract inquiry about realia, and to the effort to connect them. In doing so, it seems to me, the authors convey a fairly well-defined ideological picture to students I would characterize this picture in these terms:

1. Ahistoricism. The preferred style focuses on a truncated present moment. Things and events are frozen in an image, or they pass on the wing, coming from nowhere.

2. Empiricism. The style favors sensory news, from the surfaces of things.

3. Fragmentation. An object is just what it is, disconnected from the rest of the world. The style obscures the social relations and the relations of people to nature that are embedded in all things.

4. Solipsism. The style foregrounds the writer's own perceptions: This is what I saw and felt.

5. Denial of conflict. The style typically pictures a world in which the telephone has the same meaning for all classes of people, a world whose "rocket-age reality" is just mysteriously *there*, outside the country store, a world where avarice is a superfluous and tedious concept.

Furthermore—and I think this, too, a matter of the ideology of style— the injunctions to use detail, be specific, be concrete, as applied in these books, push the student writer always toward the language that most nearly reproduces the immediate experience and away from the language that might be used to understand it, transform it, and relate it to everything else. The authors privilege a kind of revising and expanding that leaves the words themselves unexamined and untransformed. Susan Wells has suggested that Christensen's rhetoric does not open "to investigation the relations among language, vision, and their objects,"[2] but takes those relations for granted. Her comment applies well to the use of detail recommended in these textbooks.

In an epoch when so much of the language students hear or read comes from distant sources, via the media, and when so much of it is shaped by advertisers and other corporate experts to channel their thoughts and feelings and needs, I think it a special pity if English teachers are turning students away from critical scrutiny of the words in their heads, especially from those that are most heavily laden with ideology. When in the cause of clarity or liveliness we urge them toward detail, surfaces, the sensory, as mere *expansion* of ideas or even as a *substitute* for abstraction, we encourage them to accept the empirical fragmentation of consciousness that passes for common sense in our society, and hence to accept the society itself as just what it most superficially seems to be.

Yes, it is good to keep readers interested, bad to bore them. Like Hirsch's principle of readability, the injunction to be interesting is on one level a bit of self-evident practical wisdom, not to mention kindness. Whatever you are trying to accomplish through a piece of writing, you won't achieve it if the reader quits on you, or plods on in resentful tedium. But mechanically applied, the principles of interest and readability entail accepting the reader exactly as he or she is. The reader's most casual values, interests, and capacities become an inflexible measure of what to write and how to write it, a Nielsen rating for prose. What happens to the possibility of challenging or even changing the reader? If keeping readers' attention is elevated to the prime goal of our teaching, the strategies we teach may well lead toward triviality and evasion.

Yes, I also realize that most students don't handle abstractions and generalizations well. I know that they often write badly when they try, and how depressing an experience it can be to read a batch of compositions on free will or alienation or capital punishment. And I am aware of the pressure many English teachers now feel to teach basic skills, whatever they are, rather than critical inquiry.[3] But I can't believe that the

2. "Classroom Heuristics and Empiricism," *College English*, 39 (1977), 471.
3. Obviously critical inquiry requires both abstractions and details, and a fluid exchange between them. I hope not to be taken as merely inverting the values I have criticized and recommending the abstract and general over the concrete.

best response to this pressure is valorizing the concrete, fragmented, and inconsistent world-views that many of our students bring to college with them. Jeffrey Youdelman refers to colleagues he has heard say, "They can't handle abstraction . . . and therefore I always give them topics like 'describe your favorite room.'" Youdelman continues: "Already stuck in a world of daily detail, with limited horizons and stunted consciousness, students are forced deeper into their solipsistic prison."[4] Like him, I am concerned that in the cause of improving their skills we may end up increasing their powerlessness.

4. "Limiting Students: Remedial Writing and the Death of Open Admissions," *College English,* 39 (1978), 563–4. Anyone interested in the politics of rhetoric and composition should read this excellent article and that of Susan Wells, cited earlier. I consider the present essay a supplement to theirs.

ADDITIONAL READINGS

EDWARD P. J. CORBETT, "Approaches to the Study of Style," *Teaching Composition: 10 Bibliographical Essays,* ed. Gary Tate (Fort Worth: Texas Christian University Press, 1976), pp. 73–109.

LOUISE T. MILIC, "Theories of Style and Their Implications for the Teaching of Composition," *College Composition and Communication,* 16 (May, 1965), 66–69, 126.

RICHARD L. GRAVES, "Levels of Skill in the Composing Process," *College Composition and Communication,* 29 (October, 1978), 227–232.

KELLOGG W. HUNT, "A Synopses of Clause-to-Sentence Length Factors," *English Journal,* 54 (April, 1965), 300, 305–309.

DONALD DAIKER, ANDREW KEREK, and MAX MORENBERG, "Sentence-Combining and Syntactic Maturity in Freshman English," *College Composition and Communication,* 29 (February, 1978), 36–41.

A. M. TIBBETTS, "On the Practical Uses of a Grammatical System: A Note on Christensen and Johnson," *College English,* 31 (May, 1970), 870–878.

LESTER L. FAIGLEY, "Generative Rhetoric as a Way of Increasing Syntactic Fluency," *College Composition and Communication,* 30 (May, 1979), 176–181.

ROBERT L. WALKER, O.P., "The Common Writer: A Case for Parallel Structure," *College Composition and Communication,* 21 (December, 1970), 373–379.

WILLIAM E. GRUBER, " 'Servile Copying' and the Teaching of Composition," *College English,* 39 (December, 1977), 491–497.

An Annotated List
of Some Important Books on Writing
or the Teaching of Writing

JAMES BRITTON et al., *The Development of Writing Abilities (11–18)* (London: Macmillan Education, 1975). A report of a study conducted at the University of London Institute of Education from 1966 to 1971, under the direction of James Britton, of some 2100 papers written by students between the ages of 11 and 18 from 85 different classes at 65 different schools in Great Britain.

FRANCIS CHRISTENSEN, *Notes Toward a New Rhetoric: Nine Essays for Teachers*, ed. Bonniejean Christensen, 2nd edition (New York: Harper & Row, 1978). A collection of this influential teacher's essays, including, in addition to his classic essays "A Generative Rhetoric of the Sentence" and "A Generative Rhetoric of the Paragraph," such essays as "Sentence-Openers," "Restrictive and Nonrestrictive Modifiers Again," and "The Problem of Defining a Mature Style."

WILLIAM E. COLES, JR., *The Plural I: The Teaching of Writing* (New York: Holt, Rinehart, and Winston, 1978). An exposition of a philosophy of composition by means of a narrative account of the author's experience of conducting a group of his students through thirty writing assignments designed to sharpen their awareness of themselves as users of language.

CHARLES R. COOPER and LEE ODELL, eds., *Evaluating Writing: Describing, Measuring, Judging* (Urbana, Ill.: National Council of Teachers of English, 1977). A collection of six essays by Charles R. Cooper, Richard Lloyd-Jones, Patrick J. Finn, Kellogg W. Hunt, Lee Odell, and Mary H. Beaven, explaining such innovative systems of measuring student writing as holistic scoring, primary-trait scoring, and peer evaluation.

CHARLES R. COOPER and LEE ODELL, eds., *Research on Composing: Points of Departure* (Urbana, Ill.: National Council of Teachers of English, 1978). A collection of ten essays by such teachers as James Britton, Janet Emig, Richard Young, Donald Murray, and Phillip Lopate, suggesting some of the promising areas of research into the composing process.

FRANK J. D'ANGELO, *A Conceptual Theory of Rhetoric* (Cambridge, Mass.: Winthrop, 1975). The author's conceptual theory of rhetoric developed through an exploration of the fundamental linguistic and rhetorical principles and conventions that govern the generation of discourse.

PAUL B. DIEDERICH, *Measuring Growth in English* (Urbana, Ill.: National Council of Teachers of English, 1974). Recommendations by this long-time researcher and consultant for the Educational Testing Service of Princeton, New Jersey, about how to increase the reliability of grades on student essays through a combination of objective tests and holistic evaluations of the essays.

PETER ELBOW, *Writing Without Teachers* (New York: Oxford University Press, 1973). An exposition of the author's system of enhancing students' articulateness and confidence with words through exercises in uninhibited, non-stop writing and through responses to the writing from a number of readers.

JANET EMIG, *The Composing Processes of Twelfth Graders* (Urbana, Ill.: National Council of Teachers of English, 1971). A report of an in-depth investigation of the writing habits of eight seniors in an Evanston, Illinois high school by means of questionnaires, interviews, observations, tape-recordings, and analyses of various drafts.

WALKER GIBSON, *Tough, Sweet, and Stuffy: An Essay of Modern American Styles* (Bloomington, Ind.: Indiana University Press, 1966). The author's characterizations of three types of American prose style (labeled "tough," "sweet," and "stuffy") and a presentation of his Style Machine, a schema that allows for quantitative measurements of prose styles.

E. D. HIRSCH, JR., *The Philosophy of Composition* (Chicago: University of Chicago Press, 1977). Through his research into the history of the development of the written language and into psycholinguistics, the author arrives at his ultimate criterion for judging the quality of written prose, "relative readability," a measure of the ease or difficulty that a reader has in processing a piece of writing.

WILLIAM F. IRMSCHER, *Teaching Expository Writing* (New York: Holt, Rinehart, and Winston, 1979). Sound advice from a former editor of *College Composition and Communication* and a veteran Director of Freshman English about all aspects of the teaching of writing, especially on the college level.

JAMES L. KINNEAVY, *A Theory of Discourse* (Englewood Cliffs, N.J.: Prentice-Hall, 1971; reissued in paperback by W. W. Norton in 1980). Through a wide-ranging historical review of rhetorical, logical, linguistic, and literary theories, the author arrives at a new way of classifying discourse into the four categories of Reference Discourse, Persuasive Discourse, Expressive Discourse, and Literary Discourse, each of which has its own system of logic, organization, and style.

ALBERT R. KITZHABER, *Themes, Theories, and Therapy: The Teaching of Writing in College* (New York: McGraw-Hill, 1963). Through a national survey of freshman composition programs, beginning with a detailed study of the composition program at Dartmouth College, the author assesses the state and the status of the teaching of writing in American writing in American colleges at the beginning of the 1960's.

RICHARD LLOYD-JONES, RICHARD BRADDOCK, and LOWELL SCHOER, *Research in Written Composition* (Champaign, Ill.: National Council of Teachers of English, 1963). A survey and assessment of much of the published and unpublished (e.g. dissertations) research done on composition up to the early 1960's, with some suggestions of some further needed research.

KEN MACRORIE, *Uptaught* (New York: Hayden, 1970). Through a narrative account of his experiences as a teacher of writing, this former editor of *College Composition and Communication* tells of how he developed his so-called Third Way of teaching composition, a form of free-writing that encourages unpretentious, honest writing.

JOHN C. MELLON, *Transformational Sentence-Combining: A Method for Enhancing the Development of Syntactic Fluency in English Composition* (Champaign, Ill.: National Council of Teachers of English, 1969). A research report on an experiment conducted with seventh-grade students who engaged in a series of sentence-combining exercises after being exposed to some formal instruction in transformational grammar.

JAMES MOFFETT, *Teaching the Universe of Discourse* (Boston: Houghton Mifflin, 1968). A series of essays presenting the author's pedagogical theory of discourse that became the foundation for his *A Student-Centered Language Arts Curriculum, Grades K-13: A Handbook for Teachers*.

FRANK O'HARE, *Sentence-Combining: Improving Student Writing Without Formal Grammar Instruction* (Urbana, Ill.: National Council of Teachers of English, 1973). A research report on an experiment in which a group of seventh-grade students made significant improvement not only in syntactic fluency but also in the overall quality of their writing after engaging in a sequence of sentence-combining exercises that did not require prior instruction in grammar.

MINA P. SHAUGHNESSY, *Errors and Expectations: A Guide for the Teacher of Basic Writing* (New York: Oxford University Press, 1977). Based on a study of some 4000 essays written by freshman students admitted to the City University of New York (CUNY) system in 1970 under the new policy of open admissions, this classic work describes the features of the writing of these students, attempts to account for the deficiencies of their writing, and proposes some practical ways of helping students overcome weaknesses in writing.

GARY TATE, ed., *Teaching Composition: 10 Bibliographical Essays* (Fort Worth, Texas: Texas Christian University Press, 1976). A collection of essays which point out and discuss some of the most significant literature on the following aspects of composition: Invention, The Structure and Form of Non-Fiction Prose, Style, Modes of Discourse, Basic Writing, The Uses of the Media, Linguistics and Composition, Rhetorical Analysis of Writing, Dialects and Composition, Composition and Related Fields.

LEV S. VYGOTSKY, *Thought and Language,* trans. Eugenia Hanfmann and Gertrude Vakar (Cambridge, Mass.: M.I.T. Press, 1962). First published in Moscow in 1934, this work by a Russian psychologist casts light on the cognitive processes involved in the development of verbal skills in the oral and the written media.

LINDA WOODSON, *A Handbook of Modern Rhetorical Terms* (Urbana, Ill.: National Council of Teachers of English, 1979). A fairly comprehensive glossary of the rhetorical terms that appear in twentieth-century books and articles and of the key terms from classical rhetoric. A valuable feature of the handbook is the reference in most of the entries to the books and articles in which the term figures or in which more information about the term can be found.